50 Years of India's Independence

50 Years of India's Independence

Edited by

Dr. S. Subramanian

Former

Director General : CRPF and NSG
Founder Director : Special Protection Group (SPG)
Director : National Police Academy
Minister : Embassy of India, Germany
Joint Director : Intelligence Bureau (IB)
DIG : Central Bureau of Investigation

Foreword by

Justice M. N. Venkatachaliah

Chairperson
National Human Rights Commission of India
and
Former Chief Justice of India

1997

MANAS PUBLICATIONS
New Delhi-110002

MANAS PUBLICATIONS
(Publishers, Distributors and Exporters)
4819/XI, Varun House, Mathur Lane,
24, Ansari Road, Daryaganj,
New Delhi - 110002 (India)
Ph.: 3260783, 3265523, 2523865
Fax.: 011 - 3272766 & 2927854
E-Mail: manas.vkgarg@axcess.net.in

ISBN 81-7049-094-4

First Published 1997

Printed in India at
Print Perfect, Delhi
and Published by Mrs. Suman Lata for
Manas Publications, 4819/XI, Varun House,
Mathur Lane, 24, Ansari Road, Daryaganj,
New Delhi - 110002 (INDIA)

Foreword

I deem it a privilege to subscribe a foreword to this excellent compilation on 50 Years of India's Independence. The Editor, Dr. S. Subramanian, himself a scholar of repute has applied a fitting editorial policy to bring out through the sequential arrangements of the articles, a glimpse of India's evolution down the half-century since Independence. In the range of articles, problems and perspectives of great complexity and of contemporary relevance has been debated. **Part I** is on the various democratic aspects of Indian polity and **Part II** on security dimensions by the experts in their respective fields. Likewise, the other parts contain contributions by eminent scholars on diverse subjects of national concern such as human rights, international relations, education, mountaineering, tourism and sports. The last part is a collection of selected speeches of the builders of modern India including Pandit Jawaharlal Nehru, Sardar Vallabhbhai Patel, Indira Gandhi and Rajiv Gandhi, focusing on their vision for the country.

Dr. Subramanian has had a brilliant professional career and his writings have enriched in the areas of human rights and criminology. The release of this valuable contribution is rightly timed to coincide with the Golden Jubilee celebration of India's Independence. I congratulate Dr. Subramanian for this excellent work and the valuable material that the volume offers to the reader.

August 1, 1997

Justice M. N. Venkatachaliah
Chairperson
National Human Rights
Commission of India

Preface

Free India is fifty now. It is an occasion for great rejoicing for all of us. We won freedom under the leadership of Mahatma Gandhi, and thousands of our countrymen and women had made the supreme sacrifice for achieving the same. We remember those martyrs and pay our respectful homage to them. In a developing country like India, political freedom alone does not bring happiness to the people. The people of India expected Independence to deliver them from poverty, misery and illiteracy.

Pandit Jawaharlal Nehru delineated our 'Tryst with Destiny' and had outlined the task before the nation. Under his dynamic and idealistic leadership, we proceeded on the right lines and laid the foundations of our economic advancement and progress in various fields of science and technology. On this occasion, we feel it is necessary to recall what Nehru wanted us to do and reproduce his select speeches. We owe our unity and integrity to Sardar Vallabhbhai Patel, who has been rightly described as the Iron Man of India. His speech reproduced here gives us an idea about what the Sardar visualised for the future of India..

Smt. Indira Gandhi, after a diffident start, gave purposeful direction to country's economic and social progress. She made India to be reckoned as an important power in this region. Though somewhat imperious in her attitude, at heart she had the well being of the masses. Many projects initiated by her for the uplift of the poor, have paid good dividends and brought cheer to the poor people. Her speeches in this volume give an inkling about her thinking. Mr. Rajiv Gandhi rose like a meteor in the political firmament of India and till fate snatched him from us, he held great promise to usher in a prosperous India and take her to the 21st century as a regional economic and scientific power. His ideas of strengthening India on all fronts are contained in his speech reproduced here.

We approached eminent Indians to tell us about their perceptions of the state of affairs in the Indian Republic. Justice V.R. Krishna Iyer, the champion of the downtrodden, spells out what went wrong with the Republic and suggests remedies. The Chief Election Commissioner, Dr. M. S. Gill, has outlined the basic principles governing the election system in India. Dr. Subhash Kashyap, the former Secretary General of the Lok Sabha, pleads for reforms in Parliament of India. The doyen of Indian journalists, Mr. Inder Malhotra, looks back with mixed feelings at the five decades and points out the disappointments and achievements. In a hard-hitting article, Dr. G.R.S. Rao exposes the lacunae in political populism, administrative careerism and judicial activism. Mr.Vijay Karan highlights the moral dilemma faced by the country.

The Deputy Secretary General of the Commonwealth Secretariat, Mr. K. Srinivasan, in his article emphasises the importance of 'Commonwealth of South Asia'. Mr. Bajpai, in his incisive article, deals with the Tibetan problem. Mr. C.V. Ranganathan, the acknowledged expert on India-China relations, gives his views on the retrospect and prospect of the relations between India and China. His approach is pragmatic and worthy of adoption. Mr. B. Raman explains the scope and limitations of Indo-Myanmar relations.

Dr. Asghar Ali Engineer, the crusader for communal amity in India, outlines Nehru's concept of secularism and communalism and also gives the views of intelligentsia on minorities in India. The chairperson of the National Commission for Women, Ms. Mohini Giri, highlights the need for gender equality through women's empowerment. Welfare of scheduled castes and scheduled tribes, advocated by Mahatma Gandhi throughout his life, is a matter of faith for our nation. Mr. S.R. Sankaran explains in detail what has been attempted to alleviate the sufferings of these have-nots and to bring them up economically and socially. In his article Mr. P.S. Krishnan, underlines the need for providing special measures for the welfare of the Backward Classes in India. For many, who became aware of this problem in the aftermath of Mandal Report, would find this article illuminating and educating.

Mr. T.V. Rajeswar in his article explains about the intelligence services in India and Mr. Rustamji about the urgent need for reforms for police in India. Mr. M. B. Kaushal outlines the role of Central

Reserve Police Force (CRPF) in maintaining peace and communal harmony in the country. The world renowned mountaineer, Capt. M.S. Kohli, in his article highlights India's achievements in mountaineering. The articles on the defence forces by Air Chief Marshal S. K. Sareen, Admiral R. H. Tahiliani and Lt. Gen. M. L. Chibber and para-military forces by Mr. A. K. Tandon and Mr. Divakar Prasad highlight in detail the many-faceted development taken place in these areas after Independence. Mr. D. K. Bharadwaj refers to the achievements in sports in free India.

Human Rights have come to occupy the centre stage in India. An overview of the concept is given by the Editor. Deaths in police custody occur with sickening frequency in India and is bringing a bad name to our country. How this could be prevented is discussed in an article included in this volume.

I would like to place on record my sincere thanks to Justice M. N. Venkatachaliah who rewarded this work with the foreword. I really feel honoured to receive commendation from a person of such an high intellect.

I am grateful to the eminent citizens of our country, who have contributed articles to this volume and made it a useful one.

A project of this nature requires help and support from many. Due to constraints of space I am unable to record individual vote of thanks. I wish to express my special thanks to my wife Smt. S. Jaya Lakshmi for her patience, encouragement and support to complete this project in time, Mr. G. Raj Reddy for his able secretarial assistance in preparing the manuscript, and Mr. V.K. Garg, Director, Manas Publications, for making this book possible and producing it in an attractive format in a record time.

Hyderabad **Dr. S. Subramanian**
August 15, 1997

Contents

Foreword *v*

Preface *vii*

The Contributors *xv*

PART I
The Republic

1. The Indian Republic : Retrospect and Prospect 3
   - Justice V.R. Krishna Iyer
2. Election System in India 9
   - Dr. M.S. Gill
3. Parliament of India : Case for Reforms 19
   - Dr. Subhash C. Kashyap
4. Looking Back with Mixed Feelings 23
   - Inder Malhotra
5. India's Moral Dilemmas 29
   - Vijay Karan
6. Political Populism, Administrative Careerism and Judicial Activism 33
   - Dr. G.R.S. Rao
7. Ethnicity, Plurality and Conflict Resolution 47
   - Mani Shankar Aiyar
8. Rajiv Gandhi and Panchayati Raj 82
   - Mani Shankar Aiyar
9. Are We a Market Once Again 90
   - Mohan Guruswamy

10. India's North-East : An Overview 95
- Lt.Gen. (Retd.) V.K. Nayar

PART II
Defending the Nation

11. Manning the Indian Armed Forces 113
- Lt. Gen. (Retd.) Dr. M. L. Chibber

12. Fifty Years of Indian Navy 132
- Admiral (Retd) R. H. Tahiliani

13. Indian Air Force since Independence 140
- Air Chief Marshal S.K. Sareen

14. Securing the Borders : Pains and Gains 148
- A.K. Tandon

15. Defending the Borders on Mountains 155
- Divakar Prasad.

PART III
India and its Neighbours

16. Commonwealth South Asia 163
- K.Srinivasan

17. India and Tibet 169
- G.S. Bajpai

18. India-China Relations : Retrospect and Prospect 175
- C.V.Ranganathan

19. Indo-Myanmar Relations : Scope and Limitations 183
- B.Raman

20. Indo - Pak Relations : Prognosis and Options 189
- Brig.(Retd) A.G. Krishnaiah

PART IV
Welfare of the People

21. Nehru's Concept of Secularism and Communalism 207
- Dr. Asghar Ali Engineer

22. Gender Equality through Women's Empowerment 213
- Mrs. V. Mohini Giri

23. Emancipation of Scheduled Castes and Scheduled Tribes 217
- S.R. Sankaran

24. Welfare of Backward Classes 234
- P.S. Krishnan

25. Minorities in Free India 259
- Dr. Asghar Ali Engineer

PART V
Public Order

26. Intelligence Services in India 267
- T. V. Rajeswar

27. Fifty Years of Policing : Urgent Need for Reforms 271
- K. F. Rustamji

28. Central Reserve Police Force: Peace Keepers of The Nation 275
- M. B. Kaushal

PART VI
Human Rights

29. Human Rights : An Overview 285
- Dr. S. Subramanian

30. Human Rights in Armed Forces 293
- Air Cmde (Retd) R. V. Kumar

31. Prevention of Deaths in Police Custody 299
- Dr. S. Subramanian

PART VII
Education and Sports

32. Elementary Education for Empowerment 305
- S. R. Bommai

33. Sporting Achievements in India : Bright Spots in a Bleak Scenario 310
- D. K. Bharadwaj

PART VIII
Mountaineering and Tourism

34. Fifty Years of Indian Tourism 323
- Dr. G. Sundaram

35. Mountaineering in India 330
- Capt. (Retd) M. S. Kohli

PART IX
Their Vision of India

36. Tryst with Destiny 343
- Jawaharlal Nehru

37. Building a Strong India 352
- Sardar Vallabhbhai Patel

38. Making India Strong and Great 360
- Indira Gandhi

39. Guarding the Flame of Freedom 369
- Indira Gandhi

40. Forty Years of Independence 380
- Rajiv Gandhi

The Contributors

Brig. (Retd.) A. G. Krishnaiah : A graduate of Defence Services Staff College and Master of Science in Defence Studies, held several key staff appointments in Army Hqs. and Cabinet Secretariat. He is a keen observer of Pakistan and its relations with countries of Indian interest. He writes extensively on national security.

Dr. Asghar Ali Engineer : A well-known crusader for communal harmony and welfare of minorities in India, Dr. Engineer has published 37 books and many research articles. He has lectured in numerous universities in India and abroad and is associated with many social welfare and educational organisations.

Ashok Kumar Tandon : A distinguished member of the Indian Police Service, Mr. Tandon is a Post-graduate of Delhi School of Economics. In his illustrious career he has held the appointments of Director General, Border Security Force, Central Industrial Security Force, National Security Guard and Gujarat State Police Force. He was Joint Secretary, Ministry of Labour, Government of India, and Addl. Commissioner, VIP Security, Delhi Police. Decorated with President's Police Medal for the Distinguished Service and the Indian Police Medal for the Meritorious Service, Mr. Tandon evinces abiding interest in the welfare of Police Forces.

B. Raman : Former Additional Secretary in the Cabinet Secretariat, Mr. Raman in his distinguished career served in the Union Home Ministry, and in our missions in Paris and Geneva. He was a member of the Indo-Burmese Joint Boundary Demarcation Commission (1968-72). Before joining Government service, he was a journalist for four years. Currently, he is the Director of the Institute of Topical Studies, Chennai. He writes regularly on international issues in *The Hindu, The Business Line* and quarterly journal of the United Services Institute, Delhi.

C.V. Ranganathan : A distinguished member of the Indian Foreign Service (1959-93), Mr. Ranganathan served in the Embassy of India, Beijing, in 1965-68 during the Cultural Revolution and again as Indian Ambassador in 1987-91. As head of the East Asia Division in the Ministry of External Affairs, he was closely associated with the policy matters concerning relations with China. He is an acknowledged authority on India-China relations. In his long career, he had served in New York, Bonn and Moscow and was the Head of the Indian missions in Hong Kong, Ethiopia and France.

D. K. Bharadwaj : A veteran sports writer, Mr. Bharadwaj has authored several books on sports in Hindi. A member of the Indian Information Service, he has wide experience of multi-media publicity and public relations. Also, he was the Chief Editor, *Yojana,* a leading journal of planning and socio-economic development for nearly seven years and the Chief Editor-cum-General Manager, *Employment News* for about three years.

Divakar Prasad: An IPS (1968) officer of HP Cadre, Mr. Divakar Prasad is a man of rich and varied experience who has distinguished himself in various capacities as ADC to Governor, Area Organiser in SSB, SP and DIG in CBI, as IG (Int & Ops) in Nagaland and Director (Training) in BPR & D before joining the ITBP as Inspector General - HQs in 1995. He has represented India at the Heads of Narcotics Law Enforcement Agency in Colombo (Sri Lanka) in 1985 under the aegis of UN, as member of Indian delegation for Bilateral Talks on Extradition Matters at Ottawa (Canada) in 1986 and Indian delegation in the 4th meeting of Indo-China Expert Group at Beijing (China) in 1996. Recently, on an invitation from Federal Border Guard Service of Russia, he visited their country along with the BSF Top Brass to attend the conclave of two Border Forces to share each other's experiences on border management strategies. Mr. Divakar Prasad is a recipient of Indian Police Medal for Meritorious Service in the year 1986 and President's Police Medal for Distinguished Services in 1996.

Dr. G. R. S. Rao : A researcher, trainer and consultant in the areas of public policy, democratic decentralised development, people's sector, statecraft, internal security and human rights, Dr. Rao is presently the Director of the Centre for Public Policy and Social Development, Hyderabad. He was associated with Rajaji International Institute of Public Affairs and Administration, and Administrative Staff College of India for many years. He is associated with a number of Universities. He has attended many international seminars and presented papers. He has been the Ford Foundation Visiting Fellow at Chicago University and Queen Elizabeth House Visiting Fellow at the Oxford University. He writes extensively in national and international newspapers and journals.

G.S. Bajpai : Former Chairman of Joint Intelligence Committee, Secretary to the Government of India, and Chief of the Research and Analysis Wing of the Cabinet Secretariat, Mr. Bajpai in his distinguished career held many important appointments in the Union Home and External Affairs Ministries and served with distinction in Indian missions abroad.

Dr. G. Sundaram : As a distinguished member of the Indian Administrative Service, Dr. Sundaram held many important positions; retired as Secretary, Department of Tourism in 1996. In the light of academic achievements and professional expertise, he was posted Counsellor in the Embassy of India, Brussels, and accredited to EEC, Belgium and Luxembourg for nearly three years. A Ph.D. from Delhi School of Economics, he has authored three books and contributed a number of articles in prestigious newspapers and journals.

Inder Malhotra : Specializing in defence, nuclear issues, foreign policy and national politics, Mr. Inder Malhotra combines scholarship with journalism. A graduate of the Punjab University, Nehru Fellow and Woodrow Wilson Fellow, he is the author of *Indira Gandhi - A Personal and Political Biography* (1989) and *India Trapped in Uncertainty* (1991) and his third book *Indian Security : Past, Present and Future* is under publication. In his long and distinguished journalistic career extending over 48 years, he has been Resident Editor of *The Statesman* and *The Times of India* and India correspondent of *The Guardian*. Since 1986, he has been a syndicated columnist published in over dozen newspapers in India and abroad.

K.F. Rustamji : A former member of the National Integration Council, National Police Commission and former Secretary in the Union Home Ministry, Rustamji in his distinguished career in the Indian Police held many important appointments and will be remembered for establishing the elite Border Security Force in 1965. His tenure as chief of Madhya Pradesh Police, when he eliminated dreaded dacoit gangs from that State will also be remembered forever. Recipient of many professional awards, he was honoured with Padma Vibhushan (1991) and Padma Bhushan (1971). He writes extensively on matters of public interest in the national press and participates in national and international seminars.

K. Srinivasan : B.A., MA Oxford University, Mr. Srinivasan is currently the Deputy Secretary-General (Political), Commonwealth Secretariat. He served with distinction in the Indian Foreign Service (1959-95). He was High Commissioner in Zambia and Botswana (1974-77), Consul-General, New York (1977-80); High Commissioner in Nigeria and Ambassador in Benin and Cameroon (1980-83); Ambassador to The Netherlands (1986-89); High Commissioner in Bangladesh (1989-92); Secretary, Ministry of External Affairs (1992-94) and Foreign Secretary (1994-95).

M. B. Kaushal : Joined the Indian Police Service in 1963. Served as the Commissioner of Police, Delhi from 1992 to 1995. He has worked in various capacities in Delhi Police. He was the Inspector General of Police, Goa, during 1973-76. During this period he was also made Exposition Commissioner. Served in the Railway Protection Force for about 10 years at various levels including Executive Director (Security). Was awarded the Police Medal in 1980 for Meritorious service and President's Police Medal in 1988 for Distinguished services. Shri Kaushal is with the Central Reserve Police Force since January, 1995. As Additional Director General, CRPF, he coordinated movement, deployment and utilisation of the Central Forces for Parliament and Assembly Elections in J & K in 1996. He took over as the Director General of the CRPF on 1st October, 1996.

Lt. Gen. (Retd.) M. L. Chibber : His forty years career in the Army culminated in his being C-in-C of India's Northern Command. An officer of the 5th Gorkha Rifles, he held important appointments like — the Commander of India's counter offensive force; Adjutant General, and Director of Military Operations. Was on the faculty of the Indian Military Academy and the Defence Service Staff College. Served in Korea during 1953 on the first UN peace mision. After retirement, he was Defence Advisor to the fourth Pay Commission. Thereafter, for four years 1986-89, he was the Executive Director of the Management Development Institute, Gurgaon; continues as Visiting Professor, Member of the Academic Council and Board of Studies for MBA of Sri Sathya Sai Institute of Higher Learning (Deemed University). Graduate of British Army Staff College; M. Sc. from Madras University; Ph. D. from Allahabad University. Fellow of the Inter University Seminar on Armed Forces and Society, Chicago; Jawaharlal Nehru Fellow for 1990 and 1991 to research the introduction of National Service in India, and Fellow of Arms Control, Disarmament and International Security, University of Illinois, Urbana. Authored many books and numerous monographs and articles on leadership and matters related to security, war and peace. Awarded Ati Vishisht Seva Medal in 1972 and Param Vishisht Seva Medal in 1976 for distinguished service. In 1986 was conferred the national award of "Padmabhushan" for exceptional service to the nation.

Capt. (Retd.) M.S. Kohli : India's eminent mountaineer who has led the first successful Indian Everest Expedition in 1965, which put nine men on the summit — a world record; acclaimed by Smt. Indira Gandhi as one of the six major achievements of India during the post-Independence era. During his 42 years of distinguished and varied career, he has served in the Indian Navy, Indo-Tibetan Border Police and Air India. He is closely associated with Indian Mountaineering Foundation and is Chairman of the Outward Bound Trust (India). He has been adviser to the Bhutan Government on adventure tourism. He has popularised mountaineering not only in India but all over Asia. Author of 10 books, Capt. Kohli was awarded Padma Bhushan by the Government of India.

Mani Shankar Aiyar : An ex-MP, Mr. Aiyar, after brilliant academic career in Delhi and Cambridge Universities, joined Indian Foreign Service in 1963 and served in various capacities. Joined Rajiv Gandhi as his Joint Secretary and took voluntary retirement from service in 1989 to begin his political career. He is an active member of the Indian National Congress. He was elected to the Lok Sabha and served for a full term of five years as representative of Mayladuthurai constituency in Tamil Nadu. Author of four books, he wrote a popular column 'Mani-Talk' in *Sunday* magazine, and presently writes in *India Today*. Contributes articles regularly to well-known newspapers and journals.

Dr. M. S. Gill : After a brilliant career in the Indian Administrative Service, Dr. Gill was appointed to the Election Commission of India as Election Commissioner in October 1993 and was elevated as the Chief Election Commissioner in December 1996. A Ph. D. of Punjab University and a Diploma holder in Development Studies from Cambridge University, Dr. Gill has authored three books: *Himalayan Wonderland - Travels in Lahaul; Folk Tales of Lahaul;* and *An Indian Success Story - Agriculture and Cooperatives.*

Mohan Guruswamy : Educated at Nizam College, Hyderabad, University College of Arts, Hyderabad, Indian Institute of Management, Ahmedabad, John F. Kennedy School of Government, Harvard University, Cambridge, Mass., and Graduate School of Business, Stanford University, Palo Alto. Wide ranging professional experience of nearly 25 years that includes teaching at the Administrative Staff College of India; CEO of Siel Compressors Ltd., a large light engineering company; Director of the Export Credit Corporation of India, and as a senior political advisor and analyst. Have written extensively on Defence and Economic policy issues in leading publications such as *The Times of India, Indian Express, The Pioneer* and *The Hindustan Times.* Frequent commentator on BBC and Doordarshan. Lectured on security related issues at the Indian Air Force's College of Air Warfare. Participated in the Wilton Park seminar on South Asia, 1990 and the Asia Pacific Security Conference at Vladivostock, 1991.

P. S. Krishnan : A distinguished member of the Indian Administrative Service, Mr. Krishnan is presently serving as Member-Secretary, National Commission for Backward Classes. He is a well known authority on the problems of the Backward Classes and under-privileged. He writes and lectures extensively on the subject of Development of Backward Classes. Among the many important posts he held were Secretary, Ministry of Welfare; Special Commissioner for Scheduled Castes, Government of India; Principal Secretary and Special Representative of Government of Andhra Pradesh at Delhi.

Admiral (Retd.) R. H. Tahiliani : Born on 12th May, 1930, in Karachi, appeared for Federal Service Commission Competitive Examinations in November 1947. Joined Royal Indian Navy in March 1948, and sent to U.K. for four years Naval training. On return, served on different ships; qualified as naval pilot and flying instructor and instructed in Airforce Flying College. Commanded Naval Jet Flight Carrier Borne Fighter Squadron, Indian Naval Ships, *Trishul* and *Vikrant.* On promotion to Real Admiral, he was Commander Goa Area and Western Fleet. As Vice Admiral, commanded Southern and Western Naval Commands. Appointed Chief of Naval Staff on 30th November, 1984, and retired on 30th November, 1987. Has also served as Governor of Sikkim. Decorated AVSM, PVSM. Courses Test Pilot Course at France, Naval War College at USA and National Defence College, Delhi.

Air Cmde (Retd.) R. V. Kumar : A gold medalist in law and has legal experience of over 27 years. Held the office of the Judge Advocate General in the Indian Air Force for over seven years. Honoured by the President of India with Ati Vishisht Seva Medal for services of the most distinguished order. An author of impeccable credentials, having authored various papers and educational documentaries, wrote a book titled *Safeguards for Armed Forces Personnel.*

Air Chief Marshal S. K. Sareen : Commissioned as a Fighter Pilot in the Indian Air Force in 1957, Air Chief Marshal S. K. Sareen obtained great experience of flying all types of fighter aircraft, including the state-of-the-art Mirage 2000 and MiG-29. Graduate of Defence Services Staff College, Mr. Sareen has held various important field and staff appointments including Air Officer Commanding-in-Chief of two Air Commands, and Vice Chief of the Air Staff. And finally S. K. Sareen was appointed as the Chief of Air Staff on 31st December, 1995. He was awarded the Vayu Sena Medal in 1971 for his exceptional devotion to duty, Ati Vishisht Seva Medal (1990) and Param Vishisht Seva Medal (1995) for distinguished services of an exceptional order.

S. R. Bommai : A person with vast and varied experience in different fields. He is a lawyer by profession and practiced for 30 long years. Participated in the Quit India Movement of 1942 under Mahatma Gandhi's leadership. Became a founder member of the Radical Humanist Party in 1942 and was its member till its dissolution in 1947. His experience with administration began in 1960 when for five years he became a Senator of the Karnataka University, Dharwar. In 1967, became a member of the Karnataka Legislative Assembly. Joined Indian National Congress in 1969 and became member of the Karnataka Legislative Council in 1972. When the Janata Party was formed in 1977, he became the Vice-President of the Karnataka State Unit and its President in 1981, When the Janata Dal faced crisis, Shri Bommai became the natural choice of its national Presidentship. Elected as a member of Rajya Sabha from Orissa. Since June 1996, a member of the Union Cabinet as Minister for Human Resource Development.

S.R. Sankaran : Popularly known as 'IAS Gandhi' Mr. Sankaran throughout his career in the Indian Administrative Service, strove for the uplift of the downtrodden — particularly Scheduled Castes and Tribes. Among the important appointments he held were Secretary, Department of Welfare, Government of India, and Chief Secretary, Government of Tripura. Unassuming and self-effacing, Mr. Sankaran after his retirement is quietly working for the welfare of the downtrodden. He is associated with many social welfare organisations.

Dr. S. Subramanian : A distinguished civil servant and an academic; joined Indian Police Service (IPS) in 1958 and held important positions of Director General of Central Reserve Police Force (CRPF) and the National Security Guards (NSG). He founded the elite Special Protection Group (SPG). Besides the Central Bureau of Investigation (CBI), Intelligence Bureau (IB) and the National Police Academy (NPA); served as Minister in the Embassy of India, Bonn, Germany.

A Master of Arts in Economics, and Master of Science in Criminal Justice Administration from the Northeastern University, Boston, USA, and a Doctorate in Public Administration, Dr. Subramanian has authored twelve books and writes regularly in the national Press. He serves as guest-faculty in institutions of higher learning. Decorated with the national award 'Padmashri' for distinguished public service, President's Police Medal for Distinguished Service and Indian Police Medal for Meritorious Service, Dr. Subramanian, after retirement from Government Service, has founded an NGO - Association for Advancement of Police and Security Sciences which works for observance of Human Rights in the working of Police and security services in India. He also assists International Committee of the Red Cross and UN Centre for Human Rights, Geneva.

Dr. Subhash C. Kashyap : Honorary visiting professor at the Centre for Policy Research, Jawaharlal Nehru Fellow (1996-98) and Honorary Editor, *Politics India* (monthly). He has occupied the positions of Secretary General, Lok Sabha; Director, Institute of Constitutional and Parliamentary Studies; Head CIDP (IPU) Geneva. He is author of over 40 books and lectures widely in India and abroad and writes regularly for the national dailies and Indian and foreign journals. Currently, he is writing a six-volume History of Parliament of India and a Treatise on Parliamentary Practices.

T.V. Rajeswar : Former Governor of Sikkim and West Bengal and Lt.Governor of Arunachal Pradesh, Mr. Rajeswar in his distinguished career in the Indian Police Service held many important appointments including those of Director, Intelligence Bureau; Special Adviser to The Royal Government of Bhutan; and Special Commissioner for Andhra Pradesh at Delhi. Currently he writes regularly in the national press on matters of topical interest.

Lt. Gen. (Retd.) V. K. Nayar : M. Sc. (Defence Studies) from Madras University. Participated in Indo-China war, Indo-Pak wars and Counter Insurgency operations in Mizoram, Manipur and Nagaland. He was decorated with Sena Medal for operations in High Altitude areas on our Northern borders against the Chinese. Commanded the Manipur and Nagaland Division at the height of Meitei and Naga insurgency from 1981-83, and for his services of exceptionally high order he was decorated with Param Vishist Seva Medal, while still in command. After serving a tenure as Additional Director General Military Operations from 1983-85, on promotion he took over a Corps in Punjab. in July 1985. He was promoted as GOC-in-C Western Command on 1 November, 1987, and retired on 1 November, 1989. He was also the Colonel of the Parachute Regiment and Honorary ADC to the President. He was the Governor of Manipur and also held additional charge of Nagaland. Presently he is a Research Professor at the Centre for Policy Research, New Delhi, and was awarded the Field Marshal K. M. Cariappa Research Fellowship for 1996 at the United Services Institute of India. He is the author of the book titled "Threat from Within" on India's internal security environment, published in 1992.

Ms. V. Mohini Giri : A well known social worker and associated with national and international organisations working for the welfare of the women and children, Ms. Mohini Giri is currently the Chairperson of the National Commission for Women, India. She has participated in many international conferences and seminars and presented papers covering a wide range of subjects with the core theme of Gender Justice and Welfare of Women. She is the recipient of numerous awards including the Rajiv Gandhi Excellence Award (1994) and Jawaharlal Nehru Excellence Award (1996).

Justice V.R. Krishna Iyer : A distinguished jurist who gave the judicial institutions in the country, a new orientation towards people-oriented social justice concerns and poverty alleviation jurisprudence. Adorned the benches of the Supreme Court of India and the High Court of Kerala. He was a Member of the Law Commission. As a lawyer, he was in active politics and served as an MLA and a Minister in Kerala. An erudite scholar, author of over 60 books and 300 articles. Travelled widely in India and abroad, takes active part in the activities of many legal, social and cultural organisations even today at the ripe age of 82.

Vijay Karan : In his distinguished career as a member of the Indian Police Service, Mr. Vijay Karan held many appointments including those of Director, Central Bureau of Investigation, Commissioner of Police, Delhi, Resident Director, India Investment Centre, New York, and Special Assistant to Union Home and Finance Ministers. He is known for his work in trying to humanise the rank and file of Delhi Police Force. He is the author of *'War by Stealth'* a book on terrorism.

PART I

The Republic

- The Indian Republic : Retrospect and Prospect
- Election System in India
- Parliament of India : Case for Reforms
- Looking Back with Mixed Feelings
- India's Moral Dilemmas
- Political Populism, Administrative Careerism and Judicial Activism
- Ethnicity, Plurality and Conflict Resolution
- Rajiv Gandhi and Panchayati Raj
- Are We a Market Once Again
- India's North-East : An Overview

1

The Indian Republic

Retrospect and Prospect

Justice V. R. Krishna Iyer

WHEN MAHATMA GANDHI was asked for a message for the historic Transfer of Power on August 15, 1947, he wryly replied, "he had run dry". When told again that if he did not give any message it would not be good, Gandhiji replied: "There is no message at all, if it is bad let it be so." Since 1947, we have moved down to 1997 and if the same Gandhi were to reincarnate to-day and be asked for a message for India's Republic Day he would have repeated his earlier answer with added proof of several decades of history neglecting the poor, lining the pockets of the corrupt and inviting multinational corporations (MNCs) under the cover of swadeshi-subversive New Economic Policy to substantiate his agony. Winston Churchill, when the Indian Independence Act was being passed in the House of Commons, angrily rebuked Attlee who was the Prime Minister then and said:

> "Liberty is man's birthright. However, to pass on the reins of the Government to the Congress at this juncture is to hand over the destiny of hungry millions into the hands of rascals, rogues and freebooters. Not a bottle of water or a loaf of bread shall escape taxation, only the air will be free and the blood of hungry millions will be on the head of Mr.Clement Attlee. India will be lost in political squabbles. It will take a thousand years to know the periphery of the philosophy of politics.

Today we hand over the Government to men of straw, of whom no trace will be found in a few years."

[Extracts from *The Hindu,* dated 2.11.1996]

With the hindsight wisdom we now have, if we are patriotic and sensitive about Indian humanity, Gandhiji's sad plea that he had gone 'dry', and Churchill's angry forecast of power being handed over to 'rogues and rascals' and 'freebooters', is not far-off the mark, in spite of the fact that there have been distinguished Indians, creative minds and statesmen of the tallest stature.

At this point we may recapitulate portions from Dr.Ambedkar's final address to the Constituent Assembly on November 25, 1949:

"I feel, however good a Constitution may be, it is sure to turn out bad because those who are called to work it, happen to be a bad lot. However bad a Constitution may be, it may turn out to be good if those who are called to work it, happen to be a good lot. The working of a Constitution does not depend wholly upon the nature of the Constitution. The Constitution can provide only the organs of State such as the legislature, the executive and the judiciary. The factors on which the working of those organs of State depends are the people and the political parties they will set up as their instruments to carry out their wishes and their politics. Who can say how the people of India and their parties will behave?"

[*The Framing of India's Constitution* , by B. Shiva Rao, Volume IV - p.939]

The Constitution has not failed us but the politicians have failed the Constitution. Corrupt majority, conspiratorial coalitions and economic imperialism have gained unblushing res-pectability and right to parliamentary oratory. Let me refer to another part of Ambedkar's address:

"On 26th January 1950, India will be an independent country. What would happen to her independence? Will she maintain her independence or will she lose it again? This is the first thought that comes to my mind. It is not that India was never an independent country. The point is that she once lost the independence she had. Will she lose it a second time? It is this thought which makes me most anxious for the future. What perturbs me greatly is the fact that not only India has once before lost her independence, but she lost it by the infidelity and treachery of some of her own people.........

"Will history repeat itself? It is this thought which fills me with anxiety. This anxiety is deepened by the realization of the fact that in addition to our old enemies in the form of castes and creeds we are going to have many political parties with diverse and opposing political creeds. Will Indians place the country above their creed or will they place creed above country? I do not know. But this much is certain that if the parties place creed above country, our independence will be put in jeopardy a second time and probably be lost for ever. This eventuality we must all resolutely guard against. We must be determined to defend our independence with the last drop of our blood."

[Ibid. pp. 942-943]

Communalism, casteism, economic recolonisation, with GATTastrophe and World Trade Organisation (W.T.O) have betrayed our founding fathers. Saying that India had once lost its democratic system he added:

"Will she lose it a second time? I do not know. But it is quite possible in a country like India - where democracy from its long disuse must be regarded as something quite new - there is danger of democracy giving place to dictatorship. It is quite possible for this new born democracy to retain its form but give place to dictatorship in fact. If there is a land-slide, the danger of the second possibility becoming actuality is much greater.

[Ibid. p.943]

Dr.Ambedkar, a crusader of social justice, did emphasise in his final address on November 25, 1949:

"The third thing we must do is not to be content with mere political democracy. We must make our political democracy as a social democracy as well. Political democracy cannot last unless there lies at the base of it social democracy. What does social democracy mean? It means a way of life which recognises liberty, equality and fraternity as the principles of life. These principles of liberty, equality and fraternity are not to be treated as separate items in a trinity. They form a union of trinity in the sense that to divorce one from the other is to defeat the very purpose of democracy. Liberty cannot be divorced from equality, equality cannot be divorced from liberty. Nor can liberty and equality be divorced from fraternity. Without equality, liberty would produce the supremacy of the few over the many. Equality without liberty would kill individual initiative. Without fraternity, liberty and equality could not become a natural course of things. It would require a constable to enforce them. We must begin by acknowledging the fact that there is

> complete absence of two things in Indian society. One of these is equality. On the social plane, we have in India a society based on the principle of graded inequality which means elevation for some and degradation for others. On the economic plane, we have a society in which there are some who have immense wealth as against many who live in abject poverty. On the 26th January, 1950, we are going to enter into a life of contradictions. In politics we will have equality and in social and economic life we will have inequality. In politics we will be recognizing the principle of one man one vote and one vote one value. In our social and economic life, we shall, by reason of our social and economic structure, continue to deny the principle of one man one value. How long shall we continue to live this life of contradiction?"
>
> [Ibid. p. 944]

The *adivasis*, the *antyajas* and the poorest of the poor remain the 'eternal tenants of an extortionate system'. Their only hope of deliverance is death. But there is a creamy layer which is seeking luxuries from abroad, and the disparity between the rich and the poor is widening day after day with the hollow boast that if foreign goods and consumerism flourish the whole country rises in prosperity. The reality is that the vast masses are destitutes. They are the Fourth and the Fifth World in the Third World. Women are in despair. The girl child is in perennial peril. Bonded labour is on the increase. Illiteracy of large numbers ceases to be of concern except in political rhetoric. Even the radical parties with crimson colours are joining coalitions committed to the new economic policy of 'open seasame' for neo-imperialists. Therefore, the emergence of a new massive popular upsurge is on the cards. The tidal wave of the hungry and the have-nots, of the deprived and the destitute, of the gender number victimised by the sex mafia, led by authentic patriots, not Left with the capital letter 'L' - such a pan-Indian movement inspired by the goals of the Preamble to the Constitution is the imperative of the hour.

> "The New World Human Order is based upon sacred principles which are also found in the Indian Preamble. The cornerstone of the Indian Constitutional order is thus humanist, secular, socialist and an expression of people's power."

> "Unfortunately, illiteracy about the Constitutional jurisprudence is popular among our politicians and even the bureaucrats. For them, the luminous passages of the Preamble are sufficient contemplative material. As a people, we must insist on the new value revolution being implemented so that the Constitution may become vibrant as a rule of life."

Jurisprudence cannot do it alone. It is people's militancy without violence, literacy without arrogance, sense of accountability without authoritarianism that can make the Constitution the great guarantee of people's rights.

The *Creme de la creme* of the Constitution, in its political vision, economic mission and developmental action, is what the Preamble spells out. The Preamble itself is a value-based jurisprudence in its condensed excellence.

Part IV of the Constitution also highlights the socialistic sheen of the scheme. Dr.Ambedkar referring to this part observed in the Constituent Assembly:

> "In my judgement, the Directive Principles have a great value, for they lay down that our ideal is economic democracy. Because we did not want 'merely a parliamentary form of government to be instituted through the various mechanisms provided in the Constitution, without any direction as to what our economic ideal, as to what our social order ought to be', we deliberately included the Directive Principles in our Constitution."

The Supreme Court has explained the concept of distributive justice as a means of removing economic inequalities and remedying the injustices resulting from social inequality. In Lingappa Pochanna (AIR 1985, SC 389) Case the Court stressed this aspect and Prof.Tope has said:

> "Law should be used as an instrument of distributive justice to achieve a fair division of wealth among the members of society based upon the principle. From each according to his capacity, to each according to his needs. Distributive justice comprehends more than achieving lessening of inequalities by differential taxation, giving debt relief or distribution of property owned by one to many who have none by imposing ceiling on holdings both agricultural and urban or by direct regulation of contractual transactions by forbidding certain transactions and perhaps by requiring others. It also means that those who have been deprived of their properties by unconscionable bargains should be restored their property. All such laws may take the form of forced distribution of wealth as a means of achieving a fair division of material resources among the members of society or there may be legislative control of unfair agreements."

[*Constitutional Law of India,* by Prof. T.K.Tope -2nd Edn.,p.337]

Even environment protection and unemployment presentation are part of social justice.

The Supreme Court in a case which came before it, while upholding the fundamental duty about the protection of environment, laid down:

> "We are not oblivious to the fact that the natural resources have got to be tapped for the purpose of social development, but one cannot forget at the same time that tapping of resources have been done with requisite attention and care so that ecology and environment may not be affected in a serious way. It has always to be remembered that these are not permanent assets of mankind."

A.P.High Court held that

> "Preservation and protection of natural gifts is a part of right under Article 21. When indiscriminate operation of mines prove to be hazardous to natural wealth and environment courts intervene and issue directions even as to closures of mines. Article 51-A confers a right on citizens to move courts for appropriate writs."

[Ibid p.341]

Democracy with equality on a level playing ground is never achieved where cases of elite upper classes are able to prosper leaving sandy deserts of destitutes and under-privileged in a state of despair. Therefore, dynamic intervention by the State in favour of the weaker sections from a developmental angle is fulfilment of socio-economic justice. Equality before the law is not a mere negative concept but includes a command to the State to eliminate inequalities by affirmative action. Formal equality before the law is often a sham. Likewise, unequals being treated as equals in the economic and socio fields is but a phoney homage to principles *egalite*. A giant corporation with multi-national prowess and a small scale or tiny sector enterprise can never be treated equally. Procrustean equality is inequality coupled with cruelty which is anathema to the Constitution (Art.14).

Creative equality through affirmative action is the genius of our Constitution and the Supreme Court on several occasions has established the potential for realisation of egality through such processes. Therefore the message for the managers of our Republic is the actualisation of human justice through human law.

2

Election System in India

Dr. M. S. Gill

THE CONSTITUTION of India has established a representative Parliamentary democracy under which elections to the House of the People (Lower House of Indian Parliament akin to the House of Commons in the United Kingdom) are held direct from territorial constituencies as determined under the law.

Under Article 79 of the Constitution of India, there shall be a Parliament for the Union consisting of the President of India and two Houses, namely, Council of States (Rajya Sabha) and the House of the People (Lok Sabha)

Article 80 of the Constitution of India stipulates that the maximum number of members of the Council of States shall be 250. Of them, not more than 238 shall be representatives of the States chosen by their Legislative Assemblies and the remaining 12 members shall be nominated by the President among the persons having special knowledge or practical experience in literature, science, art and social service. The existing strength of the Council of States is 245 (including 12 nominated members).

Under the provisions of Article 81 of the Constitution of India, the maximum number of elected members of the Lok Sabha shall not exceed 550. The existing strength of elected members of the Lok Sabha is 543. Of these, 530 members are elected direct from the territorial constituencies (called Parliamentary constituencies) in the twenty-five States and remaining 13 members are likewise elected direct from the territorial constituencies in the seven Union Territories. For the purpose, the country is divided into 543 single member Parliamentary constituencies.

Under Article 168 of the Constitution of India, for every State there shall be a Legislature which shall consist of the Governor, and;

(i) Legislative Assembly;

(ii) Legislative Council (Only in specified States).

The Legislative Assembly of a State, other than Goa, Mizoram and Sikkim, shall consist of not more than 500 and not less than 60 members, vide Article 170 of the Constitution. The strength of the Goa, Mizoram and Sikkim Legislative Assemblies is fixed as 40, 40 and 32 respectively.

There are also Legislative Assemblies for two of the Union Territories, viz., National Capital Territory of Delhi and Pondicherry.

The strength of the Legislative Assembly of the Union Territory of Pondicherry has been fixed as 30 under the provisions of the Government of Union Territories Act, 1963. The Legislative Assembly for the National Capital Territory of Delhi has 70 members under the Government of National Capital Territory of Delhi Act, 1991.

Under the existing provisions of the Constitution, such total number of seats in the House of People and State Legislative Assemblies shall not be re-adjusted until the relevant figures for the first census taken after the year 2000 have been published.

The members of a State Legislative Council shall not exceed one-third of the members of the concerned State Legislative Assembly, but subject to a minimum of 40. One-third of such members are elected by the members of the State Legislative Assembly, another one-third by the local authorities' constituencies, one twelfth each by the Graduates' and Teachers' constituencies and the rest are nominated by the Governor.

Five Year Duration

The House of the People and every State Legislative Assembly shall, unless sooner dissolved, continue for five years from the date appointed for its first meeting.

The Council of States and State Legislative Councils are not subject to dissolution, but as nearly as possible one-third of their members shall retire every second year in accordance with the provisions of law made by Parliament.

The election to the House of People and to the Legislative Assembly of every State are held on the basis of adult suffrage. Every person who is a citizen of India and who is not less than 18 years of age on the qualifying date and who is not otherwise disqualified under the provisions of the Constitution of India or any law made by the appropriate Legislature on the ground of non-residence, unsoundness of mind, crime or corrupt or illegal practice, is entitled to be registered as a voter at these elections under Article 326 of the Constitution. There are certain Constitutional and statutory qualifications and disqualifications. The condition for registration in an electoral roll are laid down in the Representation of the People Act, 1950.

Section 15 of the Representation of the People Act, 1950 lays down that for every Assembly constituency there shall be an electoral roll which shall be prepared in accordance with the provisions of that Act under the superintendence, direction and control of the Election Commission. In all States and Union Territories, the electoral roll for a Parliamentary constituency shall consist of the electoral rolls for all the Assembly constituencies comprised within that Parliamentary constituency.

One of the basic qualifications for candidature in an election to Parliament or the Legislature of a State is that the person concerned should be an elector. Under the law, the electoral rolls of all constituencies would have been revised and finally published well before the election programme is announced. Even after the electoral roll for a constituency has been finally published, a person whose name has not been included in the roll, has a right to apply for the inclusion of his name in the electoral roll if he is qualified for such inclusion. Such inclusion is permissible under the law up to the last date for making nominations at an election.

Qualifications and Disqualifications For Candidates

The qualifying age for the membership of the House of People and State Legislative Assemblies is 25 years and for the Council of States and State Legislative Councils is 30 years.

For the House of People/Legislative Assembly, a candidate:

i) must be a citizen of India;

ii) must make and subscribe before some person authorised in that behalf by Election Commission of India an oath or affirmation according to the forms set out for the purpose in the Constitution; and

iii) must be an elector for any Parliamentary constituency/ any Assembly constituency in the concerned State.

Under Articles 102 and 191 of the Constitution of India, a person shall be disqualified for being elected as, and for being, a member of Parliament or of a State Legislature:

i) if he holds any office of profit under the Government of India or the Government of any State, other than an office declared by Parliament/State Legislature by law not to disqualify its holder;

ii) if he is of unsound mind and stands so declared by a competent Court;

iii) if he is an undischarged insolvent;

iv) if he is not a citizen of India or has voluntarily acquired the citizenship of a foreign State or is under any acknowledgement of allegiance or adherence to a foreign State;

v) if he is disqualified by or under any law made by Parliament.

Parliament has laid down the following grounds for disqualification, viz.; (i) conviction of certain offences, (ii) commission of corrupt practice at an election, (iii) dismissal from Government service for corruption or disloyalty, (iv) subsisting contract with Government, (v) office under Government Company, and (vi) failure to lodge account of election expenses (vide Sections 8 to 10A of the Representation of the People Act, 1951).

A person is also disqualified for being a member of Parliament or of a State Legislature under the Tenth Schedule to the Constitution of India (Disqualification on ground of defection).

Election Machinery

Article 324 of the Constitution of India vests superintendence, direction and control of the preparation of the electoral rolls for, and the conduct of, all elections to Parliament and to the Legislature of every State and of elections to the offices of President and Vice-President of India in the Election Commission. The Election Commission consists of the Chief Election Commissioner and such number of other Election Commissioners, as the President may appoint from time to time. The President of India appointed two Election Commissioners in October, 1993. The Chief Election Commissioner acts as the Chairman of this multi-member Commission. But the Chief Election Commissioner and Election Commissioners enjoy equal powers and privileges in all respects and in the event of any difference of opinion amongst them in any matter, such matter is decided by the opinion of the majority.

The entire electoral machinery for the revision of the electoral rolls and the conduct of elections is provided by the Governments of the concerned States. The electoral machinery in a State is headed by a Chief Electoral Officer, who is an officer of Government. He is designated or nominated in this behalf by the Election Commission in consultation with the Government. At the district level, there is a District Election Officer for supervision of work in the district in connection with the revision of electoral rolls and the conduct of elections.

For every constituency, there is an Electoral Registration Officer for preparation/revision of the electoral roll, and a Returning officer for the conduct of elections. Setting up of the polling stations is the responsibility of the District Election Officers. Usually polling stations are set up in public institutions, like, schools, community halls, panchayat offices, etc.

The steps for the general elections are set in motion by the President of India in the case of Lok Sabha and by the Governor of the State in the case of general election to the Legislative Assembly of the State by issuing one or more notifications. In the case of bye-elections such notification is issued by the Election Commission. It is the Election Commission which fixes the time schedule for all elections under Section 30 of the Representation of the People Act, 1951. The notification fixing the election schedule is issued on the same date on which the notifications for the general elections or the bye-elections are issued. The Election Commission of India fixes the schedule of the general elections after taking into account all relevant factors. Under the provisions of Sections 14 and 15 of the Representation of the People Act, 1951, where the general elections are held otherwise than on the dissolution of the existing House of the People or the Legislative Assembly of a State, no notification calling the elections shall be issued at any time earlier than six months prior to the date on which the duration of that House would expire. The different stages of election schedule are as follows:

i) Date of issue of the notification calling the election;

ii) Last date for making nominations, which shall be the seventh day after the date of notification;

iii) Date of scrutiny of nominations, which shall be the date immediately following the last date for making nominations;

iv) Last date for the withdrawal of candidatures, which shall be two days after the date for scrutiny of nominations;

v) Date(s) of poll, which shall not be earlier than the 14th day after the last date for withdrawal of candidatures;

vi) Date before which the election is to be completed.

None of the dates mentioned at (i) to (iv) should fall on a public holiday.

The period between the last date for the withdrawal of candidatures and the date(s) of poll is utilised for campaign by political parties and contesting candidates. The minimum period of campaign allowed under the law is 13 clear days after the last date for withdrawal of candidatures. However, campaign shall cease 48 hours before the hour fixed for the conclusion of poll on the date of poll.

A period of minimum of eight hours is provided for polling on a polling day.

A person who intends to contest an election is required to file a nomination paper, in prescribed form, indicating his name, age, postal address and electoral roll number. The candidate not set up by a recognised political party is required to be nominated by ten registered electors of the constituency as proposers. Every candidate has also to make a deposit of Rs.10,000/- in the case of elections to the House of the People and Rs.5,000/- in the case of elections to the Council of States or State Legislative Assembly or Legislative Council. The amount of security deposit for candidates belonging to the Scheduled Castes and Scheduled Tribes is half of the above mentioned amounts.

The nomination paper is to be filed before the Returning Officer concerned. The scrutiny of the nomination papers is done by the Returning Officer himself or by the Assistant Returning Officer who may be specified by the Returning Officer for the purpose. Candidates can withdraw their candidatures in the prescribed form, to be filed before the Returning Officer on or before the last date for the withdrawal of candidatures. After the last date for the withdrawal of candidatures, the Returning Officer notifies the list of contesting candidates in the prescribed form.

Model Code of Conduct

As mentioned above, the period between the last date for withdrawal of candidatures and dates of poll is utilised by the political parties and contesting candidates for campaign. The campaign is to cease 48 hours before the hour fixed for the conclusion of poll on the date of poll. However, the actual electioneering starts right from the date of announcement of elections by the Election Commission and it will be over on the date of completion of election.

During the period of electioneering, the political parties and contesting candidates are to abide by the model code of conduct evolved by the Election Commission. The model code lays down broad guidelines as to how the political parties and candidates should conduct themselves during the election campaign. It is intended to maintain the election campaign on healthy lines, avoid clashes and conflicts between political parties or their supporters and to ensure peace and order during the campaign period and thereafter till the results are declared. The model code also prescribes guidelines for the ruling party either at the Centre or in the State to ensure that no cause is given for any complaint that it has used its official position for the purposes of its election campaign.

Elections to the House of the People and State Legislative Assemblies are held on the simple majority system known as 'the first-past-the-post system'. However, elections to the Council of States and State Legislative Councils are held under the proportional representation system by means of single transferable vote.

The system of voting followed in India for elections to the House of the People and State Legislative Assemblies is known as the marking system. Under the marking system, a ballot paper containing the names of all the contesting candidates and the facsimiles of their election symbols allotted to them is prepared for each constituency. The elector indicates his preference with an ink mark made with a rubber stamp on or near the symbol of the candidate of his choice, inside a screen compartment, and inserts the folded ballot paper into a common ballot box kept in full view of the Presiding Officer and polling agents of the candidates. This marking system eliminates the possibility of ballot papers being surreptitiously taken out of the polling station or not being put in the ballot box.

The facility of postal ballot papers is given to the following categories of voters:

i) Members of armed forces, persons serving under the Government of India in a post outside India;

ii) Voters under preventive detention;

iii) Special voters, like, the President, Vice-President of India, Governors of States, Cabinet Ministers of the Union or any of the States etc.; and

iv) Voters on election duty.

Part V of the Conduct of Election Rules, 1961, lays down a detailed and elaborate procedure for the counting of votes. The Returning Officers are responsible to ensure proper, systematic and accurate counting of votes. The date, time and place of counting are to be decided by the Returning Officer and he has to give prior information to the contesting candidates in this regard. For any clarification concerning counting of votes, the Returning Officer is guided only by the Election Commission. The Returning Officer exercises his functions in a quasi-judicial capacity as he has to decide on the demand made by the contesting candidates for recount of votes, etc.

The counting of votes in any Parliamentary or Assembly Constituency may be done either polling station-wise or by mixing the ballot papers of the constituency, as the Election Commission may direct in each constituency.

After the counting of votes is over, the Returning Officer declares the name of the candidate, to whom largest number of votes have been given, as the candidate returned from the constituency. Copies of this declaration are sent to the Election Commission, the Chief Electoral Officer and the Government.

Accounts of Election Expenses

Under Section 77 of the Representation of the People Act, 1951, every candidate at an election to the House of the People or State Legislative Assembly is required to keep, either by himself or by his election agent, a separate and correct account of all expenditure in connection with the election incurred or authorised by him or by his election agent between the date on which he has been nominated and the date of declaration of result of the election, both dates inclusive. The account has to be submitted to the District Election Officer within 30 days from the date of declaration of result of the election.

In a landmark judgement on 4th April, 1996, the Supreme Court of India in Writ Petition (Civil) No.24 of 1995 has held that the political parties should submit to the Election Commission for its scrutiny, the details of the expenditure incurred or authorised by the political parties in connection with the election of their respective candidates.

Failure on the part of the contesting candidates to submit the account of election expenses within the time limit and in the manner prescribed by law will invite disqualification which will debar them from contesting elections to Parliament and State Legislatures for a period of three years from the date of the Order of the Election Commission declaring them so disqualified.

Any dispute relating to an election can be decided only in an election petition which has to be filed before the High Court of the State concerned. An election petition is not an ordinary civil suit but is a contest in which the whole constituency is interested. The law provides that not only a defeated candidate but also an elector in the constituency can file an election petition and that if the petitioner seeks to withdraw the petition, any elector in the constituency who is interested in pursuing the matter may apply to the High Court for being substituted as such petitioner.

The election petition has to be filed within 45 days of the declaration of the result of election. Appeal lies to the Supreme Court against the decision of the High Court in an election petition.

According to financial arrangements that exist between the Central Government and State Governments, all expenditure in a State on the preparation of electoral rolls and the conduct of elections is initially borne by the State Government. At the end of the financial year, the Central Government shares 50% of the expenditure incurred by the State Government on items of common concern to the Central Government and the State Government. The Central Government also shares the expenditure incurred on the conduct of elections to the House of People and the State Legislative Assemblies when these are held simultaneously, including the payment of allowances to the Government servants and others deployed on election duty. But when these elections are not held simultaneously, the Central Government bears the entire expenditure incurred on conduct of elections to the House of the People, and the State Government bears the entire expenditure in respect of elections to the State Legislative Assembly. The expenditure incurred in connection with the Presidential and Vice-Presidential elections as well as the biennial elections and bye-elections to fill the vacant seats in the Rajya Sabha is wholly met by the Central Government. Likewise, the expenditure on elections to the Legislative Councils is entirely met by the State Government concerned.

Political Parties

Under Section 29A of the Representation of the People Act, 1951 any association or body of individual citizens of India calling itself a political party is required to be registered with the Election Commission.

The application for registration of a political party shall be accompanied by a copy of the memorandum or rules and regulations of the association or body, by whatever name called, and such body shall bear true faith and allegiance to the Constitution of India and to the principles of socialism, secularism and democracy and would uphold the sovereignty, unity and integrity of India.

The Election Commission issued an order providing for recognition of parties as National and State parties on the basis of their poll performance and for specification, reservation and choice and allotment of symbols at elections in Parliamentary and Assembly constituencies in all States. This order is called 'The Election Symbols (Reservation & Allotment) Order, 1968.

As per this Order, there are two categories of symbols:

i) Reserved symbols, which are reserved for recognised National parties and State parties;

ii) Free symbols, which are meant for allotment to independent candidates and candidates of registered unrecognised parties.

The symbols play an important role in elections as a large number of the electors are illiterate and symbols help them in identifying the candidates. There are eight National parties and 39 State parties at present, apart from more than 575 registered-unrecognised parties.

As mentioned above, the Constitution of India proclaims that India is a Democratic Republic. Democracy being the basic feature of India's constitutional set up, there can be no two opinions that free and fair elections to Legislative bodies alone would guarantee the growth of a healthy democracy in the country.

3

Parliament of India

Case for Reforms

Dr. Subhash C. Kashyap

THAT REPRESENTATIVE democracy and parliamentary institutions have endured in India for five decades is a great tribute to their strength and resilience. There has, however, been in recent years some thinking and debate about decline of Parliament, devaluation of parliamentary authority, falling standards of debate, deterioration in the conduct and quality of members, poor levels of participation and the like. A certain cynicism towards parliamentary institutions and an erosion in the respect for normal parliamentary processes and the parliamentarians present a disturbing scenario.

Very little effort, however, seems to have been made to examine and analyse what really ails Parliament or to find out the reasons for the erosion of the traditional authority, high esteem and pristine glory of Parliament. Certain points suggest themselves. The information explosion, the technological revolution, the growing magnitude and complexities of modern administration cast upon Parliament vastly extended responsibilities. Inadequacy of time, information and expertise with Parliament results in poor quality legislation and unsatisfactory parliamentary surveillance over administration. It is said that during the entire period of nearly 200 years of their rule in India, the British passed only some 400 laws while in about 40 years Parliament had passed nearly 4000 laws. The big difference was, as

B.K.Nehru put it, that the 400 laws were obeyed or had to be obeyed while the present-day 4000 pieces of legislation are not obeyed. Those to whom many of these laws relate do not even know or understand them. Over-legislation becomes counter-productive.

Operational Mechanics

Inadequacy of education and training in the sophisticated operational mechanics of parliamentary polity and the working procedures of modern parliamentary institutions have adversely affected the performance of both the legislators and the bureaucracy. Little effort has been made thus far to develop the essential prerequisites for the success of parliamentary polity — discipline, character, high sense of public morality, ideologically oriented two-party system and willingness to hear and accommodate minority views. Several of the archaic practices-and time-consuming procedures most unsuitable for present day needs are being continued unnecessarily. Members irrespective of their party affiliations have themselves become a new caste and part of the establishment and co-sharers in the spoils with increased perks and payments and crores of public funds at their disposal.

Legitimacy of government and of representative institutions under the system are inextricably linked to free and fair elections and to the system being able to bring to power persons who truly represent the people's will and have the necessary abilities to govern. Recent efforts notwithstanding, due to the role of mafia gangs, muscle power and money power, free and fair elections are very difficult, if not impossible. The representative credentials of our elected representatives have come to be questioned. There are hardly any ideological or programmatic considerations in voting. Almost all parties and candidates are busy building their vote banks on the basis of caste, communal, linguistic or other such identities or through clandestine control of the electoral processes. Distortions have also crept into the representative character of Parliament through the operation of the electoral system. Majority of those declared elected happen to have secured only minority of votes. Therefore, it seems it would be necessary to reform the electoral system and the political party system before Parliamentary reforms can be thought of.

Professionalisation of Politics

Politics and membership of Parliament have merged as a whole-time, highly lucrative profession for majority of those involved. Following the changed composition of the Houses, there has been faster devaluation of all the old values and increasing disorders and pandemonia on the floor during the "Zero Hour" and at other times. There is general apathy among members, ministers and public at large in the work of Parliament. Absenteeism among members has assumed alarming proportions and defections for money and office have been a common phenomenon.

Parliament is the communication link between the people and the government. Bad public relations job has resulted in a poor image of Parliament and of its members. People talk of happenings in Parliament and of the members of Parliament as things quite remote and different from themselves. There is little consciousness of Parliament being their own and members being from among themselves. A senior parliamentarian speaking of 'politics' generally, bemoaned:

> "It will not be far wrong to say, sorrowfully, that there never was a time in living memory when politics and politicians were, almost rightfully, as denigrated, even degraded, and sometimes detested, in the eyes of our people as they are at the moment."

It is, therefore, necessary to establish a new rapport between the people and the Parliament. The two must be brought closer to each other. Parliament belongs to the people and not to M.Ps. The latter themselves are responsible to Parliament and to the people outside. It is the ordinary people who have to be enabled to feel that they are participants in the decision-making and legislative processes and that through Parliament their voice can reach the Government and that it counts.

It would be necessary to take steps to improve the quality of members, reduce expenditure on Parliament and its members, improve information supply and provide other better support services to members in the discharge of their duties, plan legislative work and improve the quality of legislation, subject constitutional amendments to closer committee scrutiny, raise economic policy to non-party levels, codify parliamentary privileges, reform and regulate functioning of parties, reorganise parliamentary time table and to rationalise and modernise various parliamentary procedures.

The case for reforming Parliament is unexceptionable and, in a sense, has always been so. The real question is of how much and what to change to strengthen and improve the system. We have to be clear about the precise need, the direction and the extent of reform that would be desirable at present. It is obvious that mere tinkering, first-aid repairs and trifling cosmetic adjustments would not anymore be enough. What is needed is a full-scale review. We have to be prepared for fundamental institutional, structural, functional, procedural and organisational changes. The overriding guiding norm and purpose of all parliamentary reforms should be to make both Government and Parliament more relevant to meet the challenges of the times and the changing national needs. Precise suggestions for reforms may have to be institutionally worked out by an appropriate body of experts and senior parliamentarians.

4

Looking Back With Mixed Feelings

Inder Malhotra

DURING THE 50 years of freedom I have grown from adolescence to old age. Almost throughout this period, beginning two years after the tryst with destiny, I have had the good fortune of watching and chronicling the country's ups and downs, joys and sorrows, triumphs and tribulations, often from the vantage point of a ringside seat. It is on some of these high points and low depths that I wish to look back, but before doing so, it is necessary to make one general point.

Overall, India's record is like the proverbial glass which is half full or half empty, depending on the eye of the beholder. That we have survived in one piece, despite apocalyptic forecasts to the contrary, is a big achievement by itself. No less remarkably, except for the 19 months of the Emergency, India has remained a vibrant, if imperfect, democracy. Empowerment of the deprived sections, including women, is also a plus point. Even at the "Hindu rate of growth" the lot of most Indians has improved, as is underscored by the virtual doubling of life expectancy to just over 60 years. But the other side of the coin is dismal and stark. Four out of every ten Indians still live below the "poverty line", a euphemism for dehumanising destitution. The country will enter the 21st century with half its population wholly illiterate. Corruption, abuse of power and oppressive governance have increased exponentially. In large parts of

Bihar and Uttar Pradesh, to name only the worst examples, the State appears to have withered away, though not in the sense in which Marx had wanted it to.

It is against this mixed or mixed-up backdrop that my mind wanders back to the memories of peaks and troughs in the nation's march through the last five decades : a puzzling paradox of strides forward being followed by leaps backwards.

The mid-fifties were the golden years. India's collective mood was upbeat. Indians walked tall because they were res-pected abroad and felt confident and optimistic at home. Within the first decade of freedom, the country had solved refugee problem, caused by history's largest movement of humanity in peacetime. The word *sharanarthi* (refugee) had disappeared from the Indian political lexicon; in neighbouring Pakistan, *Mohajirs* continue to be the focus of horrendous fratricide to this day.

Of the 562 princely states left behind by the departing British, all but one had been assimilated in the national mainstream peaceably and by consent. The solitary and excruciatingly painful exception, Kashmir, haunts us still.

To cap it all, India had completed two General Elections, firmly establishing its credentials as the world's largest, and the Third World's only, democracy. The first Five Year Plan having been implemented successfully, the Second had been launched. It was to lay the foundations of the industrial and technical base. Amidst all this activity, the gigantic task of States reorganisation along linguistic lines was also completed with remarkable skill. Here also there were two exceptions: the forced marriage between Maharashtra and Gujarat was annulled speedily enough after Maharashtra's claim on the coveted city of Bombay was conceded by all concerned. The resistance to Punjabi Suba persisted much longer and led to much graver consequences which were not, however, foreseeable in the buoyant ambience then prevailing.

The architect of these achievements, and of the robust self-confidence in the country that they engendered, was unquestionably Jawaharlal Nehru. Today it has become fashionable, especially among the young who never had the good fortune personally to experience his civilised rule and noble leadership, to traduce Nehru and hold him responsible for every single ill that besets the country. Of course, Nehru had many failings and made several mistakes some of which have had lasting consequences. But which world statesman has been totally devoid of shortcomings, errors and failures? Nehru was the second greatest Indian of our time, next only to his mentor and master, Gandhi. And no amount of screaming by habitual Nehru-haters can make any difference to his exalted place in history - and in the hearts of most Indians.

Having said that, one must add that Nehru's misreading of China, combined with the Indian propensity to make foreign relations a matter of emotion rather than hard headed pursuit of national interest, led to the drift towards disaster which ultimately climaxed into the brief but brutal border war with China. No one who lived through this trauma can ever forget it. To our shame and sorrow, national morale disintegrated almost overnight.

In retrospect at least it became clear that what was believed to be an all-out Chinese assault on India was in fact only a carefully calibrated punitive exercise which, by coincidence or design, was put through while the major powers were distracted by the Cuban Missile Crisis.

Our Age of Innocence was supposed to have ended on the bleak Himalayan heights 35 years ago. But that is not entirely true. Even today there is no country across the globe so indifferent to its security as India. Surprisingly large section of the articulate intelligentsia seems to believe that there is something immoral about wanting to safeguard the country's freedom, frontiers, value system and supreme interests.

One of the worst consequences of the 1962 border war was its impact on Nehru personally. He did succeed in regaining the right perspective on the Chinese challenge, but he was a completely shattered man. The 18 months separating the unilateral Chinese withdrawal and Nehru's passing into history constituted a tragic twilight period.

Even so, Indians answered the agonising question "After Nehru, What?" with aplomb. But Lal Bahadur Shastri's tenure, during which he led the country through the 1965 war with Pakistan and back to peace of sorts at Tashkent, was sadly shortlived. He died within hours of signing the Tashkent Declaration with Ayub Khan of Pakistan. The leadership of the Congress and the country passed to Indira Gandhi.

My worst recollections relate to her first two years as Prime Minister when she was disdainfully dubbed "*goongi gudiya*" (Dumb Doll) and India underwent untold hardship and humiliation. As if two wars and two successions were not enough, the country was afflicted also by savage drought for two years running. There was no foreign exchange in the kitty to buy food from abroad. Concessional import of PL480 wheat from the United States was the only way to avert mass starvation. America eventually gave as much as ten million tons of wheat. But because President Lyndon Johnson was incensed by Indian criticism of his Vietnam policy, especially his relentless bombing of Hanoi, that he put the supply of food on a very tight leash. When someone pointed out to him that the Indians were saying nothing different from what the Pope and the U.N.Secretary-General were also saying, he retorted: "These two do not want our wheat."

Consequently, for nearly two years India lived, almost literally, from ship to mouth. With every morsel of food, we swallowed also a bit of humiliation. I was not alone during those mortifying days to believe that we might never be able to produce enough food to feed ourselves, particularly when reproduction was outpacing production, nor save enough foreign exchange to go to the world market. Nothing made me happier than to be proved wrong on both counts. In about 10 years we were in a position to export a small food surplus and foreign exchange reserves continued to rise until the late eighties when they began to plummet, reaching rockbottom in 1991. Today, a sudden shortage of wheat has surely arisen. But with $22 billion in the coffers of the Reserve Bank, there is no problem about food imports. It needs to be added, however, that though India is self-sufficient in food, millions of children do go to sleep on empty stomachs. For them the question of going to school simply does not arise.

The deep despondency that had enveloped India from the start of the sixties had begun to abate towards the end of the decade. Although the first Congress split of 1969 had caused a lot of bitterness in the body politic, Indira Gandhi, who won a massive election victory in early 1971, on the magic slogan of 'Garibi Hatao', looked a symbol of hope for the future. By the end of that year, she had surpassed the wildest expectations of her supporters. With India's luminous and lightning victory in the War for the Liberation of Bangladesh, the melancholy national mood turned into one of unbridled euphoria.

This was Indira Gandhi's finest hour. The Dumb Doll was now hailed as the invincible Durga, even by her inveterate critics. Having reached the Olympian heights of national esteem and international recognition -- *The Economist* described her as "Empress of India" -- she had nowhere to go but down. However, who could have thought that her fall would be so swift, spectacular and shattering? Or that having been overthrown ignominiously in 1977, she would return to power with a two-thirds majority in Parliament a short three years later, only to be assassinated by her own security guards? Or that her son and successor, Rajiv Gandhi, would meet a similar fate at the start of the nineties?

Let me not dwell on history that is well known. But I do wish to stress, with all the emphasis at my command, that the 19-month long Emergency was one of the worst wounds inflicted on eternal India. Elsewhere, I have called it Indira Gandhi's cardinal sin, and I see no reason to change this opinion. Time is doubtless a great healer. But, sadly, the Emergency's poison has not yet been fully washed out of the Indian system.

The key point is that Indira Gandhi was driven to the crass blunder of imposing the Emergency because of the collapse of her moral authority within a short period of the tremendous triumph in Bangladesh. She had allowed her cohorts, acolytes, hatchetmen and hangers-on to give a virtuoso display of what I had then called their "gift of the grab". They collected tons of black money. Eventually, thanks to the Maruti car project of younger son Sanjay, the stain of corruption was brought to the Prime Minister's own door.

Since then the scourge of corruption and abuse of authority with the single-minded objective of amassing ill-gotten money has increased in geometric progression. There is no need to labour the point if only because over the last two years India has become "a scam a day" country. The loot is both egregious and brazen beyond belief. Even those who have occupied the highest positions in the land are facing criminal charges -- but only because of public interest litigations and judicial activism. Otherwise, the doctrine that politicians in power and the bureaucrats collaborating in their crimes are above the law would have continued to operate. What greater condemnation of the rulers of yesteryears can there be than that a Minister known to be harbouring terrorists in 1993 should have continued to sit at the Cabinet table for more than a year thereafter and was shown the door on charges of involvement in the sugar scandal? Or that another Minister of the once great Congress Party should have left crores of rupees lying around in bedsheets and plastic bags?

As I write these lines, the morning paper has two chilling news stories. One gives the frightening dimensions of the scams under investigation: Rs.950 crore in the fodder scam with Laloo Yadav resolutely refusing to accept that anything wrong has happened; Rs.2,000 crore in the telecom scam; Rs.5,000 crore in the securities megascam; and so on. The urea scam is in a class by itself.

A sum of Rs.133 crore was electronically remitted to international crooks in the dead of night without any bank guarantee, insurance or safeguard of any kind. Not a granule of the desperately needed fertiliser arrived in this country or ever will. Nor is there any likelihood of a single paisa of the poor tax-payer's money being recovered. A son of the then Fertiliser Minister was at least arrested though he is now on bail. But a son of the then Prime Minister, also alleged to be involved in the dirty but lucrative deal, is merrily strutting around.

The other news story, based on an affidavit filed by the Income Tax Department in the Supreme Court, gives the list of the highly placed beneficiaries of the Jain Hawala largesse which reads like a who's who of Indian politics in the highest echelons. The list is exceedingly long. It will be simpler to catalogue those who are not involved.

In short, while in most other respects India has moved two steps forward, one step back or vice versa, in the department of corruption and graft it has been a relentless and remorseless downward slide. Not to put too fine a point on it, the brazen loot in this country has assumed the proportions of tyranny in Hitler's Germany or Stalin's Russia. Under these circumstances, something has got to give. Let there be no mistake about it, as the second half-century of Independence begins.

5

India's Moral Dilemmas

Vijay Karan

SADLY, INDIA'S electoral politics has repeatedly shown how power can corrupt almost everyone, even the best of people. And criminalization of politics is but a consequence of the politics of power. National parties of all hues, even those claiming to be somewhat upright, have acquired a vested interest in the criminals, if only with the objective of winning elections.

History has shown that no value system can be lasting and is vulnerable to degeneration very quickly. Though India has been strong on values, historically and culturally, its value systems have fluctuated with every turn of history. For instance, after the collapse of the Mughal empire and till the eventual consolidation of the British rule over the country, there was an interregnum during which there was a frightening explosion of criminality in India. The absolute authority of the Mughal emperor had collapsed and the smaller rulers and petty landlords had been reduced to local tyrants. Anarchy prevailed over much of India and crime and criminality were on rise. The most notorious among the criminals were the thugs, who committed highway robberies and combined them with murder with macabre finesse. At one stage, it was estimated that about 10,000 thugs were on the rampage in the Gangetic region alone, killing and robbing about 30,000 travellers every year. It took much determination and effort on the part of the British to crush them.

Then there were the Pindaris, who were just bands of freebooters and marauders. The Pindaris would move about in large armies sweeping across towns, villages and settlements, indulging in rapine, torturing one and all, including children, ravishing women and destroying what they could not carry away. It is said that entire villages would prefer to commit suicide rather than go through the hell of facing them. In course of time, they had become militarily so strong that various local rulers including the Scindias of Gwalior and the Holkars of Indore enlisted their services for furtherance of their military and political objectives. Thus, there were the Scindiashahi Pindaris and the Holkarshahi Pindaris, symbolising in a way an early example of criminalization of politics.

The freedom movement came not long thereafter and it had a wonderfully cleansing impact on the country. Cutting across almost the entire population, it generated high idealism, sacrifice and heroism. Along with it came several Hindu revivalist movements, like the Brahmo Samaj of Raja Rammohun Roy and Arya Samaj of Swami Dayanand Saraswati, which too restored values among the Indian people. The times were such that they produced giants among men never perhaps witnessed in the annals of Indian history. Gandhiji exemplified the ethos of the times with his principled politics in the struggle for freedom.

However, it did not take long for the value system of that period to disappear. Ironically, it seemed to disappear with the advent of India's Independence, showing how tenuous and vulnerable even the most noble of value systems can be.The very same men who fought for freedom succumbed to the trappings of power with scarcely a moral fight. A rat race and a virtual free-for-all ensued, for the riches and luxuries and patronage that came with power.

In our present democratic system, everyone wants to win elections, by means fair or even foul. That means spending enormous sums of money, which in turn results in spawning an entirely new culture of corruption. The criminal was also brought in, mainly to intimidate some sections of voters into either not voting or into voting for a particular candidate. Later, as the use of the muscle increased, the criminal was used more extensively for rigging and booth capturing. As the nexus with the criminal grew, the criminal's exposure to politics naturally increased. Soon enough, the criminal realised that proximity to power or better still, electoral victory could bring him power too and that power seemed to bring everything and almost total unaccountability. You could do almost anything and get away with it, if you had some degree of political power. The criminal saw that he could commit murders and rapes with impunity, caring little for police cases registered against him, so long as he was an MLA or an MP. Bail came just for the asking and if his party was in power, he could get the case against him dropped or diluted or put on the back-burner.

The godman phenomenon may at first glance seem natural only to the Indian environment. But if one looks at world's history, the clergy have tried to dabble in politics everywhere. The Popes of Rome often functioned like monarchs and some even went to war to retain their stranglehold on political power. Russia had a charismatic evil priest called Rasputin who was the lover of the queen and wielded enormous power. In Iran, the priesthood still rules the country. In much of Africa, the witch doctor was a very powerful man. Our godmen, though equally interested in power and money, are of somewhat different kind. They are more in the nature of astrologers and *tantriks* who are able to impress and influence those seeking or retaining power into believing that they can propitiate the gods or manipulate the stars in their favour. Today, the godman may seem on the run, but considering the high stakes of political power, he can be expected to bounce back sooner than later.

Meanwhile, things had come to such a pass in the country that a reactive process was inevitable. The Jain Hawala case and a succession of scams were the last straw. Judicial activism followed and seemed to shake the corrupt and venal political system. Today, a former Prime Minister and several former Ministers are facing trial for bribery and corruption. Such a situation was inconceivable a few years ago. The CBI, which would not dare to look at political corruption earlier, has suddenly acquired teeth, courtesy the judiciary.

However, things seem to be happening only in the higher reaches of the judiciary. At the lower levels, nothing seems to have changed. The collapse of the criminal justice system continues. Today, cases just do not come up for trial for several years. And if they do, the trials go on for umpteen number of years without result. As a result, witnesses are either compromised or they just fade away, leading to failure of the cases. Every year at the present rate, about a million criminal cases are charge-sheeted or put on trial and every year a mere 2,00,000 cases are disposed off. The rest are added to an already bulging backlog. In such an ambience, the political criminal finds it even more easy to get away.

Everyone talks of electoral reforms to reduce the role of the money and the muscle from politics but nobody seems to be serious. Seshan did chasten the politicians to some extent but without meaningful electoral reforms, the sway of money and muscle will continue, and the criminal will continue to get elected to the top political positions. Unfortunately, our electoral system is so aberrant that it costs a fortune to fight an election. It also costs another fortune to keep one's political constituents and supporters happy. Visit a *neta's* house on any morning and you will see throngs of people seeking favours, most of which are far from genuine or legitimate.

Nobody seems to genuinely want a Lokpal either. Since 1968, as many as five Lokpal bills were introduced in the Parliament but, quite obviously, only for the sake of appearances. When Charan Singh became the Home Minister during the Janata regime in 1977, he was keen to see a strong Lokpal bill through. He was an honest and determined man but within a few months, he had to succumb to the pressure of his party MPs. V.P.Singh's Lokpal bill was so diluted that it was called the *naqli* Lokpal bill. No wonder all the bills have met the fate of obfuscation. We have to see whether the present government really means business and whether it will be allowed to create an effective Lokpal.

India completes its fifty years of Independence and enters the next millennium in this somewhat bleak scenario. And yet, things do not seem all that hopeless. Judicial activism could yet be a catalyst that could considerably cleanse our value systems once again. Who knows, the present climate may throw up another movement of the kind that India has repeatedly witnessed in its history, bringing in a new wave of morality. India also still functions in an open and rather transparent democratic system. India's media and the non-governmental organisations (NGOs) are becoming increasingly articulate, reflecting the prevailing public mood. Hopefully, the current climate of economic liberalisation would also bring in greater transparency in government functioning, reducing misuse of power and reducing corruption.

6

Political Populism, Administrative Careerism and Judicial Activism

Dr. G. R. S. Rao

AS INDIA stands at the threshold of a new era, with her spirit inherited through myriad years of unbroken history, revived by a century of reform movement, assimilation of humanist and democratic ideals, and having carved out a constitutional blueprint for social development, the cardinal issue that has emerged to the fore before the citizens today is : how soon can India get the individuals who are momentarily manning the institutions of the Republic to appreciate and practice the ethics of Rule of Law enunciated by the Constitution, as the bedrock of the process of democratic social transformation?

There are five parallel tracks on which the process of social change is taking place, today. These tracks are not mutually exclusive, but are activated concurrently by different groups of people. The nature of density of these five tracks is shifting with the changing dispositions and patterns of use of these tracks reflect the quality of democracy and degrees of anarchy in India.

Track One: Constitutional-Democratic Mode

In a constitutional democracy, such as the case of India, the constitutional scheme provides the direction, the pace, and the mechanism for bringing about social transformation; the legislative, the executive and the judicial instrumentalities of the State perform different and yet complementary tasks in order to achieve their inseparably common objectives. Representative, decentralized political process, and a responsive and responsible executive with accountability for results and transparency in performance operating as the "first-court-of-justice", almost makes the role of judicial institutions redundant except where validity, interpretation and application of law or the constitution are involved as a part of the process of dispute settlement and conflict resolution.

Dedication to the constitutional values, goals and processes on the part of the functionaries manning these three institutions would promote social harmony and (harmonious) development, as the two wheels of social transformation. In the background of this ideal canvas, what is the Indian reality?

Political and Legislative Process

Under ideal conditions, the democratic process is nourished and sustained by the political/legislative process, harmonizing the diversity and conflict of values and interests. Mahatma Gandhi had stated that the "lives of millions of people constitute my politics". Politics thus equated with the service to society inspires the manifestos of political parties, influences the mandate of the people, shape the programmes, the well-being of all the citizens, and quality of life of the community as a whole — enhancing the sense of citizenship through processes such as decentralization and participation.

In reality today, the wide-range of distortions in the political/ legislative process can be summarized thus: (a) a shift in the motive-force of political process from 'public-service' to 'personal-power', acquisition of power at any cost, and retained at all costs (as reflected by increasing degrees of money and muscle power, muscle-power getting into the legislatures, converting people into vote-banks, and competitive populism) leading to the disastrous consequence of fracturing society; expanding patterns and intensity of corruption (covering recruitment, postings, transfers and promotions, to gas and telephone connections, to railway berths); devaluation of intrinsic value of votes and, as of now, purchase of votes within the legislatures, and corrupting even the system of parliamentary and legislative committees. In sum, politics has defected from the people; political parties have become the single largest 'corporate' activity geared to the amassment of power and pelf; 'power' has become the prime-mover of politics with no place for social development and nation-building. The potential threat of corruption to democracy in India emerges from the fact that citizens have become collaborators in corruption, thus debasing the democratic base.

Indian Parliament did not, repeat not, have to bring about the 73rd and 74th amendments to the Constitution in order to set in motion the process of decentralized, participative, self-reliant, sustainable development. The process of amendments with all the political breast-beating was a redundant exercise. And, having brought in the amendments, they have been already aborted, nay snuffed out, à la infanticide through authoritarian political process and even worse, centralized bureaucracy. Anti-defection legislation was an equally redundant measure; no true democracy ever had to invent such a measure; having brought it into existence, it is being abused in a manner precisely contrary to its proclaimed objectives.

Indian legislatures, including the national, are churning half-baked legislation; occasionally with the privately admitted hope, that such legislation would be questioned in and quashed by the judiciary. The avalanche of legislation is not backed up by the intention and ability to implement, in spite of the knowledge that such legislation can only backfire. Social transformation is mocked through churning of political declarations. Indian political process today has become anarchic at all levels. The impression that sections of politicians project today is that even crimes such as a gang-rape or a dacoity can be got condoned or even legitimised by manipulating numbers in the legislatures, as if numbers is all about democracy.

Administrative Process

When the gravity of the political process is firmly rooted in society, it is adequately, if not absolutely, supported by the administrative structure, systems and processes in translating political will, into delivery of efficient and effective service, thus promoting justice — political, economic and social. Under ideal conditions, administrative process is characterized by commitment to the Constitution and to the policies of the party in power as mandated by the people, responsive to the problems and needs of the people; responsible to the elected representatives; transparent in performance and democratic in style. Under ideal conditions, administration can truly operate as the change-agent, the instrument of social transformation and as the 'first-court-of-justice'. 'Feedback' is provided to the political executive and to the legislatures on the inadequacies and unintended distortions in the policies and programmes so that appropriate mid-course corrections are provided by the political/legislative processes. People's 'problems', 'grievances', or 'complaints' at the individual as well as the systemic levels are received and processed as the built-in 'management information system' in providing correctives to the administration and thus preventing recurrence. Such an ideal disposition on the part of administration would eliminate the need for citizens to seek either 'politicization' of their problems, or to secure the intervention of the judiciary.

An alert administration committed to the constitutional mandate could check the abuse of power at the political level, monitor and control the factors that cause social turbulence and violence leading to breakdown of law and order, and thus uphold the Rule of Law - the quintessence of democratic social transformation. Thus, under ideal conditions, administration should aim at zero complaints and grievances against the State.

In reality, the democratic constitutional republic is distorted and aborted by the executive as well as through centralization, authoritarianism and non-responsive disposition, sans accountability and transparency. In spite of the 73rd and 74th amendments to the Constitution, adopted on the basis the experience and wisdom of seven Five Year Plans that development cannot be effectuated without democratic decentralization, development effort continues to have been effectively neutralized by the centralized bureaucratic structures, systems and styles. The political executive, irrespective of party affiliations, has consistently charged, *ad nauseam,* that bureaucracy in India has become the major impediment to social transformation.

Administration has not merely remained an impediment or a barrier to social change, it has also effectively negated all attempts at reform. The Republic is left with several Prime Ministers and Chief Ministers lamenting the fact, as if they were helpless. The citizens are left with the committees and commissions that only resulted in escalated charge on the public exchequer, and volumes of wisdom converted into garbage by the efflux of time, belying and burying the hopes of reform. The only change that the administrative apparatus of the State has been affected, with deadly periodicity, is through a series of Pay Commissions. The administration in India has grown into a mighty self-serving corrupt citadel of power.

The 'average citizen', including women and children, works for 350 days in India; the government servant pushes the files for not more than 150 days; government servants take more than 85 paise out of every rupee revenue of the State, the community gets something out of the balance of 15 paise. Alas, in the Indian Republic today, 'public servants' do not seem to consider themselves as citizens of the Republic; they are not accessible to the 'average citizens'; they look down upon the citizens as lesser mortals.

All the ombudsman institutions ranging from anti-corruption bureau, grievance and complaint mechanisms, vigilance cells and commissioners, Lok Ayuktas and the much debated Lok Pal, and a wide range of other national and state level commissions (Women, Human Rights, Minorities, et al) and institutions have not been able to mitigate, much less eradicate the problems of citizens with the administration. Even worse, there has emerged a pattern of equations between the political and administrative functionaries in the form of collusion, the latest scenario reflected in the Vohra Committee Report as 'nexus'; politicians and the administrators have entered into collaborative exploitation with extended participation by the criminals. There is a visible and measurable slide in the umpiring of Indian democracy, belying the efforts and hopes of the Founding Fathers of the Republic.

The 'average' citizens' disposition towards the political/legislative as well as the administrative institutions and processes is characterized by alienation, antagonism and hostility leading towards a fatalistic withdrawal on the one hand, or an inclination towards partnership in corruption with the politicians and the administrators, or even worse, taking law into their own hands on the other, with disastrous consequences to the polity. The fourth category, increasingly becoming a declining minority, goes to the judicial institutions in the hope of either providing a corrective, and/or securing justice. This category is tending to become not only a declining minority, but also 'cynical', for the other categories of citizens mock at them as the 'unwise', and offer to 'tout' their cause — a process of negative 'conversion'.

Track Two: The Judicial Process

When the political/legislative process is lost in competitive populism, and in the exclusive pursuit of power at an enormous social cost and the administrative process has become self-serving, the damned social problems explore alternative tracks, in search of solution. That is how, in India today, the judicial process seems to have moved to the centre-stage.

Under conditions of a democratic decentralized polity, the ideal of 'Rama Rajya' should have been 'empty-court-rooms' and 'zero-litigation' between citizens as well as bet-ween citizens and the State.

In reality, we are not only carrying on with an antiquated legal system and judicial process without even an alibi available after 50 years of Independence for its continuance with its adversarial, litigation-prone, time-consuming, hierarchical layers of the system. The system frustrates the law-abiding citizens most; the conscientious members of the judiciary are equally frustrated with the realization that they are manning a system that has become dysfunctional and counter-productive. All this in spite of accumulated knowledge, experience and wisdom borne out by the volumes of reports being churned out by the national and state level law commissions, and various other commissions and committees that invariably end up, inter-alia, with a beaten path of recommendations viz., (a) amendments to the existing provisions of law, (b) improvement in the content and quality of legal education, and (c) increasing the number of judges at various levels. An adjunct to this set is the reform of the judicial structures, processes, training and continuing education for members of judiciary at all levels, India has excelled all other countries (developed and developing), and itself, in creating ever new institutions, an institutional proliferation, but certainly not in creating a 'work-ethic'.

That the statistics of pending cases of litigation presented to the Parliament and to the state legislatures, periodically and in a routine manner, are not only staggering, but are also grossly misleading is known to everyone. Everyone — lawmakers, law-enforcing functionaries, justice administrators, law-breakers, and the hapless citizens — is aware that for everyone 'problem' that contributes to the statistics of pending cases, there is at least, one, if not two, that has not entered into the official statistics. Knowledgeable and wise citizens recognize that taking their problems to the judicial institutions will lead to more frustration, more expenses, aggravation of conflict, and that the court system, if ever, can be expected to deliver justice to the second generation of litigants.

There is not merely a tremendous amount of filtration (complaints are not registered, often the aggrieved party is slighted, insulted and even abused in a variety of ways beyond the verbal in police stations) but also distortions galore at the chambers of advocates, and in the court premises; it is corruption all the way not merely monetary, any more, but corruption in all its Indian manifestations. It has become proverbial, and continues to be, that it is the rich, influential and knowledgeable who threaten the poor, the weak, the innocent and the ignorant, that they will be 'dragged to the court'. That is why in the reality of life, people opt out of the system, making the statistics of pending cases most unreliable and misleading. The innocent, who have no other means of pursuing redressal of their problems, are aware that it is the rich, the influential (haven't we got anticipatory bails for criminals) and the underworld who are abusing, and are allowed by the system to abuse the judicial process. There was a judge who while dealing with alienation of tribal land, rather unwittingly stated "but what would happen to the 'poor' people who invested a lot of money on the lands?"

Even more dangerous to the Republic is the image, that is gaining ground, of systemic inadequacies and distortions in the appointments, transfers and elevations of members of the judiciary, and increasing degrees and myriad forms of corruption creeping into the system.

True to the extant culture of governance in India, transfer as an effective instrument of 'punishment' is being used even in the case of judiciary. Even worse, post retirement appointments have emerged as 'rewards' alongside the liberalization of the Indian economy. Providing legislative cover to such appointments represents another form of degeneration, and loss of credibility of the judicial system.

People's Initiatives and Declining Standards of State Institutions

True to the inherent attributes of democracy, which is otherwise vibrant at its base, the alert citizens aided by the more 'concerned' functionaries manning the legislative, administrative and the judicial institutions, are activating the two complementary institutions viz., citizens' initiatives (variously called non-governmental organizations, community-based organizations, etc.) and earlier the print and now also the electronic media, constituting the vital Fourth and Fifth Estates respectively of democracy. While people's initiatives are taking several paths, they found the judicial institutions more responsive, contributing to the emergence of Public Interest Litigation as the third track of social transformation.

The vibrancy of democracy in India is reflected, interalia, on three occasions in the short span of five decades; first, when the dictatorial tendencies in the form of 'emergency' had been nipped in the bud by the people; second, when the legislation seeking to censor the media had to be withdrawn; and third, efforts to curb Public Interest Litigation were made futile by strong public opinion. That there are distortions even in the functioning of the media and the community-based organizations cannot constitute a base against their role and place in democracy.

Track Three: Public Interest Litigation

Public Interest Litigation (PIL) cannot be legislated, for if and when an attempt is made to do so, it ceases to be PIL, but becomes a part and parcel of the formal legal system and of judicial process. It can retain its creative character only when it is operated outside the formal legal system. And, as long as it is not statutorily defined, opinions are bound to vary about the concept and its role and place, including its tenability and desirability. Even if and when it is defined and regulated, the citizens of the Republic should be given the credit for the gift of innovative exploration of alternatives, options and choice; and equally, members of the judiciary are bound to explore and innovate creatively, as has been the case during the four decades, though conditioned by individual dispositions and varying styles in their effort to respond to the dynamics of society. Article 32 of the Constitution provides a safety-valve in the best interest of the Constitutional Republic.

Under ideal conditions, PIL should operate as a safety-valve, as the third track of social transformation, under, and in tune with the spirit of the Constitution. It speaks of the good sense of the government of the day that the (ill-conceived) proposal to regulate and restrict the scope of Public Interest Litigation has been dropped. But, an inherent danger to the PIL becoming counter-productive could emanate from the judicial institutions itself, rooted in the citizens' experience with the clogged, dilatory, non-responsive character, and image distortions of the judicial process, systems and styles. While Public Interest Litigation has to be allowed to operate in an atmosphere of judicial innovation, the ebb and tide of PIL is already being attributed to the populist dispositions of individual members of higher judiciary. It is also acquiring the colour of judicial surfing into the realm of policy, that belongs to the political process.

Thus, unless and until the clogged channels of the judicial system are quickly cleared and made adequate, and the philosophical premises and judicial dispositions are crystallized with a large measure of sharing, the third track also may get distorted as indeed there are indications, going by the labelling of Public Interest Litigation variously as judicial activism, populism, extremism, absolutism and adventurism.

Quality of Democracy and Degrees of Anarchy

The three tracks viz., (i) political/legislative and administrative, (ii) the judicial institutions and processes, and that of (iii) public interest litigation are perfectly within the realm of democratic constitutional mode of social transformation. However, the pattern of their activation at any given point of time reflects the quality of democracy.

Inter-institutional and intra-institutional tensions, contributing to their relative efficacy, provide for the germination of alternative paths of social change, leading to varying degrees of anarchy. Democracy as well as anarchy can coexist to some extent, and for some time. In India today, the processes of governance and social transformation are showing clear signs of rapid slide from the democratic mode to the anarchic path. There are two discernible tracks - (a) the extra-legal-institutions and processes, and (b) various shades and streams of extremist organizations and processes that are tending to bypass the legitimate modes in constituting the fourth and fifth tracks leading the Republic in the direction of anarchy. Any bypass would, sooner than later, lead to, making the original dysfunctional, leaving the substitute as the only path of social transformation in political process (blood circulation in physiological terms). It is not only that the quality of democracy is showing signs of degeneration, but the degree of anarchy is rising fast and the system of governance as well as the policy are heating up.

Track Four: Extra-Legal Institutions and Processes

An 'average' Indian citizen today does not respect a police constable as the symbol of the majesty of law; citizens fear the police and would like to avoid any contact, or a visit to a police station for a variety of reasons; yet, the police is approached if circumstances so compel not knowing where else to go. The image of police is that they operate as an extra-legal force; the constabulary believe and opine that they are not protected by their own leaders if they act under conditions of strict legality. It is not only the police, but the entire range of institutions designed to sustain law and promote justice.

The Founding Fathers of the Constitution had the vision to provide for constitutional machinery with immense design safeguards in forms such as the Tribes Advisory Councils, comprising the elected representatives of the tribal communities in order to protect the interests and to promote the welfare of tribal communities. But, the impact of five decades of their 'existence' can be summed up in that they have not only failed to fulfil their constitutional role, but in fact proved counterproductive in more ways than one. The cancer of corruption is illustrated in cases such as prohibition — excise officials themselves indulging in the trade of illicit liquor; and the vigilance and anti-corruption officials conniving with and protecting the corrupt.

The extra-legal institutions and processes can be seen as emerging from disuse, abuse and misuse of the statutory and constitutional processes by all the instrumentalities of the State.

Abuse of legal institutions can at best be illustrated in terms of partisan dispositions and other inadequacies leading to the emergence and growth of private armies; 'modernization' of the police forces to the utter neglect of the compelling need for professionalization; and abuse of the police leading to their awareness of their declining image and efficacy with the disastrous consequence of demoralization, giving vent to their frustrations in the form of brutal violence against and on unarmed innocent citizens. The paradox of public policy and police in India is that in five decades the state governments have been dismissed or administration has been taken over more than a hundred times, on grounds of breakdown of law and order; all political parties in office had been accused by all parties in opposition of misusing and abusing the police force (in a variety of ways); yet, no political party has brought in the 'State Security Commission' as a buffer between the political process and the police, designed to protect both, and to help enhance impartiality and accountability of police. Strangely, the leadership of police organizations has also not so far made it an important issue, thus giving the impression that they are comfortable with their own political equations, even if resulting in disastrous consequences to the Rule of Law, loss of morale of the police forces, and increasing incidents of State terrorism. In the case of judiciary ground distortions are creeping into the system through instances such as 'bail' being abused, and is being allowed to be so abused, especially by the affluent. The ever shifting policy and practices in regard to appointment, transfer, elevation and appointment to commissions and the mix-up between privileges and prerogatives have not enhanced the image of the judiciary among the citizens. Judicial activism may be a response to the distortions emerging from political populism and administrative careerism. But such activism acquires credibility only when the institutions of judiciary operate with a measure of transparency. Such credibility is a *sine qua non* for judicial activism to gain acceptability and legitimacy.

Issues of privileges and contempt, of legislators and the judiciary have long crossed the canons of democracy. The citizens believe that both the legislators and the judiciary are not inclined to codify their ever expanding privileges; this tendency amounts to 'contempt of the citizens' in any Republic. The privileges, self-proclaimed, almost in a competitive spirit, by the legislative, executive and judicial functionaries are mostly unrelated to their roles and responsibilities. The most vulgar display of these privileges takes place on the streets, in utter contempt of "we the people".

Where functionaries of the State misuse, disuse, abuse and distort law, people tend to take law into their own hands; they tend to develop respect for 'people's courts'; and where the umpiring, elaborately set out by the Constitution, slides or fails, the institutions suffer loss of legitimacy and credibility. This is the social reality in India today. If this trend is not arrested - of which there is not even a mute indication, things do not stagnate, they further slide into extremism of various hues, and intensities in forms such as terrorism. We had several Chief Ministers who had advised citizens to take to arms. In place of social transformation, as designed and proclaimed, we could end up with social turbulence and anarchy.

Track Five: Extremism

Legislators, administrators and judges buying peace with extremists (of various hues) is an all-India phenomenon today. While leaders seek and secure the support of extremists in order to get elected in some places, elsewhere elected representatives either desert their constituencies or resign from their elected offices out of fear of extremists. Police who are supposed to protect the citizens, wind up their shops from 'extremist' affected areas and move to 'safer' places. While police do not 'enter' the villages as long as the extremists are within the villages, as if a convention of 'safe passage', in some other places police are the informers and suppliers and sellers of weapons to the extremists. These are signs not merely of withdrawal of the State, and defeat of democracy, but represents the process of decay of both democracy and the State.

An Agenda for Ethics Committee

India is the largest democracy, so says the world, and we seem to be enjoying that status, 'quantitatively' so to say. At the advent of 21st century, the entire humanity — the global society — appears poised to move in the direction of global democracy.

Shall India merely struggle to retain its quantitative primacy, or aim at qualitative excellence and radiate the 'democratic' ethics all around the globe? Indian society is quintessentially democratic, secular, and egalitarian not because, but in spite of divisive political processes. Political process ought to be the prime-mover of social transformation, engine of the democratic Republic. For us to be able to keep our Republic on the right path, the political process has to gain and retain its legitimacy and credibility. That is the agenda before the Ethics Committee.

The pollution of the political process in the polity is the cardinal cause of declining ethics of the parliamentary process. Hence, ethics within the House cannot be promoted and sustained for as long as the source and the base of legislature remain polluted. Looked at it from an entirely different angle, who else, if not the legislatures and the legislators, can cleanse the political process and its polluting influences from spreading all over the body politic? We have to quickly convert our quantitative democracy into qualitative democracy. It will be out of place to carve out and elaborate an action plan here. But some of the elements of an agenda for the Ethics Committee can be indicated.

Supremacy of Institutions

In the seemingly endless debate over 'individuals versus systems' we need to recognize that individuals have to take the initiative to strengthen the systems; systems and institutions are supreme and individuals are merely and momentarily instrumental and trustees in making institutions endure and sustain. Under conditions of democracy, institutions have to be made autonomous, accountable and transparent in order to acquire and retain their legitimacy and credibility.

In a Constitutional Republic, the three instrumentalities of the State are assigned different but complementary roles with common, inseparable objectives and goals. Such a complementarity and constitutional balance gets disturbed, if not disrupted, when individual functionaries, momentarily occupying positions, tend to arrogate to themselves the attributes of hierarchy and superior-subordinate dispositions. There may be, and will be, situations and instances of intra and inter-institutional conflict which can and should be resolved through democratic conventions and within the framework of constitutional culture, and even more importantly, through creative interaction across the table.

In the Indian experience, one gets the impression that the political leadership has always been inclined to resolve areas of divergence of opinion, and inter-institutional conflict, but the judicial leadership has tended to maintain that such conflicts have to be resolved in the court-rooms alone. However, if and when 'creative' dialogues are undertaken, needless to say that the fact of such dialogues must be transparent, so that the citizens do not get an impression that inter-institutional conflict is converted into 'personal-agenda'.

In the case of conflict between the elected and appointed executive, the impression is: either there has been a sense of withdrawal, of conflict, or the other extreme of collusion, but not complementarity. The most adverse impact of the process of governance on the democratic Republic arises not from the growing conflict between the legislature and the judiciary, but from an utter imbalance in the relationship between the elected and the appointed executive. The mass transfers of senior administrators as much as at the field level (such as police Station House Officer) almost as the first act after the swearing in of any new Chief Minister has not merely diluted the efficacy of bureaucracy, but even worse, has led to either demoralization, or total submission to the party in power, with the adjunct consequences of collusion and partnership in corruption.

Indian democracy suffers disproportionately from conflict between the 'ruling' and 'opposition' parties, as though the 'opposition', constitute the enemies of the country, and that the 'ruling' represent the preferred darling of democratic process. The distortions of the political process that are reflected as the 'negative vote' in the electoral process, almost consistently during the first five decades of the Republic should make our political leaders think that we need to legitimize and institutionalize the role, status and thus the image of 'opposition' in the legislatures and in the process of governance. Over a period of time, opposition (and all parties have been in opposition) has started conducting itself as though they have to 'oppose' everything, even the policies that they had carved out while in government. The party/parties in 'power' tend to treat those in 'opposition' as though they are enemies of the nation and traitors, not recognizing that all the parties and their representatives have gone through the 'same' electoral process.

The Ethics Committee of the Parliament has to concern itself, in order to do justice to itself, with (a) democratic conventions, (b) constitutional propriety and (c) fault-lines of social transformation while setting standards for the complementary tasks of the instrumentalities of the State, within the framework of their common, constitutional objectives and the vision of India.

7

Ethnicity, Plurality and Conflict Resolution

Mani Shankar Iyer

THE CENTRAL issue of governance in post-Independence India has been, and will continue to remain, at least for several decades, the consolidation of the nationhood of India. The single most important portfolio that any Prime Minister of India holds is his responsibility, at the helm of the ship of the State, for the unity and integrity of the nation. The litmus test of an effective Prime Ministership is the contribution made by the incumbent to strengthening unity and assuring what Jawaharlal Nehru called the "emotional integration" of our people.

We start with a great advantage. The idea of India is millennia old. Our ancients began their prayers — the *Sankalpam* — by sitting themselves in the continent of "*Jambudweep*" and the land of "*Bharatavarsha*".

> ..... *Jambudweepe, Bharatavarshe*
>
> *Bharatakhande, Merohu* .....

Geography defined the land: the gigantic mountain ranges to the north, penetrable only through isolated passes; the broad seas to the three sides of the subcontinent. Interestingly, the definition of "India" rested on geography rather than race, language, culture or religion. It did not rest even on history, as the idea of India pre-dates much of what we now know as the history of India. This geographic definition of nationhood imparted the characteristic which gives India its unique character among the world civilizations : unity in diversity.

There are other civilizations perhaps more ancient than ours, notably Pharaonic Egypt and Mesopotamia. There are other civilizations as continuous as ours, notably, the Graeco-Roman civilization of Europe and the Han civilization of China. But ours has uniquely been the civilization that has sought to be inclusive, as distinct from exclusive, in its definition of itself, that has not sought unity through uniformity but unity through recognition, acceptance, preservation and, eventually, the celebration of its diversity is celebrated, and whose unity is weakened every time its diversity is sought to be straitjacketed. Thus, all who live in *Bharatavarsha,* whatever their race, whatever their colour, whatever their provenance — indigenous or outsider, whatever their language or dialect, whatever their culture or sub-culture, whatever their religion, belief, creed or superstition, so long as they were of our land they came to be regarded as integral to *Bharatavarsha.*

Yet, it is only in contemporary times that there has been a measure of correspondence between the idea of India and the political entity we call the Union of India. Through much of our history, much of the land was divided into a congeries of often competing and usually conflicting kingdoms, more often than not at odds with the central authority that was attempting to establish its political hegemony over the land. To this was added the repeated invasions to which the land was subjected, till the sixteenth century AD through the mountain passes and, since the Portuguese capture of Goa, increasingly through the sea routes to India.

For the Europeans, the "discovery of India" lay in finding the sea-route of India - the overarching political objective of Europe after the fall of Constantinople to the Caliphate (Khalifat) in 1453, which blocked the overland route to Asia on which not only did European commerce depend but on which, thanks to the importance of pepper in the preservation of meat, physical survival itself depended. For contemporary India, on the other hand, "*The Discovery of India*", as in the title of Jawaharlal Nehru's celebrated book, written in the climactic run-up to the establishment of Independent India, lay in translating into the principles of modern statecraft the underlying forces in India's millennial civilization which had helped preserve her civilizational unity through centuries of political discord, economic turbulence, repeated foreign invasions and even two centuries of colonial occupation.

First and foremost of these forces was the uniquely Indian genius for synthesis. Unity in diversity rests upon a capacity to recognize, welcome and integrate alien influences which are desirable in themselves even if their origin lies in military conquest or political domination. Indeed, the civilizational continuity of the land had been assured through repeated periods of political and economic turmoil primarily because of the Indian penchant for synthesizing the new ideas, mores, values that come from outside without losing the essence of what went before; a penchant which invariably so worked on the outsider that he found himself subject to the same process of synthesis, however much of an iconoclast he might have been on first entering the land. India was, thus, politically conquered often enough in her history, but the invader found it impossible to convert political conquest into civilizational conquest because India's indigenous civilization synthesized what was desirable in what came from without, thus Indianizing the outside influence and, indeed, Indianizing the outsider himself.

It is not that successful synthesis was always the outcome. It was the overall trend but there were exceptions. The politically most significant exception as India came to freedom was the Pakistan Movement, based on the "Two-Nation Theory", which held that the Hindus and Muslims constituted distinct "nations", leading in 1947 to the creation of separate state called Pakistan as the price to be paid for the liberation of the rest of India from colonial thralldom.

We accepted Pakistan as a political reality, as we had so often in history acknowledged political realities not in concordance with the transcendental civilization reality. But that only reinforced the imperative of Independent India setting its domestic house in order in the light of the political victory scored by forces not representative of the overall civilizational trend towards synthesis which had characterised our history.

How were we, on the basis of the principle of unity in diversity, to react to the exclusivism that had led to the partition of India? By abandoning millennia of synthesis to assert nationhood on the basis of the majority religion, as Pakistan had done, or by going back to first principles and building the contemporary nationhood of India on our civilizational tradition of unity in diversity? Synthesis in civilizational terms came to be called "secularism" in the vocabulary of modern India's statecraft. It has remained the dominant theme in the building of modern India, as much in the time of Jawahralal Nehru as during the Prime Ministership of Rajiv Gandhi. This is the basic thesis that informed Rajiv Gandhi's vision of India.

The Post-Assassination Riots

Rajiv Gandhi became Prime Minister on the evening of the day his mother was assassinated by two members of her security detail. Both were Sikhs. Both were incensed, it would seem, over her decision in June 1984 to deploy troops of the Indian Army to evict the armed terrorists who, in the guise of religious fundamentalists, had occupied the Golden Temple at Amritsar. Even as he was being sworn in as Prime Minister, mobs began roaming the streets in the capital and elsewhere in search of Sikhs on whom to exact vengeance. By next morning, the situation had dangerously deteriorated, with innocent Sikhs being killed and maimed, their property ransacked, looted and set on fire. The Army had to be called out. It took a day or two to restore security. The riots left a lasting scar on the Sikh psyche.

There were three broad elements to Rajiv Gandhi's handling of the situation. First, the restoration of civil peace — by appeal to the people, by setting a personal example, by deploying force against the rioters. Second, the adoption of long-term measures to forestall the recurrence of such events and restore confidence in the hearts and minds of the affected community. Third, action to resolve the underlying political problems that were, in part, causes of the violence and, in part, caused by violence.

The appeal to the people began with his very first address to the nation on the 31st October, 1984, hours after being sworn in as Prime Minister :

> "The foremost need now is to maintain our balance. We can and must face this tragic ordeal with fortitude, courage and wisdom. We should remain calm and exercise the maximum restraint. We should not let our emotions get the better of us, because passion would cloud judgement. Nothing would hurt the soul of our beloved Indira Gandhi more than the occurrence of violence in any part of the country. It is of prime importance that every step we take is in the correct direction".

Notwithstanding the inherent security risks involved, he personally toured several of the worst-affected areas in Delhi and, eventually, not satisfied with the measures taken by the authorities directly concerned, took personal charge of measures to quell the rioting. He followed this up with a second appeal two days later, invoking Indira Gandhi's own words: "Do not shed blood, shed hatred". He said:

> "Indira Gandhi gave her life so that a united India should live and prosper. Anything that creates a division between brother and brother comes in the way of national unity. This violence is only helping the subversive forces to achieve their ends. Communal madness will destroy us. It will destroy everything India stands for. As Prime Minister of India I cannot and will not allow this."

And he did not. Civil peace was restored. Relief camps were established. There was no exodus of Sikhs from different parts of the country to Punjab, as some were predicting and others were encouraging, even abetting. However, there was some adverse comment about his phrase "when a mighty tree falls, it is only natural that the earth around it does shake a little"; it is, therefore, important to recall the context in which the phrase appeared:

> "Some riots took place in the country following the murder of Indiraji. We knew the people of India were very angry and for a few days it seemed that India had been shaken. But, when a mighty tree falls, it is only natural that the earth around it does shake a little. But, from the way you put a stop to it, from the way India has been brought back to the path of unity with your help and is able to stand unitedly together again, the world can see that India has become a genuine democracy."

It is also important to recall the credo set out in his major broadcast to the nation a week before the speech cited above:

> "Nothing is more important than the unity and integrity of our nation. India is indivisible. Secularism is the bedrock of our nation. It implies more than tolerance. It involves an active effort for harmony. No religion preaches hatred and intolerance. Vested interests, both external and internal, are inciting and exploiting communal passions and violence to divide India. Answering communalism with communalism will only help these subversive and secessionist forces. The combined might of the people and Government will thwart their designs. There is only one India. It belongs to all of us."

We may now turn to the long-term measures taken to forestall the recurrence of such incidents. While the riots of the first few days of November 1984, certainly do constitute an indelible blot on the history of the nation, equally it is to be noted that they never recurred. There was provocation enough for such recurrence. Through the remaining years of Rajiv Gandhi's Prime Ministership, there were numerous incidents in Punjab which could, without deft handling, have led to communal rioting, both in Punjab and outside. There were also numerous incidents outside Punjab, beginning with the serial bomb blasts in Delhi in May 1985, that also could, without deft handling, have led to communal violence inside and outside Punjab. It is a measure of the success of the administrative, security and political steps taken to deal with the situation that there was no such recurrence. It is also a tribute to the innate belief in, and practice of, communal harmony as the norm among our people at large. Above all, it is the clarity with which the nation's leadership insisted on secularism and rejected all forms of communalism that set the tone of both the administration and the people.

Allied to this was the determined effort launched, soon after the elections of December 1984, to find an enduring basis for the resolution of the political problems which were inextricably enmeshed with the violence in Punjab and its spin-off effects in other parts of the country. A senior politician was appointed Governor of Punjab. Rajiv Gandhi visited Punjab (23 March, 1985) and Sant Harchand Singh Longowal was released from detention soon after. The nation went delirious with the news on 24 July, 1985, that an Accord had been signed between Sant Longowal and Rajiv Gandhi to bring the turbulence in Punjab to an end. Tragically, Longowal was assassinated a month later. His death undermined, as it turned out, a major prop to the Accord. Undeterred, Rajiv Gandhi went ahead with the elections to the State Assembly required to bring into existence a representative state government through whom the Accord could be implemented.

Initially, implementation was smooth but ran into rough weather in January 1986, over the question of Chandigarh and the sharing of river waters. The impasse over the implementation of the Accord, the renewal in violence, and the succumbing of those in authority to the threats and blandishments of the terrorists led to the suspension of the Assembly and the imposition of President's Rule in April 1987. Over the next two years, policy was founded on three important parameters: unrelenting police and security action to contain and eliminate terrorism; subterranean contacts with militants to persuade them to give up violence and come to the negotiating table; over-the-table discussions with the dissident elements who were prepared to eschew violence and accept the basic tenets of the Constitution, in particular, the unity and integrity of the Union of India, in exchange for full integration into the country's democratic process; and, perhaps most importantly, sensitivity to religious, cultural and ethnic sentiment, the emphasis being on *Punjabiyat* as the shared heritage of all the people of Punjab.

We have here the essential ingredients of the Rajiv Gandhi approach to conflict-resolution : unswerving firmness in confronting violence with the full coercive apparatus of the State, best exemplified in the swift and clean surgery of Operation Black Thunder II which liberated the Golden Temple from its terrorists stranglehold; simultaneous amnesty, even rehabilitation, to those who give up violence without necessarily giving up their political beliefs, short of those beliefs that undermine the unity of India; emphasis on the political process, specifically the democratic electoral process, as the necessary precondition for successful coercive action against violence; and total respect for religious, cultural and ethnic diversity as the basis for preserving the unity of the country.

The problem of violence in Punjab was not solved during Rajiv Gandhi's Premiership, but the gains recorded were summarized in his report to Parliament on 3 March, 1989, during the course of his reply to the debate on the Motion of Thanks:

> "We have given no quarter to terrorists. Terrorists have been faced with tougher force than ever before ... The terrorists have ceased to be a political force in Punjab. They are a criminal force, mixed up in drug trafficking, in smuggling, and in looting. Amongst the people, there is widespread revulsion at such criminal activities."

Specifically:

> "The Golden Temple has been restored to its pristine purity. The full *maryada* is being observed in the Golden Temple after a very long time."

> "The Gurudwaras are no longer sanctuaries."

> "Schools and colleges are normal or near to normal."

> "Now that the political linkage has been broken with the terrorists, now that religious fundamentalism and terrorists have been separated, it is time, we feel, to start a normalization process in Punjab".

To this end, he announced:

- the release of the remaining Jodhpur undertrials;
- the withdrawal of prosecution for making objectionable speeches;
- the removal of restrictions on entering and moving around Punjab under the Foreigners Act;
- geographical limitations on the applicability in Punjab of the Disturbed Areas Act and Special Armed Forces Act;
- the withdrawal of the National Security Act;
- the establishment of a monitoring mechanism against alleged excesses by the security forces;
- the setting up of Village Defence Organisations; and
- elections to the panchayats in May (these were not held, but Punjab participated fully in the general elections of November the same year).

The House was also informed that in respect of the investigations into the anti-Sikh riots of November 1984, 225 cases had been registered with 2300 accused. Eleven cases had been concluded, with 90 convictions, including six sentences of life imprisonment.

The seeds laid during Rajiv Gandhi's period of office sprouted during the subsequent Congress regime. The problem of violence in Punjab now stands substantially resolved. The enduring basis for a resolution of the remaining political problems continues to be the Rajiv-Longowal Accord.

The Assam Accord

The other major problem which Rajiv Gandhi had inherited was the student agitation in Assam, which began during the last days of the Janata Party regime and had assumed menacing proportions in the last two or three years. Elections held in February 1983, had returned a Congress government to office but in the midst of escalating violence and widespread boycott — voluntary and involuntary — of the polls. The essence of the agitation was a problem central to the building of the modern nationhood of India : the preservation of ethnic particularities while integrating parts of the nation with the whole of the nation. In Assam, the presence of large numbers of "outsiders" and "foreigners" had led to widespread apprehension, stoked by the student agitators, that the identity of the indigenous Assamese was being swamped and, unless drastic steps are taken, the Assamese would be reduced to a minority in their own home-State. The attempt to disabuse the Assamese of the exaggeration had not succeeded and the student movement was clearly snow-balling.

Subterranean contacts were established with the student leaders to obtain an accurate perception of their concerns. Open negotiations were then undertaken with them to arrive at a mutually acceptable outcome. An Accord was eventually concluded in the early hours of Independence Day 1985. The Accord fell in two parts. The first set out a *procedure* for resolving burning political issues, including the vexed question of detecting and deporting foreigners. The second addressed itself to *specific issues* such as a second refinery, the future of a paper mill, an Institute of Technology and other such bread-and-butter questions.

What distinguished the Assam Accord from the Punjab Accord was that it did not attempt to find comprehensive solutions to specific problems so much as lay out the framework within which the search for specific solutions would be pursued. The essence of this procedural approach was giving the agitationists an opportunity to themselves take the responsibility for working out solutions to the problems they were agitating for, subject only to the democratic requirement of first securing a mandate from the people to do so. The elected government of Hiteshwar Saikia still had more than three years to run. Notwithstanding this, and notwithstanding the strong possibility that the Congress would lose the elections, Rajiv Gandhi ordered the dissolution of the existing Assembly and fresh elections.

As widely predicted, the Congress lost and the political front of the student movement, the Asom Gana Parishad, took office. That Government held office for a full five years. In the elections of 1991, the Asom Gana Parishad was ousted and the Congress re-elected. Most of the political problems facing the State were, in fact, left unresolved by the AGP government and it is the subsequent Congress government that is entitled to much of the credit for the substantial progress made in recent times towards ending violence and finding political answers to political questions, as indeed the resumption of economic growth and social development in the State. The process began with the Assam Accord.

The Assam Accord illustrates further facets of Rajiv Gandhi's approach to conflict-resolution. First, the primacy he accorded to the recognition and resolution of the problem of identity over any short-term gains. He recognized that the student movement had touched a sensitive chord in the hearts of the people of Assam and could not be wished away. Second, his acknowledgement of the right to pursue their ends by agitationists whose perceptions he did not share. They were in no way outlawed by their views, nor even by the violence they had unleashed and abetted. The important thing was to bring their differences into the democratic arena by enticing them into the democratic process. This was most easily possible by holding out to them the prospect of real political power through elections. Third, it illustrated Rajiv Gandhi's belief in the sobering effects of responsibility. Agitationists out of power can demand the earth; once in office, it is no longer for them to demand but deliver.

That the AGP did not deliver is another matter. They were afforded the opportunity of doing so; had they succeeded, they might have ousted the Congress indefinitely from the corridors of power. It was a risk Rajiv Gandhi was prepared to take in the larger national interest. The AGP did not fulfill the expections roused by their electoral victory, but the democratic process helped the people of Assam rid themselves of their unwarranted fears while, at the same time, addressing some of their problems that were real. Further, agitation accompanied by violence to secure the demands of the student agitators made them subject to the same devices by those, like the Bodos and Karbis, dissatisfied with the performance of the student agitators as holders of government office. It also bred violence of the ULFA kind as the Frankensteinian consequence of earlier violence. At the same time, it opened for those who cared to see, the way to solving the problems of the micro-minorities of Assam along the lines spelt out in the Accord for solving the major concerns of the dominant ethnic community of the State. Overall, the Assam Accord stands as a contribution of great significance towards conflict-resolution in a pluralistic, democratic State beset by problems and perceptions of ethnic identity.

Resolution of Mizoram Problem

The third major Accord of Rajiv Gandhi's Premiership was the Mizoram Accord. Back in 1966, as a direct consequence of the failure to effectively tackle the problem of drought and even famine in the State, an armed insurrection had persisted, backed by substantial assistance from East Pakistan. Attempts since the mid-seventies to find a political road to ending the insurgency had floundered. Rajiv Gandhi broke the impasse by offering to share power with the rebels as a prelude to inducting them into the political process. The essence of the Mizoram Accord of June 1986 was to surrender the Chief Ministership of the State to the leader of the rebels, Laldenga, with the duly elected Congress Chief Minister stepping down voluntarily to become Deputy Chief Minister to the very person he had hunted as an outlaw!

The composite government was then charged with organizing the elections of February 1987, in which Laldenga's party, the Mizo National Front (MFN), secured a majority and formed a duly elected government. Midway through its term of office, the MNF lost its majority. A mid-term poll was called for January 1989. Laldenga lost. Lalthanhawla of the Congress returned as Chief Minister. It did not lead to Laldenga or his associates returning to the *Maquis.* The MNF continues to be an important political force in the State, but as part of the democratic process with violence and rebellion a thing of the past. The extent to which democracy has taken root in the State is, perhaps, best exemplified by the remotest district of the Indian Union, Chhimptuipui, having recorded the highest voter turn-out (92%) in the elections of November 1993.

The Mizoram Accord marks a further evolution in Rajiv Gandhi's approach to conflict resolution. He was here dealing with an insurgency all of two decades old. True, it was an insurgency that was petering out, its cadres deserting in droves, the desire for peace overwhelming among the people. Rajiv Gandhi, however, resisted the temptation to turn the weakening of the militancy into an opportunity for military triumph or any kind of revenge. Instead, reliance was placed wholly on the democratic electoral process. The personal security of the former insurgents was guaranteed; those who came overground were assured of generous treatment; not only an equal and honoured place but also assistance for the rehabilitation of themselves and their families. Total transparency was ensured. Faith was demonstratively reposed in the democratic credentials of yesterday's outlaw. Narrow, local party interests were sacrificed in the cause of the greater national good. There was no patronizing of a distant outpost of the Indian Union. The implementation of the Accord was not assumed to be Central responsibility to the detriment of local involvement. Implementation in letter as in spirit was left wholly to the local democratic process.

This respect of the local population, this evident reposing of full-fledged trust in them, and the sensitivity with which ticklish matters of the ethnic micro-minorities such as the Chakma, the Mara, the Lai and the Hmar were handled, was reflective of Rajiv Gandhi's larger concern for celebrating the diversity of India as the precondition for ensuring its unity. It made for a deep-rooted, sincere and very moving identification of the local population with him, and of him with the local people, transcending all barriers between the geographic mainland of the country and the people of its geographic periphery. This was clear during the many visits he made as Prime Minister to Mizoram. It also contributed to the general sense of identification of the people of the North-East with the Prime Minister of the country and, through him, with the people of India as a whole.

Darjeeling Autonomy

In the Darjeeling Hills, a crisis had been building up for some years, which burst upon the national consciousness with full force in 1986. The Gorkha National Liberation Front (GNLF), led by Subhash Gheising, demanded Indian citizenship for all Gorkhas resident in India, including many whom the authorities held to be Nepalese citizens; complained of discrimination at the hands of the State Government of West Bengal and accordingly sought separation from the State and took up the cause of Gorkhas in other parts of the country, such as Meghalaya, where there had been trouble between Gorkha residents and the local population. The agitation began acquiring an increasingly violent colour leading to a strong reaction all over West Bengal. In August 1986, all political parties in the West Bengal Assembly, including the legislative party of the Congress, joined hands in passing a resolution deploring the agitation and its objectives. The movement was condemned as "anti-national". Everyone's eye was on the forthcoming elections to the West Bengal State Assembly which would determine whether the State, already under the CPI(M) rule for a decade, would opt for a change of government.

Rajiv Gandhi reached Calcutta on 18 September, 1986, on what was to prove to be the first of a series of forays into West Bengal aimed at attempting victory at the polls for the Congress. At a press conference in Raj Bhavan that evening, he was asked about the situation in the Darjeeling Hills. He refused to describe the GNLF as "anti-national". It was a stand of principle for which a significant political price had to be paid. It repudiated the popular view in West Bengal. It repudiated the stand taken by the State unit of his own party. And it led to no immediate dividends in Darjeeling, as witness the paltry crowd that turned up to greet him when he went to Darjeeling in December 1986 to address a public meeting.

Yet, in the long run, there is no denying that his refusal to trim his sails to populist winds infused in the Gorkha minority a confidence in his *bona fides* which played a critical, probably crucial, role in bringing Subhash Gheising around to a position of accepting Rajiv Gandhi's equally firm insistence that there could be no redrawing of the boundaries of West Bengal. Instead, through the tripartite agreement negotiated between the Union Government, the GNLF and the State government, an unprecedented measure of autonomy was granted to the Darjeeling Gorkha Hill Council to deal with the bread-and-butter issues that underlay the discontent in the Hills. Violence was brought to an end. A micro-minority's apprehensions about its identity and status were allayed. Pressing questions of economic and social development, which had been given a political dimension by the agitation, were addressed to. Above all, the responsibility for attending to these matters was, in substantial measure, devolved upon those who had agitated for these matters. Rajiv Gandhi visited Darjeeling again in May 1989 to a rapturous reception to inaugurate the building of the Hill Council. He may have lost the elections to the State Assembly but he had restored peace, infused confidence in a minority, devised an innovative way of dealing with minority grievances, preserved the political boundaries of West Bengal and ensured the integrity of India. It was proved to be a precedent for resolving the Bodoland and Karbi Anglong agitations in Assam and the Jharkhand agitation in Bihar; a possible model for all such situations anywhere in the country. The list of subjects devolved to the Hill Council contributed to the listing of subjects for devolution to Panchayati Raj Institutions through the Eleventh Schedule to the Constitution. "It is sometimes necessary" as Rajiv Gandhi once drily remarked, "to lose today to win tomorrow".

Insurgency in Tripura Ceases

Another secessionist insurgency the country has been confronted with for some years since 1981 had been in Tripura where the tribal leader, Bejoy Hrangkhawl, of the Tripura National Volunteers (TNV) had been captured but then mysteriously allowed to escape. Tripura, till Independence and Partition, had been virtually a totally tribal State. The influx of refugees from East Pakistan had, however, dramatically altered the State's demographic profile. Tribal discontent, centred on questions of ethnic identity and related economic, social and political issues, had fuelled the insurgency. By the time Rajiv Gandhi became Prime Minister, much of the steam had gone out of the militancy but tribal discontent was still of alarming proportions. The elections of January 1988 focussed on these matters. An alliance of the Congress and the Tripura Upajati Juba Samiti (TUJS) gave the tribals of the State a forum for articulation of their grievances; the electoral victory of the alliance, leading to the formation of a coalition government, gave them a share of governance.

In this setting, the Tripura Accord of September 1988 brought the insurgency to a definitive end, restored balance between the tribal *indigenes* and the settler population, substantially allayed ethnic apprehensions, and set the course for the peaceful evolution of the State's polity. It was a good example of a judicious combination of firm anti-insurgency action by the security forces, well-thought out Intelligence contacts with the insurgents, deep sensitivity to minority aspirations and determined political action in full recognition of the fact that the only enduring solutions are political solutions that invoke the democratic, electoral process.

Jammu & Kashmir Situation

The situation in Jammu & Kashmir during Rajiv Gandhi's Premiership has been overlaid by the crisis that developed within days of his laying down office. Some trace the roots of the crisis to events that occurred when he was in office; others attribute the course that crisis took to the abandonment of the course he had charted. It might be best to confine this overview to a kind of summary of his approach to the problem.

A few months before the assassination of his mother, serious differences had developed between the State Government, led by Farooq Abdullah, and the Central Government. A split in the ruling party brought Farooq Abudallah's brother-in-law, Gul Shah, to the office of Chief Minister. But this only generated further instability. This was the situation that obtained when Rajiv Gandhi became Prime Minister.

Rajiv Gandhi was persuaded that the situation in this sensitive border state demanded as close a measure of cooperation between the nationalist political forces in the valley and the Central authorities as could be secured. The voice of the nationalist forces was undoubtedly the National Conference. The only all-India party with a significant political presence in the Valley was the Congress. Accordingly, Governor's Rule was imposed on the State and protracted contacts between the two led to the announcement of an alliance in September 1986 in preparation for the polls scheduled for the spring of 1987.

There is the alternative view that the National Conference lost some of its legitimacy to be regarded as the authentic voice of J&K nationalists by entering into an electoral pact with the Congress. On the other hand, it was the National Conference-Congress alliance that defeated the fundamentalist-sectarian-secessionist challenge at the hustings. Allegations of electoral malpractices have been persistently made. The number of disputed seats would not have altered the NC-Congress majority.

The forces defeated by the ballot resorted to the bullet soon after. In this, they were heavily abetted by the Pakistanis. The fomenting of communal strife was their prime objective. Security in the Valley did deteriorate. Yet, the situation was sufficiently under control for the Valley to receive in October-November 1989, the largest number of tourists ever in the autumn season.

Rajiv Gandhi had sharp differences with the successor regime about their handling of Kashmir. These might, perhaps, be summed up as under:

- confrontation with the forces of secession requires the cooperation of a strong and authentic representative of the Kashmir people; secession cannot be successfully fought by sidelining political forces in the Valley;
- there must be trust in the people of Kashmir; secession cannot be fought by generalising distrust of Kashmiris or marginalizing them in administration and security operations;
- there must be a total eschewal of communal bias or communal prejudice; Kashmir is the symbol of our secularism and must be treated as such;
- stern action against terrorism must be combined with genuine compassion for the people; a civilized government does not wage war against its people, only against terrorists; the level of force must be graded and calibrated to the requirements of the situation;
- as military solutions cannot be found to political problems, resort to force must be accompanied by at least outlining the framework of a political settlement. Therefore, military action must be seen as stage-setting for a political solution; hence, the door to political settlement must be kept firmly open, seen as being kept open, through all anti-insurgency and anti-terrorist operations;

- the ultimate answer lies in the democratic process and the democratic process alone; every malcontent should have the assurance that if his is, indeed, a representative view, the electoral process will give him the opportunity of himself participating in the redressal of his grievances; and
- the Constitution, however, is sacrosanct and the democratic process presupposes that the unity and integrity of India will not be called into question; on everything else there can be flexibility.

Shah Bano Case

Two of the most complex problems of pluralism, identity and nation-building which Rajiv Gandhi had to contend with were the Shah Bano case and the Babri Masjid/Ram Janmabhoomi controversy at Ayodhya.

The facts relating to the Shah Bano case may be stated easily enough. A Muslim woman, Shah Bano, on being summarily divorced by her husband, sought compensation under the vagrancy provisions of the Criminal Procedure Code, whose provisions were over a century old but which had been codified again as recently as 1973. The Sessions Judge in Indore had awarded her a small sum of money. Her husband challenged the award in the High Court at Jabalpur, which gave verdict in favour of Shah Bano and enhanced the payment due to her to Rs.179.20 per month. The case went to the Supreme Court, where a bench headed by the Chief Justice upheld the High Court judgement, leaving the compensatory amount untouched. In passing judgement, however, the Chief Justice made some remarks about Islam, the Muslim community and the *Shariat* which many Muslims found offensive. The moot legal point was whether Muslim Personal Law could be modified by court judgements pertaining to provisions of the law that dealt with other matters, specifically whether the provisions of Islamic jurisprudence with respect to compensation on divorce could be impinged upon by invoking the vagrancy provisions of the criminal law.

A minority community, like any other community, speaks in several different voices. Not surprisingly, therefore, the Shah Bano judgement sparked a debate within the Muslim community which ranged from the straight forward humanitarian issue of the obligations of a husband towards an abandoned, indigent divorcee to complex matters of theology and jurisprudence. The argument within the

Muslim community found reflection in Parliament where a lively debate began on a Private Member's Bill brought by a distinguished representative of the Indian Union Muslim League. A Muslim Minister of the Rajiv Gandhi government sought and was given permission to participate in the debate in a personal capacity. While asserting that the issue at hand did not impinge on Muslim Personal Law and that for him, as for all Muslims, the Holy Koran was "everything", the Minister pleaded with his community to take a liberal and non-dogmatic approach to these questions.

Another Minister of the Rajiv Gandhi government, also a Muslim and highly respected for his long and distinguished contribution to nation-building, sought and was given permission to participate in the same debate. As discussions on Private Member's Bills are not always held continuously, his participation in the debate came some four months later. He took a stand very different to his colleague's insisting that the key issue was to reassure the minority community that Muslim Personal Law would not be eroded by court judgements on extraneous matters.

In between, the Shah Bano case had become a matter of high controversy not only within the Muslim community but in the country at large. There were those who felt that the Supreme Court having pronounced its verdict, no alternative other than proceeding rigorously with its implementation should be considered. Others held that it was the function of the legislature to legislate; and that if a court judgement placed an interpretation it to be, it was the right, indeed, the duty of the legislature to ensure that suitable clarifications were legislated. In the instance case, attention was drawn to the statement of the Minister of State for Home Affairs, who while moving the 1973 legislation, had given the explicit clarification that no provision of the Criminal Procedure Code was intended to impinge on Muslim Personal Law. Associated with this was argument over the import of the constitutional provisions relating to the protection and safeguarding of community-based Personal Law and the Directive Principle which, without specifying a deadline, called on the State to progressively evolve a uniform civil code.

Over and above these somewhat arcane legal and constitutional questions was the underlying tension between liberals who would not countenance custom, usage and religious sentiment as a barrier to what they saw as a matter of human rights, and conservatives who insisted that the matter at issue was not of human rights but the right to identity of a minority community. Indeed, liberal opinion found itself so often in the company of communal sentiment, which saw in the controversy a golden opportunity for the ventilation of anti-Islamic and anti-Muslim views, that it became difficult to disentangle the one from the other. Equally, on the other side, legitimate concern over the imperative of protecting identity in a pluralistic, secular democracy often found itself in the company of a blind and harsh assertion of dogma. Sections of our largest minority came to see themselves as a community under siege, denigrated for their beliefs, under threat of having key constitutional safeguards undermined. Large sections of the rest of public opinion in the country dismissed these concerns as unfounded, as a mere cloak for reaction. A discussion of overwhelming national importance came, thus, to be clouded in an idiom that was often destructive of calm, rational consideration and dangerous for national integration.

It was at this juncture, and in these circumstances, that Rajiv Gandhi stepped into the picture. The populist thing to do clearly was to go along with the substantial majority view. He, however, held that the primordial duty of a leader of a pluaralistic democracy was to reassure a minority, big or small, that it was not required to sacrifice its identity as the price to be paid for belonging to the nation. This was the larger question of nation-building and conflict resolution. He told one senior Chief Minister that, if the Chief Minister were right, 85 per cent of the non-Muslim population of the country would find no cause for approbation in the steps he took; and that if the Chief Minister were right, the female half of the remaining 15 per cent would be against him too; and that at least a proportion of the 7.5 per cent male Muslim electorate also would not approve! So, where did the question of a vote-bank come into this?

There were of course, important questions of social reform, women's rights, and the uniform civil code involved, but the atmosphere generated by the Shah Bano controversy seemed hardly the most appropriate in which to resolve these larger issues. For one thing, any community resents being told by others what is wrong with itself; each community has its own methodology of self-advance; the concept of each community deciding for itself the direction in which it should go seems crucial to the preservation of identity in a pluralistic society, to the upholding of the fundamental principle of unity in diversity.

In the immediate aftermath of the Shah Bano judgement, this process of introspection and self-examination was what appeared to be taking place within the Muslim community. But the idiom and arguments used by many of the proponents of change from without the community vitiated the atmosphere and changed the context of the argument from the social issues involved to the preservation of the identity of a minority community and its constitutional right to a Personal Law of its own.

Governance often involves Hobson's choices; statesmanship lies in choosing the option that serves the long-term interests of the nation even if it involves sacrificing short-term gains or temporarily postponing specific measures of reform. That, at any rate, was how Rajiv Gandhi appears to have approached the issue. The immediate imperative appeared to him to be to reassure substantial segments of our largest minority that constitutional safeguards for their Personal Law were not being eroded, that they were not being called upon to subject the *Shariat* to civil jurisdiction as the price to be paid for continuing as honoured and equal citizens of the country.

This, he believed, could best be achieved by the dangerous red herring of an alleged "threat" to ethnic identity being put out of the way of nation-building so as to clear the path for the real issues.

In the instant conjuncture, there were three such real issues that had been clouded over by the controversy over constitutional safeguards and the mutability or otherwise of Muslim Personal Law. First, carrying forward the process of introspection within the Muslim community by the time-honoured process of *ijtehad*. Second, addressing anomalies in the extant secular law which had resulted in an indigent divorcee receiving only Rs.179.20 per month as compensation under the vagrancy provisions of the Criminal Procedure Code. Third, promoting an atmosphere in which the issue of a uniform civil code could be considered in a calm, rational, harmonious way, the key question here of nation-building being that a uniform civil code could only be evolved by consensus, however long that might take, not imposed by a majority on a minority, however expedient such a step might appear at the hustings.

The Muslim Women (Compensation on Divorce) Act certainly stilled fears about identity and constitutional safeguards that had permeated sections of the minority Muslim community. Unfortunately, continuing controversy over the Act itself stalled progress in the three directions described above. While the need for progress in all these three directions cannot be overstressed, it is not without significance that no successive regime to Rajiv Gandhi's ever contemplated repealing the Act; and no political party but one has declared its intention of doing so. The task for the future appears to be the one signalled by the Rajiv Gandhi Government: pluralism and our composite culture demand that, in nation-building, we allay misapprehensions or misperceptions about any threat to the identity of any community while pressing ahead with social reform. Otherwise, even the most well-intentioned measures can recoil on the unity and integrity of the nation, the preservation and strengthening of which is the most important portfolio held by any Prime Minister of India.

Babri Masjid/Ram Janmabhoomi

More or less in tandem with the burning controversy regarding the Shah Bano judgement, the long pending dispute over the Babri Masjid / Ram Janmabhoomi site in Ayodhya came to the boil.

The proximate cause for the revivification of the Ayodhya question was the Faizabad Session Court's decision in February 1986, instructing the administration to unlock the gates which had remained barred (by court order) since 1950. Over the previous 36 years, numerous cases had been filed involving Hindu petitioners against Muslim defendants, Muslim petitioners against each other, public interest petitions, and petitions relating to private property rights. This plethora of litigation had, over the previous three decades or more, effectively stalled political action to resolve underlying communal tension.

The revivification of the controversy tragically stoked the very tension which had been largely kept under control after 1950. The Vishwa Hindu Parishad took the initiative in mobilising a country-wide movement, heavily backed by a political party; this was inevitably opposed country-wide by almost everyone in the Muslim community and a substantial majority of public opinion in the country at large.

Rajiv Gandhi's priority was to defuse communal tension while remaining deeply sensitive to religious sentiment, from whichever quarter such sentiment emanated, Hindu or Muslim. He evolved a two pronged approach: first, facilitate an amicable settlement among the contending parties; second, expedite the resolution of the legal issues pending in the courts. With these twin objectives in view, a dialogue was set up between the All-India Babri Masjid Action Committee and the Vishwa Hindu Parishad under the aegis of the Home Ministry; secondly, a special bench of the U.P.High Court was constituted at Lucknow to expeditiously, but of course judiciously, dispose of the litigation which had been pending for decades.

Towards the end of September 1989, it looked as if a breakthrough had been achieved in the dialogue being facilitated by the Home Minister. How fragile was the settlement apparently reached became evident when the apparent consensus broke down almost immediately thereafter. Meanwhile, the stipulated date for the *shilanyas* was approaching. It fell in the middle of the electoral process. On the basis of the assurance given to the Prime Minister by the local authorities that the site of the *shilanyas* was not in the disputed area, and without prejudice to the eventual authorization for the construction of the temple or the location of its *garbha griha* at the site of the *mirab* of the mosque, the *shilanyas* was permitted amid strict measures to ensure the physical protection of the mosque.

The decision was not a popular one and perhaps contributed to the reverses which the Congress party suffered in the elections in November 1989. The situation, however, dramatically worsened during 1990, reaching crisis proportions with the Rath Yatra of September-October 1990, and the *kar seva* at Ayodhya at the end of October 1990. Rajiv Gandhi responded by undertaking a series of journeys all around the country, the *Sadbhavana Yatra,* which captured the imagination of millions across the land and contributed crucially to the retention of an ethos of secularism in the face of perhaps the most serious challenge that secularism had encountered since the dark days of Partition.

The National Front government fell on 7 November, 1990, and was succeeded a few days later by a minority government supported by the Congress. After holding intensive consultations with his colleagues, and informally sounding many of the principals involved, including the Sunni Waqf Board, the Babri Masjid Action Committee, leading Shia personalities, the Sankaracharyas of Dwaraka and Kanchi Kama-kotipeetham, and others, Rajiv Gandhi wrote to Prime Minister Chandra Shekar on 30 November, 1990, outlining a way out of the impasse. He suggested that a Commission of Inquiry comprising three sitting judges of the Supreme Court be constituted to adjudge the validity of the claim that Babar's commander, Mir Baqi, had in 1528 demolished an extant *mandir* at the site of Ram Janmabhoomi to build in its place the Babri Masjid. Alternatively, said Rajiv Gandhi, the President might be requested to refer the question to the Supreme Court under Article 138 of the Constitution for a binding verdict on the subject. He indicated that his soundings had given him reason to believe that the findings of either the proposed Commission of Inquiry or the Supreme Court would lay the controversy to rest. Moves in this direction were initiated, but not in the particulars of the proposal made. They did not fructify. The rest is history.

Secularism As Bonding Adhesive

No single issue of nation-building preoccupied Rajiv Gandhi more than the role of secularism as the bonding adhesive of our nationhood. He spoke about it often. He held long and detailed, sometimes agonized, consultations with his colleagues about the nuances of the concept and its application to evolving circumstances. The attention he accorded it merits considered treatment even in a brief overview such as this.

Rajiv Gandhi defined secularism in terms that derived from the millennial history of our country. He said:

> "India goes back thousands of years, the boundaries have changed, the politics have changed but still India has remained India. It is an inner spirituality that makes India. No matter who conquered us, no matter if we were enslaved, that concept and that idea was not threatened and did not die and that is our strength today - the idea that all people from all faiths, all castes, all languages, all cultures are equal and must get equal opportunity; the concept that there is always something more that we can learn from outside to assimilate and to absorb, to enrich our own culture".

He explained:

> "Conquerors have been attracted to India throughout history by its rivers, by its fertile plains, by its deltas, by the knowledge and wisdom that prevailed in India. But from every conqueror we gained something. In battle, in war, you might win some, and you might lose some, but ultimately the concept of India, the idea of India was so powerful that no matter who won the battle or who lost the battle, it was India that gained and became stronger - culturally stronger... It is this idea, this concept of mingling the old with the new, which has given us a fusion, new inputs, new developments in our civilization while keeping alive our own culture, our heritage, what we have always valued, whether we go back to Alexander and the Bactrians whose culture was synthesized into the Gandhara culture, or the Suryavamsha and the Chandravamsha clans from whom arose the Rajputs. Our Christian community in Malabar is much older than the Catholics of the West.

Whether it is the Arabs, the Mongols, the Turks, the Persians, or those who brought us the Bhakti movement and the Sufi Ulema, it has always been a history of infusion of the new into the old, never rejecting one culture or one civilisation completely, as has happened in many other areas of the world. It is this that gives us our strength today."

Apart from our tradition of synthesis, Rajiv Gandhi saw our secularism as deriving from our ancient fidelity to the concept and principles of nonviolence. He said:

"We must not forget what Gandhiji taught us about nonviolence. Nonviolence is not merely absence of physical violence. Gandhiji's interpretation was that you must not even think of violence."

And he added:

"Any kind of violence is wrong, but the worst kind of violence is that which takes place in the name of religion. This in fact is a fraud on religion. True religion stands for love and tolerance, love for all fellow beings and respect for all faiths. Different religions are only different paths leading to the same destination. God is reached through many paths."

India of Rajiv Gandhi's vision was an India that rejected uniformity as the path to unity. Instead, it was in the joyous celebration of diversity - racial, linguistic, cultural and religious - that had always found its road to unity. He said:

"Unity does not mean uniformity. It does not mean obliteration of differences of identities. It means the independent development of each of our cultural systems within an integrated whole for the development of India. Tolerance, coexistence, interaction, enrichment are what will give our system strength."

He pointed out that:

"In every village of India, in every *basti* and in every *mohalla,* there are people of different faiths, of different languages, of different cultures who live together as neighbours. Secularism is a condition of our existence. It is the essence of our tradition. We are a multi-religious society, we are a multi-lingual society, we are a multi-cultural society, but we are not a multi-national society. We are one people, we are one nation, we are one country and we have one common citizenship."

And thus he came to the conclusion that:

> "Secularism and our nationhood are inseparable."

Rajiv Gandhi took great pains over defining "Secularism" as an uniquely Indian concept. He said:

> "It is also important to understand how India sees secularism. How do we understand secularism?"
>
> "First and foremost, our secularism is not anti-religious or irreligious. We have a deep and abiding appreciation of the rich vein of spirituality that runs through our culture, that runs through every religion of India. It runs through our history, it runs through every person who is an Indian. That rich vein of spirituality is the source of our moral values, of our ideals and our standards, of our goals and of our objectives. We vene-rate this spiritual tradition. We cherish its moral values. We respect all the different forms in which this spirituality manifests itself. The cardinal principle of our secularism is equal respect for all religions : *sarva dharma sambhavana.*
>
> "Our second great principle is that we respect all religions equally. No religious community is singled out for favours by the State, no religious community is subjected to any disability or disadvantage by the State. The State has no religion. The State is above religion. For the State, religion is a private and personal matter for the individual. Whatever religion an Indian professes, whatever faith an Indian propagates, for the State it is a personal matter. The State is concerned only with full protection to all, with equal opportunity for all, with equitable benefits for all. For the State, all Indians are Indian, equal in the eyes of the State.
>
> "The third principle, which flows from the first and second, is that religion has high value but must remain in the sphere of private and personal life. It has no role to play in the politics of the country.
>
> "Injecting religion into politics is the poisoning of our body politic. Mixing religion with politics is against the traditions of our civilization, the canons of our Constitution and the survival of our State."

Rajiv rejected the notion that an Indian's religion had anything to do with his patriotism. He said in Parliament:

> "There is no quota for patriotism. Everyone in India is a patriot - whether he is a Hindu or a Muslim, a Sikh or a Christian, a Parsi or a Jain or a Buddhist, or of any other religion. There are no restrictions on being a patriot. We have to see that no community pretends to monopo-

lise patriotism. Over the years our people have shown that patriotism is not reserved for any one community; it flows in the blood of every Indian. We cannot allow the deliberate acts of a few people of one community to colour everyone of that community. Because if we do that, we play straight into the hands of the terrorists."

He went on in another speech in Parliament to say:

"A patriotic Indian is a secular Indian. A nationalist Indian is a secular Indian. A dedicated Indian is a secular Indian. A disciplined Indian is a secular Indian."

Just as Jawaharlal Nehru in Ahmednagar Fort turned most of all to Maulana Azad in writing his immortal *The Discovery of India*, so did Rajiv Gandhi look to the speeches and writings of the great Maulana in guiding both the minority and majority communities to amicable friendship and brotherhood as Indians. On Maulana Azad's birth centenary, Rajiv Gandhi observed:

"Partition was a traumatic experience for the entire country. But the most traumatized of all was the Muslim community. Overnight, they found themselves divided between two countries, brother separated from brother, mother from son, father from daughter. There were all the complications of resolving family identity with national identity, national identity with religious identity, minority interests with national interests. There was also the aftermath of the riots to cope with, the loss of property, the loss of near and dear ones. On the one hand were the fundamentalists urging the community to retreat into an Islamic shell. On the other hand were those who urged that the Islamic identity of the Muslim community be subordinated to an identity which abstracted from all religious affinity. Both courses were wrong. Both courses were dangerous.

"This crisis brought out the best in Maulana Azad. It was, in many ways, his finest moment. He synthesized in his being, in his mental make-up and in his profound patriotism, the best of Islam and the best of India's millennial civilization. He showed the Muslim community of India how they could be good Muslims and good Indians at the same time. He showed the other communities of India what was meant by the expression: an 'Indian Muslim'.

"That India remained steadfastly secular despite the trauma of Partition, owed a great deal to the leadership and statesmanship of Maulana Azad, to his symbolizing the Indian synthesis, to his being the personification of India's composite culture. In a famous speech at Delhi's Jama Masjid, a few months after Partition, Maulana Azad said:

'Come, let us take the pledge that this country is ours, that we belong to it, and that fundamental decisions of its destiny will remain incomplete till we participate in them'.

"Four decades after that famous speech, we can say with pride that the Muslims of India have stood by India, and that India has stood by its Muslims. We are the second largest Muslim country in the world. Muslims have participated fully in the life of the country. The Muslim community and millions of individual Muslims have made an invaluable contribution to the building of modern India, to the progress and development of our country."

It was this composite culture of India, this unique heritage that Rajiv Gandhi saw as being threatened by the emergence and spread of communalism and communal forces. He warned:

"We proclaim and celebrate the unity of India. It is a fact of transcending significance. But is it not also a fact that most of us, in our daily lives, do not think of ourselves as Indians? We see ourselves as Hindus, Muslims, or Christians, or Malayalees, Maharashtrians, Bengalis. Worse, we think of ourselves as Brahmins, Thakurs, Jats, Yadavas and so on and so forth. And we shed blood to uphold our narrow domestic walls of religion, language, caste and region, blocking out the clear view of a resurgent nation. Political parties, State Governments and social organisations promote policies, programmes and ideologies which divide brother from brother and sister from sister. Bonds of fraternity and solidarity yield to the onslaughts of meanness of mind and spirit. Is this the India for which Mahatma Gandhi and Indira Gandhi sacrificed their lives?"

The answer, said Rajiv Gandhi, lies in ourselves:

"Our greatest asset in fighting communalism is that our people are overwhelmingly not communal. We have a long tradition of tolerance and brotherhood. Our composite culture is a reality. We have five thousand years of experience of unity in diversity. Communalism is the work of a few misguided elements who sometimes succeed in inciting communal passion by exploiting specific social disorders and tensions. To marginalise the communalists, we need vigilance of the local community and the local leadership, we need an administration that is impartial and seen to be impartial, that is seen to be firm and determined in dealing with violence. And, above, all, we fight communalism by fostering and preserving the values and standards embedded in our culture and our traditions."

And he cautioned the nation against those who wanted to adopt the methods of communalists to fight communalism. He said:

> "We will not become communal ourselves to counter communalism. That is the important thing."

And added:

> "If we raise a counter communal force, we do not kill communalism; we only increase communalism. What we have to do is to bring the fringe elements into the mainstream of our society. We have to make them feel involved."

And he further explained:

> "Answering communalism with communalism will help these people. There is only one India. It belongs to all of us."

Again and again, Rajiv Gandhi asked us to search in our own heritage for the inspiration to continue our secular traditions. He recalled our ancient seers:

> "Our ancient seers taught us, both as a matter of personal ethics and as a guidance for the organisation of society, that there was a valid alternative to the corroding emotions of fear, hatred and avarice. They taught tolerance and respect for diversity. They taught the benefits of synthesis. They taught the virtue of regarding nothing as alien, of taking the best from all that was new or different, and so synthesizing it into one's being that no reason remains for fear or hatred of that which is not one's own."

He recalled the Buddha:

> "The Buddha's enduring lesson was the substitution of fear by confidence, hatred by compassion, and greed by sharing as the basis for organisation of human society."

He recalled Adi Sankaracharya:

> "Adi Sankaracharya was a *sanyasi* but he was no recluse. He was devoted to action. He walked the length and breadth of India. He met millions of persons and talked to them. He was born in Kaladi, in Kerala, but he went to Shringeri, Badrinath, Puri, Dwarka, Srinagar and Kanchi - all over India. His life was linked with our entire country. Wandering across the plains of India, across its forests, its deserts, its

plateaux, and the Himalayas, he experienced the oneness of India with his own eyes. Through his message and his deeds, he made this oneness a reality. In the unity of India, he visualised the integrity of the universe. In his discourses and his poetry, he highlighted this oneness of all creation. Through his works we get an insight into the universe, into the truth of the cosmos."

He recalled Sri Narayana Guru, the great religious social reformer of Kerala:

"Sri Narayana Guru's response to oppression and conflict in the name of the religion constitutes one of the great sources of modern Indian secularism. Sri Narayana Guru was keenly aware of the evils in the name of religion but he did not reject religion for that reason. He saw these evil practices as weeds in a garden of religion to be pulled out and thrown away."

He recalled Panditji:

"Panditji was the great unifier of the Indian people. India is the home of many great religions. Her many-splendoured mansion of unity rests on the bedrock of secularism. Like a great teacher, he expounded in simple language the philosophy of secularism. He repeatedly warned the nation against communalism. To him, secularism was the beacon light when waves of passion threatened to submerge us."

He recalled his mother:

"Indira Gandhi gave her life so that a united India should live and prosper. Anything that creates a division between brother and brother comes in the way of national unity. Violence only helps the subversive forces to achieve their ends."

He recalled the people of India:

"India is one of the few countries where, as an expression of faith, people from one religion visit temples, mosques, gurudwaras, churches of other religions; Sikhs go to temples, Hindus go to gurudwaras; Sikhs, Hindus, Muslims, everyone goes to mosques. The fact is that in India faith is so deeply ingrained that we find religion in every religious place, we do not have to be confined to our own narrow parameters."

And, above all, he recalled Gandhiji:

"Gandhiji fought for our traditional values, he fought for our heritage, he fought to uphold our culture, our traditions. But, at the same time, he saw that there were many things in our society that needed to be changed. Gandhiji, although he was a staunch Hindu, fought against casteism. He fought against the suppression of women. He fought to bring the Harijans and women into the mainstream of our freedom movement, and it was this that gave our freedom movement its real strength. He saw clearly that a society that discriminates against any group of its own people cannot progress, cannot develop, cannot prosper. And he fought all his life to break these barriers that had been built. It is a homage that we pay to him when India stands strong and united, with its diversity being its main strength."

Rajiv Gandhi is no more but his words reverberate in our ears as we build India of his dreams. "India is strong," he said "because it is secular."

Cultural Challenges

Plurality in our society, stressed Rajiv Gandhi, did not end with secularism. There were many other facets of our diverse but, nevertheless, unified civilization that needed attention at the highest level of governance. Material progress, however, desperately needed in a poor country like ours, was in itself perhaps the single most important challenge the nation had ever faced to the continuity of our civilization. He said:

> "Throughout history, we have coped with invasion and occupation, political turbulence and economic disruption, but the challenges we are faced with today are more subtle, perhaps even more serious, than those we faced in earlier times. The challenge is to maintain and keep one's traditional values despite the changes brought about by economic development."

He went on to describe in detail this challenge:

> "For the first time, millions of Indians are leaving their traditional homes, going to new areas, new towns, looking for different types of occupations, occupations which have not traditionally been their family or home occupation.... and in doing this creating tremendous geographic uprooting in our society. In the past, the vast majority of our population spent their entire lives within few kilometres of their homes and their village. Today there is mass movement. It is the dominant fact of our national life... Millions who would not have come into contact with people from outside their own immediate environment are today going to different States. Millions are living with, meeting with, working with people from different castes, different religious communities,

> different regions, different linguistic groups, different cultural traditions. This to a degree has meant much greater knowledge of each other. (But) it has also led to millions competing with each other... So the challenge to national integration is in preventing this great movement from becoming a platform for individual rivalries, community rivalries or linguistic rivalries."

He also stressed:

> "Roots (are) lost when people leave their villages. When they go to urban areas, they get cut off from their traditional culture. They are faced in their new environment with the breakdown of their traditional values, breakdown of their links with their old culture."

One answer to this challenge which he began exploring was the establishment of a chain of seven zonal cultural centres whose primary objective was to facilitate access for all, however remote the hamlet or however economically or socially deprived the individual, to the many facets of our vibrant composite culture. This would also promote a cross-fertilization of ideas and art forms within and between regions. Besides, no other comparable institutions had earlier been established nation-wide to help rural, mofussil, folk and tribal artistes preserve, present, enrich and document the many-splendoured variety of our proud heritage.

While completing the institutional framework for this celebration of our most precious inheritance - the very civilization of India - Rajiv Gandhi set in train a high-powered review of the major cultural institutions that had been built since Independence. He chaired the Trust established to build the Indira Gandhi National Centre for the Arts, the most prestigious cultural centre that the country is to have. And although most of the Festivals of India held abroad had their conceptual origin in Indira Gandhi's time, it fell to Rajiv Gandhi to inaugurate many of them.

The personal involvement of the Prime Minister in such cultural activity was not always understood or appreciated. If, however, the celebration of our cultural diversity was a much-noted and much-commented on aspect of his Premiership, it was because Rajiv Gandhi was deeply persuaded that culture, particularly the performing arts, was not so much a matter of entertainment as of contemporary nation-building. Modern India would be built - or broken - in the mind of India; that was a mind with a millennial past but confronted now by challenges without precedent in its hoary past. Measuring up to that challenge by preserving, in the face of rapid material progress and cultural globalization, the essential values which had ensured the continuity of our civilization was, in Rajiv Gandhi's vision, a central obligation of political leadership for at least two basic reasons.

One, without broad-mindedness, tolerance, compassion, and our unique genius for synthesis, it would be impossible for a society as diverse as ours to survive; these values could not be preserved merely in a didactic mode: they had to be consciously propagated through the medium of culture. This required a living, throbbing, continuous nation-wide celebration of the glorious diversity of India.

Second, India had a special message to give humankind in an era where science and technology had not only converted our planet Earth into a global village but also placed in humanity's hands the capacity to self-destruct in hours or days in the event of a nuclear war. Throughout history, international relations had been based on the quest for dominance. The quest for dominance, in turn, is based on a segmenting of humankind between those who will exercise dominance and those over whom domination is sought to be imposed. The struggle between the dominant and the dominated had acquired an entirely new complexion in the era of nuclear weapons because they had made annihilation possible. Therefore, humankind would survive, perhaps even surmount, the era of nuclear weapons only if there was a fundamental change in the mindset, a change away from the quest for dominance towards the alternative of peaceful coexistence. And peaceful coexistence, observed Rajiv Gandhi, was posited on unity through diversity, as opposed to unity through uniformity.

It was a lesson, he was convinced, the world needed to learn from India:

> "Most civilizations posit nationhood and diversity as antithetical. The single greatest contribution of India to world civilization has been to demonstrate that there is nothing antithetical between diversity and nationhood. Through 5000 years of living experience, we have demonstrated to the world that our unity in diversity is a vibrant reality."

> "Today's world is in desperate need of learning from India's experience. Peace and survival in the modern age depend on nonviolence, on tolerance, on compassion and understanding, on peaceful coexistence between diverse philosophies and diverse ways of life. Through technological development the world is becoming smaller and is growing into a global village. The world is equally in need of unity and diversity.

"India's secularism is a global secularism. It is inseparable from human survival, it is inseparable from global cooperation."

Micro-minorities

The problem of the minorities - religious, linguistic, regional, and cultural - looms large in contemporary India's perceptions of nation-building. Not quite the same attention is always given to the micro-minorities, such as the Anglo-Indians, the Nicobarese, the Onges, the Minicoyans, the minority tribal groups of the North-East, the followers of the Donyi-Polo faith in Arunachal Pradesh, and other tiny groups whose minuscule numbers, in relation to the population as a whole, calls for extra attention in a democracy where the number game might lead to witting or unwitting neglect. Rajiv Gandhi believed that the problems of these micro-minorities required particular notice at the level of the Prime Minister, not any lower, since their very lack of numbers deprived them of constituencies to champion their causes.

Of course, it is not lack of numbers alone that lies at the root of neglect and discrimination. The most neglected and discriminated against segment of our society, he often said, was the women of India. The provision of reserving a third of the seats in local bodies for elected women representatives was, perhaps the most decisive step taken during his Premiership to bring women into a central role in the public life of the country. He outlined the Indira Mahila Yojana at a press conference at the All-India Congress Committee on 19 November, 1989, which would have been a major highlight of his second term of office had the electorate, and Fate, let him have a second term of office. The Indira Mahila Yojana was designed to conscientize and empower women to take charge of their own lives and themselves become the prime arbiter in determining priorities and modalities for programmes of women and child development. It was aimed at debureaucratizing these programmes and making them participatory. It would have touched the lives of every woman in the land, wherever she lived and whatever the economic or social segment of the society to which she might belong. The Yojana remains a manifesto commitment of the Congress Party and a commitment made by Government through the President's Address.

The other segments of society that have suffered millennia of neglect and discrimination not for want of numbers but as a consequence of inhuman prejudice are the Scheduled Castes (SCs), the

Scheduled Tribes (STs) and the Other Backward Classes (OBCs). With respect to the SCs and STs, Rajiv Gandhi's task was one of consolidation, building on specific steps taken by the Father of the Nation during the struggle for Independence and his Prime Ministerial predecessors since Independence. Administrative measures included appointment of a Commissioner and special recruitment drives to fill vacancies. Education received particular attention. Reservations were extended for another ten years at least, while steps were taken to endow reservations in local bodies with constitutional sanction. The Congress party's Election Manifesto 1989 spelt out these achievements in detail:

- no post reserved for SC/ST communities will be dereserved;
- recruitment in just six months of 45000 SC/ST candidates through special recruitment drive;
- Scheduled Castes and Scheduled Tribes (Prevention of Atrocities) Act;
- remedial and special coaching classes;
- National SC/ST Finance and Development Corporation;
- One Million Wells scheme for small and marginal farmers of SC/ST communities;
- Indira Awas Yojana : dwelling units for SC/ST communities;
- Kutirjyoti scheme : Single-point light connection for SC/ST communities;
- Tribal Cooperative Marketing Development Federation; and
- mobile teams to enforce the Protection of Civil Rights Act which made "untouchability" illegal.

Measures to implement the long-pending Mandal Commission recommendations were taken up in August 1990 in a manner which Rajiv Gandhi regarded as unfortunate. His disapproval was manifest in the resolutions of the Congress on the subject and his intervention of over two hours in the Lok Sabha. The position of the Party in respect of this burning social issue was detailed in the Party's Election Manifesto, 1991:

> "The Congress has always been at the forefront of the struggle for social justice and in the fight against social and economic inequality. It has been an integral part of the struggle for emancipation of socially and

> educationally backward classes from the very inception of that struggle. The Congress reaffirms its unshakeable commitment to this struggle (and) unequivocally declares its continued commitment to reservations as an important instrument of social justice. The Congress party's commitment to undertaking special measures in favour of socially and educationally backward classes - including reservation in jobs - was first made over 40 years ago and has been successfully implemented by Congress governments in several States. This commitment will be a basic plank of the Party's policies at the Centre. In implementing these special measures, preference will be given to the poorer sections among the backward classes, while ensuring that, if candidates are not available from the poorer sections, the benefit will go to other members within the backward classes. The Congress is also committed to ensuring that the bene-fits of reservation are provided to other economically backward sections of our people who are not covered by existing schemes."

This constitutes the basis on which reservations for the OBCs in the Central Government employment were introduced by the Rao Government with none of the bloodshed and social tension that had marked the period August-October 1990.

We are now in a position to evaluate Rajiv Gandhi's vision of India in the light of his approach to issues of ethnicity, plurality and conflict-resolution in democratic India which, as much during his Premiership as during any Premiership in the building of our modern nationhood, constitute the central issues of political leadership.

Towards the end of his term in office, Rajiv Gandhi more than once articulated his vision of India. It might be summed up as the determination to restore India by the 21st century to its traditional place in the vanguard of human civilization.

Mark the words carefully : not to "take" India but to "restore" India to that position; for through most of its history, indeed, for all but the last two and half centuries of its 5000-year history, India has been in that position. In the perspective of history, therefore, these 250 years must be seen as something of an aberration. It follows that restoring India to that position is no impossible dream but mere rectification of a recent and unnatural distortion. That position is, of course, a vanguard position; not, however, a position in the vanguard of political domination or economic hegemony or military might, but a position in the vanguard of human civilization, a civilization to which India has contributed so much and so uniquely in the past and to which it must again contribute in full measures.

Rajiv Gandhi was proud of India, proud of being an Indian. It was in the ancient genius of our ancient civilization that he sought solutions to the problems of the present; at the same time, he recognized that since today's present is yesterday's future, it is in terms of today's reality that tomorrow's future must be built. Every moment in time throws up its own challenges; a mindset mired in the past cannot find the right answers to the present challenges; at the same time, a mindset ignorant or ashamed of its past cannot move into the future; the mind must be alive, independent and proud if the past is to move seamlessly through the present into the future, keeping the nation alive, independent, united and proud. That remains the enduring insignia of Rajiv Gandhi's brief but decisive contribution to building the India of the 21st century.

8

Rajiv Gandhi and Panchayati Raj

Mani Shankar Aiyar

THE ORIGINS of Rajiv Gandhi's decisive contribution to the establishment of constitutionally-sanctioned Panchayati Raj may be traced to his first broadcast to the nation after winning the elections of December 1984. Repeatedly, Rajiv Gandhi returned in that speech (5 January, 1985) to the theme of a "responsive administration", a preoccupation which found reflection in the inclusion of the concept in the new 20-point programme which he announced on the Independence Day, 1986.

At the time, Rajiv Gandhi appears to have regarded administrative reform as largely a managerial matter. He was much impressed by what a young Collector had done in Ahmednagar to impart a human face to administration. He seems to have thought that the fine-tuning of such innovative managerial techniques, combined with training administrators to sensitize them to the felt needs of the people, might result in an administration which responded to the people rather than remain wrapped in its own cocoon of perceptions and priorities.

Primarily with a view to ascertaining what administrators themselves believed to be the right managerial techniques to make administration people oriented, Rajiv Gandhi embarked on a programme of face-to-face interaction with District Magistrates drawn from every district of the country. It started dawning on him at the very first of these encounters, in December 1987, that the best of our administrators felt handicapped most by the absence at the grassroots of a machinery for determining the will of the people. Administration in a democratic country was being carried on without effectively consulting the people or their elected representatives on the issues that most immediately impacted on the people. Even the best of administrators had to go by what they thought the people wanted instead of basing themselves on a well-articulated programme of priorities as desired by the people.

This helped Rajiv Gandhi fit in his mind the different pieces of the jigsaw puzzle of people in democracy and development which had evidently been preoccupying him at least since his advent into the country's political life. As a newly elected MP, he had spent months on end driving to every nook and corner of his constituency, sipping tea at the wayside *dhabas* and chatting with the constituents on village *chaupals*. These conversations made clear to him the vast chasm separating the people from the administrative system that was supposedly designed to serve them. Four decades into Freedom, the steel-frame was as much in place as when the British, who devised it, were ruling the country. Was this, perhaps, the reason that the people felt almost as distanced, even alienated, from their own democratically elected Government, be it at the Centre or the States, as in colonial times?

Rajiv Gandhi's experiences as a constituency MP were only reinforced by what he saw of the political culture spawned by the absence of representative government at the grassroots. It was a political culture famously decried by him at the centenary session of the Congress (December 1985) where he tore into the "brokers of power". Clearly, if a vast chasm separated the elected representatives from the people, the chasm would have to be filled by those who made a profession of interceding with the authorities on behalf of those without access to authority. These were the power brokers, who may have succeeded in making the administration res-ponsive to some but only because the administration was so cut off from the many.

By the time Rajiv Gandhi had completed his second workshop with the District Magistrates (February 1988), his mind was more or less made up that the problems of a non-responsive administration, which concerned him as the head of the country's system of governance, were intimately linked to the problem of marginalizing and, hopefully, eventually eliminating the power brokers, which was a priority item in his political agenda. It was the non-representative character of the power system at the grassroots that had necessitated the power brokers. If power at the grassroots were to be exercised by the people's representatives, the empowerment of the people would itself eliminate the imperative for the brokers of power. It followed that the search for a responsive administration should begin not with the managerial solutions being sought hitherto but by a systemic revolution that would vest power in the hands of the people.

One has only to read Rajiv Gandhi's address to the All India Panchayat Parishad in September 1986 (close to a year before his workshops with District Magistrates and close to a year after his centenary speech) to see how clearly he had thought through the system of Panchayati Raj which he would have wished to see flourish in the country. Yet, that speech does not disclose any specific appreciation of the link between Panchayati Raj as a system of governance and the evolution of a responsive administration or the marginalization of the power brokers. That link became clear to him only at and through the workshops. It transformed the workshops from what might otherwise have been an interesting experiment into a truly seminal breakthrough.

Focussing, then, on Panchayati Raj as the systemic answer to the systemic deficiencies in our system of governance, Rajiv Gandhi, at no time, attempted to lay any claim to originality in conceiving or elaborating the concept of Panchayati Raj. On the contrary, what intrigued him was the failure of Panchayati Raj to take root in Independent India despite its having been the fundamental prescription of the greatest Indian of the 20th century, Mahatma Gandhi, and the priority political objective of the second greatest Indian of the 20th Century, Pandit Jawaharlal Nehru. Why had democracy at the grassroots so palpably failed when, equally palpably, democracy at the Centre and in the States had taken such deep roots that India could justifiably lay claim to being the world's largest democracy?

By the time he came to the Third Workshop (April 1988), Rajiv Gandhi had come to the conclusion that the answer to that conundrum lay in our Constitution. Democracy had flourished at Delhi and in the State capitals because the Constitution made detailed provisions for the institution and protection of democracy at these levels. However, the same Constitution treated local government in a most perfunctory manner, confining all mention of the subject to a mere three lines - and that too not in any obligatory or mandatory part of the Constitution but in the non-binding chapter on the Directive Principles of State Policy. The entire responsibility for Panchayati Raj having been vested in the political will of the States, it was the tug and pull of political compulsions in the State capitals that had determined the fate of Panchayati Raj, not any prescriptive provision of our Constitution. In consequence, most States had played ducks and drakes with self-governance at the grassroots, rendering it a plaything of narrow political exigencies instead of making it the forum for the determination of the people's will. The solution lay in making Panchayati Raj as much a constitutional obligation as democracy in Parliament or the State Assemblies.

Rajiv Gandhi quickly discovered that his quest for such a systemic revolution was a rather lonely quest. Few of the senior administrators he initially consulted shared his perception of the imperative of root-and-branch reform. Few of his political colleagues shared his enthusiasm for the programme. In State capitals, there was positive hostility to what was correctly seen as a move that would rob State ministers and State legislators of many of their powers. And the Opposition, by and large, condemned the workshops as an unacceptable transgression on States' rights and his Panchayati Raj plans as an insincere political gimmick designed to distract the nation's attention from Bofors and other such matters.

Rajiv Gandhi, therefore, mounted a major campaign to build a nation-wide consensus on what he increasingly came to see as the single most important platform of his domestic agenda for taking India into the 21st Century as a nation worthy of its traditional place in the vanguard of human civilization.

Since the workshops were being run by the Ministry of Personnel a sub-committee of the Consultative Committee attached to that Ministry was established under the chairmanship of Shri P.K.Thungon, a long-standing MP from Arunachal Pradesh. The Report of that sub-committee then became the basis on which to carry the campaign further afield. A Working Group of the Congress Parliamentary Party was constituted to elicit back-bench reaction to the programme. The theme was taken up in public speeches and party forums. Meanwhile, some of the more positively inclined members of the Planning Commission were drafted informally into fleshing out the concept. The Council of Ministers was sensitized into an appreciation of the significance of the endeavour underway.

It was, thus, not till the last days of December 1988, all of one year after the first workshop and close on nine months after he had made his mind clear at the third workshop, the Rajiv Gandhi felt the coast to be sufficiently clear to ask the Department of Rural Development (then a part of the Ministry of Agriculture) to begin the exercise of drafting the Constitution Amendment. Simultaneously, he made sure the exercise was not reduced to bureaucratic or legal technicalities by putting the same officials who were doing the drafting incharge of organising what was undoubtedly the most profound attempt ever at ascertaining the perceptions of the people on any single issue through face-to-face interaction bet-ween the Head of Government and the general run of people's representatives. It is estimated that, in all, some 25,000 Panchayat representatives, drawn from every region of the country, and including representatives of the scheduled castes, scheduled tribes and women, met, heard and had their voice heard by the Prime Minister in a series of conferences held in different parts of the country. The country was woken up to the significance of the systemic revolution being launched.

Within the ruling establishment, there were two different trends to counter. On the one hand were those who wanted to adopt the minimalist approach of urging State governments to launch a fresh initiative but not having the Centre itself too embroiled in the details. On the other, there were those who favoured a Constitutional Amendment but wanted this to be as brief as possible, confined essentially to the question of ensuring that elections to the Panchayats were held on schedule. At the other end of the spectrum were a few who wanted the Central Government to go well beyond constitutional stage-setting and, in effect, draft the country's municipal law and local government.

The guidelines given to the drafting group were to prepare as detailed constitutional provisions as were required but not to alter the constitutional place of Panchayati Raj, namely, its position in the State List. In other words, the proposed Amendment would ensure full constitutional sanction and protection to the institutions of local government in rural India but leave it to the States to work out the modalities for decentralization and the devolution of power.

During the course of months devoted to detailed drafting, during which Rajiv Gandhi gave freely his time and energy at every stage of the process, he decided that the Constitutional Amendment must ensure uniformity in bringing Panchayats into existence, uniformity in provisions for dissolution and reconstitution by election within a reasonable period of time, uniformity in regard to the legitimate life of the Panchayats after which elections must be held, and uniformity in regard to the system for the representation of the scheduled castes, the scheduled tribes and women. Initially, there was no particular desire to ensure uniformity in the structure of the institutions of Panchayati Raj. But it gradually became evident that there could not be uniformity in reservations for the three identified disadvantaged groups unless there was uniformity of structure. Thus, for example, if some States had only two tiers, or even only one, while others had three tiers, clearly the representation of the people would be different in different States and, equally representation for the weaker sections of society would also be different in different States. This Rajiv Gandhi regarded as indefensible since, in principle, there was no reason why Tamils should find direct, elected representation at the village and intermediate level only while Bengalis found direct, elected representation at the district level also; or for reservations to operate through a direct election process at the intermediate level in Karnataka but not in Uttar Pradesh because the middle tier there was composed ex-officio of the village pradhans (heads). Uniformity in election schedules thus got married to uniformity in the structure of Panchayat Raj institutions and the system of reservation in these institutions. It also eventually led to uniformity in the method of electing representatives to these institutions and the methodology for electing office-bearers and the composition of the electoral college for this purpose. In determining the shape that such uniformity should take, Rajiv Gandhi was persuaded that, if a parliamentary system was favoured at the State and Central levels, a similar system should be introduced uniformly in the Panchayats in preference to a presidential model, advocated by many, of having the chief executive of the panchayat institutions directly elected by the electorate instead of, as in the parliamentary system, indirectly by the members of the panchayat body.

To secure consensus on these basis systemic changes was no easy matter. He particularly relied on a determined band of scheduled caste and scheduled tribe Ministers to bring sceptics and doubters around to this point of view. He demonstrated in Cabinet that the protection of the interests of the weaker sections was not possible uniformly without uniformity in systems, such reservations being the key to ensuring that feudal elements and gender bias did not result in Panchayati Raj becoming exploitative rather than representative. In the process of evolving this consensus, he had to concede two points that have since detracted from the degree of uniformity in systems. One, he was obliged to leave it to the States to devise their own patterns of representation for the Other Backward Classes (OBCs). This has led to various anomalies in State legislation. He also agreed to leave it to the State legislatures to determine the mode of election of the village panchayat president : some have favoured direct elections, others have gone in for the parliamentary mode.

At the end of the day, however, it is remarkable how much uniformity in the system has been secured in contrast to the systems devised under earlier dispensations. Of course, assured representation for women is the single most important conceptual breakthrough. It is important, though, to appreciate the significance of the other major conceptual change: SC/ST reservation is now proportional to the population of SC/ST in each panchayat area, not weighted to some national average in the State as a whole. The domination of panchayats in SC/ST areas by non-SC/ST elements has, thus, been kept in check.

While questions relating to the structure and design of Panchayati Raj institutions (PRIs) compelled Rajiv Gandhi to call upon all his reserves of persuasion to secure consensus within his government, curiously the far more important provisions relating to decentralisation and devolution for development had much smoother sailing. No one doubted that the primary function of the PRIs must relate to planning and implementation of schemes of economic and social development, nor that social justice (that is, equity in regard to beneficiaries from all classes), must be integrally built into the planning and implementation process. Despite his many other preoccupations, Rajiv Gandhi spent some three hours going over every entry, with a fine tooth-comb, as it were, of the proposed Twelfth Schedule illustratively listing the subjects to be devolved to the PRIs. His painstaking attention to this crucial detail fully justified itself. Not only did the Twelfth Schedule emerge unscathed from repeated examination by successor governments and Parliament's Joint Select Committee, but every State in its State legislation had incorporated each of the entries in every particular into the legal scheme of their patterns of devolution. This is, perhaps, an even more enduring and significant contribution to Panchayati Raj than establishing the irreversibility of Panchayati Raj in the warp and woof of our policy.

Rajiv Gandhi was now ready to go before the most crucial forum of all, the Chief Ministers of the country, the group most likely to have reservations over this encroachment into what had hitherto been their virtually exclusive preserve. The country was, however, so firmly behind his endeavours that, some criticism of specifics notwithstanding, he was able to build a substantial measure of agreement at the meeting. Indeed, the meeting was chiefly notable for a query posed by the Chief Minister of Uttar Pradesh, Shri Narain Datt Tewari. Why, he asked, had the Prime Minister concentrated exclusively on Panchayats for the rural areas? Why not a similar Constitutional Amendment for the Nagarpalikas?

Rajiv Gandhi immediately initiated consultations for such an Amendment and the process was every bit as intensive for the municipalities as it had been for the Panchayats, although concentrated within a much shorter time span.

The 64th and 65th Amendments had an easy passage through the Lok Sabha but ran into serious straits in the Upper House. This had been anticipated as the Congress lacked the requisite two-thirds majority in the Rajya Sabha. The initial strategy had been to take the Amendments to the Rajya Sabha by Independence Day 1989, in the hope that the larger cause of Panchayati Raj would prevail over narrower partisan political considerations. But despite Rajiv Gandhi's very generous acknowledgement of the contribution of non-Congress governments in shaping his ideas, such constructive cooperation was not forthcoming. The initial strategy was to force the issue whatever the outcome, win or lose, and go to the country on the issue at the next elections. Subsequently, however, a determined effort was made to secure the required two-third majority. On the night of Friday,13 October, 1989, these efforts came to nought as the Rajya Sabha fell five votes short of the required target. The following week, Rajiv gandhi went to the country. The rest is history.

It was Ayodhya rather than Panchayati Raj that dominated the elections of 1989. But so firmly had the seeds of Panchayati Raj been planted that, in December 1992, Parliament passed into law a new part of the Constitution consecrated to the Panchayats and the Nagarpalikas, which in all but some matters of detail, was the scheme born out of Rajiv Gandhi's dreams and ideals. The new part IX of the Constitution remains the most enduring monument to Rajiv Gandhi's stewardship of the nation.

9

Are We a Market Once Again

Mohan Guruswamy

AT THE TIME OF Independence the population of India was around 320 million. Today after just fifty years it is more than three times of that and continues to grow at 1.9 per cent each year. Today 352 million Indians or 36 per cent of the population, most of them born after Independence, are considered to be living below the official poverty line earning less than Rs. 264 per month. Over 400 million are now illiterate. If we use a more humane yardstick to define poverty such as the UNDP's 'capability poverty index' which factors in education, health and other basic support indices, not less than 61.5 per cent or 554 million Indians can be considered to be living in poverty. The Founding Fathers of our Republic had expectations of erasing poverty and illiteracy within twenty-five years. A quarter of a century seemed too long for the many that believed the State could do more and do it quickly. Now it seems that we will need a hundred more years to reduce poverty to an acceptable level. As India ranks a very low, i.e., 135 in terms of development keeping company with countries of sub-Saharan Africa and South Asia, there is little reason to believe that we have made significant progress in relation to others in the past fifty years. We must ask ourselves the question as to why is it that this nation which boasts of the world's oldest and most enduring civilization, and which for the most of known history was far ahead economically and socially than other nations, finds itself in this unenviable position?

Well before the first millenium this nation was so powerful that even the all-conquering Alexander turned back at the Indus rather than face the Mauryan army. That period lasted almost a thousand years and ended with the assertion of region over nation. We became a divided people, organized into mutually antagonistic and warring principalities. Unfortunately this largely coincided with the spread of Islam. The power and greatness so dwindled that since 1000 AD when Mahmood of Ghazni first conquered parts of north India, our country has almost continually been under the domination of alien powers. Persians, Turks, Uzbeks, Mongols and Europeans followed the Afghans. What the great Greek army could not do was achieved by several conquering armies with far fewer numbers and increasing ease. The final ignominy was when the East India Company took all India from Calcutta to Quetta with Indian troops led by the British officers giving us the dubious distinction of being the first country to be conquered by a commercial enterprise. In 1947 India once again became a free nation.

We might have gained political freedom, but have our minds been freed from the malaise that cost us our place in the world? What we see all around us are signs of disintegration and fragmentation. We are now mostly castes, religions and regional nationalities. Enormous and ever growing economic disparities compounded by regional imbalances have further divided us. Like before the elite's are once again entirely focussed on obtaining the most if not all without regard to those less advantaged and supplanting those who might seem more advantaged than them. Recently there was a great deal of euphoria generated by the latest budget proposals, the most notable features of which were steep reductions in personal and corporate income taxes, customs and excise tariffs simultaneously accompanied by sharp reductions in the expenditures for agriculture, irrigation, health, education, infrastructure and poverty alleviation. This is only the further evidence of an unconcern once again for the masses and the elevation of selfishness to a State philosophy.

This unconcern for the poor masses and ruthless preoccupation with oneself was the main characteristic of feudalism. In the days of the past these political doctrines were sanctioned by suitable adapting religion to serve the narrow interests of the rulers. Nevertheless oppression even if it were sanctioned by religion still remained an injustice and the oppressed found ways to exit from the vicious cycle by taking whatever opportunity that came their way. Not surprisingly national systems that sanctioned the oppression of the people and the perpetuation of injustice wilted against the onslaught of more egalitarian doctrines. Islam arrived in India with the invader's sword, but it found acceptance among vast sections of Hindu society because it seemed to represent a way out of the miserable situation they were in due to the stratified arrangement of society allegedly legitimized by divine ordainment. The conquest of India was also made easy for the invaders by the willingness of various ruling elites to put their limited and immediate interests ahead of larger relationships. Many Indian rulers therefore actively collaborated with the invaders, be they Muslim or European, because of this preoccupation with oneself. One must wonder if the outpourings in support of globalization, the sellout to the multi-nationals and the unconcern for the plight of the majority are yet another manifestation of this mentality? The doctrines might have a new name but the underlying motivations of those who propounded them then and those who seek to endow virtue and good sense to uncaring and divisive policies now seem to be the same.

It is fifty years since the British left. We no longer enjoy the luxury of blaming our ills and the continuing wrongs upon the colonial master. Fifty years may be a short period in history but it is a long enough time to remake society if a people were determined to do so. Many other countries have done so, some even in lesser time. Japan remade itself twice in the past century and a half. Korea and China ravaged by occupation and war have done so under two entirely different systems. Cultural homogeneity alone cannot be the reason for this, as Malaysia which is undergoing a similar transformation is a multi-cultural and multi-ethnic State. Even paucity of resources is not a constraint in breaking down the barriers of backwardness as countries like Sri Lanka which despite not being much more better off than India have managed to substantially improve the physical quality of life of its citizens. Sri Lanka boasts of life expectancy, infant mortality and literacy rates that compare favourably with those of many of the advanced nations. Even within the country States like Kerala despite of their relative economic backwardness have shown that high human development standards are achievable if leaders have vision and the commitment to back it up with action. After all development is not entirely about economic growth. It has also to do with improving basic living standards and equipping people to realize their potential. Equality of opportunity, which is integral to democracy, only makes sense when equality is not merely an abstract notion and when ones place in society is not determined by accident of birth.

Those who determine our economic policies, be they be in India or abroad, seem to have either inadvertently or deliberately misread history or have their own agenda. Japan and South Korea which are unique in that they made great economic and social development advancements in short time spans have done so by emphasizing human development, self-reliance and economic nationalism. War ravaged Japan did not accept the huge financial aid offered under the Marshall Plan and preferred to depend on domestic savings for financiang its industrial rebirth. By rejecting the unbridled entry of Western capital they gave their industries a chance to grow and become powerful global players. If Japan had opened itself up to the RCA's and General Motors in the early 1950s then it is very likely that there would have been no Sonys and Toyotas like we know them today. We see the reverse happening in India today. There are few Indian products in the market. Cars, refrigerators, television sets, soaps and shampoos, toothpastes, coffee and tea, and whatever else are a part of our everyday lives are all mostly foreign brands. One must define what Indian products mean. Products made by multinationals under license in India are merely made in India. All the real benefits of production accrue to the parent corporation and its national economy. Products that are designed, manufactured and branded in India utilizing local technology, skills, raw material and parts to the maximum extent possible are truly Indian products because the benefits of value addition accrue here and serve the process of economic development in a far more significant manner. Japan and Korea achieved what they did in the industrial sphere was by adopting hardheaded policies built on the cornerstone of economic nationalism.

A nation's greatness owes to its sense of self-esteem and self-respect. Its leaders, therefore, must not only think big but must also walk tall. In the recent days we have seen disquieting evidence of this lacking. The manner in which our social, economic and political elite clamoured to be around Bill Gates just because he was the richest man in the world was a pathetic exhibition of craven and obsequious behaviour. Must the Prime Minister and the Finance Minister go each year to the so-called World Economic Conference at Davos to sell India as a destination for foreign capital? At one time it was an annual ritual for our leaders to go with a begging bowl to the so-called Aid India Consortium. Now it seems that we must do it in Davos! We no longer seem to be in a hurry to make its tryst with destiny. Now we seem to be merely a market waiting to be taken.

On August 15, 1947, a colony became a nation. Let it not be recorded in history that in just fifty years this nation became merely a market for exploitation by neo-colonial mercantile forces. If at one time force was needed to capture markets, now it is competitive advantage bestowed by technological lead and larger capital resources that captures markets. For the exploited the result remains the same.

10

India's North-East

An Overview

Lt. Gen. (Retd.) V. K. Nayar

THE SITUATION in the North-East in the last decade has become more complex and the problems have multiplied. In order to focus on major problem areas of the current situation, it is important to refer to some of the generic and historic causes of the ferment in the region.

The very first problem is the factor of isolation. North-East has stood at the crossroads of history as much as the North-West of India with one basic difference that the interaction of the immigrating population with the indigenous remained confined to its natural boundaries due to its geographical vastness and abundant natural resources. In the North-West the invaders and immigrants intermixed with the local population and got assimilated. Even the great Vaishnavite surge, Bhakti cult of Sankaradev during the Sixteenth to Eighteenth century AD remained confined to the Brahmaputra Valley, which later the Manipuri Kings integrated into the plains of the Imphal Valley. Annexation by the British in the 19th century did not mean administrating the area, rather it was essentially to protect their interests in the plains. The Inner Line Regulations 1873, Government of India Act 1919 and Excluded Area Act 1935, resulted in perpetuation of physical, social, political and economic isolation. Since Independence the efforts to break it have been halfhearted and disjointed.

The second factor is the diversity within the region. There are over 200 ethnic groups, and over 400 languages and dialects are spoken in the area. In addition, there is a vast cultural and religious diversity. The area is inhabited by a high percentage of the scheduled tribes: 93 per cent in Mizoram, 84 per cent in Nagaland, 80 per cent in Meghalaya, 70 per cent in Arunachal Pradesh, 28 per cent in Tripura, 27 per cent in Manipur and 10 per cent in Assam. We need to appreciate that the North-East is not a homogeneous region with common political, social or economic system and perspectives. Therefore, search of a North-East identity will be fallacious. While searching for a solution and a holistic perspective, we must be conscious of the fundamental differences at the ground level in the constituent areas of the region.

In the socio-political field both the good and the bad effects of modernisation have manifested; unfortunately the process has not been harmonised and the past values and systems are in conflict with the modern forces. The major fallout that the traditional rural elite has been replaced by a centralised and formal system.

It may be pertinent to mention that one of the major inbuilt constraints of most of the tribal areas, particularly of the hill tribes, is the close and federal nature of society. Generally people have been traditionally suspicious of anything from outside, and the period of assimilation is a long term process; trust and credibility have high value in their minds. The major outside constraint is the ignorance, lack of detailed knowledge of each constituent State and its heterogeneous inhabitants and their requirements. These not only impose constraints on influencing the solution but pave way to exploitation by the parochial elements.

Increasing Alienation

By and large the major area of concern for the entire North-East is the increasing alienation of the people of the region from the national mainstream. Primarily, it is due to our failure to recognise the peculiar historical, social and cultural factors of each area in the North-East with the common effect of isolation. Various facets of this isolation vary from area to area; of this the factor of physical isolation impinges on the minds of the people the most. The communications and railway network are totally inadequate. Movement into and within the region is restricted and puts people to economic and social harassment by the neighbouring States.

In the tribal areas, apart from the political and economic causes, the very federal nature of society where each ethnic group has led an independent existence, the suspicion of outsiders persists. The tribal society is a classless society; while it is getting modernised, the federal structure still remains. There is a widespread demand for political independence/autonomy but they find it difficult to accept the emerging economic class structure. Literacy, awareness and modern political system have been accompanied by corrupt administration — both civil and political — and mounting economic bankruptcy and unemployment have provided fertile ground for exploitation.

Neglect and lack of real economic development have provided incentives for exploitation, which has been accentuated by the influx of foreigners giving rise to ethnic parochialism. Under these conditions the question of identity has come to the forefront. The identity crisis is fermented by the fear of cultural submergence and economic and social insecurity.

Alienation of land is one of the root causes of the alienation. In the plain areas of the North-East, particularly in Assam, alienation of land is primarily due to perpetuation of the colonial land policy, continuation of land based developmental process and unchecked immigration. In the hills and the tribal areas, it is the result of the perversion of traditional jurisdiction of community on land and land based resources due to greed and manipulation of the local political elite and political economy of the neighbouring countries.

To break the alienation of the people of the North-East, first and foremost is the requirement of honesty of intention and sincerity of purpose. This needs to be backed by a pragmatic policy framework based on correct inputs recognising the genius of the divergent societies that inhabit the area. The key element is to break the physical isolation.

Institutional Degradation

The area has very democratic and well established social and cultural institutions regulating all activities at the village and community level. However, their authority and effectiveness have been eroded under the pretext of modernisation and the modern democratic set-up. We have neither absorbed them into the system nor replaced them with new ones. The motive is clear; if these are effective then they will question the politicians and the administration, who want a free hand in exercising power and utilisation of meagre resources for their selfish purposes. Without rejuvenation of the institutional structure at the grassroots level, neither genuine participation by the people in the democratic system and the development process can be ensured nor alienation of the people be reduced. The enactment of the 73rd and 74th amendments to the Constitution on Panchayati Raj and Municipalities is a step in the right direction. However, it can only succeed if there is a mandatory financial devolution and there is no overlap in the functions between these institutions and the State Government Departments to prevent political interference.

Student power and student politics always had a role in these areas. These were broad based, democratic and secular. The high point of students' movement was the formation of the AGP Government in 1985 by the student leaders of Assam. Since then student movement in Assam and other States has fragmented on ethnic and communal lines. This has happened because of the failure of the democratic parties to comprehend the dynamics of these developments. The fragmentation and its aftermath have generated their own social tensions; this is being exploited by the local politicians, particularly in the smaller hill States.

Deteriorating Political Ethos

Since the 1980s there has been entirely the politics of expediency and both political parties and individual loyalties have been frequently purchased. This has led to instability and bad governance. Government resources have been essentially used to gain, retain and consolidate power.

Insurgent factions have been used in the power game by most leaders and parties; this has provided them unlimited opportunity to gain financial and other resources at the cost of the people. This has worked to the double advantage of the insurgents. Firstly, their resource base has widened. Secondly, due to denial of economic benefits of developments, people feel alienated and are vulnerable to insurgent influence and propaganda.

No discussion of the current political ethos will be complete without touching on electoral politics and blatant corruption. Political will and perceptions are only confined to winning elections and perpetuating power. It has lost its sancity and meaning as the most sacred and fundamental democratic function. In a closed society divided into small ethnic groups, particularly in smaller States, electoral politics and corruption have effected each individual and spared no one. With limited economic base, political leadership, bureaucracy and insurgents are digging into the common limited kitty. Financial mismanagement is of the highest order. There is no ethos of systematic utilisation of funds meant for specific purposes and there is no monitoring. Denial of opportunity to entrepreneurs in some of the hilly States has resulted in benami contractors operating on behalf of the local people(mostly people in power or their relatives), who pay large sums to the local frontmen and insurgent nominees out of the meagre development funds. Political permissiveness and corruption are eating into the society and feeding insurgency.

Nationalism in all its connotations and of various varieties is the most exploited sentiment in the North-East, particularly in the smaller hill States. Broadly speaking two versions of nationalism which are doing the maximum damage to the national cause and the interest of the people of the area merit special attention. First one is, wherein the local political leaders pose as true nationalists while in Delhi and profess that national interest will suffer without them. They justify it on the basis of the propagated threat by the insurgents, the very same people are doing the maximum damage to the national and local interest. The motive is entirely to perpetuate power, with a free hand in utilising resources(totally provided by the Central Government) for selfish purposes. The second is the one locally propagated, which is of different varieties of local sentiments or sub-nationalism. This is exploited by the politician in power and out of power and the insurgents to gain local support. In recent years, the Central Government has shown undue tolerance to these elements for short term political gains, which has resulted in greater turmoil in the area. Real nationalism is not detrimental or exclusive of the local interest and identity. There are a large number of political and public leaders, particularly in the younger generation, who have faith and are convinced that their future lies with the Indian nation. But power brokers have continued to keep them away from the positions of prominence and power. A review of the last decade and a half is a testimony to it. The current deteriorating situation in the North-Eastern States is an outcome of it and entirely related to the selfish motives and actions of such political leaders.

Status of Insurgency

In all cases of insurgency in the North-East, the initial phase of violence had been arrested before it blew up, and full scale armed expression of insurgency was controlled by the Army. However, it is continuing as a more sophisticated brand of terrorism and subversion, an ideal combination in the current disturbed environment of the North-East. Insurgency has thrived while retaining its low key posture, which is the peculiarity of the North-East. Although we have had limited periods of high intensity violence and situation remaining under control for prolonged periods, insurgency which germinated in Nagaland spread to Mizoram, Manipur, Tripura and Assam. The insurgents have learnt their lesson well by experience that the classical guerrilla tactics are not cost effective in our environment; control of population and subversion accompanied by planned acts of violence and terrorism are rewarding at minimum cost. This also gives the Government, administration and security forces a sense of complacency, but they must realise that taming violence is not the same as liquidating insurrection.

Since the inception of insurgency in the North-East, its complexion is changing from those of local unrests to that of collusion amongst them. Howsoever ineffective our system of democratization and economic development in these areas may have been, it certainly has demolished the myth of free sovereign tribal states due to their political and economic nonviability. The halo of great and noble cause of freedom has become more or less defunct. It has been replaced over a period by new slogans like 'Pan Mongoloid','Seven Sisters Movement', socialist or communist ideology, foreigners issue, greater autonomy and ethnic integration in the shape of greater Nagaland and greater Mizoram and tribal reserved areas. These may not be as glamourous but are equally lethal. A study of these will reveal a secessionist and anti-Indian sentiment; of these, foreigners issue has received the widest recognition as it helps in raising the question of identity. The cause to unite against foreigners of India is a negative one. Within this framework local issues which provide anti-government slogans will continue to be exploited.

Another issue that need to be clearly understood in this regard is that when we talk of anti-India feelings and sentiments, it is really anti-government, both local and Central, and is essentially related to policy issues which are inflicted on them by default. The level of motivation of these may not be high to cause a long-drawn-out violent explosion but it will provide enough fire and smoke for insurgencies to continue at a low key which are aided and abetted by local politicians and bad governance.

The support base of the insurgents has undergone both a qualitative and quantitative change. On the one hand, people want peace and tranquility and look forward to the benefits of development, on the other hand, they want to exploit all issues to gain maximum benefits. The youth in the changed environment is losing the will to face hardships of an insurgent's life in the jungles. Without a support base, not only their survival but the very meaning of their existence may be lost. Therefore, their covert presence must not only be effective but sophisticated. The emphasis has shifted to exploitation of ethnic bonds to influence events in the area, whether these be political, economic, social or cultural. Insurgents have influenced elections in Manipur and Nagaland and established links not only with the politicians but also with the administration and elite in other spheres. Financial and other resource base has shifted from the rural areas to the urban areas, the main source being government money which is passed by dubious means.

Insurgent movements require not only highly dedicated, committed and robust leaders capable of sharing and standing the greatest physical and mental privations but people of impeccable moral character. Of all the current insurgent leaders, only Muviah has the potential to rally the Naga insurgents, but due to tribal affiliations, he being a Thangkhul Naga from Manipur, his ability to gain full dominance over the Nagas of Nagaland and other insurgent groups of the North-East is constrained.

At the tactical level, the growing potential of the NSCN(I), the most potent of the North-East insurgent groups, is of special interest. The NSCN(I) in collaboration with its sympathisers has been exploiting the sentiment of Naga identity and interest, particularly in Manipur and Naga inhabited areas in Assam to expand its area of influence. A combination of misconstrued Naga sentiment, threat and Kuki baiting has been effectively employed, to dominate Naga inhabitated areas. In this, some Naga leaders of Manipur have played a dubious role. The partisan attitude of the present Government of Nagaland in favour of Khaplang factions is having its own reaction and is acting as a boost for the NSCN(I). The NSCN(I) has reliable contacts for arms procurement in Thailand and other South East Asian countries; it also has well-established links for transportation of arms and material to camps in Bangladesh. The NSCN(I) participation in UNPO in July 1993 in Vienna and subsequent representation in Indigneous Peoples Forum has given them openings to international fora and avenues of support. They have reportedly established offices and representatives in Nepal, Hong Kong and some European capitals in addition to Bangladesh and Pakistan to project themselves.

Geopolitical Environment

The changes in the neighbouring geopolitical environment of the North-East are of relevance. Emergence of Bangladesh, change in the attitude of the Chinese towards the insurgent groups of the North-East due to thaw in Indo-China relations and negotiations by the Myanmar authorities with most insurgent groups have certainly acted as a dampener to the insurgents and forced them to rethink their strategy. The centre of insurgent activites has shifted west-wards from the eastern border with Myanmar to inside Nagaland and Manipur and is spreading within Assam. Similarly, their bases have shifted to Chittagong and Sylhet in Bangladesh. This has resulted in the manifestation of a more cohesive and potent threat of regional dimensions. Both the validity and relevance of Indo-Burmese Revolutionary Front(BRF) is questionable due to changed situation and new imperatives. The United Liberation Front of Seven Sisters(ULFSS) when consolidated will be greater threat.

In spite of the progress in talks between India and Bangladesh on the Chakma issue, the attitude of Bangladesh towards North-East insurgents in respect of providing safe sancturies, help and facilities for training and resource mobilisation is one of total benevolence. Establishment of camps by the NSCN(I) in Chittagong and Sylhet by Meitel Extermists(ME), provide ready help for transportation of weapons and men through their area to NSCN(I), ME and ULFA and association of DG Field Intelligence of Bangladesh and ISI of Pakistan with the insurgents is a definite sign of belligerent attitude towards India. The freedom with which ISI is operating from Bangladesh for anti-India activities add further dimensions to the insurgency problem. Apart from active diplomatic measures, we also need to think and consider punitive measures against Bangladesh in the long term.

Myanmar's attitude is entirely conditioned by their requirements at the ground level, their limited capability against their own insurgent groups and recent negotiations with most of them. Shelter to pro-democracy refugees at Leikun, so close to the border in Manipur, has been a sore point with the Myanmar Government. They suspect our connivance in their activities against them. Tactically, in Myanmar's perception, KIA and NSCN(K) in the north and Karen, CNA and Muslims in the south are a bigger threat. Our failure to appreciate their concern has changed their stance to be pro-NSCN(I) in certain border areas at the local level.

The traditional transborder trade is another area which is causing antagonism. We should resolve it generously by identifying commodities and crossing points and permit it with least restrictions as it will be to our advantage. With the signing of the MOU and opening of trade at Moreh and Champai, it should result in better management of the border and also help us in controlling narcotic smuggling and contraband trade, resulting in denial of at least some of the dubious resources to the insurgents. At the ground level, we should fully activate our informal and formal level contacts with the Burmese Army as in the past for better cooperation in joint transborder activities against insurgents.

The presence of large immigrant Bangladeshi population over the entire North-East, a fertile ground for ISI's anti-Indian designs with full connivance of Bangladesh Field Intelligence exists. ISI has established outposts in the border areas of Bangladesh and is spreading its tentacles in Assam and bordering areas of Manipur, Nagaland and Meghalaya. Mizoram though peaceful but due to Hmar trouble and its location is vulnerable as in Tripura. The threat has acquired regional dimensions which needs to be countered both at the strategic and tactical levels.

Because of the varied perceptions of the divergent insurgent groups and the people of the North-East, there can be no common cause for the insurgent groups in the same area or insurgent groups of different areas. In the absence of a common cause and ideology, the nature and dimensions of the collusion amongst the insurgent groups will be confined to common interests and requirements. The areas of collusion in the near future will be confined to sharing of material and training resources, mutual support for infiltration and providing safe areas and sanctuaries to insurgents of neighbouring areas, when under pressure from security forces. Cooperation at tactical level for joint operations will be limited to insurgents of a particular area within the area. To counter it, the main thrust at a strategic level should be well coordinated intelligence operations covering not only areas within our national boundaries but beyond into Bangladesh and Myanmar. Along with it there is a crying necessity of counter-intelligence operations planned on long term basis over the entire North-East and adjoining areas of relevance.

In the overall context, special areas of attention for the region as a whole are North Cachar Hills as they form a vital corridor for infiltration into the southern and eastern Meghalaya, north Tripura, north

Mizoram and western borders of Manipur and Nagaland. Complete coordination of operations in the border areas of these States is essential. In this context, there is an urgent need to resolve the inter-State boundry disputes between Assam and Meghalaya, Mizoram and Nagaland.

From the above it should be clear that the potential of the "Low Key Insurgency" in the North-East is that of a slow poison which requires thorough and prolonged treatment.

Core Areas

The grave problems that the region is facing cannot be resolved by wishful thinking and quick-fix solutions. These have been fermenting for decades and with the passage of time developed graver dimensions and complexities. One gets the impression that these have been permitted to linger on for short term political gains which is also responsible for negative responses from the local people. The feeling amongst the local politicians and their henchmen at the Centre is that if unrest and insurgency dies down then the North-East and they will be forgotten. For me, who has been close to the people and seen the manipulations of these elements, this is nothing but exploitation of the situation both at the local and national level. There can be no short cuts for resolving the problems.

Absence of a declared policy has resulted in disjointed responses both by the politicians and bureaucrats and inconsistent and motivated projections. It has led to expediency and tardy execution. In the economic and developmental fields it has resulted in disorientation, circumventing the system and malpractices with corruption as the ugly fallout. Unless there is fusion of a well-defined and credible policy based on correct inputs, political will and an efficient and responsible machinery to implement it, success will be difficult. This coupled with the fact that political power is the master, both in principle and practice, lays the responsibility squarely on the political leadership.

A Government must function to a mandate and be accountable for the same. Our failures in the North-East like elsewhere are due to this reason. In the absence of a policy on the North-East or for that matter on Manipur, on imposition of the President's Rule in Manipur on December 31, 1993, a policy framework was laid down based on my assessment of the situation and a directive was issued to the administration and security forces, covering all aspects of the problem. We were able to achieve a substantial lot, if not all our tasks, the year 1994 has been acclaimed as a year of progress and development in Manipur. Without a policy framework there can neither be accountability nor correct orientation of the organs of the State apparatus.

Responsive Machinery

The State machinery and the administrative set-up to be efficient has to be manned by people of high calibre, integrity and dedication; it is just the opposite in these areas. Similarly, to get positive responses and generate peoples participation, credibility, trust and a high degree of involvement are essential which are conspicuous by their total absence. It is a subject in itself; suffice it to say that basic ingredients are political will and a change in ethos. Shuffling of people is the least requirement, an exercise the Government undertakes often for public consumption.

There is a perceptible change in the functioning of the States and their administration since the 1970s, wherein the emphasis has shifted from administration with involvement by the old IFAS cadre to that of bureaucratic white collar impersonal management by the IAS cadre. Neither people's requirements are identified nor are these met by people's participation. The central service cadres are not only weak but the system has broken down. Cadres are over subscribed by local officers who are inducted and empanelled due to ethnic and parochial considerations. Such a situation is convenient for the local politicians who treat the administration as an extension of their personal, political and ethnic designs. As such, upright and professional officers are eliminated as it has happened in Nagaland in recent months.

Administration at the district level in the smaller hill States is virtually non-functional due to structural defects, wrong manning and influence of local politicians, ethnic elite and insurgents. This will require reorganisation, reorientation and revamping.

To improve the machinery, apart from above measures special emphasis will be required to train the administrative cadres in financial management and monitoring, human resource development, planning, education and employment generation. In the field of economic development planning, grassroots level knowledge of local requirements, attitudes and how to generate peoples participation are essential. Another area of special attention is of youth development, unless we take it in hand, our problems of unemployment and unrest will escalate.

Our process of economic development and strategy for the same have failed to achieve the desired results in the North-East. The process has failed because of wrong orientation and bad implementation. While with each plan fund allocations have increased but there is no cumulative effect in any field. There is unchecked increase in non-plan expenditure due to mismanagement, and transfer of outlays on large employments and infrastructure under plan projects to non-plan for political considerations.

An assessment of the increasing unemployment in the North-Eastern states, particularly the smaller hill States, would reveal that along with stunted and lopsided economic growth, no employment opportunities were created. The only employment is in the organised sector mainly in the Government departments. Neither employment opportunities were created in the unorganised sector, nor people were prepared for self-employment. This is due to lack of a policy and wrong orientation of the education system. The education system needs a scientific and technological orientation, and facilities for vocational training needs are required to be established.

Our development strategy should recognize unique features of the area and not be a replica of what is followed in other areas. Geographical isolation and constraints of hill area economies with local complexion of each area needs to be recognized. The region's continued dependence on rest of the country needs to be catered to. Due to terrain the cost of infrastructure development may be higher but it can be offset by simultaneous development of vast hydel power resource, forest and other natural resources. Potential for clean industries based on power is high. While the technology may be primitive, the manpower is literate and proficient. As such, upgradation of the technological base will not only be easy and cost effective but will be productive. The seven States of the region need to develop a system of mutual support for each other's requirements and act as sub-systems for regional requirements. We should also be conscious of the fact that the process of economic liberalisation and induction of free market economy in the North-East will be slow as flow of private investment depends on level and quality of administration, social and economic infrastructure. In addition, in some of the areas, private investers are reluctant to venture due to disturbed security environment. Therefore, certain safeguards and considerations for these special category States will have to continue. Within the above parameters, a strategy to meet the challenges of economic development of the region needs to be worked out.

Our approach to economic development should be on two planes. At the macro level, emphasis should be on development of the core sectors of communication, power, human resource and education. At micro level, emphasis should be on small scale industires, processing industries in agro and horticulture sector and fisheries, improvement in civic facilities like water, sanitation, community development and health, duly supported by an efficient public distribution system. Due to physical constraints of the area, Public Distribution System (PDS) unless managed well has proved the main cause of corruption and deprivation. Weaving is the mainstay in the cottage industries sector, where every household is equipped with a loom but yarn availability is limited. Spinning mills, run properly, have great potential. Employment generation should form a part and parcel of economic development strategy and it should be an area of major thrust.

Trading is an important part of economic activity. This is in the hands of Marwaris and Banias particularly in the hill States who are acting in collusion with the politicians. As trade with Myanmar is opening up; it has vast potential economically as well as for employment. This will entail export of finished goods preferably of local origin, embargo on export of raw material and greater participation of locals in trading. A beginning was made in Manipur in 1994 to train educated Manipuri youth in trading, management and creation of communication and secretarial infrastructure for the same. Unless benefits of value addition come to the people of the area, it will create yet another area for exploitation.

Keeping the above parameters in view, a special package for economic development in Manipur, spread over the next seven years at a cost of Rs. 1600 crore, with employment generation potential of 251 lakh man-days was submitted to the Government of India in July 1994. This contained a special allocation of Rs. 51 crore for schemes for self-employment.

Tackling of insurgency requires a holistic approach with all sinews of the Government playing their part. It involves removing the people's grievances in the political and socio-economic fields. The termination of insurgency situation at the military level only will lead to wrong conclusions.

In spite of our years of experience in the North-East and having been associated with the changing complexion of the problems at each stage in the past so many decades, we seem to make a fresh start with each explosive situation in the same area or similar situation in different areas of the North-East, rather than building up on the past. I attribute it primarily to the lack of a high sense of involvement and certain amount of disorientation. More time and energy is spent on questing the situation and legitimatisation of actions than in handling the situation. These attitudes have permeated down and blunted our capability. I have discussed these at length and corrective action has been taken in the recent years.

Security and effectiveness are key areas for the administration and security forces. Security embraces all aspects of public life and it should be understood and implemented in all its connotations of physical, economic, social, ethnic and religious security. Similarly effectiveness not only means physical effectiveness, in addition, it encompasses positive contribution by the Government and all its instruments to the economic, religious, cultural and social well being of the people. The guiding principal in securing the environment is that you cannot be secure unelss you are effective. In any disturbed environment physical security and effectiveness are the foundations on which action in other fields are built up, it cannot be otherwise.

Securing the environment is the whole canvas in which anti-insurgent operations are only a part. By carrying out anti-insurgent operations, you are only fulfilling a part of the overall task of securing the environment. Foundations of securing the environment and all military operations are laid by controlling the area.

Control of the area of responsibility of one's command is the key to success in counter-insurgency environment. Without control neither can you gather intelligence, nor can anti-insurgent operations by security forces and counter measures by administration be successful. The word control should not be understood in its restricted or defensive sense; it really means total domination of the area, whereby security forces and administration provide protection to the population, and are aware of all happenings and can predict and forestall or influence events in every field of activity. The essence of control can be summed up as, "Nothing can happen in the area without our knowledge and without we being aware of it in time to counter and influence it". This largely contributes to the physical isolation of the insurgents and creating a secure environment.

There are other areas of interest like intelligence, civic actions, public relations, human rights, psychological operations.

In the North-East a crisis of credibility is fast emerging and the people's alienation is turning into a sentiment of negative responses to the Government and its instruments. The primary reason for this state of affairs is political expediency overriding all other considerations resulting in instability and bad governance, the major manifestations of which are denial of resources to the people, exploitation of ethnic and local sentiments by the local leaders for parochial and selfish purposes and impetus to insurgency.

The North-East requires an integrated and holistic approach in keeping with its regional requirements and peculiar problems of each of its constituent States to meet their requirements in the socio-economic, cultural and security fields.

The status of contemporary insurgency, its spreading manifestations both areawise and collusionwise, needs to be understood and countered effectively by securing the environment on long term basis. Political will has to be displayed by our leadership to safeguard the interest of the people and national interest, an essential part of which is not only to deactivate but completely incise the anti-national and anti people elements in the body politic of the North-Eastern States and its elite echelons. Without it neither the national interest can be safeguarded nor peoples alienation removed.

PART II

Defending The Nation

- Manning the Indian Armed Forces
- Fifty Years of Indian Navy
- Indian Air Force Since Independence
- Securing the Borders : Pains and Gains
- Defending the Borders on Mountains

11

Manning the Indian Armed Forces

Lt. Gen. (Retd.) M. L. Chibber

THE INDIAN ARMED FORCES we inherited at Independence were among the finest in the world. They are still so. However, not easily perceptible to those who have not been in the battles, over the years they are slowly losing that shine. Today if radical remedies are not speedily implemented the decline may become so precipitating as to go beyond control. It was not for nothing that the Deputy Leader of the Opposition, Jaswant Singh, speaking on the motion of confidence moved by the then Prime Minister on April 11, 1997, observed that "the security situation that we face today is similar to what prevailed on the eve of our debacle in 1962."

He should know, because in the early nineties he headed a committee that studied defence problems. He is well aware of the sorry state of the armed forces — particularly in their manning policy.

How had this come about? The answer is startling but obvious. Our political leaders have from the early years after Independence continually shown an apalling lack of understanding of matters military. The malaise began with Nehru. When Sir Robert Lockhart, the first Commander-in-Chief of Independent India, presented to him a paper on the perceived threats to India and the size and shape of the army needed to counter these, Nehru's response was, "Rubbish. Total rubbish. We don't need a defence plan. Our policy is non-violence. We foresee no military threats. Scrap the Army. The police are good enough to meet our security needs". The Pakistani tribal invasion of Kashmir a few days later almost fortuitously kept the Indian Army in being!

The record at the military level has been no better. It is stating the obvious that as true professionals the higher echelons of the military should have formulated policies that would ensure an efficient fighting machine. Even more important, it was their moral responsibility to educate their political masters to accept and adopt such policies. Failure to do so should have prompted them to give up the office. They did neither. They are thus equally culpable.

The civil service — the bureaucracy — readily exploited this great divide. They are in effective control of the levers of governance and they have used this power to systematically downgrade the military and erode its status.

The profession of Arms requires a commitment and dedication monastic in its intensity. It is a full time calling. It cannot indulge in the luxury of trade union hours. The most vital ingredient of any fighting machine is the quality of its officers and men. Quality that is reflected in the battle winning attributes of tone, style and elan that the Army must acquire. This write-up shows how this can be achieved. In the current state there are five areas of concern that need attention.

- Wearing the country's uniform to defend the country is no longer a matter of pride and elan. From being a calling which inspired and compelled the men to be ready to die for the 'safety, honour and welfare' of the country soldiering has degenerated into a mere job in the market in a situation of acute unemployment. Erosion in the status of the soldier has had a malignant impact on this deterioration.
- We have an aging military. Commanding officers, the cornerstone of any military system because they directly lead their men in battle, are in the age group of 45 years plus/minus whereas they should, as per the experience of combat all over the world, be in the age group, at the most, of 35 years plus/minus. Similar is the situation with soldiers, sailors and airmen after the colour service was increased from seven to seventeen years.

- Experience of war also indicates that it is the unmarried officers and men in the age group of 18 to 27 years who make the maximum contribution to winning the battles. Now over ninety percent of the soldiers, sailors and airmen are married. Compared to this, the system which we inherited, provided for only fourteen percent of men to be married. There are, of course, numerous examples of great heroism and gallantry displayed by married individuals. However they are exceptions that prove the rule that a married soldier avoids taking risks and tends to side step in situations of danger; it is but a natural phenomenon.
- We have created the most expensive system in the world to man our military. Before long we will have two disgruntled pensioners for every one serving person in the Defence Forces. Over 70 percent of the budget allocation for Defence is already being spent on manpower related costs (including pensions). It is of little consolation that Pakistanis are the gold medalists in this folly and we are only the silver medalists. Even among the richest nations in the world alarm bells ring the moment manpower related costs exceed 50 percent of the Defence budget.
- The cumulative impact of the above is noticeable in the huge shortage of officers in the Army. Against an authorised strength of 44,000 there is a shortage of 13,000. In addition around 6000 officers are in low medical category or, are a demotivated lot because there are not enough vacancies to promote them and they have been superseded. Thus, the Army is expected to fight and win battles with virtually only 57 percent of the authorised strength of officers. Similarly the Air Force is short of over 1000 officers and the Navy over 600 officers. Among the senior ranks, there is a flood of non-statutory and statutory complaints against non promotion and numerous officers have gone to the courts on this account.

Let us learn from what happened in the economic field. The bureaucratic stranglehold on India's economy almost ruined our enterprises in the public and private sectors. When we were moving towards economic bankruptcy the Indian democracy woke up. Despite a determined subterranean rear-guard battle still being waged by the bureaucracy to retain power without accountability, our economy is being progressively liberated from its shackles. We have now to liberate our National Security System from the vicelike grip of this octopus. Malignance is inherent in the very concept of bureaucracy which is a necessary evil in any organisation. However, it has to be strictly controlled, periodically pruned and at suitable intervals beheaded.

The Manning System in 1947

The manning system that we inherited in 1947 was evolved during a period of about a hundred years, not only in India but the British Commonwealth as a whole. Two major experiences played an important role in the evolution of the system that we inherited :

1. The disastrous performance of the British Army in the Crimean war against the Russians. The gallant but the foolish charge of the Light Brigade and many other such faux pas opened the British eyes. The experience triggered a few reforms.
2. The disaster that struck the British Army once again in 1899 in the opening stages of the Boer War in South Africa. After the war, a Royal Commission was set up to enquire into the poor performance of the Army in South Africa to take remedial steps.

Far reaching organisational reforms particularly in the Higher Direction of the Armed Forces were recommended and adopted. The experience and lessons of the World War I were later built into the system which was eventually stabilized for the Indian Army from 1920 to 1939 when the Indian Army entered the World War II. The major principles of the policy for manning the Armed Forces were :

> Pride in the profession and status in society are the crucial inputs for inspiring a man to be ready for the supreme sacrifice for the "safety, honour and welfare" of the country.
>
> A youthful profile is an absolute must for an effective military. The most youthful segment in human life is approximately from 18 to 27 years of age and it has no relationship with low or high life expectancy. The famous military author John Master while analysing this factor during the World War II in Burma concluded that the best Brigade commanders were in their early thirties. Today they are around 50 years plus/minus.
>
> Terms and conditions of service were tailored to fulfil the above principles and compensated the soldier for being subjected to the military law, turbulence and rigours of employment and injected pride in wearing the country's uniform.

When translated into terms and conditions of service the major features of the above policy need a brief discussion.

Up or Out System

A jawan was enrolled for seven years of colour service. After the period of seven years he was retained only if he was to be promoted. Otherwise he left the service to be in reserve for a few years when he came back for refresher training every year for short periods.

This system worked well for a small Army till the World War II. The colonial administration in the districts went out of the way to grant preferential treatment to those who had served in the Army. This ensured that, by and large, those who joined were from the land owning class. They were happy to do their time in the Army to earn the special status and prestige which were a sufficient rewards in themselves.

In the cantonments the authorisation of family accommodation was only for 14 percent of the soldiers. It was hundred percent only for those who were promoted as noncommissioned officers (NCOs). The proportion of NCOs was however, very small. The result was that the bulk of the jawans were unmarried. We shall later discuss why we changed the colour service from seven to seventeen years but it is of interest to discuss how the figure of seven years was originally evolved.

When the Royal Commission after the Boer War went into the concrete reasons responsible for the poor performance of the soldiers they found that the major cause was the length of the colour service of a soldier which was seventeen years. Examination of this problem showed that after about seven years of soldiering, the rigours of service which still continued included less than three full nights of sleep in bed per week (as every soldier had to take his turn to undergo night training as well as night sentry duties) took a heavy toll and his elan declined. Being subject to the military law also imposed an extra psychological burden unlike in other occupations; it imposed unlimited liability to go wherever he was ordered to go. The colour service was consequently reduced from seventeen to seven years because thereafter the decline became sharp.

After a soldier was promoted to become an NCO, the policy governing his subsequent stay in the service was 'up or out'. For example, a Naik was either promoted to become a Havildar if he was fit for promotion and there was a vacancy before he completed 15 years of service or he retired after 15 years of service. Similarly, if a Subedar after completing 28 years of service did not become a Subedar Major he was retired with a compensatory pension. This progressive culling at each rank ensured that the Army did not have men on active service beyond a specified age if they were not promoted. This policy thus ensured a youthful profile and added to the effectiveness of the hierarchy as, by and large, no superseded individuals were retained in the Army.

The 'up or out' system worked well primarily because of the very high prestige which a retired Army Havildar and above enjoyed, the colonial administration made sure of this.

Status and Prestige

The main policy which was adopted to have a motivated set of officers was to provide them status and prestige. Some of the steps which were institutionalised need a mention.

In the Warrant of Precedence, military officers were given their rightful place even when the civil servants were mostly British; the status of military officers was high.

Place in Warrent of Precedence (1947)	Rank/Appointment	Remarks
14th	Chief Justices of High Court	
16th	Army Commanders (rank of Lt. General)	
24th	Other Lt. Generals	
26th	Major Generals Commanding Districts (now called Areas)	In their own jurisdiction
	Secretaries to the Government of India	Secretaries have now moved up to be equated with Army Commanders
59th	Major	A Major no longer figures in the Warrent
	ICS officers with 12 years standing Superintendents and Deputy Commissioners of Police of more than 15 but less than 20 years standing.	

What is really significant is that there was no political leadership during the colonial period to exercise and be accountable for exercising executive power. The civilian officers, who were mostly British, consequently exercised executive powers. Despite this burden of governance borne by the bureaucrats, the Army officers were given their due place in the warrant of precedence basically in recognition of the responsibility shouldered by them, their accountability, as also to inject pride in their profession which, as we have discussed, is the main input for high morale and dedication to lead men in a battle. A few examples will show as to how our present bureaucracy despite executive powers and accountability having been taken over by the political leaders, have managed to crawl up in status.

A military officer automatically became a member of the club as soon as he arrived in a station. As far as terms and conditions of service were concerned the main features were :

- An Army Officer had a higher starting salary compared to the civilian officers and this edge was maintained at commensurate levels of service.
- Officers were not allowed to marry before they were 25 years of age.
- After becoming a Major the subsequent promotions (by selection) were governed by a policy of 'up or out'. If an officer could not be promoted he retired with a compensatory pension. The following table illustrates the point. It is pertinent to remember that 85 percent of the officers needed in the Armed Forces are in the ranks of Major/Lt. Commander/Squadron Leader and below:

BALANCED SYSTEM IN 1947

Rank	Age/Tenure for Retirement Combat Arms Officers	Pension as percentage of pay	Remarks
Major	45 years	75 %	On the civil side no
Lt. Col	48 years or 4 years tenure whichever is earlier	76.7 % to 88.9 %	pension was more than 50 %.

In the above table the significant point to note is pertaining to a Lt Colonel which was the rank for commanding units and the fact that a commanding officer is the corner-stone of any military system. An officer selected to be promoted as a Lt Colonel could serve for a tenure of four years as substantive Lt Colonel or the age of 48 years whichever was earlier. He retired with a compensatory pension which was upto 88.9 percent of his salary. Compensatory pension for a truncated career was the key of the policy of 'up or out'. Those who retired earlier had a higher compensation. The major purpose of this policy was to maintain the youthful profile of the military.

How did We Ruin the System

Our political leaders who led India to freedom were men of great idealism and were inspired by the great Indian heritage of 'tyaga' (the sanskrit word which embodies in it a combination of sacrifice and selflessness). Most of them like Tilak, Gandhi, Nehru, Patel and Jinnah were legal luminaries but had no administrative experience of governance. When we became Independent in 1947 we inherited a well established administrative system structured by the British in about 200 years of colonial rule in India. With this system, we also inherited an experienced civilian bureaucracy. However hardly any Indian had any experience of participating in the higher direction of Defence. After the so called 'mutiny' in 1857, Defence matters were virtually placed out-of-bounds to the Indians. It took determined efforts by our political leaders to make a start in inducting Indian officers into the Indian Army and this began as a mere trickle after the World War I in 1918. By 1947 there were only a handful of officers who had just reached the rank of Brigadier. In view of this background the civilian bureaucracy became the most experienced and indispensable instrument for evolving systems of governance in free India. It exploited this situation to the hilt.

Two other factors also contributed to erode the effectiveness of the military and were fully made use of by the bureaucracy :

1. Nehru, one of the tallest leaders of India, played a prominent role not only in the movement for Independence but also in consolidating the nurturing democracy in the country with deep love, care and conviction. His idealism, unfortunately, was far ahead of the times. He had an innate distrust of the military as an organ of the State. Even when he was shattered by the Chinese betrayal of his trust in 1962 by inflicting a humiliating de-

feat on India, his scepticism about the military was undiminished. In December 1962, when the country undertook a programme of rapid expansion of the Army to make up for the neglect of 15 years, Nehru wrote to Bertrand Russel and said "the danger of military mentality spreading in India and the power of the Army increasing" bothered him.

2. Nehru's innocence of matters of national security and his reservations about the role of the military in the post World War II emerging world, led to several mistakes for which we are still paying the price. For example, we literally threw away Tibet into the lap of the Chinese. What is relevant to this paper is the fact that the bureaucracy played on his fears of a military coup. In the garb of increasing civil control over the military, they increased the bureaucratic control of the apparatus of Defence. Progressively, over the years, they degraded a career in the military and this effort, as is apparent from the recommendations of the Fifth Pay Commission, is still continuing. Having had the privilege of formally being an adviser to the Fourth Pay Commission, the author is aware of the machinations of the Commission secretariat which is merely an organ of the bureaucracy.

In view of what we have discussed, India became a classic case of democracies where "group interests compete with each other. In public services this competition is essentially between the bureaucracy on the one side and the professionals like academicians, doctors, engineers, industrial managers and military officers on the other". This is a universal phenomenon; "the modern official, according to Webber, always strives for salary attainment and for distinctly elevated social status. Here the aspiration of the modern bureaucrat and the modern military professional converge; both are searching for social esteem and corporate endownment." This results in various organs of the States to becoming competitive rather than complementary.

Countries where political leadership has the wisdom to overcome this competition and make these organs work in harmony, achieve the most efficient and cost-effective State apparatus.

While the successive Pay Commissions have reviewed the conditions of service of the civilian employees of the Central Government and have evolved their emolument structure based on these reviews, no such examination has been carried out in totality for the Armed Forces. Their pay structure has been arrived at by mere extension of civilian scales based on certain arbitrary and distorted relativities. This has been attributed to the fact that such an examination is an extremely complex process. This aspect was noted by the Raghuramaiah Committee in 1959 who nonetheless recommended that such an examination should be carried out at a time convenient to the Government. However a full, thorough and integrated examination has not so far been undertaken. Thus their terms and conditions have not been tailored to suit their needs but remain 'consequential'.

Our Constitution provides a safeguard to an employee of the State for full working life provided the person has been in employment for a period exceeding ninety days. It is virtually impossible to terminate the service of a person in a Government job once he completes 91 days of service.

This provision, unfortunately, is not available to the men in uniform. It's adverse impact started to grow in the lives of Jawans. With the huge expansion of the Indian Army during the World War II, the bulk of the recruitment shifted from land owning sections in rural India to those seeking employment for a living. Thus, after giving the best seven years of their youth to the country, they were, so to say, retrenched and thrown out on the street. This gross injustice was not set right for over a quarter of a century. Slowly however the plight of these men was driven home to our politicians who periodically went around rural India in search of votes.

It was during the mid-seventies that this problem eventually came to a head when Bansi Lal became the Defence Minister in Indira Gandhi's cabinet. He belongs to Haryana which is a high recruitment area for the Armed Forces. The fateful decision to increase the colour service from seven to seventeen years was taken primarily on one consideration. That it would enable every man who joins the military to earn at least some pension instead of being thrown out after seven years. However, this, truth was never recorded in files. The case was processed on the plea that the reserve system did not work well in 1965 and 1971 wars which, of course, was true.

This decision was precipitated by the determined efforts of the bureaucracy to resist the absorption of the released soldiery in civilian jobs in the government sector. While on paper reservations were made for the ex-servicemen in civilian jobs but when it came to implementing these provisions nothing really happened. In the event, we put the clock back to 1902 when the British Army, because of the colour service being 17 years, performed disastrously in South Africa.

This single step essentially taken as a 'welfare measure' has, over a span of about 20 years, contributed to the sad state which we discussed in the introductory part of this chapter.

Grave Concern

The cumulative effect of ruining the system we inherited is obvious. The Army is expected to defend the country with 57 percent of the authorised strength of officers. A career in the Armed Forces repels the youth because of the continuous erosion in the status and emoluments of officers. This is despite the fact that constant employment of the Army in operational areas and protracted counter insurgency operations makes their work far more demanding than ever before. The military has even lowered the standards of selection but the shortage have kept on mounting.

It is significant that the concern expressed by the Deputy Leader of Opposition on 11 April, 1997, in Parliament was brought to the notice of the Government of India almost fifteen years ago by the three Service Chiefs. In a joint letter to the Government about the quality and morale in the Armed Forces, they said words to the effect that 'the erosion that has taken place in this field in recent years has caused us grave concern and we would be failing in our duty if we were not to bring this to the notice of Government'. Nothing significant was done.

The first major blow to the system which we inherited was struck in the early fifties. The Armed Forces Pension Revision Committee in 1949 eliminated the compensatory pension for early termination of a career. However, the policy of 'up or out' was still retained. It took more than a decade for the military to realise its adverse impact on the morale of the officers.

The remedy that was adopted was to throw the 'up or out' system out of the window and adopt a slow creep up of the ages of retirement. A Lt Colonel now goes out at the age of 52 instead of 48 or even earlier and a Major (Time scale Lt Colonel) now retires at the age of 51 instead of 45 but with no compensatory pension. Little wonder that a career in the military has become extremely repellent. It is well to remember here that 85 percent of officers needed for the Armed Forces are in the ranks of Major/Lt Commander/ Sqn. Leader.

The adverse impact of the higher ages of retirement has made the task of the Commanding Officers extremely difficult. He has to weld a team for combat in which a number of majors are either in low medical category or are those who have not been promoted and at times both. In peace stations this situation is particularly bad.

Options to Revive the System

In the evolution of mankind, there is an irreversible mega trend towards unity of man, global economy and earth citizenship. As we stand on the brink of the information revolution, the signs towards this end are becoming increasingly clear. Compulsions for the move have been very clearly articulated.

However, the process of change is likely to produce severe frictions. India must not forget the experience of the first fifteen years of our Independence. We then spent less than two percent of our GDP on defence. Our rulers naively believed that the United Nations established after the World War II would take care of the national security problems; there was hardly any need for the non-productive military. We were shaken out of this self-created delusion in 1962. The Army lacked boots leave alone effective weapon systems. The bewildered higher command sulked and retreated into self-imposed isolation because of the inept handling of the defence matters by Krishna Menon, the Defence Minister. We suffered a humiliating defeat at the hands of the Chinese when a distinguished bureaucrat, a mere joint secretary, issued written orders to the Army to throw the Chinese out!!

A shattered Nehru breathed his last in May 1964 and in 1965 our friends in Pakistan concluded that they could wrest Kashmir by force from a demoralised India. They launched operations Gibraltar and Grand Slam to capture Jammu and Kashmir. That war ended in a stalemate.

In 1971 we won a decisive victory against Pakistan which gave birth to Bangladesh. It was possible because we had Field Marshal Manekshaw as the Army Chief who had the moral courage to say 'No' to the political masters when directed to intervene in East Pakistan in the month of April, 1971. Indira Gandhi had the wisdom to listen to him. There were huge defeciencies of weapons, ammunition and equipment. He insisted on making these up and concentrating a much superior land and air force strength against Pakistani troops deployed in East Pakistan. Of course the insurgency in that country at that time also greatly helped in our success.

The most worrisome consequences of ruining our manning system is the aging and much married military and the shortage of 13,000 officers. Many studies have shown the reasons why good qulity youth are not coming forward to join the Armed Forces as officers. These include :

- Numerous high paid opportunities are available in our growing economy in a variety of fields;
- Severe erosion in the status of military officers;
- A truncated career in which around ninety percent of the military officers have to retire at the age of 51/52 when their social obligations to settle their children are at the highest;
- Poor emoluments;
- Very disturbed family life due to postings in forward areas, frequent moves and it's adverse impact on the education of children;
- Being subject to the severity of Army, Navy and Air Force law which imposes unlimited liability and seriously curtails freedoms of an individual; and
- High risk of loss of life or limb.

During the decade 1988 to 1997 the percentage of GDP allocated for Defence (in real terms) has declined from 3.37 percent to 2.26 percent. Little wonder that the Deputy Leader of the opposition in Parliament sounded an alarm about our ill-prepared and ill-equipped Defence capability. What can be done ?

An Empowered National Commission

Military is a complex organisation. During 1975-76, the author was a member of the three-man expert committee along with Generals Krishna Rao and Sunderji to restructure the Army. In 1986, he had the opportunity of advising the Fourth Pay Commission. It is a fact that even the most experienced senior officers in uniform are innocent of the total process of manning an effective military machine. The bureaucracy and the members and the secretariats of the Pay Commissions are totally oblivious of it. The first need consequently is to set up an empowered National Commission on manning the Armed Forces. Like the Finance Commission it's recommendations should be enforceable.

The Commission of three members should be made up of captains of society. The head should be a senior statesman in the country enjoying the support and confidence of all the major political parties. Bureaucracy should be kept well away from the Commission. Even the secretariat should be hired from the market. It should undertake its work in two phases :

Phase I - Policy Reforms.

Phase II - Implementation of policies.

Phase I - Policy Reforms

The goal of the policy should be to evolve a manning system to ensure that :

- Approximately sixty-five percent of the officers and jawans in the Armed Forces are always less than twenty-seven years of age.
- Thirty-five percent who stay beyond twenty-seven years of age should be governed by the policy of 'up or out'. Those who go out should be given adequate compensatory pension or a civilian job for full working life.
- Emoluments of officers and men should keep pace with the prevailing compensation at various levels in society plus an extra bit for the rigours of service (the most common term used for this monetary edge in various countries is 'military service pay'). This monetary compensatory edge varies from 10 to 15 percent in various countries and its purpose is two fold:

One : convey to the military men that society and the State appreciate their special role of winning victory in war and deprivations imposed on them to be ever ready for this purpose.

Two : generate a sense of pride in them so that they do not hesitate to lay down their lives to uphold the safety, honour and welfare of the country.

In this context it is well to remember the words of Sardar K. M. Panikkar about the officers of the Army, "it is necessary to emphasise that unless the officer cadres feel that their interests are safe in the hands of the civil authority, the whole morale of the Army as an instrument of civil government may be undermined. It should never be forgotten that without the officer cadre, the Army is but a collection of men - a mob". Officers must be motivated to lead their men in battle and be prepared to die.

The Warrant of Precedence should be revised to restore the dignity of military officers commensurate with their 'responsibility and accountability' as shown in the Warrant of Precedence which prevailed till the late forties. Secondly, higher direction of our Defence Forces is ponderous, flabby and archaic. Two reforms are essential to ensure that sound and rational policies for National Security are pursued :

1. Restructure the Ministry of Defence to bring it in line with modern management practices. In a nutshell it means integrating the Service Headquarters and the Ministry as one entity to abolish duplication in examining problems and to speed up decision making. There is a model available in the UK and nearer home in the system of the Railway Board. There is also the comprehensive Arun Singh Committee report gathering dust in some office.

2. There are three Service Chiefs without an empowered full-time professional coordinator. In the field there are 13 regional commanders-in-chief of the Army, Navy and Air Force running their fiefdoms. This anarchism needs restructuring.

For arriving at the basic policy to man the Armed Forces, the commission may consider two options :

- Option advocated by Justice P. N. Shinghal, the Chairman Fourth Pay Commission.

- National Service as enshrined in the Constitution of India.

Justice Shinghal Option : Full Life Career

When Justice Shinghal applied his mind to the manning problems of the Armed Forces, the learned judge felt most uncomfortable. After his visits to the military formations all over India, discussions with senior Armed Forces officers and discussions with some of the political leaders in the country, he felt that there was a need for statutory provision to guarantee to the man in uniform a full-life career and yet have a youthful profile. He was of the opinion that in our soft State nothing can be enforced unless there is a sound legal provision for it. He consequently drafted, in his own hand, an amendment to the Army Act (also to be incorporated in the Navy and Air Force Acts) dealing with Terms and Conditions of Service of a soldier. He felt that a similar provision could be formulated for officers. The effect addenda to the Army Act reads as under :

> "With a view to maintaining the professional efficiency and youthful profile of the Army, enrolment of various categories of personnel in the regular Army shall be for such periods as may be prescribed by the Central Government; provided that every person, on termination of the prescribed period of his enrolment, shall commensurate with his status in the Army at the time of such termination, be given alternative employment, or appointment or an office under the State, subject to such terms and conditions as may be prescribed. The term 'the State' shall have the same meaning as defined in article 12 of the Constitution of India."

It will be noticed that most of the major policy issues stipulated for maintaining an effective military get resolved once this amendment is incorporated. Knowing the concern of our political leaders for National Security such an amendment is likely to be passed by Parliament with great despatch. Unfortunately, when it came to putting this recommendation in the commission's report, the learned judge said in distress "my secretariat tells me that such a recommendation would be outside the terms of reference of the Pay Commission". Such are the ways of the bureaucracy!

National Service Option

This option is based on the proposal crystallized in the book 'National Service for Defence, Development and National Integration of India'. The book is based on a research project supported by Jawaharlal Nehru Fund for two years. Our Constitution makes the following provision for National Service :

> "Every citizen of India shall be obliged to defend the country and render National Service when called upon to do so."

Shri R Venkateraman, our former President, in his foreword to the book says:

> "Country has been eager to implement National Service ever since we became Independent ...... I am glad that the author has recommended a model which is pragmatic and is a step by step approach .... I sincerely hope that the authorities at various levels will have the wisdom and vision, courage and dynamism to implement this attractive scheme."

In a nutshell, the book, after studying National Service all over the world, suggests that in a large and soft State like India we have to tailor our own method to introduce National Service. However, before discussing this method there is a need to correct an erroneous impression in India that National Service is related only to the military. Since Independence we have got obsessed with our fundamental rights and totally ignored our obligations. National Service has been defined as under :

> "National Service is a civic obligation which entails the full-time undertaking of public duties by young people — whether as citizen soldiers or civilian servers — who are paid subsistence wages."

As the first step in India, the book suggests three areas to be served :

- Primary education in villages,
- Ecological camps to revive our degraded land and forests, and
- Defence.

Initially National Service may be rendered by the two segments in the country who derive the maximum benefit from society. These two segments are :

1. College students who get education which is highly subsidized by society. This segment is confined to service for one year only for primary education in villages and not relevant to this paper.
2. Government servants in the States and Centre including public sector undertakings where they get guaranteed employment for life.

In India as a whole there are 19 million employees of the State - teachers, railways and other public undertakings, police and paramilitary forces in the States and Centre, a variety of bureaucrats in the States and Central services and so on. To sustain this work force, approximately six lakh and thirty thousand persons are selected each year to replace the retired persons and other wastages. The suggestion is that those entering the employment of the State may continue to be selected as per the existing systems. However, once selected they should be required to render National Service for the prescribed periods in the three areas identified above. After satisfactory completion of National Service they may continue the rest of their working lives in the jobs they are selected for.

The minimum period of National Service should be three years. However, those inducted into Defence would serve from three to nine years with appropriate incentives for those who are kept for durations over three years. Very broadly the needs of Defence may be met as under :

(a) **Three years** - Doctors and Engineers as officers.

(b) **Five years** - As soldiers, sailors and airmen and officers. The bulk will be from those selected as teachers, police and officers in various services and public enterprises.

(c) **Nine years** - Air Force Pilots and other high skill jobs for which the Armed Forces undertake their training for long periods.

Phase II - Implementation of Policies

To revive and restructure the national security apparatus and its organs which have become flabby, ponderous and wasteful in half a century of mishandling will take a considerable length of time. However, the empowered National Commission should continue to guide and monitor the implementation till the process is completed. For this national cause, our political parties have developed enough maturity to fully back and support the National Commission which should be headed by a senior statesman.

Whichever option the country adopts will give us youthful Armed Forces and that too at a very much lower cost. However there is a difficulty.

In a soft State like India any attempt to revive the manning system of the Armed Forces through either of the two options will be resisted by the influential and the affluent sections of society. As is well known the most influential segment in India is still the bureaucracy. It is a worldwide phenomenon that the influential and affluent segments do not like to dirty their hands. They like to pass on the honour to defend and die for the country to economically poorer sections of society. They resist by ingenious arguments, sponsored and doctored studies producing piles of statistical data and surreptitious lobbying.

The fact that we will get a far more effective Defence Force at about half the present manning costs matters very little to them. They are only interested in their rights and privileges; they cannot see beyond themselves. That was the conclusion of Gibon when he wrote his famous words :

> "When Athenians finally wanted not to give society, but for society to give them; when freedom they wished for most was freedom from responsibility, then Athens ceased to be free."

Fortunately there is some hope in a democracy. When people understand what is good for the country, they can influence policies by the irresistible power of one-man-one-vote. But they have to be informed before we are again forced to learn a lesson like we did from a disaster in 1962. It is the duty of the enlightened media, political leadership, retired Armed Forces officers and enlightened citizens to bring this problem to the notice of our voters and persuade the Government to undertake the reforms.

12

Fifty Years of Indian Navy

Admiral (Retd.) R. H. Tahiliani

THE GROWTH OF the Indian Navy has been a series of peaks and troughs not unlike the passage of a ship in a some what stormy sea. Independent India found itself with a modest sized Coastal Navy consisting of six old frigates and sloops and a handful of minesweepers. Some 538 officers — most of them recruited for hostilities only — and 4,121 sailors made up the Navy's manpower strength. Since most of the training establishments had been located in Karachi and now belonged to the Pakistan Navy, the infrastructure for training fresh manpower was also meagre. The only strength the Navy had, was a reasonably competent Naval Dockyard in Bombay for maintaining its ships.

The fact that India found itself so poorly placed for its security at sea was understandable. In the British scheme of things, maritime security for India was the concern of the Royal Navy. The Royal Indian Navy, as it was called then, had a lot of British officers too, who were recruited in Britain for serving in the Indian Navy. The seniormost Indian Officers in the Navy were of Captain's rank. Rear Admiral J.T.S. Hall R.N. was the Flag Officer Commanding Royal Indian Navy on the day of India's Independence on 15th August, 1947.

India's maritime heritage dates back to the Indus Valley Civilization nearly 3000 years B.C. Excavations at Mohenjo-daro and

Harappa have revealed positive evidence about maritime activity in this period. The people who lived in the coastal areas of the subcontinent were adept at the use of the seas for fishing and trade with the neighbouring countries. The Chola Kings in the South were able to maintain an armada of ships and spread the Hindu culture and civilization to Malaysia, Java and Sumatara during the ninth to eleventh centuries A.D. It was an Indian navigator, who helped Vasco de Gama reach Calicut from the East Coast of Africa on 11th May, 1498.

Early invasions in India came over the Himalayan passes. Most of these invaders made the more hospitable and fertile Indo-Gangetic plains their home and were assimilated in the population. The Portuguese, the Dutch, the French and the British who came to India by sea, ostensibly for trade, proceeded to carve out their areas of influence and dislodge the local chieftains. The British eventually established total rule over the whole Peninsula with the exception of small territories which remained with the Portuguese and the French. This process happened so gradually that the Indian psyche finds it difficult even today to comprehend that any potential lack of preparedness of the Indian Navy can have any security implications.

Fortunately India's first Prime Minister Pandit Jawaharlal Nehru fully appreciated the need for India to have a Navy commensurate with the country's size, coastline, island territories and trade. The first fifteen years of Independence saw the addition of two cruisers and six destroyers, acquired from the Royal Navy. Eight new frigates and some minesweepers were also ordered to be built in the British yards. The most significant addition, however, was the aircraft carrier VIKRANT (formerly HERCULES) armed with Seahawk fighter jets and Alize turboprop anti-submarine aircraft. Britain's desire to sell three aircraft carriers which were laid down in 1943-44 and which it did not need after the war, and Mountbatten's friendship with Nehru, no doubt helped in this acquisition. With this addition, the Indian Navy took the first step towards becoming a three dimensional Navy. Its share of the Defence Budget which was 4.8 per cent in 1950-51 increased gradually to a peak at 12.68 per cent in 1959-60.

The 1962 war with China in which neither the Navy nor the Air Force played any part, saw the fortunes of the Navy decline rapidly. Its share of the Defence Budget declined to less than four per cent in the mid-sixties. The only redeeming feature of this bleak era was the start of indigenous construction of a Leander class frigate in Mazagon Dock in Bombay.

A truly balanced Navy has to have submarines as an essential third dimension. Although the Indian Navy had been scouting around for buying one of these, its traditional source of hardware supply — Britain — was reluctant to sell India a reasonably modern variant. The embargo which the Western nations placed on arms supply in the post 1965 war between India and Pakistan, ensured that India would have to look elsewhere for a submarine. The U.S.S.R. seemed a logical choice as the Indian Air Force had already acquired MIG aircraft from this source. For the next quarter of a century the U.S.S.R was to be the Indian Navy's principal supplier of submarines, destroyer type of ships, missile boats, minesweepers and shore based maritime reconnaissance and anti-submarine aircraft. The arrival of the first submarine in India in 1967 saw the Navy graduate to being a three dimensional force.

The Naval leadership had always been conscious that being a buyer Navy was a great weakness for the country. The first indigenously built Leander was commissioned in June, 1972. From then onward five more Leanders were commissioned in a span of eleven years. The last two were armed with a big single package Seaking helicopter which could detect and attack a submerged submarine. This was a most creditable achievement for the Indian designers and engineers. During a visit to India in 1981, Admiral Gorshkov, the principal architect of the U.S.S.R. Navy, was so impressed with the Seaking carrying Leander that he went back and asked the U.S.S.R. designers to emulate the Indian example.

The basic Leander hull having performed well, it was logical to improve on this and to build the next three ships by lengthening and broadening the hull marginally, to carry two Seaking type helicopters, in addition to medium range surface to surface missiles and surface to air missiles. Successful integration of weapons and electronic systems from eight different countries gave a lot of confidence to the Naval design and system integration staff. The next step was to embark on designing and building a missile destroyer from scratch. The first ship of this type is about to be commissioned, although there has been considerable delay in its completion owing to uncertainty and delay in the supply of some weapon systems consequent to the break up of the U.S.S.R.

Having just one yard for building major war vessels like frigates, was not enough to build the modest strength which Naval plans envisaged. A second yard, Garden Reach Shipbuilders, which had hitherto built ships like Survey Vessels and landing craft was, therefore, pressed into service. This yard is currently building a modified version of the broadened Leander which would be capable of operating two helicopters.

By early eighties the Navy's design organization was bristling with confidence to design bigger ships and it was given the task of designing an aircraft carrier as a replacement for VIKRANT. A French Shipyard (DCN) was commissioned to study the suitability of the Cochin Shipyard for building such a ship. Severe Defence cuts from 1987-88 onwards have put this scheme on hold. Otherwise the Indian Navy would have commissioned this ship in India's fiftieth year of Independence.

Designing and building submarines are specialized skills which the country lacked. With a view to diversifying its sources of supply, a contract for the supply of two HDW submarines to be built in West Germany and two more to be built in Mazagon Docks was signed in 1981. The Navy's intention was to follow the Leander learning route and carry out incremental improvements in subsequent submarines and thus acquire the knowledge and confidence to be self-sufficient in this field also. Unfortunately for the country, this scheme came unstuck with the discovery of kickbacks in the original contract. Mazagon Docks has had expensive submarine building infrastructure lying idle and some of the trained manpower has probably been wasted out, since no more than the first two submarines have been built there. Goa Shipyard has contributed its bit by building missile craft for the Navy.

The aircraft and helicopter requirements of the Navy are too small to warrant any initiatives independent of the Air Force. Very early in the sixties the Navy adapted the Hindustan Aeronautics built Alouette III Helicopter for match role duties from Leanders in preference to buying a more proven helicopter like the WASP from Britain. For training aircraft as well, the Navy has gone along using what was produced for the Air Force. The Navy lent full support to HAL's Armed Light Helicopter programme. Likewise the Navy has pitched in its staff requirement for the carrier borne Naval version of the Light Combat Aircraft. The Navy has been all too conscious about the logistic problems and additional costs involved in the maintenance support of too many types of aircraft in its inventory.

Starting with a negligible training infrastructure, the Navy has in these five decades built some of the finest training establishments one can find anywhere in the world. In the beginning, the Navy's training doctrines were essentially British. Induction of Soviet hardware necessitated adopting the best in the Soviet system to our needs. The Navy has also had the benefit of seeing how the Americans tailor their training inputs and has modified its own to include the best in the American system. The training systems are constantly updated as newer generation of weapons make their appearance in the service.

On the operational front the Navy's first exposure to "Ops" was during the action against the Portuguese in Goa in 1961. Faulty intelligence (a constant bane of our system) and the anxiety to get into the act, caused one of our frigates to pump a few shells into the Portuguese Frigate "Alphonso de Albuquerg" which would have hoisted the white flag anyhow.

The 1965 war with Pakistan did not earn the Navy any laurels. The Indian Fleet found itself in the Bay of Bengal on 1st September when the shooting war begun. This came about because the then Chief of Army Staff did not deem it necessary to share with his Navy and Air Force colleagues the happenings in the Valley where operation "GIBRALTAR" had been mounted by Pakistan. On the night of 6th/7th September a Pakistani warship lobbed a few shells on Dwarka which mercifully caused no casualties or damage. The Navy Chief sought the approval of Prime Minister Lal Bahadur Shastri to take retaliatory action against Pakistan. He was, however, not given such a clearance on the plea that we wanted to limit the sphere of hostilities.

The war in 1971 saw the Navy play its part to the full and redeem its somewhat tarnished image in the 1965 war. The brilliantly planned and executed missile attacks on Karachi demoralized the Pakistan Navy and confined it to Karachi Harbour for all intents and purposes. Bottling up of the erstwhile East Pakistan and not allowing any reinforcements from reaching there demonstrated the potential of an aircraft carrier in Sea control over large expanse of the Bay of Bengal. In addition, VIKRANT's aircraft bombed shipping in Chittagong and Khulna Harbours and sealed any possible escape routes for Pakistan's beleaguered army. The actual battle on land was won by the Army with the support of the Air Force. The Navy played its classic role of ensuring that the war was brought to a speedy and desired end.

The decade of the sixties had been a lean period as far as funding for Navy's projects was concerned. The seventies did see some marked improvement when the Navy's share of the Defence Budget increased to 9.65 per cent in 1977-78. It also saw creation of the Indian Coast Guard in 1976 to handle regulatory functions and tackle smuggling and pollution control. However, it was only in the eighties that the Navy reached the two digit figures which it had had for a couple of years in the late fifties. In 1989-90 the Navy's share was 13.53 per cent, the highest it had reached till then. The commissioning of a second aircraft carrier - VIRAAT - in 1987 made the Indian Navy a modest sized blue water Navy. Loan of a nuclear submarine for three years from the U.S.S.R gave our officers and men valuable training in this highly specialized field. This will stand us in good stead if and when the Indian Navy decides to add nuclear submarines to its fleet.

Budgetary figures and types and numbers of warships, submarines and aircraft do not and cannot give a true indication of the fighting potential of a service. A better way to pose the question would be to ask whether the nation has got the optimum in terms of security from the modest investments it has made in its Navy. The answer, sadly, would be an emphatic 'No'. For a poor country with competing demands from the social sector, this must be deemed to be an area of grave concern. At the macro level the planning for the Armed Forces has been totally ad hoc. More prosperous nations deem it necessary to take a holistic view of security, debate the options in their national security councils, adopt achievable goals and then secure the means to bring these about. Our political parties pay lip service to setting up such institutionalised mechanisms for national security. The reality on the ground is that in our half-a-century of Independence we have not been able to do so.

In countries like the U.S.A. and Britain, there have been periodic reviews about the organizational structures in the armed forces. The initiatives and the drive for these have come from their political leadership and have resulted in more cost effective answers. We have been content to carry on with what we inherited from our colonial masters. The only change we made was in the nomenclature of our Service Chiefs whom we called Chiefs of Staff and not Commanders-in-Chief of their respective services. We did this without the concomitant organizational changes which are necessary for such a progressive step.

The Services have from time to time urged the integration of the Service headquarters with the Ministry of Defence as obtains elsewhere in the world. This has fallen on deaf ears because the Ministry of Defence bureaucrats have a vested interest in status quo and the politician has no time to apply his mind to such an important issue. From time to time the Defence portfolio has been kept by the Prime Minister, a sure recipe for neglect. One of India's Prime Ministers went so far as to justify on the floor of the House, that he had kept the Defence portfolio with himself because of its importance.

If, in spite of wholly wasteful, inefficient and slow organizational structures, the Navy and the Armed Forces as a whole have performed well and given a good account of themselves, it is because of the dedication of the Armed Forces cadres.. Our manpower, particularly our men, are some of the best anywhere in the world. They continue to do their duty in peace and war with total disregard for their comfort and safety, secure in the knowledge that their countrymen do value their sacrifices even though the political masters only pay periodic lip service to them.

In the first four decades after Independence, the Navy's strength grew in fits and starts, and from a tiny coastal force, the Indian Navy became a small blue water Navy. The wanton neglect in the next decade caused the last Chief of Naval Staff to give public expression to his anguish. While our shipyards remained without orders, we were obliged to buy a second hand Leander class frigate from Britain. Frigates are the workhorses of any Navy and it is not appreciated that in our environment this type of ship takes five to six years to build after the design stage. The Navy's peak frigate strength was 23 in 1985. At the rate at which we are going we could reach a single digit figure by the turn of the century. With VIKRANT already retired from service and with no sanction for its replacement yet, we run the risk of putting the clock back to the fifties.

The Navy is a tiny part of our great and diverse country. If the Navy finds itself in dire straits in India's fiftieth year of Independence, the fate of the country as a whole is no better. On the plus side we have a democratic structure — no mean achievement — but the minuses are colossal. Our human and material resources are mired in a low productivity corrupt system with total lack of accountability. Poverty alleviation, primary education and environment have received scant attention and such meagre resources which have been committed to these have gone into enriching the few. We live in a "scam a day" year, with an unbelievable syndrome of not being able to bring the guilty to book for lack of permission. Our archaic laws, many of them owing their origin to a colonial era will witness a confluence of three centuries as we "march" into the 21st century in less than three years' time. The one redeeming factor is the ten good monsoons which have shown that the weather gods are concerned about our plight. Let us hope that the second half century of Independence will see some enlightened handling of the nation's security concerns. History has shown that whatever power controlled the Indian Ocean had in the first instance India's seaborne trade at her mercy, and in the second India's very Independence itself.

13

Indian Air Force Since Independence

Air Chief Marshal S. K. Sareen

Hyderabad, 1947: The eastern horizon was glowing pink at Begumpet airfield when Sqn Ldr A. R. Pandit, DFC, the Commanding Officer of 3 Squadron, finally finished briefing, by lantern-light in the Ops Room tent, the two young Flight Lieutenants flying with him that morning. The previous day, the Chief of the Air Staff had directed him to fly his eight piston-engined Tempest fighters from Poona to Hyderabad to carry out operations in support of the Army against the rebels at Hyderabad. The three pilots, their parachutes slung over their shoulders, walked out into the dawn to their Tempest fighters, engines ticking over, already warmed up by the Flight Sergeant in charge of the ground crew. Pandit climbed onto the wing and stood for a moment before climbing into the cramped cockpit, his eyes narrowing against the slipstream of the idling propellor, breathing in the cool, clean morning air flavoured with the fumes of burnt 100 octane petrol. Life was good, he mused; his country on the threshold of Independence, and himself a commanding officer of one of the nine fighter squadrons in the Indian Air Force (till recently, the Royal Indian Air Force) . A little later, his two wingmen positioned a few feet on either side of him, he opened ful throttle on the runway, checking his engine before commencing the take off. Glancing to either side, he saw his wingmen, their eyes on him, giving him the thumbs-up signal signifying their readiness for take off. Raising his left hand for the signal for take off, he brought it down in a swift chopping motion, released his brakes and felt the aircraft surge forward. Accelerating on the take off roll, he saw, from the corner of his eye, that his wingmen were in perfect position on either side of him. The three aircraft soon rose into the air, their wheels foldiing up in unison as the roar of their 18 cylinder 2520 hp Bristol piston engines faded to a hum while they turned away in close formation towards their target in the southwest.

Fifty years later

Pune, 1997: Wg Cdr Unnikrishnan, Commanding Officer of No. 24 Squadron (recently eqipped with the Su-30 multi-role combat aircraft) and his co-pilot-cum-Systems Operator, Sqn Ldr Verma, walked out of the darkened, air-conditioned briefing room into the warmth of a Pune afternoon along with the other Su-30 crew. They had just finished briefing for a practice maritime air defence sortie, where they were to safeguard a Task Force fleet, which would include an aircraft carrier, against enemy marauders simulated by Jaguars of No. 6 Sqn. Walking to his sleek Su-30, Wg Cdr Unnikrishnan reflected on how the very role of the Air Force had changed. From the Tactical Air Force of a half century ago, today, under Air Chief Marshal SK Sareen PVSM AVSM VM ADC, the Chief of the Air Staff and appropriately the Commodore Commandant of No. 24 Sqadron AF who is spearheading this revolution, the IAF is well on its way to becoming a Strategic Air Force, a separate entity in its own right. The sortie was to be flown at medium level, and the briefing had included exhaustive details on radar operation, target identification, missile guidance and launch tactics, communication procedure, etc. The Jaguars were simulating an enemy Harpoon sea-skimming missile attack; hence, the marauding aircraft would have to be intercepted and electronically interrogated while more than a 100 kms away, as the radar guided missile would be launched by the Su-30s at a range of about 100 kms. In an actual situation, the Su-30 pilots would never see the aircraft they were shooting down; hence the need for positive identification. A short while later, both the Su-30 fighters rolled onto the runway. To the leader's radio calls of "Rolling...NOW", and "Reheat...NOW" both aircraft commenced their take off roll, engaging reheat and getting airborne almost immediately.

The Early Years

When India attained her Independence in 1947, the IAF had already progressed from a small, dedicated band of pioneers flying dilapidated Wapiti and Hawker Hart biplanes (outdated even then) to the then-contemporary Hawker Hurricanes, Spitfires and Tempests. From six and-a-half fighter and one transport squadrons at the time of Independence, the IAF rapidly expanded within the next fifty years to 35 fighter squadrons and a similarly enhanced strength of helicopter and transport Squadrons. In 1950, under Air Marshal RI Chapman (the first Indian Chief of the Air Force), the IAF inducted its first jet fighter the Vampire, and under the yeomanship of the late Air Marshal Subroto Mukherjee IAF had its fighter fleet in 1959. The next milestone was the transition from a transonic to a supersonic Air Force; 28 squadron, known ever since as the "First Supersonics", ushered in the supersonic age with the MiG-21 . Along the way, many of the world's aviation classics have rendered yeoman service to the IAF, like the Spitfire, Hurricane, Hunter, MiG-21 Mirage-2000, MiG-29 and, to usher in the 21st century, the Su-30. Among the transport and bomber aircraft were the famous Dakota, Super Constellation, B-24 Liberator and the Canberra. Today, the IAF has taken its rightful place as the fourth largest Air Force in the world.

Role of the IAF Today

During the formation of the IAF (then RIAF), the role envisaged for the Air Force was the support of ground operations; however, the IAF soon came into its own as an independent entity. With the development of air power, history is replete with examples emphasizing air superiority as a prerequisite for victory in any battle, be it over land or sea. The Gulf War is the most convincing demonstration of this basic tenet, as, compared to the air war, the ground battle paled into inconsequence.

The primary responsibility of the IAF is the air defence of the national airspace, and the safeguarding of our assets from attack from the air. Condensed into the simple statement made above are myriads of complex functions and variables like air defence, air interdiction, tactical and strategic reconnaissance, offensive air operations including counter-air operations and battlefield air strike, air transport, air maintenance of the forward areas like Siachen, paradropping operations and many more. While some of the fleets of combat and other aircraft are old, a few are new and state-of-the-art, like the Su-30. The strike role is done by the Jaguar, MiG-27, MiG-23 BN and

MiG-21 aircraft, while the air defence tasks are carried out by the MiG-29, MiG-21, MiG-23MF and Mirage-2000 aircraft. Our transport fleet consists mainly of Avro-748, AN-32 and IL-76 aircraft, while helicopters like the Mi-8, Mi-24 gunship and Chetak form the bulk of the rotary wing inventory. Maintaining a viable capability in all these areas is a massive effort involving a constant process of training, evaluation and consolidation.

The IAF is also committed to render aid to civil authorities during natural calamities, movement of troops to maintain law and order, as well as the ever present requirement of air maintenance of our troops in inaccessible border outposts. Time and again, pilots and crew of our helicopter and transport squadrons have rescued marooned soldiers, tourists and moutaineers from the certain death, while operating in abysmally bad flying conditions and weather.

Air Defence : The Constant Vigil

In implementing its primary role of safeguarding India's airspace, the IAF goes through many activities at various levels. At higher Headquarters, a constant process of threat evaluation and assessment of the capabilities of our potential adversaries calls for constant changes in tactics, and, often, changes in equipment as well.

At field level, a high level of vigilance ensures that selected bases along the border remain at instant air defence readiness to deal with any violations of national airspace. At such bases, at least two armed fighters along with their pilots are maintained on high alert in special underground shelters (called operational Readiness Platforms (ORPs), to be "scrambled" at a moment's notice when required. Such "scrambles" to investigate a suspect aircraft picked up on radar are not uncommon, as civilian aircraft are often known to stray from their assigned corridors. In addition, all fighter, transport and helicopter squadrons as well as ground based missiles and radars remain in a state of high alert at all times. Planning of various activities like training and exercises are done so as to ensure the capability of all units to swing into action at short notice.

An Air Defence pilot needs to be well versed in the art of aerial combat and tactics arising from a number of possible exercises; he could be a part of an element escorting a formation of strike aircraft (laden with bombs and unable to fend for themselves) to their target, or scrambled to intercept intruders, or a part of a Combat Air Patrol (CAP) to protect a Vulnerable Area or point from enemy air attack.

The Air Defence Pilots thus spend a great deal of their time practicing air combat in different combinations, like 1 vs 2, 2 vs 3, 2 vs 4 and so on, in a variety of realistic simulated scenarios. While a mock combat would typically last only a minute or so, each aspect of it is painstakingly debriefed and dissected on the ground subsequently so as to derive the maximun training benefit at lengthy debrief sessions. With the average pilot flying two to three such sorties a day (a supervisor would fly even more) it is no wonder, then, that the fighter pilots often work for 12-16 hours a day. Interceptions at night, executed using a combination of control from the ground radar terminating in the attack by the interceptor using its own radar have their own special demands.

Delivering the Punch : Strike Operations

The cutting edge of an Air Force is its offensive arm; history and Confucius both agree that a strong offensive capability is the best deterrent and guarantor of peace. The IAF has the latest fighter ground attack aircraft capable of delivering a lethal blow to the enemy; the Jaguar, MiG-23BN, 27 and 21, and even the Su-30 and Mirage-2000 can be used for this role. The Jaguar has also been successfully modified for the maritime strike role, both by day and by night.

Strike pilots need to devote a lot of time and study in preparation for even their training missions. From preparation of maps and flight planning to weapon delivery skills and defensive air combat tactics, the required level of expertise is above and beyond the basic skills required to fly with a pinpoint accuracy a mere 50-100 meters above the ground at speeds of upto 1000 kmph, while carrying out other complex tactical and system management activities. Not all ground attack flying is at low level; depending on the distance of the target, hostile air defence and weapons to be avoided as well as employed, the mission could also be flown at medium levels or a combination of low and medium levels.

Helicopter and Transport Operations

Our transport fleet ensures round the year lifelines to numerous remote and inaccessible areas, delivering vital provisions and evacuating critical casualties while often operating in very marginal weather conditions. From a single squadron of the venerable Dakota at the time of Independence, the IAF now boasts of a total of seven transport squadrons including aircraft like the IL-76, AN-32, Avro, Boeing 737 and Dornier 228. The heavy lift capability of the IAF has been tested more than once, like during the IPKF operations in Sri Lanka and the Maldive operations. During the Gulf War, the IAF IL-76s carried out many evacuation sorties from Kuwait.

Likewise, the helicopters are employed in a wide range of environments from maritime (till recently, in support of Bombay High Operations), desert, jungle and high altitude. The "choppers", as they are affectionately known in the IAF, have also done more than their share of mercy-missions, whether it is during times of natural disasters like floods and cyclones, or evacuation of hundreds of marooned pilgrims on the Badri Nath trail during 1996.

Maintenance

Behind every minute of an aircraft's flight lies hours of laborious, painstaking dedicated maintenance work. Besides aircraft, there are a myriad other systems and types of equipment ranging from sophisticated radar and missile guidance systems, mobile radars, communication and other related electronic systems, computers and a whole range of backup technology, vehicles and many servicing laboratories and workshops. Manning, training and operating the maintenance infrastructure is a mammoth project. The maintenance branch, in spite of the severe constraints and considerable load and pressure, has consistently delivered the goods, allowing the complete and unrestrained use of the IAF's weapon and other systems.

Training

To keep the cutting edge of the IAF finely honed to achieve peak performance, a rigorous training programme is adhered to and strictly monitored to ensure combat worthiness of man and machine at all times. To fully exploit the enormous potential of its skilled manpower, the IAF has brought about judicious changes in the training of pilots in all streams, introducing an 'applied' stream for trainees selected for the fighter stream. For flying branches, training is imparted in three prestigious flying colleges around Hyderabad, which train Flight Cadets of the IAF and foreign Air Forces, as well as officers of the Army and Navy. The quality of training has been vindicated more than once during the two Indo-Pak wars. On Ist Sept. 65, the IAF, led by Air Chief Marshal Arjan Singh DFC, responded within an hour to a Pakistani armoured attack; again, on 3rd Dec. 71, in response to a surprise air attack by Pakistan, Air Chief Marshal PC Lal DFC led the IAF to victory.

Numerous ground establishments located all over the country ensure the *abinitio* as well as periodical follow-up and advanced training of various disciplines of the other non-flying branches.

IAF Personnel : Our Greatest Asset

The burning zeal, determination and dedication displayed by the pioneers of the IAF as well as successive generations continue to motivate the men and women of the IAF today, who constitute the greatest asset of this Service. The most famous example of valour, of course, is the saga of Fg Offr NJS Sekhon, who took off during an air attack by the PAF in December 1971 to do battle with half a dozen Sabre jets. Fg Offr Sekhon was shot down and killed; for his extreme courage and valour, he was awarded the Param Vir Chakra posthumously, the first such award in the IAF.

Coming from all walks of life and all religions, the IAF effectively bonds its personnel into a dedicated, enthusiastic homogeneous community which, in today's turbulent, multipolar society, is a shining example to the rest of the country. The proof of the pudding has been seen time and again when the coutry was rent by communal unrest, during which the personnel of the IAF, as those in the sister Services, stood united. The quality of the personnel manning the IAF permits the pursuit of all goals and targets with vigour and zeal, and the relentless accomplishment of the many tasks and responsibilities of the IAF.

Modernisation and Indigenization

Modernisation in any area is a continuous process; however, what is unique to the field of aviation alone is that in no other area is the technology of the day so apparent in all aspects of development. As a consequence, financial outlays are often inadequate, as the constant strive for dominance in the world of military aviation generates an enormous financial burden, one that is often difficult to bear; in addition, the extremely low useful life cycle of a modern aviation-related system due to technological obsolescence is a major limiting factor. Despite the financial constraints, however, the IAF has launched a vigorous modernisation drive, especially in the mid-life upgradation of aircraft and other systems (the MiG-21 update programme is a case in point) and the review of deployment and utilisation to create a more "lean and mean" force.

To increase operational effectiveness, the IAF has gone in for many new inductions like the Su-30 multi-role fighter and new aircraft systems which would enhance the IAF's capabilities in the areas of night attack, electronic warfare and navigation. Many radar and missile systems are also under upgradation.

All these areas would be out of reach unless considerable progress in indigenization is achieved. The efforts of the Self- Reliance Implementation Council (SRIC), the Joint Planning Council (JPC) and executive organisations like DRDO, ADE and HAL are of crucial importance in the drive towards indigenization. These organisations gave India her first jet fighter, the HF-24, in the late sixties; the Advanced Light Helicopter (ALH) has already flown and the Light Combat Aircraft (LCA), albeit delayed due to unavoidable reasons, is definitely progressing well. Other important projects are the Indra series of low looking radars, various items of Electronic Support equipment, the Airborne Early Warning (AEW) system, and the now-well known Prithvi and other series of missiles.

Conclusion

In the last fifty years, the nation has been through many significant changes. The IAF too, from a small band of dedicated men, has become a large, well organised fighting force known for its professionalism and dedication. In a fitting symbol of progress, the IAF has ushered in the next century with the induction of one of the most lethal multi-role fighters in the world, the Su-30, leaving no doubt of the IAF's constant endeavour to "Touch the Sky With Glory".

14

Securing the Borders

Pains and Gains

A. K. Tandon

THE CHINESE AGGRESSION in 1962 showed the need to improve and revitalise the defence preparedness and border management of the country. It brought to focus the politico-strategic threat and pressure a neighbouring country could exert on India. The need was further reinforced when confrontation with Pakistan in the cheerless Rann of Kutch in early part of 1965 took place followed by infiltration in Jammu & Kashmir. The events evoked a national response for effective management of the security of the borders. Perception of border security, the deployment of multi-purpose specialised force, adoption of security developmental complementary model, need to enlist public support of border population, augmentation of strategic responses of the armed forces, need for different standard of security based on threat level and geo-political compulsions, provision of graduated deterrences and adoption of institutionalised conflict resolution framework led to the evolution of a border security system. The perceptions and the in depth study conducted by a study group, consisting of Gen. J. N. Choudhary (the then Chief of Army Staff), Shri L. P. Singh (the then Home Secretary) and Shri K. F. Rustamji, provided a model for raising the Border Security Force.

The model was designed to create a unified, organised paramilitary force to serve in the country's remote intractable frontiers from

Kutch and Kargil in the west to Assam, Bengal, Meghalaya and Tripura in east during peace and war. It was envisaged that this Force will be controlled by the Centre and administered through two-tier system i.e., Directive level (Force & Frontier HQs) and Operational level (Sector and Battalions). This model was converted into a reality by Shri K.F.Rustamji on 1 December, 1965, with the constitution of the Border Security Force (BSF).

When the ground was being prepared to sow the seeds, Pakistan gave a rude shock of infiltration early in August 1965 followed by a full-fledged attack in September 1965. The State Armed Police troops who braved the bullets and tackled the situation with sheer guts formed the part of the BSF and provided fertilizer to grow the seed into the largest paramilitary force of the democratic world today. These troops brought home the lessons in collection of hard intelligence and future role of BSF in war — holding out in concentrated groups at strategic posts under the overall defence plan.

A team consisting of Shri Nanda, Shri Kamraj and Shri L. P. Singh, Home Secretary on visit to Assal Uttar Sector in Punjab in an attempt to assess the intelligence prowess, demanded one of the Units earmarked for embodiment into the BSF to produce a daily newspaper from Lahore on 9th September, 1965. Sure enough two daily newspapers were brought from Lahore and delivered to VIPs next day — the day of famous tank battle.

Initial Stage

It was a time of almost unbeatable mounting tension, crisis, nerves and expectations. The father founder of the Force set out on the task of provision of basic infrastructure to mould the new Force and provision of accommodation in the inhospitable terrain (deserts, forests, salt swamps and back breaking mountain ranges), assessed need of funds, communication, logistics and administrative support and above all the elan of the Force to convert heterogenous force into a homogenous one. Systems were designed to improve productivity and health of the organisation. This challenging task gave birth to the honing of innovative skills - the bedrock of the BSF culture. The entire border of India hummed with activities ranging from training chores to the Research and Development and production/fabrication for self-reliance. The Central Training Institutions - BSF Academy, TCS Hazaribagh, Signals Training School, Operational Support Units — Water Wing, Air Wing, National Training centre for Dogs and

Printing Press were raised. The BSF Act was passed and training of future leaders i.e., Asstt Comdts (Direct Entry) started. Soon a 'shield' was forged, with specific role — security of the borders and matters connected therewith, vigorous spirit of kinship, adventure and commitment, which has over the years displayed its awesome power many a time. The Force which started with 25½ Battalions is now having 157 Battallions and full-fledged administrative, logistics and operational support systems.

Early in 1966, the BSF launched a tremendous sports fostering programme with the help of old athletes and coaches. Its sportsmen learnt the latest methods of improving athletic excellence. As a matter of fact the BSF has become the power-house of sports in India. In many disciplines like hockey, athletics, football, volleyball, equestrian, basketball, swimming and shooting, its sportsmen have become Asian Champions. The hockey team consisting mainly of the BSF boys became Olympic champions in 1980. Its sportsmen have been given Arjuna awards and a large number of them have represented India in international events and won laurels.

The BSF, while involved in the teething troubles of border management, was assigned the task of dealing with the Delhi Police strike in 1967, Pheruman's 'Death Fast', Sant Fateh Singh's fast and the highly explosive activity, i.e., support at the time of demarcation of the Fazilka belt. When Indian survey team was finding it difficult, the force provided not only technical but also the operational support in demarcation of Gujarat-Pakistan border immediately after 1965 operations.

Technical Expertise

Innovativeness, resourcefulness and self-reliance are three cornerstones of the BSF culture. The Chinese principle of mass innovation and Japanese principle of 'Small Scale Industries' have been introduced to develop and modernise the Force. This concept has activated all ranks to improve their equipment and functioning through innovations and the result was the BSF could develop prestigious equipment like Rocket Motors which could hit upto 17.4 Kms, Tear Smoke Munition, Multi Barrel Launchers, fibreglass and sophisticated electronics equipment, etc. BSF-made rockets were used in 1971 operations and Tear Smoke Munitions are being used by all Police/paramilitary forces in the country and exported too. BSF has its own Communication set-up, R&D base, a chain of workshops as a part of total Quality Management System and Electronics Data Processing Wing.

The Hot-water Scenario

The Punjab, prior to 1971 war, was in serious ferment and full of nasty law and order problems. The Naxalite menace loomed large and wanted to disrupt the stability of the State so as to bedevil the war efforts when hostilities broke out. The BSF with its Punjab Police comrades was able to crush the activities of the criminal renegades and 'sanitized' the State before December 1971 War. During hostilities, the BSF supplied rich intelligence on the internal activities from across the borders.

The liberation of Bangladesh is a well-known history. But very few are aware that the BSF was very much a part of that history as well. This was the organisation which received Col. Osmani, Maj. Shaffiullah (Later Army Chief of Bangaldesh), Maj. Khalid Musharraf, Maj. Zia (later President of Bangladesh) the then East Bengal Rifles Officers in March 1971, and conducted training of the Mukti Bahini during the initial stages when it was barely a five years old Force. This added a new dimension to its role and scope of duty. On the western front, the BSF was suddenly faced with the first fury of Pakistan's full ground and air attack. The fledgling force unflinchingly stood its ground, repeatedly repelled heavy shelling with outdated weapons, participated in infantry offensives and successfully captured enemy territory. In Rajasthan, the BSF's fearless Camel Unit - with a strength of 100 'Desert Ships', armed with LMGs — played a critical role in the harsh desert warfare. In the East, streams of refugees poured into the BSF outposts, seeking shelter, food and medical assistance. Its courage, innumerable acts of bravery and compassion are legendary in Bangladesh, even today. Despite its total lack of experience, inadequate arms and ammunition, the young Force came through its first ordeal with honour, fought well in 31 independent operations, sacrificed lives of 135 personnel. Its 392 personnel lost limbs and 423 personnel were decorated for their distinctive role. The BSF has carved a permanent and proud place for itself not as India's second line of defence, as had been formally defined in 1965, but as the country's first line of defence that bears the brunt and first fury of the enemy's onslaught.

The BSF assisted Government in conduct of a unique experiment full of risks by enrolling General Zuhoto and his associates of Revolutionary Government of Nagaland. The experiment not only won the hearts of the undergrounds, it brought them into the mainstream of the nation as part of the BSF. This group later became the mainstay of counter-insurgency operations in Nagaland.

In the eighties another dimension was added to the BSF portfolio. The Force was called upon to handle prestigious security-cum-ceremonial duties for ASIAD 1992, NAM, CHOGM and SARRC summits. In April 1990, the BSF joined the UN Police Monitors in Namibia. There, the BSF helped conduct fair polls, preserve law and ease the transition towards independence. The BSF also provided active support to UN Missions in Cambodia, Mozambique, Angola and Bosnia - Herzegovina and earned a name at the international level.

Tackling of Critical Issues

The communal riots in Ahmedabad, Moradabad, Bhagalpur etc., Railway strike in 1974, militancy/terrorism in Punjab, J&K, Bihar, Assam, Andhra Pradesh, counter-insurgency operations in Nagaland, Manipur and Tripura are some horrendous events, which have been tackled with professionalism, characteristic restraint and tact by the BSF.

Today as never before, the integrity of the country is being threatened on several points. The BSF is therefore, guarding troubled borders and its hinterlands, dominating hotbeds insecurity afflicted States, reassuring civilians and local authorities through intensified operational activities. It has augmented its Units, fenced and fortified vulnerable border segments and improved detection, intervention and alarm systems through upgradation of technology and modernisation. The BSF efforts in the last seven years have caused interception of 291703 Bangladesh/Pak nationals, killing of 1285 intruders in encounters, seizure of contrabands worth Rs.657.7 crore, 420945 ammunition and 2507 arms. The major seizures were of narcotics and gold which clearly indicate the starting of narco-terrorism.

Days in Inferno

The attitude of the dominant fundamentalist lobby, after effects of 'Operation Blue Star', role of Pakistan ISI, adoption of 'entanglement theory' by militants/terrorists, narco-terrorism, mushroom growth of terrorist gangs to earn easy money and flooding of modern weapons and equipment both in Punjab, Jammu and Kashmir have kept the BSF busy in fighting counter-insurgency operations. With its meagre resources, task is being performed with utmost professionalism. The BSF has played a major role in bringing back political stability both in Punjab and Jammu & Kashmir by following path of humanism and principles of human rights. In the last six years, 678 troops have sacrificed their lives and 3381 their limbs. When major intelligence network shifted from Srinagar to Jammu, it was the BSF Intelligence set-up which sustained the pressure on militants and helped the Centre in countering militancy. The BSF Intelligence has helped in apprehension of dreaded militants and its concerted efforts have led to surrender of 600 hardcore militants and seizures. Since 1990 BSF has apprehended 9678 militants, killed 2417 militants and have captured 9383 arms, 144908 ammunition and 776 Rocket Bombs during conduct of various operations. These arms could have created havoc, if left with the terrorists.

The disputes between Assam and Nagaland led to tension on the inter State border. A war like situation was created and it became difficult to contain it. Keeping confidence of both the State Governments, BSF was deployed on the State border to bring peace between these States.

The BSF deals with human beings with compassion, consideration and care. Its assistance during the natural calamities and hour of crisis has left stories of praise.

The BSF Praharis, selected through a well-conceived, scientific system of induction, cast into a steel mould through rigorous training, are tough, resilient, highly skilled and resourceful. They readily perform any task, anytime, anywhere with vigour, efficiency, drive and dedication. Their motto is "Duty unto Death" and their pledge is "I will not disgrace the Borderman's arms nor abandon the comrade who stands at my side alone or with many. I will defend every thing that my country holds sacred".

Major factors responsible for rapid development of the BSF include faith in systems approach, learning through own and others experience and scientific temper. From the very beginning, motto of self-reliance, innovation and resourcefulness has been followed in the Force which has resulted in commissioning workshops in armament, electronics, mechanical transport.

Managing Role Diversity

The responsibility of policing highly volatile borderlines for over three decades has helped the BSF garner a reservoir of unique skills and experience. Recognised as one of the finest border patrolling forces today, it has redefined its scope of duties and tackles the most critical issues of national concern. In an environment charged with uncertainty, where terrorism, aggression and communal disharmony raise daily alarms, the BSF uses its inherent strengths to ease the tensions with characteristic restraint and tact.

The Force was born from the ashes of a conflict with Pakistan. Yesterdays *raison d'etre* for the BSF is no longer relevant today although conflict at the border is still there. The BSF is moving forward under the influence of its own cultural impact, a coherent strategy and systems approach. Its birth has paved the way for India's integration — through the safety of its frontiers and borders.

15

Defending the Borders on Mountains

Divakar Prasad

THE INDO-TIBETAN Border Police (ITBP) is the child of perfidious Chinese attack on India. It saw the light of the day on October 24, 1962, within 5 days of the lacerating trauma this unsuspecting nation was thrown into the Force was raised under the CRPF Act/Rules and originally administered by a joint director of the Intelligence Bureau (IB) designated as special Inspector General, but shifted to the operational and administrative command of Director General(Security) in 1965 before finally passing under the wings of the Ministry of Home Affairs on September 3, 1971.

Incredible though it may appear, the ITBP literally took off as a micro outfit with just four battalions on its roll. It picked up two more in 1964 and became eight-Battalion strong by 1971 with three training centres feeding it. Nothing changed until 1978 when the force was re-structured within its existing strength at the time. Restructuring resulted in the creation of nine Service battalions (4 Coy pattern), one Telecom battalion, one Transport Battalion, one SPT battalion and one Supply and Service battalion, a base hospital, three SHQs, one Force Headquarters- including Central Record Office and Clerical Training School. One Battalion was sanctioned to strengthen surveillance on Jammu and Kashmir and Uttar Pradesh border, and another six were raised at the rate of two battalions each year in 1988,

1989 and 1990. Government sanctioned six battalions on the pattern of unattached battalions of the Central Reserve Police Force (CRPF) for safeguarding banks having currency chests all over Punjab. Two Battalions were added to the force in 1990 for internal security duties in J&K. In 1994 another battalion for HQ Sector came through. The total strength of force at present stands at 30367.

Terrain and Deployment

The raison d'etre of the ITBP is axiomatic, viz, guarding of the India-Tibet border implying it is there to scout for discovering possible chinks in the now vulnerable Himalayan armour, and help plug them primarily by pre-emptive measures. And what kind of a topography the jawans are required to serve in?

A solid 2115 km of staggering mountainscape with astounding varities of dizzy heights ranging between 9000 to 18000 feet, chilly locales where mercury plummets to 40 degree C, bottomless gorges, abysmal ravines, tempestuous rivers, treacherous glaciers, craggy steeps overshadowed by hazards truly cliff-hanging - that is the typical theatre of operations the ITBP men and officers spend two-third of their service career in . It extends from Karakoram Pass (old trade route to Tibet) in J&K to Lipulekh Pass (on Kailash Mansarovar route) in UP.

The ITBP has its forward posts much ahead of the Army defences and well deep inside the Inner Line areas. Men have to constantly contend against Nature's fury in the shape of rampaging snow blizzards, high velocity storms, lightning, avalanches, and landslides which, though overawe them, imbue in them as well grit and stamina a net gain without doubt, though expensively purchased. When severe winter cuts off the posts from the outside world, they have to depend on air dropped supplies which offer tinned rations in the absence of fresh vegetables and fruits and milk products.

A Multi-dimensional Force

The role of the Force has evolved out of three distinct phases.

During 1962, the Force reconnoitred the entire length of borderline, surveying and selecting suitable sites for border posts. It embarked on civic action programmes to instil confidence among the border people, collected intelligence and geared itself up for the prescribed role of non-conventional guerrilla organisation.

In 1965 and 1971, the Force saw action. In the Indo-Pak conflict (1965), it fought the enemy away from the border, conducted combing operations against Pak infiltrators and paratroopers, and guarded vital installations. In the 1971 war, two of its battalions performed earmarked "special tasks" of sealing certain areas, detection and destruction of infiltrators, bases in Srinagar valley and Poonch sector a maiden mission which earned plaudits.

National imperatives in 1978 redefined the Force's role afresh and what followed was a change in its charter. Tasks of great variety and content were handed down to its making it a multidimensional force.

The ITBP protects the IB in its operations, joins them in combating trans-border crime and traffic, interrogates smugglers and infiltrators and conducts joint patrolling-cum-covert missions along the international border/Line of Actual Control (LAC). As it has to function in close conjunction with Army in sensitive areas, it attunes and gears itself professionally in peacetime to deal with situations of insurgency, secessionist and subversive designs and terrorism. It participates in the Army's operational planning and patrolling and exchanges tactical information with it.

To provide a "sense of security" to the border population, the ITBP nurses the sick, repairs roads, bridges and hutments ravaged by natural calamities.

In a war situation, the ITBP is to function in a role similar to that of the Border Security Force (BSF). That implies bearing the brunt of enemy's first attack until the Army takes over, to organise limited aggressive action against enemy paramilitary or irregulars and conduct guerrilla operations behind enemy lines. Guarding the Prisoners of War (POWs), arranging escort and maintaining law and order in the enemy territory administered under the Army control, are some other tasks to be executed. The Force safeguards important banks and currency chests in Punjab, movement of cash, protects VIPs and vital installations, assists civil police in operations against insurgents and work to restore law and order. Search and rescue of mountaineers and civilians lost in mountains and avalanches, medical and communication cover for the Kailash Mansarovar Yatris, and making available liaison-cum-security-coverguides to foreign expeditions and the Ministry of External Affairs also fall in the job content of the ITBP.

Four Pillar Structure

The structural paradigm of the ITBP rests on four pillars combat elements, logistic and communications and support elements, administration and training.

Combat elements comprise 25 service battalions and 19 companies of support weapons. They are distributed in five sectors. Jammu and Kashmir with HQ at Srinagar covers a total area of 1570 km; Himachal with HQ at Shimla covers 200 km in length; Garhwal which also covers a border 200 km long, Dehradun is HQ; Kumaon, headquartered at Bareilly, mans 145 km of frontage in district Pithoragarh. Punjab is the last sector to emerge in the Force, thanks to the sponsored terrorism in the eighties. Headquartered at Chandigarh, the Force protects 175 nationalised banks in the State.

The sector relating to logistic, communication and support elements has its HQ in Delhi and mobilises resources like telecommunications, support weapons, transportation and supplies for the Force. Telecom Battalion, stationed at Shivpuri in Madhya Pradesh (MP), runs necessary professional courses for the personnel and procures telecom stores. Mortar and MMG fire support is provided by the Support Battalion, located at Karera(MP). It makes one company available to each border battalion except bank security units in Punjab. The battalion functions as central arms and ammunition depot. Mechanical and animal transport is catered to by the Transport Battalion based at Chandigarh. The Supply and Service Battalion looks after the requirements, procurements and supply of rations including items of high altitude clothing and equipment to the Force besides managing transit camps all over.

For training the personnel in required disciplines, the ITBP runs three institutions. The ITBP Academy, Mussoorie, is today's face of Advance Training Centre established way back in 1964 at Shivpuri as the most modern and premier institution of uncoventional warfare and guerrilla operations in the country. Shifting to Mussoorie in 1976 and rechristened as High Altitude Defence and Survival Academy, it runs specialised courses in tactics, karate, field engineering, intelligence, map reading, demolition etc., as also on rock climbing, identification and handling of bombs and commando training for the benefit of other Central Police Organisations (CPOs) and the State Police Forces as well.

The Mountaineering and Skiing Institute at Auli (Joshimath) at a height of 9708 feet organises basic and advance training in skiing, snow combat, mountain methodology and warfare, and rescue and survival which together constitute the core of a typical ITBPean. Antarctica bound expeditions also receive specialised training here. Army and other organisations benefit substantially from these courses. Conversely, ITBPeans attend some two dozen courses at the Army training institutions and some other under the BSF, CRPF and DCPW.

The Basic Training Centre at Bhanu (Ambala) conducts conventional basic training for recruits and other ranks. It also organises courses on judo, physical training, drill, sniping, bugler and junior and senior cadre courses.

Weaned in IB culture, the ITBP is a low profile organisation, though it has traversed 34 years which reads like an inspiring saga of glory, selfless service and achievements nonpareil. The Force has kept the India-Tibet borderline scrupulously inviolate. It is the sole repository of tactical and strategic information concerning the area it is deployed in. The personnel live off the land, on edible and medicinal herbs, roots and others plants. Special ski techniques for accomplishing swift raids have been developed. In Indo-Pak wars of 1965 and 1971, the ITBP not only drew enemy blood, but shone in defending its positions as well. Our commandos have won laurels in protecting high risk international events taking place in India, like ASIAD-82, NAM and CHOGM. The Kailash-Mansarovar Yatris rely on the ITBP for escort, medicine and communication. No bank-breaking has occurred in Punjab since ITBP took charge of their safety. In the strife-torn J&K, the personnel have repeatedly demonstrated exemplary discipline, steadfastness and functionality of junior leadership. Foolproof safety attends Jawahar Tunnel, the lifeline of the Valley. The credits redound on the sterling discipline of the Force characterising its mainstay. One happily recalls in this context how the Force had distinguished itself by remaining cool and aloof when almost every CPO was thrown into a crisis of discipline in the "70s".

A historic event we lovingly cherish is the presentation of colours to the Force by the late Rajiv Gandhi, then Prime Minister of India, in Kulu on June 20, 1987. Professionalism has ITBPeans don UN berets and do India proud on various occasions as custodians of peace in Namibia, Cambodia, Mozambique, and constitute, at present, the largest contingent of India's police presence perhaps in the burning cauldron of Bosnia-Herzegovina. In Colombo, Sri Lanka, the Indian High Commission continues to enjoy our commando umbrella since

1988. The latest assignment to come our way is security of Punjab and Haryana Secretariat at Chandigarh.

The silent sentinels of the Himalayan snows speak through their deeds. As Many as 342 men and officers have been decorated for gallantry, fire service, distinguished and meritorious services rendered in the cause of the nation. Two of our officers have been awarded Padmashri.

Spending better part of their service career in intractable Himalayan heights, at the mercy of stark elements, and remaining away from family takes its toll. The Force shares the concerns of the jawans and ensures they do not lose their sleep over them. Men are rotated from hard to soft postings, and from heights to plains. Stringent medical checkups, speedy evacuation and a good tie-up with the Army hospitals helps. The Medical Assistance Scheme for Pensioners, a recent bonanza in any CPO, entitles retirees to receive Rs. 12,000 annually for 20 years.

Adventure Sports

The ITBP is a byword for international mountaineering. It has hoisted the Indian Tricolour atop more than 100 world class mountains including Everest (4 times) and Kanchenjunga, India's highest peak in the Himalayas and those in the Alps, Iran and USA. The first police-woman "double Everester" belongs to the ITBP which has pioneered the concept of international police expedition by launching one on Nun in 1991. Skiing is our forte. National champions for years, we recorded the first ever ski-down from Kamet peak, and represented India in the World Police Winter Games at Trento, Italy and at the skiing carnival at Chamonix, France.

History was created in river-rafting (1991) when the ITBPeans led Indo-Japan Brahmaputra Rafting Expedition, sailing down 1100 km. of moody, turbulent white-waters bristling with 6-grade rapids. The Army selected our boys, of all the CPOs, to sail down 327 km of river Indus in -10°C temperature in Ladakh as part of the multiforce expedition HIMEX (1995). We have also been wintering in Antarctica, the replica of the Ice Age, for as long as 18 months.

PART III

India and its Neighbours

- Commonwealth South Asia
- India and Tibet
- India-China Relations: Retrospect and Prospect
- Indo-Myanmar Relations: Scope and Limitations
- Indo-Pak Relations: Prognosis and Options

16

Commonwealth South Asia

K. Srinivasan

COMMONWEALTH South Asia comprises Bangladesh, India, Maldives, Pakistan and Sri Lanka — countries that have played a crucial role in the evolution of the modern Commonwealth. The five member countries from the region are immensely diverse each with distinct identity of its own. However, historical experience has resulted in an underlying unity in this diversity that has stemmed from similarity, not in their national make-up, but in their nation-building process.

The nation-builders of South Asia, in the arduous and sometimes heartbreaking task of translating their vision into reality, arrived at a common political idea of nationhood. There was not only a general consensus on the principles of democracy, but also on institutional structures, constitutional conventions and the ordering of public life. The colonial era planted the concept and institutions of parliamentary democracy and the rule of law, and spread the use of the English language as a medium of communication in all parts of the subcontinent. This meant that the people of these countries could read the same books, study the same cases, follow each other's debates and share similar ways and methods of conducting business.

However, although the seeds of parliamentary democracy were sowed by the colonial administration, it did not nurture them. The demand for parliamentary democratic institutions was raised from within the independence movements in these countries. Parliamentary democracy was adopted in Commonwealth South Asia not because these countries borrowed their institutions from Britain, but because each country created of its own free will a political system of which parliamentary democracy was an integral part.

The Post-Colonial Decades

A year or so after Independence, India had to decide whether to continue its membership of the Commonwealth. In the days of the Independence struggle, leaders of the nationalist Congress party had wanted a complete severance of the Commonwealth tie. But Indian opinion eventually veered towards some form of association with the Commonwealth. In 1948, at the end of the Dominion Prime Ministers' Conference, Prime Minister Nehru said, "We may not agree about everything, but it is surprising what a large measure of unanimity there was, not only in the objectives to be aimed at, but also on the methods to be pursued. This meeting has shown me that there is great scope for the Commonwealth".

In December 1948, speaking at the annual session of the Indian National Congress, Nehru declared that membership of the Commonwealth would not involve any interference in India's foreign policy. He strongly advocated remaining in the Commonwealth, particularly as a formula was found which enabled India to be a member even as a Republic. Nehru's decision that India should remain a member of the Commonwealth after it became a Republic was a defining moment for the association. It set a precedent and provided a framework for accommodating nationalist sentiments in the post-colonial era.

The Commonwealth Prime Ministers' Conference in London, in April 1949, recorded that when India under her new Constitution became a sovereign, independent Republic, she would, in accordance with her own wishes, remain a full member of the Commonwealth and would acknowledge the British monarch as a symbol of the free association of its independent member nations and, as such, the Head of the Commonwealth. The Indian constitutional settlement was important because it reconciled constitutional forms with political realities and showed a new way. Thereafter, many countries opted to follow the same course and the 1949 London Declaration paved the way for their membership of the Commonwealth. Thus, 1949 is regarded as the year of birth of the modern Commonwealth.

Pakistan was committed to the Commonwealth membership from the outset. The Quaid-e-Azam (as Mohammad Ali Jinnah, Pakistan's founder, was popularly known) had been explicit on this matter all along. Pakistan became a member of the Commonwealth in 1947; it became a Republic in 1956, (Pakistan chose to leave the Commonwealth in 1972, following the latter's recognition of Bangladesh, and returned to the fold in 1989).

Ceylon, as Sri Lanka was then known, was the first crown colony to achieve independence. (While India could be classed with the colonies of administration as distinct from the 'dominions', it was never a crown colony in the proper sense.) As such, the independence of Ceylon was in its own right an event of importance in the Commonwealth and set the precedent for crown colonies in much the same way as Canada's independence had for the dominions. Bangladesh joined the Commonwealth in 1972, immediately after it achieved nationhood. On the other hand, Maldives acceded to the association in 1982, several years after its independence in 1965.

South Asia: A Profile

South Asia is by far the most populous region of the Commonwealth. It includes its largest member, India (900 million), and two countries, Pakistan and Bangladesh, with populations of 123 million and 117 million respectively. Together, the subcontinent accounts for about three-quarters of the total population of the Commonwealth. All five countries of the region are multi-party democracies, and India and Sri Lanka have enjoyed a virtually uninterrupted 50-year span of democratic rule. The democratic ethos is deeply embedded, and a free and lively print media thrives everywhere in the region. Civil society is also extremely well developed with a proliferation of effective non-governmental organisations. The countries of South Asia share much in terms of common heritage, tradition and culture, while displaying unique national characteristics and identities. The region has been characterised by both inter and intra-state tensions which have constrained economic cooperation, but in recent years all five South Asia Commonwealth members have made significant progress in macro-economic management and in improving the material well-being of their peoples.

The countries of the subcontinent have embarked upon wide-ranging reform programmes designed to stabilise their economies and to increase efficiency and boost competitiveness. Fiscal consolidation has been an important feature of the stabilisation packages. Stabilisation efforts have been supported by the liberalisation of the trade, payments and investment regimes. The private sector is increasingly playing the locomotive role in achieving sustained growth. There has been a sharp increase in private investment flows to the region which underlines the confidence of international investors in the region's growth potential and the credibility of its reform efforts. These flows represent a major opportunity to increase investment performance and hence to raise growth rates. Economic prospects for South Asia in the coming decade will depend on the spread and acceleration of the reform process.

The Indian economy is expected to enter a period of sustainable growth averaging five per cent per annum over the next decade. The Indian government has been remarkably successful at engineering a major transformation of India's economic policies without the disruption that has been known to accompany such a process elsewhere in the world. The government in Pakistan has also confirmed its adherence to the reform process. It is moving towards full currency convertibility and establishing a favourable investment environment. High priority is also being attached to increasing social sector investments, particularly in education and health. Bangladesh has promoted foreign investment, with a simplification of bureaucratic procedures for the approval of new investment, the establishment of export processing zones and approvals for full foreign ownership. In Sri Lanka, all current account transactions were liberalised in 1993 and considerable strides have been made towards creating a business friendly economic environment. Maldives has sought to diversify its economy by giving high priority to the development of its human resources, tourism, and physical infrastructure. Privatisation is on the subcontinent's agenda and progress is being made. The reform programmes in South Asia have received the strong support of the Bretton Woods institutions.

The economic prospects for the region have been enhanced through the signing of the South Asian Preferential Trade Arrangement (SAPTA), in December 1995, within the framework of the South Asian Association for Regional Co-operation (SAARC). The challenge now is to translate this into concrete action thereby reversing the loss of several years' time in this area that has plagued the Association. Progress is however being made to enhance cooperation in other fields, including transport, communications, anti-poverty programmes and infrastructure development.

Functioning Democracies

All countries in the region are functioning democracies, consistent with the Commonwealth values, notwithstanding past and current political problems faced by some of them. The Commonwealth election observer missions have included distinguished persons from Bangladesh, India, Pakistan and Sri Lanka. The Commonwealth has been invited to observe recent elections in Bangladesh and Pakistan. The Commonwealth South Asia has played a major role in all aspects of the Commonwealth agenda. These countries have had a particular interest in the socio-economic development programmes of the Commonwealth due to the high levels of poverty and illiteracy in most parts of the region. The Commonwealth Heads of Government, at their Auckland Summit, called on the Commonwealth Secretariat to facilitate the adoption by more member countries of successful self-help schemes to mobilise the energies of people for alleviating poverty. The South Asian region has adopted innovative approaches to poverty reduction. A Constitutional Amendment relating to Panchayati Raj in India has endowed local level institutions with financial and other powers to enable them to function as effective institutions of local governance in rural areas; and equally worthy of note are the Grameen Bank Scheme in Bangladesh, the Orangi Project in Pakistan, and the Janasaviya and Samurdhi programmes in Sri Lanka.

South Asian countries have been important contributors to the Commonwealth Secretariat Assessed Budget (7.2 per cent); Commonwealth Fund for Technical Co-operation (3.2 per cent); Commonwealth Youth Programme (5.3 per cent); Commonwealth Science Council (11.2 per cent); and Commonwealth Foundation (7.9 per cent). (These figures relate to financial year 1994/95).

The Commonwealth Secretariat's operational arm, the Commonwealth Fund for Technical Cooperation (CFTC), now in its 25th year, is an outstanding example of effective South-South cooperation. The majority of experts of CFTC, a pioneer of technical cooperation among developing countries, are from developing member countries of the Commonwealth. The CFTC has proved to be flexible and relatively less bureaucratic in the administration of technical assistance, and has the capacity to complement the work of others by filling gaps in assistance and focusing on areas which larger agencies have difficulties in addressing on a micro basis. A further advantage is that a central element of its mode of delivery is counterpart training and transfer of skills. The CFTC is able to provide assistance at any stage in the process of policy making and implementation, and has rendered technical assistance to the level of over £6 million in support of development activities in South Asia over the last five years. About 20 to 25 per cent of CFTC-funded experts originate from South Asia and over 15 per cent of CFTC's training programmes, many of which benefit the wider Commonwealth, are hosted by institutions in the region.

South Asian members have been in regular attendance at all Commonwealth gatherings. Not only have they participated actively in the Heads of Government and Ministerial meetings, but have made substantial contributions to the work of various Commonwealth Expert Groups, Committees, and Task Forces. India hosted the Commonwealth Summit in 1983 and the Commonwealth Science Council in 1995. Maldives hosted the Commonwealth Finance Ministers meeting in 1984 and Commonwealth Youth Ministers meeting in 1993. Pakistan played host to Senior Officials and Education Ministers in 1994. Bangladesh has hosted the Senior Officials in 1986, and the Commonwealth Parliamentary Association held its 1995 annual conference in Colombo, Sri Lanka.

South Asian countries have played a central role in the evolution of the modern Commonwealth. They have demonstrated a commitment to the fundamental values of the association and have made a significant contribution to the affairs of the Commonwealth from the 1940s onwards. The enlarged association faces the dawn of the next century strengthened in its resolve and clear in its purposes, and the five nations of South Asia must form an essential part of that future.

It is worth noting in passing that cricket, the quintessentially a Commonwealth game, has a passionate following in the subcontinent and all the three test-playing member-nations, India, Pakistan and Sri Lanka, have at different times been the World Cup champions.

17

India and Tibet

G. S. Bajpai

AFTER INDEPENDENCE on August 15, 1947, the new Government of India inherited from the British Government all existing treaty rights including extra territorial rights and obligations in regard to Tibet. Thus it had the right to keep a representative at Lhasa and maintain Trade Agencies at Gyantse, Yatung and Gartok with military escorts; to lease lands for the building of houses and godowns at the marts; maintain a chain of rest houses and telegraph lines between trade marts and the frontier; hold courts at the Trade Agencies to try cases of Indian nationals involved in crimes at the marts or on the trade route, and to hold joint enquiries with the Tibetan authorities into disputes involving Indian and other nationals. In a letter to the Tibetan Government, sent in August 1947, the Government of India sought an assurance that the Tibetan Government would continue relations on the existing basis, and the Tibetan government confirmed their acceptance of the former relationship with the new Government of India.

Tibet, at that time, was to all intents and purposes an independent country and had enjoyed a large degree of sovereignty. It was ruled by the Dalai Lama only with the nominal assistance of the Chinese resident. The Chinese had hardly any real control over Tibet. Even in 1904 it had acted independently of China and had concluded a treaty with the British, the validity of which was never questioned by the Chinese Government. Only for a brief period of about seven years, between 1904 and 1911, when Tibet's military resistance was completely broken down due to the Younghusband expedition, the Chinese had established some authority over the Tibetan administration and its external affairs. It was during this period that the 1906 Convention was signed by the British with the Chinese Government so that the latter did not obstruct or interfere with those special privileges which the British had secured for themselves in Tibet. Similarly, the next year, a convention relating to Persia, Afghanistan and Tibet was signed with Russia, and in order to prevent the emergence of any direct relationship between Tibet and Russia, it was resolved that both the parties could negotiate with Tibet only through the intermediary of China. These developments had given China a free hand in Tibet and encouraged it to invade Tibet in 1910 and to forcibly occupy certain areas. That occupation was, however, very short lived, and, with the fall of the Manchu dynasty in 1911, Chinese authority in Tibet had collapsed once again, and the Tibetans had expelled all Chinese officers and troops from their country. With that, all existing links between China and Tibet were severed, the old relationship of the patron and the priest had disappeared and Tibet had re-emerged as a fully sovereign state. A formal declaration of independence was also made by the Dalai Lama in 1913.

On October 1, 1949, the Central Government of the People's Republic of China was proclaimed, and the Government of India extended its official recognition to it on December 30, 1949. One of the first tasks on the agenda of the Communist China was to "liberate Tibet", though Chou En-lai did assure K.M.Panikkar, first Ambassador of India to the Communist China, that "his Government was anxious to secure their ends by negotiations and not by military action. However, the Chinese Army was soon ordered to advance into Tibet, and on October 25, 1950, Peking Radio announced that the process of liberation of Tibet had already begun. The next day the Government of India sent a note to Peking deploring the Chinese invasion and pleading for "slower but more enduring methods of peaceful approach". The Chinese Government immediately retorted: "Tibet is an integral part of Chinese territory. The problem of Tibet is entirely the domestic problem of China. The Chinese People's Liberation Army must enter Tibet, liberate the Tibetan people, and defend the frontiers of China. This is the resolved policy of the Central People's Government ... and no foreign interference shall be tolerated." The Government of India assured in reply that they did not intend to interfere in China's internal affairs and that "they had neither any political or territorial ambitions as to Tibet nor did they seek any novel privileged position for themselves." However, China's tone remained unchanged. China rudely reiterated that liberating the Tibetan people and defending the frontiers was the "sacred task of the Chinese People's Liberation Army and in doing so the Chinese Government was only exercising its sovereign rights." To quote Panikkar, "both parties made their point of view clear, and were content to rest there."

While all this was happening in Tibet, a Tibetan Goodwill Mission was on its way to Peking. On May 23, 1951, a 17-point agreement was signed between Tibet and China. By this Agreement the Tibetan people were to "unite and drive out imperialist forces from Tibet... (and) return to the big family of Motherland — the People's Republic of China", the Lhasa Government was to "actively assist" the PLA to enter Tibet and consolidate the national defenses; the Tibetan Army was to be merged in the PLA, and the Chinese Government was to handle all external affairs of Tibet in future. The Government of India did not fail to realise that those provisions were to change the entire course of history of India-Tibet relations but they seemed absolutely helpless. "Many things happen in this world", Pandit Nehru said in the Lok Sabha, "which we do not like, and which we would wish were rather different, but we do not go like Don Quixote with lance in hand against everything we dislike; we put up with these things because we would be, without making any difference, merely getting into trouble."

In December 1953, India proposed to China that negotiations might be held to settle some of the outstanding issues. About four months later, a Trade Agreement was concluded between the two countries on April 29, 1954. The major thing about that agreement was the preamble which laid down the five principles, namely, recognition of the sovereignty and territorial integrity of each country, mutual non-aggression, mutual non-interference in each other's internal affairs, equality and peaceful co-existence, which were to govern the mutual relations and approach of the two countries. The agreement itself dealt with the opening of Trade Agencies by both the countries, the definition of trade marts, routes and passes of entry and facilities to be extended to pilgrims, customary traders, and border inhabitants of India and Tibet, but it was supplemented by an Indian Note which declared that the Government of India would withdraw, within six months, the military escorts of the Trade Agents stationed at Yatung and Gyantse, hand over to the Government of China the Postal, Telegraph and Public Telephone Services and all the rest houses built between Gyantse and Sikkim border. Independent India felt that those extra-territorial privileges which it was surrendering had been imposed by the strong British Empire on a weak Tibet, and India, as a free and non-aligned country, would not like to keep such "relics of imperialism in any country in the world". "By this agreement", Pandit Nehru declared, "we ensure peace to a very large extent in a certain areas of Asia ... (which) could be spread over to the rest of Asia and indeed over the rest of the world".

While India's stand with regard to Tibet was strictly governed by the spirit of the Panchsheel, articulated in the preamble of the 1954 Trade Agreement, China looked at Tibet purely from offensive considerations. In possession of the Tibetan plateau the People's Republic would stand at the apex of the orient. In the event of conflict with either India or Russia, Tibet as the central and highest ground, would prove an invaluable platform from which to launch an assault.

Chinese soldiers were therefore ordered to advance into Tibet. They brought with them the artillery, tanks and trucks and moved to all important and strategic areas. They systematically employed an entire arsenal of methods to intimidate the local population. The Tibetan clergy were tortured; monks were either deported to labour camps or even burnt alive. Entire villages were erased and wiped off the map. Lhasa was swamped by the continuous influx of refugees from all over.

On March 7, 1959, the Chinese Commander in Lhasa, General Dan Guansau, invited the Dalai Lama to attend a theatrical show in the PLA Headquarters. The Dalai Lama was informed to come only with two unarmed attendants and not to be accompanied by his bodyguards. This kind of invitation resulted in rumours that the Chinese planned to kidnap him. Angry crowds therefore started gathering outside the Potala palace and Norbulengka. They even attacked some of the known Chinese collaborators and raised slogans demanding an end to the Chinese occupation. The Dalai Lama urged the crowds to disperse but there was no slackening of tension.

On March 17, the Chinese began shelling the Norbulengka. The same night the Dalai Lama decided to leave for India. After an arduous journey, he entered the Indian soil across Tawang in NEFA on March 31, 1959. In India there was a groundswell of popular sympathy for the Tibetans. The Government of India, therefore, decided to grant him asylum. He was, however, not permitted to use India as a base for the Tibetan independence movement.

As soon as the Dalai Lama's flight came to their notice, the Chinese applied naked force to rapidly and thoroughly integrate Tibet with China. Energetic massive purges were organised to decapitate the religious hierarchy and Tibetan aristocracy and to crush any hint of dissent. The city exploded in street-to-street fighting. The Tibetans were slaughtered by the thousands and the wounded were left to perish in agony, unattended. The chaos that ensued is a tale of destructive fury that ravaged Tibet causing excruciating suffering.

China's attitude towards India, which had given asylum to the Dalai Lama purely on humanitarian grounds, also changed. It alleged that the Dalai Lama had been "blatantly abducted" and "held under duress" by the rebels who were acting under orders from India, Taiwan and the United States. It accused India of inheriting the shameful legacy of the British imperialists for carrying on aggression against China.

In the years to come the People's Liberation Army stationed in Tibet became more and more aggressive all along the Indo-Tibet border. It was now abundantly clear that the Chinese ambition did not extend only to the annexation of Tibet but also to the adjoining territory. After making Tibet as their firm base, the Chinese now started using force in assertion of their supposed claims. On July 29, 1959, a party of six Indian Army personnel which was on a routine patrol was apprehended by the Chinese from inside North Ladakh. Less than two weeks later, on August 7, 1959, a strong armed contingent of about 200 soldiers committed a violation of the Indian border at Khinzemane (NEFA). On August 25, 1959, a strong Chinese detachment crossed in to the Subansiri Frontier Division of NEFA, encircled the Indian post at Longju and opened fire at it, killing some of the occupants.. This was followed by the Chinese letter of September 8, 1959, which claimed, for the first time, vast areas of India which had so far been vaguely included in some of the Chinese maps. Soon thereafter there was one more incident. On October 21, 1959, the Chinese forces advanced 40 to 50 miles west of the traditional Indo-Tibet border in the Chang Chenmo Valley of Ladakh and opened sudden and aggressive fire on an Indian Police patrol party, killing nine and capturing ten of its members.

Events had taken a strange turn. The monument of friendship on which India had built high hopes, had proved to be an illusion. In spite of all the sympathy for its cause, India could not save Tibet. As Nehru confessed in the Rajya Sabha, "Words like Bandung and Panchsheel had begun to lose their shine and to be hurled about without meaning, even as the word peace had become almost a thunderbolt."

18

India-China Relations

Retrospect and Prospect

C. V. Ranganathan

FOR THOSE of us who have enjoyed the privilege of dealing with China in official capacities, in this author's case from the early sixties, the transformation of prevailing negative domestic consensus on China in that decade, amongst political, intellectual and opinion making circles to a consensus seeking positive improvements in India-China relations from the mid-seventies, is a very welcome development. The reasons for the earlier negative consensus are not far to seek. Newly liberated China's actions in Tibet leading to the Dalai Lama's refuge in India, the unfolding public disputation over territorial questions and the resort to armed clashes, domestic developments within China in the later "erroneous" years of Mao Zedong, the severity of the bitter Sino-Soviet dispute were some of the causes. An autarchic inward-looking China caught up with a convulsive movement of internal destruction of institutions led to very negative perceptions in India whose charismatic leader since its Independence was driven more by idealism than by an informed understanding of a resurgent China which sought to redress what it saw as historical wrongs. The movement towards the building of a new and positive consensus on China started in the mid-seventies and it is to developments since then that this author will now turn.

In 1976, when Indira Gandhi was Prime Minister, a decision was taken to bring the abnormality in diplomatic relations between India and China to an end, which existed from 1961. This was the decision to reassign an Indian Ambassador to China after a gap of 15 years and K.R.Narayanan, our present Vice-President, was sent to China. Indira Gandhi lost her Prime Ministership in 1977 and a Janata Party Government under late Morarji Desai took over, and A.B.Vajpayee became the Foreign Minister. From this date, continuity and broad consensus with reference to China has been a constant feature of Indian foreign policy over the last two decades.

One recalls here the visit of Vajpayee, now one of the seniormost leaders of the Bharatiya Janata Party (BJP), to China at the invitation of Chinese Foreign Minister Huang Hua in February 1979. That visit was the first high level bilateral exchange between the two countries in almost two decades.

The visit of Vajpayee and the substantive results achieved in breaking the ice pertaining to frozen relations between the two countries was unfortunately overtaken by more dramatic developments pertaining to the China-Vietnam armed conflict and its negative fall-out on Indian public opinion. However, fairly soon thereafter in 1981, Foreign Minister Huang Hua visited India at the invitation of a different Government in India, this time under the Congress Party led by Indira Gandhi. That visit led to the beginning of annual dialogues at the Vice Ministerial level and restoration of relations in various fields such as trade and culture.

The visit to China of former Indian Prime Minister Rajiv Gandhi in 1988 at the invitation of Premier Li Peng is the well acclaimed turning point in India-China relations. The first visit by an Indian Prime Minister to China since 1955, that visit led to a perceptible improvement in the atmosphere. It prepared the conditions for increased mutual understanding and frequent political, economic, scientific, cultural and military exchanges. The visit also set into motion machinery to both resolve outstanding problems and expand cooperative ties in various fields of mutual interest. Following up on this visit, Chinese Premier Li Peng visited India in 1991 and former Prime Minister Rao visited China in 1993. The President of India visited China in 1992, its Vice President in 1994, its former Defence Minister in 1992 and also other leading Indian Ministers have been to China. From China, the Chairman of the National Pecple's Congress, Quiao Shi, Vice Premiers Li Raui Huan and Qian Qichen (twice), Defence

Minister Chi Haotien, Minister of Trade Wu Yi have visited India. High level Chinese dignitaries who visited India in 1990 paid tributes, both in public and in private, to Rajiv Gandhi for his initiative to open a new chapter in India-China relations, when a different government under V.P.Singh was in office then. This once again reaffirmed the consensus cutting across different political parties on the importance attached to India-China relations and the wish to sustain improved relations with China.

The vast transformation in relations leading to normalisation, is marked by the intensified political interaction at bilateral as well as multilateral fora, institutionalised negotiations on pending problems through the Joint Working Groups at the Vice Ministerial level and other official levels and the deepening of trade and economic relations. Together all this has laid the basis for a regime of confidence and security building between the two countries. This includes the firm resolution that territorial differences would be settled peacefully through negotiations and that pending such settlement, peace and tranquility would be maintained along the Line of Actual Control. The September 1993 Agreement to Maintain Peace and Tranquility along the Line of Actual Control is a major development that brings together the political achievements of diplomatic negotiations that began in 1981, the political normalisation since 1988 and programmatic discussions on Confidence Building Measures (CBMs) in the nineties. The net effect of all this is that military stability prevails all along the India-China boundary. A border security environment has been created that is the most relaxed in nearly four decades.

Since 1991 direct and regular contacts between the defence establishments of the two countries, involving exchanges of visits by the Defence Ministers, Indian Army and Naval Chiefs and groups of high ranked Generals, symbolise serious attempts by the Governments of both countries to allay suspicions inherited from the past, build up trust and confidence in each other's intentions and to bring in transparency and mutual understanding of the broader directions of military preparedness in each country. Given the background of events in the sixties, such direct communications at senior professional levels of the armed forces are invaluable inputs to the process of establishment of stable political relations between the two countries.

The next major landmark in India-China relations was the visit to India in November 1996 by President Jiang Zemin and a high level delegation which included Vice Premier and Foreign Minister Qian Qichen. Four agreements were signed during that visit:

i) Agreement on Confidence Building Measures (CBMs) in the military field along the Line of Actual Control (LAC) in the India-China border areas;

ii) Agreement concerning the Maintenance of the Consulate-General of India in the Hong Kong Special Admini-strative Region of the People's Republic of China;

iii) Agreement on Cooperation for combating illicit trafficking in narcotic drugs and psychotropic substances and other crimes; and

iv) Agreement on Maritime Transport.

The political significance of the agreement on CBMs along the LAC needs emphasis. It reflects an attitude displayed by both sides which is informed by realism and a strategic wisdom and elaborated in some details in various parts of the agreement. Earlier commitments from 1988 and 1993 not to use or to threaten the use of force against the other by any means has been expanded into a categorical avowal that neither side will use its military capability against the other side. Some of the provisions include a pledge by both sides to avoid holding large scale military exercises involving more than one division in close proximity to the LAC. Significantly if such exercises are to be conducted,the strategic direction of the main force involved shall not be towards the other side. The two sides have also agreed to reduce or limit their respective military forces within mutually agreed geographical zones along the LAC to mutually agreed ceilings. Major categories of armaments either side deployed along the LAC would be subject to ceilings. Flights of combat aircraft are prohibited within 10 kms of the LAC except by prior notification. Other provisions of the 1996 Agreement reconfirm the 1993 agreement on meetings of local commanders, exchange of information, etc.

The full implementation of this Agreement, which needs to be worked out by expert groups would go a long way to remove prejudices on both sides who still refuse to allow the events of 1962 to fade.

In calling for a cooperative and constructive partnership between India and China into the 21st Century, President Jiang Zemin indicated Chinese desire to ensure a peaceful neighbourhood in South

Asia from which all the countries could benefit. In Pakistan in an address at the Senate, he emphasised that while differences between neighbours should be settled amicably, if certain issues cannot be resolved for the time being, they may be shelved temporarily so that they will not affect the normal State-to-State relations. He pledged China's support to South Asian Regional Cooperation, the establishment of a South Asian Nuclear Free Zone and to the Indian Ocean Zone of Peace.

President Jiang Zemin has, since the death of Deng Xiaoping, become the acknowledged leader of China and holds the dominant position as the Head of State, Party and military affairs. He will be on the scene for some years to come. The visit to India by him is bound to give an all-round direction to relations in the years ahead.

A rising curve in trade and investments underpin these welcome changes in political and military spheres. Real growth in trade volumes have taken place over the last three years. While the overall trade balance favours China, India's own comfortable foreign exchange situation since the introduction of economic reforms in 1991, can sustain the potential growth in trade. In 1995-96, two-way trade between India and China is expected to cross the billion dollars mark. It is a healthy sign that businessmen in both countries frequently voice the opinion that this figure is still far below the potential of the vast economies of the two countries. The commodity basis of Indian exports is gradually diversifying and holds the promise that Indian products are increasingly acceptable to the Chinese consumer.

While determined bilateral efforts on the part of both Governments to improve relations have borne fruit from 1988 when Rajiv Gandhi visited China, the vast changes in the international environment have been conducive to the improvement in relations. The end of the Cold War followed by a common recognition of the dangers posed to large societies which are composed of diverse ethnic and cultural groups leads to sharing perceptions on challenges which face India and China. The leaderships of both countries have followed policies aimed at coming to grips with various successor States of the erstwhile Soviet Union. Good working relations between China and Russia and between India and Russia and with the Central Asian States are parallel paths to contribute to peace and stability in a vast area which is vital to both countries.

The end of the Cambodian conflict and the initial successes of the conscious policy adopted by the Rao Government in India to look eastwards have brought in its wake closer political and economic ties between India and ASEAN countries and between India and East Asian countries. The entry of India in ASEAN and ARF Fora, in which China was already present earlier, provides India and China an opportunity to interact constructively to contribute to the building of a stable political and security structure in the neighbourhood through constructive dialogue with members of the ASEAN.

Another welcome feature in contrast to past decades is the relative absence of intrusion of third country issues or issues not directly related to India and China in the overall India-China relationship. Scrupulous adherence to the Five Principles, founded by India and China, and in particular to the principle of non-interference in domestic affairs has immunised relations from various strains felt in both countries in maintaining the unity and integrity of our vast countries. Each of us does not seek to exacerbate the other's domestic problems which exist either as hold-overs of past history or which are brought about by the transitional phases of the modernisation of our vast economies.

Future Prospects

Turning to future prospects in India-China relations, we need to deepen understanding of the dynamics of each other's domestic economic development in the period after the enormous changes brought about by reforms in each country. There are so many obvious similarities our two countries share as we review our experience in reforms. At the same time we must not lose sight of the long distance our two countries have still to traverse to spread the benefits of economic reforms to vast sections of our populations.

There could be many such parallels between India and China in the challenges both countries face in the process of modernising their economies and taking the appropriate steps to facilitate their growing participation in the process of globalisation. Given the prevailing flux in the international economic situation and the evolving international trade regimes, the outstanding results achieved by the countries of South East and East Asia, the shift of international focus and attention on Asia and the Pacific and the interests of India and China, there is ample room for dialogue and exchange of experience between Indian and Chinese socio-economic experts.

Looking beyond such exercises however our experts also need to interact on growth models which are appropriate to our large continental-sized economies. Given the enormous regional disparities which have come into being in the reform era in both countries, there is evident need of following an alternate model, a middle path, which will allow vast segments of our populations to catch up with the advanced areas in our countries. Essentially this would imply the search for viable models, which would facilitate prosperity in rural areas from accessible resources, while being in harmony with overall national patterns of growth. In addition there has to be a new balance between modern technology and tradition. Advances in relevant technologies and attention to more scientific and systematised application of traditional skills may yield far greater benefits to our rural areas than the imitative practices of commercial competition that are witnessed in cosmopolitan cities. These are not areas susceptible to the application of the global-market matrix, if we search for answers from available economic models. There is therefore enormous room for a distinctive Sino-Indian approach to questions of rural and agricultural development. Such an approach would be a contribution, second only to the Five Principles. Our thinkers could set in motion a wide-ranging dialogue on these aspects.

It is common place to recognise that the trade and investment between our two countries is below the potential, impressive though the growth in these areas has been in recent years. Many conventional paths are under active exploration to increase interactions between businessmen representing various sectors and channels for enhancing trade and mutual investments. Given incomplete understanding of the circumstances in each country, the process of increasing trade and mutual investments is understandably slow. Businessmen in both countries are more comfortable dealing with traditional and long established partners, rather than invest the time, energy and money in exploring complementarities between India and China. We therefore need an infusion of fresh ideas to propel economic cooperation in areas, where each country needs the other to supplement its vast indigenous base of home-grown technologies and skills. While each of us are following parallel paths for the importation of advanced technologies for our industries and services there is not a similar effort to look at each other's rich technological achievements and inventions. We have to find institutional mechanisms to facilitate commercial interactions with respect to scientific and technological breakthrough, which each of our societies has achieved.

Lastly both India and China need to take advantage of the factors of geographical contiguity. Hitherto geo-political compulsions have prevailed at the cost of geo-economic objectives. In recent years China has setup diverse transborder linkages across China's borders in all directions. The time has come in India-China relations to explore possibilities of such linkages between the two countries. While a beginning has been made in border trade between India and the Tibet Region of China, more points remain to be opened. To the east of India and to the south-west of China there is a vast populated region, including Myanmar and some countries in ASEAN, where India and China could cooperate in building up infrastructural and communication linkages, trade and investments to the benefit of the area as a whole. Our two governments and leaders of trade and industry should open up to the realities of geo-economics in order to bring the needed development to an important area in the neighbourhood of our countries.

19

Indo-Myanmar Relations

Scope and Limitations

B. Raman

INDIA'S RELATIONS with Myanmar under the State Law and Order Restoration Council (SLORC), as the ruling military Government is called, have passed through three phases.

In the initial phase, between 1988 and 1991, India made no secret of its moral support for the pro-democracy forces and expressed itself in favour of a peaceful transition to democracy. While the embassies in the two countries continued to function, bilateral interactions were disrupted.

The second period from 1991 to 1993 saw a re-appraisal by the Government of India of its policy. It was caused by an increase in the activities of the insurgent groups of India's North-East from sanctuaries in Myanmar. There have been reports of contacts of some of these insurgents like the Bodos and the United Liberation Front of Assam (ULFA) with the Karen insurgents through Thailand and the smuggling of arms and ammunition allegedly procured from smugglers in Cambodia by sea to Bangladesh with the help of the Mon insurgents of Myanmar.

This re-appraisal led during the third phase after 1993 to a re-activation of official level contacts with the SLORC to promote co-operation in dealing with trans-border insurgency and narcotics smuggling.

In 1994, the two countries reportedly agreed to the establishment of VHF communication between the Indian border post at Moreh in Manipur and the Myanmarese post at Tamu in the Upper Chindwin District. This was for the exchange of information on narcotics smuggling and joint operations for trapping narcotics smugglers through controlled delivery of narcotics. However, there have been no significant results as yet on the ground in respect of counter-insurgency.

The bilateral interactions on trans-border insurgency and narcotics control were followed by increased contacts to promote trade across the border as well as by air and sea. There has consequently been an improvement in bilateral trade mainly due to increased Indian imports of teak and wood products. For its imports, Myanmar continues to rely on China, Singapore and Japan. As a result, the balance of trade has been heavily adverse to India. In 1995-96, India's exports to Myanmar amounted to Rs. 85 crore only as against imports from Myanmar worth Rs. 530 crore, leaving an unfavourable balance of Rs. 445 crore. Trans-border trade, now permitted across Moreh-Tamu in the Manipur sector and Champhai-Hri in the Mizoram sector, is yet to pick up significant momentum.

As against this, in 1993-94, Myanmar's bilateral trade with China amounted to US$490 million (Rs. 17.1 billion), of which $295 million (Rs. 10.3 billion) was across the border.

In matters of trade with Myanmar, be it by air, sea or across the border, India would continue to be at a disadvantage as compared with China due to the following reasons:

i) Myanmar's foreign trade is overwhelmingly in the hands of companies owned by overseas Chinese, either exclusively or jointly with Burmese State firms controlled by the military. They prefer dealing with the overseas Chinese trading networks in the ASEAN countries, Hong Kong and Taiwan as well as businesses owned by the State or by their relatives and contacts in China. In contrast, the overseas Indian community in Myanmar (420,000) is an insignificant economic force.

ii) In the pre-1979 period, Yunnan was one of the regions preferred by Beijing for locating industries in order to protect them from the reach of the US Pacific Fleet. The preference given to the coastal regions after 1979 has not led to any diminution in the interest paid to industrial development in Yunnan. As a result, Yunnan has flourishing consumer and other industries from which cheaper-priced goods flow into Myanmar. In the past, smuggled Chinese consumer goods coming from Yunnan via the Shan and the Southern Kachin States used to sell cheaper in Manipur and Mizoram than goods manufactured in the rest of India and transported to Manipur either by air or by train/road via Dimapur. Due to the insurgency and other reasons, India has not been able to develop manufacturing industries worth the name in the North-East bordering Myanmar.

iii) The purchasing power in the Shan State is relatively much higher as compared to the Chin Hills Division, the Upper Chindwin District, the Burma Naga Hills and the Kachin State due to the large flow of drug money, the better development of the area in which the military has always had a better presence etc. This has led to better economic development of the area. On the contrary, the Chin Hills, the Upper Chindwin District, the Burma Naga Hills and the Kachin State, which would constitute the natural market for Indian consumer industries, are the most impoverished, with no economic development and with road communications and other infrastructure practically in the same state in which they were left by the British in 1948.

iv) China has always attached great priority to the upgradation of road communications between Yunnan and the Shan State of Myanmar. Apart from the strategic importance of the road networks from the military point of view, another objective was to enable the manufacturing industries in Yunnan to send their goods by road right up to Lashio. In contrast, development of road networks on our side has not received the required attention from the trade point of view and the project for the upgradation of the road link from Dimapur to Moreh has not made significant progress.

The Political Impasse

Politically, Myanmar is in an impasse with the SLORC and the pro-democracy forces, led by Daw Aung San Suu Kyi, sticking to their respective positions with no move for reconciliation. With Myanmar's admission into the ASEAN Regional Forum (ARF) and its entry into the ASEAN expected in 1997, the SLORC finds itself at least regionally, if not internationally, rehabilitated despite its misdeeds and feels itself under no pressure to make concessions to the pro-democracy forces.

Daw Aung San Suu Kyi still projects an optimistic picture of the eventuality of the success of pro-democracy forces. Her optimism is based partly on the devoted support from her followers in Myanmar despite brutal harassment by the SLORC and the determined anti-SLORC campaign of foreign-based support groups and partly on her assessment, which is now shared by some Western analysts, that Myanmar's economic development has either already reached or is about to reach a plateau. As such, it may not continue to be as attractive to foreign investors as it was till now. It remains to be seen whether this assessment proves to be correct or would turn out to be wishful thinking.

In the meanwhile, her support groups outside have stepped up pressure on Western investors to withdraw from Myanmar. Their stated objective is to make Myanmar "the South Africa of the 1990s". Since 1989, their campaign has passed through two stages. Between 1989 and 1994, in their campaign against the SLORC, they over-projected the increasing Chinese influence in the political, military and economic fields. Spectres of Myanmar as "an emerging Chinese colony", and a "second Tibet", etc., were consciously painted before the world, often with the help of obliging Western analysts. They were hoping this would provoke the West and the ASEAN into pressurising the junta to make way for the political forces.

On the contrary, these tactics proved counter-productive. Anxious not to drive the SLORC further into the hands of China, the ASEAN countries, Japan and even the West gradually ended the total isolation of Myanmar and set in motion the policy of constructive engagement. As a result, the support groups no longer play upon the Chinese factor. In their recent campaign, they have instead been projecting Myanmar as an ethical and moral issue similar to what South Africa was in the 1980s.

Would the new tactics succeed? One is skeptical because of the tremendous difficulties faced by Daw Aung San Suu Kyi. For one thing, unlike the ANC in South Africa which had built for itself a capability for achieving its objective through violent means if peaceful means failed, she has consciously abjured resort to violence. For another, the anti-apartheid movement in South Africa enjoyed the support of the third world and particularly the regional countries or frontline states, which were prepared to undergo economic hardships and risks of retaliation by the regime in South Africa for their co-operation with the ANC.

Myanmar's regional neighbours do not view the problem in the country in the same ethical or moral terms as they had viewed South Africa. They, therefore, do not feel themselves under moral pressure to help in the success of the pro-demo-cracy movement on the terms set by Daw Aung San Suu Kyi. On the contrary, in the interest of regional stability and prosperity as perceived by them, the regional countries would not be averse to democracy in SLORC colours ultimately emerging as a solution to the problem.

The Myanmarese economy cannot develop beyond certain limits without the development of the infrastructure which would entail huge investments and without currency and other structural reforms for which it would need assis-tance from the international financial institutions. While her supporters in the West have failed to prevent the oil companies from making major investments in Myanmar, they have so far succeeded in preventing any assistance for infrastructure development and structural reforms. They are hoping this would ultimately force the SLORC to seek reconciliation with her.

Would such difficulties ultimately make the army more amenable to a compromise with pro-democracy forces? If past experience is any guide, one is doubtful. For nearly 27 years, it did not hesitate to keep Myanmar in enforced isolation even if that meant tremendous hardships to the people. It may not hesitate to do so again if it feels that it is the only way of keeping power in the hands of the military.

Dilemma for India

Myanmar poses a cruel dilemma for Indian policy-makers. Influenced by her stay in India in her youth and by her admiration for India and its leaders, Daw Aung San Suu Kyi has consciously chosen the democratic path. To forsake her and her movement would be to forsake our own moral and ethical roots and our claims to the moral leadership of this region.

Unfortunately, politics is not just a moral play. We have vital strategic concerns which do not blend with our moral concerns. Northern Myanmar is the buffer of buffers between our sensitive and even now troubled North-East and Yunnan, and the Andaman and Nicobar are too close to the Tennasserim region of Myanmar for comfort. An impoverished, ill-governed Myanmar, with large pockets of political, administrative and military vacuum in these regions thereby leading to Chinese inroads or a better-governed, prosperous Myanmar owing the better governance and prosperity largely to the

Chinese with a consequent increase in their influence would equally add to the threats to our security and vulnerability.

How to safeguard our strategic interests while at the same time ensuring that our moral leadership is not diluted and that the hopes of Daw Aung San Suu Kyi and her followers who look up to India are not belied? That is the question before our policy-makers. Anyone who claims to have a totally satisfactory answer to this question would be less than honest with him/herself. However, putting all eggs in the SLORC basket, in deference to our strategic concerns, could prove counter-productive. While not diluting our interactions with the junta, we should build up and strengthen the network of our relationships with the pro-democracy elements inside Myanmar as well as abroad--not for helping them in their campaign against the SLORC, but for bringing the two together for promoting national reconciliation.

After the recent reconciliation between a section of the Filippino Muslims and the Manila Government in which Indonesia played an important behind-the-scene role, there has been talk that Indonesia and possibly other ASEAN countries too could play a similar role in promoting reconciliation in Myanmar. Culturally, Myanmar has more in common with India than with any of the ASEAN countries, barring Thailand. It would be a thousand pities if India finds itself reduced to the sidelines due to lack of vision and inaction. India and Thailand could play a more beneficial role in this regard than any other country. Encouraging Myanmar to associate itself with the SAARC could also further this goal.

20

Indo-Pak Relations

Prognosis and Options

Brig. (Retd.) A. G. Krishnaiah

THE COMMUNAL violence and holocaust that followed immediately after the partition of the Indian subcontinent into India and Pakistan ironically due to a generally non-violent freedom movement, the distrust and disbelief of Pakistan in its own identity as a nation State in the wake of religion-based two nation theory, and obsession with Kashmir to perpetuate its survival as a viable political unit, continue to haunt bilateral relations between India and Pakistan. Never in the history of nations, the division of a natural, geographical and historical entity was force-broken and accepted as a political alternative against all strategic calculations to carve out a smaller nation for Muslims, when equally large number of them preferred to stay back in India. The characteristic treachery with which Pakistan launched its invasion backed by Pathan and Afridi tribesmen to annex Jammu and Kashmir within less than three months of its birth in October 1947, created a permanent hiatus that punctuated bilateral relations ever since. The three Indo-Pak wars, the ongoing proxy-war launched by Pakistan in the state of Jammu and Kashmir and Pakistani Inter Services Intelligence's (ISI) covert campaigns covering many facets affecting India's integrity, secularism and sovereignty to break up political cohesion, communal harmony and defence preparedness, have all influenced shaping a firmer base for the development of normal State-to-State relations between the two countries. The other characteristic includes Pakistan's much-vaunted view of equality and parity with larger India, its alignment with the USA in a self-seeking effort of military preparedness exclusively to force military solutions on India, its equation with other Islamic countries to periodically discredit India's well established secular credentials and above all its fear of assimilation in the event of normalisation of trade, cultural, social and other people-to-people contacts in the subcontinent, continue to vitiate political, diplomatic and economic harmony that should exist amongst nations. The underlying causes of confrontation with and animosity against India may not be eliminated with the solution of Kashmir problem but will have to be found based on more lasting platforms of mutual coexistence, religious tolerance and non-interference in each others' internal affairs, with a total commitment to the territorial integrity of both nations. The cognisance of the strategic security spectrum of South Asia as a region in its entirety can only form a mutually advantageous and continuing framework within which the Indo-Pak relations will have to be orchestrated. In this context, the sensitivities of much larger country — India and all other smaller nations including Pakistan will have to be articulated on a regional basis without extra territorial influences and other extraneous considerations. A right and earnest beginning in this direction is yet to be clearly charactered and progressed and this will stem mainly from sagacious and pragmatic political understanding, recognizing the realities of strategic compulsions and economic imperatives of South Asia in particular perspective and of individual countries in general objective. Though a good start has been initiated through South Asian Association for Regional Cooperation (SAARC), it has yet to fructify to its full potential, the main obstacle being Pakistan's intransigence and procrastination.

Kashmir Issue

Forced by Pakistan sponsored tribal invasion to annex J & K State, the otherwise hesitant Maharaja acceded to India, which remains irrevocable to date. Seeking military solutions to integrate the State to bolster its Islamic domain in the region, sui generis, Pakistan, *inter alia,* unfolded its three-fold strategy. One, the annexation of Muslim majority J & K State will substantially enhance its identity as well as geographical area and give a degree of legitimacy to the unviable Pakistan as a nation. Second, the success of this violent adventure would have assured Pakistan leadership amongst the Muslims of the world in general and Indian Muslims in particular. Lastly, and most importantly acquiescence and forced acceptance by the then utopian Indian leadership would have provided much-sought-after *raison d'etre* for the balkanisation of India through eventual targeting of Muslim populated areas in the name of Jehad and Umma with Pakistan as the leader of the flock. These feudal designs and inchoate foreign policy perceptions appear to underline Pakistan's thinking in its bilateral relations and dominate its responses on trade, cultural and other issues. Emboldened by their perceived success in the withdrawal of the Soviet troops from Afghanistan and encouraged by the events that led to the disintegration of the former Soviet Union, Pakistan masterminded Operation 'TOPAC' to systematically incapacitate Indian military power through a well-planned and thought-out "three phase" plan. The death of General Zia in August 1988 did not lead to the abandonment of this vicious scheme but found its activation with more concerted efforts through the 1990s. Even as the phase one of TOPAC is being actively pursued by Pakistan ISI, a vigorous and forceful response by the Indian security forces over a period of six years led to holding of peaceful elections and restoration of elected Government under Farooq Abdullah, notwithstanding the fact that militant activity is being still supported by Pakistan and its ISI.

On the other hand, India being a large country of South Asia with internationally avowed and credible secular credentials, could ignore Pakistan 1947 invasion only at the peril to its integrity and sovereignty. Despite its overall known capability to force a destructive withdrawal on Pakistan, India, for reasons of international image and protection/projection of political ideals of Indian leadership, accepted a UN sponsored tenuous but holding ceasefire leading to a constant source of threat to bilateralism and drain on our developmental programmes, besides being a *casus belli* for Pakistan military adventurism. As time passed and after 50 years of Independence both countries find themselves in a quagmire of Himalayan proportion. Neither of the two nations could now grant any concessions least the Government (or party in power) doing so, be completely mauled and consigned to flames in the frenzy of respective domestic politics. While status quo sucks Pakistan into a continuing anti-India syndrome characterised by confrontation and distrust preventing logical development of good neighbourly relations, any change except in their favour is not likely to be accepted by either of the two nations. This peculiar situation continues to be an impasse in Indo-Pak bilateral relations. The rapid strides in media processes with extensive access to common public and acute political awareness, combined with the ability of the opposition parties to exploit people's sensitivities and nationalist emotions would make it difficult for any Government to find an acceptable formula by mutual adjustments and concessions. In the context of the Indian stand of J&K being an inalienable part of India, the Kashmir problem now essentially revolves around the issue of the return of Pakistan-occupied areas. This would stand unaltered unless a pragmatic Pakistan Government sees in its wisdom, probably under compelling circumstances, the need to vacate its unprovoked aggression of 1947 and then, then only, bargain for any territorial or other adjustments, which could however be negotiated before such return to pre-August 1947 position. As this is unlikely to happen in the foreseeable future, Kashmir would be an unmitigated and severe source of irritant in bilateral relations.

The US Connection

Since 1950, the USA, initially considered Pakistan as a fulcrum in its strategy towards containment of communism and later as an essential conduit and adjunct in its Afghan and West Asian policies targeted in limiting the influence of the former Soviet Union. As Pakistan played a willing part for a price in terms of supply of military hardware essentially, it had even manipulated the US support to further its military designs against India. The defence assistance programme of 1950s — the famous four and a half division militarisation plan coupled with the provision of Sabre jets to its Air Force and Patton tanks to the army was mainly responsible for Pakistan's aggressiveness during 1965, leading to a major war. Despite embargoes by the USA during 1965 and 1971 wars, an undercurrent of active political and defence cooperation always underlined the US-Pak relations. The Soviet occupation of Afghanistan provided an ideal opportunity to bolster declining bilateral relations and the US acquiesced in more ways than one to enlist Pakistan cooperation to further its strategic interests in the region. Their nuclear programme, Chinese missile technology transfers, human rights violations, political vendetta against Mohajirs and ethnic violence have all been deliberately ignored and silently viewed. The waiver of the US Pressler Amendment during 1995 enabling supply of embargoed military hardware is a reflection of reactivation of defence and alliance relationships with Pakistan and is a part of overall American strategic response in the post cold war era in the Central, West and South Asia. Such US-Pak relations would impact on Indo-Pak relations as Pakistan always became intransigent and truculent and even went to war whenever the US support was at its zenith to force a military solution on Kashmir. Some salient issues that may have influenced reactivation of the US-Pak connection in the region affecting India may include the following :

- The strategic requirement of a close time-tested and willing "ally" to provide support facilities (defence and aerial coverage, a la U-2 flights in 50s and 60s and intelligence operations) bordering the Soviet dominated Central Asian Republics, Afghanistan and emerging super-power, China.
- Growing strategic and economic relations of Russia with China and India provides an ideal opportunity for the threat-starved USA to initiate responses providing perpetuity to its uni-polar stature; in this, Pakistan plays a vital role in the region especially to further the US interests in its Afghan Policy. This is the reason for deliberate American and Western tolerance and even tacit support to blatant and flagrant interference in Afghanistan to establish a pro-USA albeit Islamic fundamentalist Government.
- Play up of Indo-Pak relationships in an effort to prevent emergence of India as an economic and power centre in South Asia and Indian Ocean Zone (IOZ) and enable ever eager and opportunity seeking Pakistan in any destabilization and balkanisation process of India, when considered appropriate in the aforesaid scenario.
- Prevent close defence, economic and regional collaboration with Iran in consonance with the US Iranian policy.

While the US interest in Pakistan may be to meet its strategic objectives of Russian and Chinese containment, economic compulsions and preventing emergence of regional power centres, Pakistan would derive major advantages in pursuing its nuclear weapon programme, missile acquisition plans and continuing its proxy war in the J&K with tacit but silent support from the USA. These do not augur well for normal evolution of Indo-Pak relations and we need to consider them in the formulation of our policy perceptions *vis-a-vis* Pakistan.

Sino-Pakistan Axis

As against characteristic vicissitudes in the US-Pak alliance, the emergence of Sino-Pakistan relationship has all along been stable, pragmatic, all encompassing and more responsive to Pakistan aspirations. As India-China 1962 war provided the expected spark to fuel Chinese South Asian perspective, Pakistan entered into an unholy but mainly defence collaboration to strengthen its anti-India campaign to keep the latter embroiled in a bleeding feud and confrontation and maintain "balance of power" in the sub-continent, Pakistan felt gratified to see its might militarily boosted. India's immediate attention continued to focus on threat from a much smaller country diverting from a larger, long-term and more vicious designs and "strategic encirclement" by China to keep India generally isolated in South Asia itself and containing it as such politically, militarily and even economically. Pakistan initiation of 1965 and 1971 wars with India was based on its perceptions of specific and positive support from China, though naivety of such an understanding was proved to be its undoing. While the Sino-Pakistan alliance and defence relationships are to be considered as any normal State-to-State relations, strategists and policy makers will have to always see through the true meaning of apparent normalities — generally unpublicised with a view to protecting national interests and vital areas by developing responsive policies and strategies. While China may positively maintain a degree of non-interference with limited diplomatic and threatening postures in any Indo-Pak adverse and war-like situation, one cannot and should not expect a similar Pakistan stance in any such India-China situation. Pakistan will leave no-stone-unturned to exploit such an adverse situation ruthlessly to further its own known objectives. The ceding of about 2000 square miles area in Pakistan Occupied Kashmir (POK) to China involved the latter in an otherwise bilateral issue. The Chinese strategic objectives - which define India as one of the potential threat areas in South Asia need to be analysed in proper perspective to clearly discern joint Sino-Pakistan anti-India propensities and orientations so that Indo-Pak relations can be developed in the desired direction to further Indian policy perceptions.

Pakistan Psyche

While it is not the intention to trace out the history of both 1965 and 1971 Indo-Pak wars and apportion the blame for these conflicts, it is necessary to identify Pakistan's compulsions and strategies forcing her to launch pre-emptive wars on both the occasions so that one can deduce with a degree of certainty the Pakistan national psyche and ethos that guides its foreign policy specially towards India. Without a fair view of Pakistani intentions, it may be difficult to evolve a responsive and pragmatic policy towards that country. Though 1948 invasion may not technically be termed as a full-fledged war, this was the immediate reflection and spontaneous response to the Pakistan national leadership to settle the J&K issue in their favour by use of military force and present a *fait accompli* to India and force international recognition. Such instinctive national responses have dangerous connotations that need to be addressed in their entirety.

Some of Pakistan's visualisations and perceptions to initiate these conflicts are:

- Despite the Panchsheel and the Gujral Doctrine now, Pakistan views India as an usurper of Pakistan Islamic and other Muslim rights, holds it in contempt to disparage its image at every domestic, regional and international fora and seeks to exploit India's perceived vulnerabilities through military force and proxy war to further its national objectives and vital interests.
- The settlement of Kashmir problem alone may not lead to true normalisation of bilateral relations. The issues of support to Indian Muslims, the treatment of Mohajirs (original Indian Muslims) in Pakistan, the trade arrangements, external influences by the USA and China and above all domestic compulsions to retain political cohesion, unity and internal harmony would continue to force Pakistan to maintain its anti-India syndrome for a long time to come.
- Pakistan military hierarchy, which has great stakes to maintain its strength and hold in internal governance may not willingly allow restoration of good neighbourliness with India.
- Pakistan harping on a solution of the Kashmir problem first is really meant a settlement favourable to and on its terms only. Pakistan is unlikely to be sensitive to the strategic concerns of India. Despite their public overtures and known stands, the USA and China would like, as a normal strategy of statecraft, to allow Kashmir issue to continue to haunt India, with a view to preventing latter's emergence as a regional power centre.
- Whenever Pakistan feels militarily strong with assured external support and perceives India's political, economic and military vulnerabilities, it will endeavour to force a military solution specially on the Kashmir issue.
- Pakistan always feels threatened by mightier and powerful Hindu India and utilises every possible opportunity to reduce

such threat levels by a process of political, economic and military destabilisation and if possible, balkanisation, to maintain permanent peace in the sub-continent.

While it is pragmatic to be aware of likely Pakistan strategic thinking, it will be prudent to articulate Indo-Pak relations in such a way as to cater for possible adverse eventualities. Diplomatic nuances and development of bilateral relations based on mutual trust and economic well being of the people should, however, continue to be the sheet anchor of our foreign policy initiatives. Indian defence preparedness and capabilities, to thwart Pakistan designs, as and when they unfold, should be essential ingredients of our military strategy.

The issue of minorities in India and Pakistan of Muslims and Hindus respectively has always been governed by emotional and religious considerations with subterranean strong political undercurrents. Pakistan by a deliberate and well orchestrated social, political and economic pressure manipulations has almost cleansed its country of Hindus to almost 1.5 per cent of its total populace, whereas in India, Muslims form 14 per cent population — may be slightly larger than the total Muslim population in Pakistan itself. Ironically, India remains a mute helpless spectator to the recent influx of Bangladeshi Muslims to India. When we refer to the issue of minorities in the Indo-Pak context, it is essentially Pakistan's perception about Indian Muslims and efforts to arrogate to itself the leadership and spokesmanship of Muslim Umma of Indian sub-continent. The issue of Hindu minority in Pakistan, has generally been limited to the destruction of Indian shrines, as and when some issues flare up in India involving Muslims. With almost largest Muslim population in South Asia, India should be the centre of Islamic culture and act as a watchdog to obviate fundamentalist orientation vitiating the culture and ethos of Muslims in the Indian sub-continent. Though, this is a laudable ideal, it may not find ready acceptance even from the majority of Indian Muslims. It should not however, deter us, as a secular democracy, to raise our voice in support of oppressed Muslims in the region.

Some of the issues that merit our serious consideration and action are :

- Suppression of women's rights in the name of Shariat should be opposed and meaningful publicity campaign should be launched under Indian Islamic auspices.

- The denial of Muslim status to some known Islamic sects like Ahmadias should be questioned at appropriate international Islamic fora and necessary religious *fatwas* or injunctions should be issued against the government of Pakistan.
- Mohajirs are original Indian Muslims with their roots still entrenched mostly in Bihar, Uttar Pradesh, and Hyderabad. They were the ones who fought and got Pakistan. Denial of their legitimate rights in that country and suppression and elimination campaigns by Pakistan security force, should be of natural and serious concern to India. The need to ensure proper civilized response by Pakistan government towards them should be taken up.
- The political exploitation of Sikhs and a small number of Hindu pilgrims to visit shrines and worship in Pakistan should be stopped.

SAARC and Bilateral Trade

The evolution of SAARC in South Asia is a significant development aimed at cooperation mainly in economic, cultural, communications and other areas amongst the seven number states. It should have been logical to enhance the level of cooperation in all fields of industrial and economic development. While some progress has been made, the South Asian Preferential Trade Agreement (SAPTA) has yet to take off to optimise full potential of regional economic cooperation. Pakistan's hesitation in reciprocating specially with India, appears to have stalled Indo-Pak bilateral trade. It may be noted that informal trade between India and Pakistan is of the order of Rs.2,000 crore annually. Only the consumer in Pakistan gains and the Pakistan government revenue suffers. Reciprocity in trade is an essential ingredient for harmonious and healthy growth of bilateral trade on a long term basis. Pakistan's reluctance to open up its "trade gates" to India despite several mutual advantages, underlines its suspicion of possible assimilation of its smaller economy into larger Indian economic super-structure. It is, therefore, essential that integration of Pakistan into South Asian cooperative structure should be essentially through the route of SAARC. While Pakistani corporate houses, industrial organisations and business community generally appear to be enthusiastic of bilateral trade, Pakistan's political leadership and civilian and military bureaucracies are hesitant to take the right leap forward. Historical perspectives and machinations of vested interests more than economic compulsions are the obstacles towards the positive movement in this direction. Concerted diplomatic efforts coupled with extensive people-to-people contacts would, in the long run, yield and bring about much needed change in Pakistan outlook. All available economic factors indicate that there is an increasing awareness amongst Pakistan public in general and the business community in particular for enhanced bilateral cooperation with India. What is required is the political will and direction to overcome bureaucratic hurdles by strong Pakistani national leadership. Any progress in this regard would have favourable impact on otherwise threat-based and eye-for-eye bilateral Indo-Pak relations.

The Military Line-Up

Instead of tabulating the known force and military hardware levels of India and Pakistan, we seek to highlight some important aspects that have long range impact on defence analysis and appreciation. Firstly, Pakistan's fixation to seek "parity" with India and "equate" their force levels in comparative terms. Secondly, while entire Pakistani military capabilities can be applied against India, India has a "three front" security commitment as Pakistan and China constitute two major "fronts" which need to be addressed simultaneously; and the "third front" being the internal security commitment in eastern and northern/ western India.

Despite vast and qualitative as well as quantitative differences in threat levels and perceptions, Pakistan's efforts to seek "force level equality" is a well-contrived publicity stunt both to show India's military preponderance and its lower and inadequate force structure with a view to enlisting support of the USA and Western nations to secure defence assistance. Some general "criteria yardstick" to analyse security commitment of individual countries need to be considered to judge the issue in proper perspective.

	India	**Pakistan**
Borders with neighbours (in kms)	15,500	6,500
Coastline to be guarded (-do-)	7,700	1,400
Economic exclusive zone-EEZ (sq.kms.)	2.1m	0.3m

Pakistan with almost one-fourth of security commitments is seeking parity with India and many defence strategists accept this on its face value. A broad analysis would reveal that:

- Pakistan spends about 36 per cent of its central revenue on defence compared to about 12 per cent in India. Its military spending is as much as $2.8 per person as against $0.7 by India.
- Presently, Indian defence forces have a minimum of two front obligations which inter alia require them to protect the security of borders both with China and Pakistan; a strategic concurrent commitment.
- Comparatively, Indian forces have much heavier internal security commitments on their borders with no such major requirement for Pakistan.
- Number of soldiers deployable per km of border would be 65 soldiers on Indian side and 80 on Pakistan side with a definite advantage to Pakistan in that it needs deployment of regular soldiers only on half of its border with India, with Iran and Afghanistan being "no-threat" borders for a foreseeable future.

As Pakistan has strategic advantage in the deployment of its forces whose peacetime locations are just near the borders, it derives considerable force-multiplier effect to enhance its war waging capabilities. However, what is more important in this scenario is that specious argument and proposal by Pakistan harping on "reduction" of force-levels which would further degrade already inadequate force structure of India.

A significant factor affecting the overall prosperity of both the countries is their large defence budgets. While India should "freeze" its force levels at the present scale, there is every scope for Pakistan, whose economy is fully stretched and at the breaking point, to "curtail" its force levels and its defence budget. As Pakistani force structure is reorganised based on progressive demobilisation of forces, simultaneous verifiable mechanisms with utmost transparency can be put in place to assure Pakistan's integrity and inviolability of its international borders with India. Pakistan needs to take Indian guarantees with all seriousness they deserve and enhance the overall well being of its people. This is one of the peaceful options Pakistan has, should it wish to steer a course on good neighbourliness and prosperity. Sheer dependence on inadequate military might will in any case, not enhance Pakistan's security and sovereignty.

The Gujral Doctrine

The articulation of a good neighbourhood policy in August 1996 by Mr. I. K. Gujral contains major elements of Panchsheel duly incorporated and has come to be known as "The Gujral Doctrine". Of the five critical ingredients of the doctrine, four stand violated and continue to be so, by Pakistan. Firstly, Pakistan Occupied Kashmir, NWFP, the Punjab States of Pakistan are being used for operation of training camp for Kashmiri militants. There were known to be about 120 such camps in Pakistan at the height of insurgency. Similar facilities were being extended to Taliban. Secondly, by launching a proxy war in Kashmir, abetting Punjab extremists, supporting fundamentalist Muslim elements to vitiate Hindu-Muslim amity in India and its ISI operations reflect direct and blatant interference in the internal affairs of India. Thirdly, by claiming constitutionally and legally acceded State of J&K and occupying part of this State by armed aggression, Pakistan violated the territorial integrity and sovereignty of India. Fourthly, by seeking military solution of the Kashmir issue and harping on third party mediation, the question of peaceful bilateral negotiations stands rudely shaken by Pakistan. What is left of the doctrine for Pakistan is India giving all it can in good faith and trust without asking for reciprocity; hoping for the best.

The Gujral Doctrine as such should form an ideal base for economic cooperation and strategic partnership of the group of the countries in South Asia, provided the countries involved are prepared to follow its key elements and not violate them. In the case of Nepal, Bangladesh, Bhutan, Maldives, and even Myanmar, the applicability and relevance must be appreciated. In case of the Indo-Pak relations the same has no relevance as of today all the four major provisions stand completely trampled by Pakistan. A South Asian initiative for adopting the basic elements of Gujral Doctrine as a policy for all the regional countries may be called for. Such an initiative could form part of SAARC objectives. Only combined diplomatic efforts can convince Pakistan of the genuineness of the Doctrine for the ultimate peace in the sub-continent. Such a move would enlarge both the scope and nature of association of SAARC.

The lamentable course of the Indo-Pak relations since 1947 was beset and interspersed with long interruptions and intense strain a la the pangs of their violent birth. India has all along followed a defensive posture in its responses to Pakistan's aggressive diplomatic as well military movements and designs. The result is that what would have been a closed chapter in 1948 was allowed to torment bilateral relations during the last 50 years. It is time to analyse the underlying causes and identify options so as to set harmonious and mutually beneficial tone in our relationship. The Pakistani psyche and ethos towards bilateral relations with India will have to undergo a drastic change. The latter has set the ball rolling by the timely enunciation of the Gujral Doctrine, which could be the first stepping stone to initiate measures in this direction *de novo*. Some of the issues that may come to impair such a process may be the following estimates of Pakistan's responses.

- In the overall interests of both nations, the Kashmir issue will have to be placed on the back-burner. Pakistan will have to accept development of normal relations without making Kashmir a prestige or core issue, as it defies an immediate solution. This is unlikely to be accepted on its own volition by Pakistan.

- Pakistan, as a minimum and elementary response, should stop its proxy war in J&K. It must stop all types of support to anti-national elements in India specially Punjab, and North-East. Pakistani political leadership may be powerless to do this in the immediate future.

- Pakistan's support to fundamentalist Islamic elements must stop. Supply of arms, ammunition, explosives and funds will be an "Act of War" against India's integrity and secularism. Pakistan's political will for a reversal of such a policy is debatable.

- Pakistan should see the strategic realities of South Asia in the correct perspective. The security interests of India — the major player in the region, need to be given due consideration. Pakistan will have to confine its geographical limits to the four States of Punjab, NWFP, Baluchistan and Sindh. India will have to extend adequate guarantees to ensure such territorial integrity. The more Pakistan insists on J&K and on the leadership of Muslim Umma specially Indian Muslims, the more will be the strains on already eroded Indo-Pak relations. The writing on the wall must be seen clearly in the interests of the well being and prospects of common people. Pakistan may not toe the line of such a strategic perception in the near future unless it becomes a "failed" State, the hazy signs of which are on the horizon.

- Pakistan's fixation for "parity" and "equation" with economically stronger, militarily mightier and politically stable India will lead to its ultimate ruination. It will have to abandon such a course in the interests of its own people. The earlier it happens, the better it is for the region. The moot question is whether Pakistan will see the reason?

- India did not respond to Pakistan's constant and blatant interferences in India's internal affairs, and its efforts to internationalise Kashmir issue in a way that a big and powerful neighbour should have. The "Right of Pursuit" into and launching of "Punitive Actions" against terrorist training camps — a normal defensive reaction - had not been exercised. The internal situation of Pakistan involving Mohajirs and Sindhis in Sindh, Saraikis in Punjab, Shia-Sunni sectarian differences and ethnic differences in the NWFP and Baluchistian have not been, by a deliberately taken policy decision, exploited in any retaliatory and revengeful responses. A host of other counter actions would have led to Pakistan's disintergration and balkanisation. Yet, Pakistan, on every small available pretext humiliates India, be it malicious harassment of innocent diplomatic personnel and exploitation of religious pilgrims to shrines — leave alone its constant support to Kashmir, Punjab, and North-East extremists or supply of arms and explosives to Islamic fundamentalists in India. A well articulated campaign involving the Ministries of External Affairs, Information and Broadcasting, Home, Defence and other agencies should be launched to make a positive impact on the people of Pakistan and more importantly on their Government and Army. A change in the national outlook of Pakistan eschewing violent and clandestine means to interfere in India's internal affairs is a *sine qua non* for a healthy development of our bilateral relations. On Pakistan's cooperation and her will to follow a normal good neighbourhood relations would help the well being of the common man in Pakistan, who is groaning under the weight of the civil and military bureaucracies and ever increasing erosion of revenues through expanding defence budgets.

As a country with a long history of peaceful governance for the welfare of their people, India has been exercising every restraint against Pakistan and should continue to do so in the future. Our ultimate political objective in South Asia is to establish the rule of international and regional laws, in which all countries are guaranteed of their territorial integrity and sovereignty. Joint economic and culture endeavours aimed at the prosperity and well being of poverty-stricken people should underline the SAARC efforts. India should continue to originate confidence building measures by taking the unilateral initiatives, as hitherto. More transparency in our defence, nuclear and missile capabilities may be thought of, to make it clear to Pakistan the futility of following a course of confrontation with India and the need for a peaceful coexistence and good neighbourly relations. The State-to-State dealings are to be from a plank of equality with no "Big Brother" syndrome, business like and above all "statesmen like". Then only South Asia will again be at the center stage as was the case in the past. As a policy, some of the options that may be considered for India may, inter alia, include the following:

- The policy of tolerance and understanding of Pakistan's sensitivities should continue to dominate our foreign policy responses. The sincerity of our policies of peace and economic development need to be made more transparent and acceptable to Pakistan through a series of diplomatic campaigns, political interactions, cultural exchanges and people-to-people contacts. The Kashmir issue needs to be left as it is for seeking a solution at a later point of time.

- The pace of normalisation of economic and cultural relations through the SAARC and SAPTA should be accelerated by mutual consultations and understanding. India will have to take the initial steps to dispel Pakistan's distrust and suspicions. The Gujral Doctrine and earlier principles of Panchsheel could form the basis, to start with.

- Be that as it may, Pakistan may continue its clandestine assistance and proxy efforts to expand its support base in Kashmir, specially under the garb of favourable response to India's peaceful overtures. We should strengthen our warning and intelligence systems in India particularly in the border States of J&K, Punjab and Rajasthan. We should not lower our guard, as we are usually wont to do.

- Pakistan's involvement in Afghanistan and emerging developments there are of strategic as well as immediate concern to us. Should Pakistan succeed in its efforts to establish pro-Pakistan and pro-Western Taliban-led government, be it fundamentalist, Pakistan will be emboldened with expected tacit understanding of the USA to again experiment similar strategy in Kashmir. We need to articulate a pragmatic Afghan policy so as to steer the Indo-Pak relations on an anticipated course. The nuances of Indian diplomacy will be put to severe test to create favourable environment in a complex situation.

- We need to take unilateral measures — with or without Pakistan, as a part of the SAARC and independently - to develop cordial relations with other member countries of South Asia. Agreements on Ganga waters with Bangladesh and on water and power with Nepal are right steps in this direction. Paradoxically, such steps may form part of confidence building measures with Pakistan to dispel its distrust of India.

- Interestingly, our strong and close relations with Iran, Afghanistan and China would have a favourable impact on the Indo-Pak relations. Our stand on Afghanistan may have to be activated. The India-China relations will have to be further underscored with increasing economic content and cultural initiatives. A responsive relationship with Iran will be a contributory factor for better Indo-Pak relations.

The Indo-Pak relations are based not only on exclusive self-interests of respective countries but Pakistan susceptibilities to the US, Islamic and Chinese influences that have come to exercise an overriding influence in their shaping and chartering. This makes its course extremely complex and changing perceptions of extra-territorial powers and interests would subject it to unpredictable stress and interruptions. Concurrent with the evolution and progress of the Indo-Pak relations is the inescapable requirement of taking appropriate counter measures and initiatives against surprising possibilities of behind-the-back, unpublicised and silent anti-India actions, be it in Kashmir, Punjab or support to fundamentalistic elements. A longer period of peace and tranquillity specially in the border and frontier regions may be the only answer to dispel such continuing Indian suspicions. Despite the ominous beginning at the time of Independence and good neighbourhood policy, the Gujral Doctrine can provide the spark to make such an auspicious beginning now.

PART IV

Welfare of The People

- Nehru's Concept of Secularism and Communalism
- Gender Equality Through Women's Empowerment
- Emancipation of Scheduled Castes and Scheduled Tribes
- Welfare of Backward Classes
- Minorities in Free India

21

Nehru's Concept of Secularism and Communalism

Dr. Asghar Ali Engineer

IN THIS FIFTIETH year of our Independence it is highly necessary for us to be aware of what the Founding Fathers of our nation thought on the basic issues and how far those thoughts are relevant to us. Among those who laid the intellectual foundation of our nationhood, Jawaharlal Nehru was, no one can deny, among the most important one. And among the founding values of Indian nationhood, secularism was the most important value. Though secularism was accepted as the founding philosophy of Indian National Congress from the very beginning, no one had systematically theorised about it as Nehru did. Secularism at the initial stages of the founding of the Indian National Congress was nothing more than giving proportional representation to the members of various communities.

It was Mahatma Gandhi, Jawaharlal Nehru and Maulana Azad who applied their minds and propounded systematic ideas about secularism though from different perspectives. While Mahatma Gandhi and Abul Kalam Azad thought from their respective religious perspective, Nehru was the first person to accept the Western notion of secularism and strongly advocated the cause of separation of religion from politics. His ideas about secularism found great approval among the intellectual elites in the country. Not only that Nehru's secularism found acceptance among the minorities as well, particularly the Muslims. It is quite interesting to note that Jawaharlal Nehru was always looked upon by the Muslims, both orthodox as well as those modernised, as their protector. No wonder than that in post-Independence India, Muslims generally voted for the Congress led by Nehru despite its poor record of governance and even of protecting minorities. Nehru's intellectual struggles against communalism had greatly attracted them (the Muslims).

In view of importance of Nehru's seminal intellectual contribution to the Indian secularism it is necessary to throw some light on his ideas and struggles for promoting it. It is particularly more important to acquaint the post-Independence generation of Indians with Nehru's contribution to Indian secularism. It needs to be stressed here that though Nehru was agnostic and consequently indifferent to religion he was fully aware of the contribution of religion to Indian socie-ty and its grip over the minds and hearts of Indian people. He fully acknowledged the role of religion in Indian society. It is in this light that his reply to a query on secularism by a student at the Oxford in the mid-fifties should be seen.

When an Indian student asked him as to how he will define secularism in the Indian context, Nehru replied, "equal protection by the State to all religions" which was quite an insightful answer keeping in view the Indian conditions. It was for this reason that even those who had profound faith in religion were also attracted towards Nehruvian concept of secularism. However, in his personal views, Nehru was not only indifferent to religion but even hostile to the organised religion.

Thus he observes in his write-up "Religion, Man and Society" in *An Autobiography* (Allied Publishers, 1962, pp,374-80)"... organised religion, whatever its past may have been, today is very largely an empty form devoid of real content. Mr.G.K.Chesteston has compared it ... to a fossil which is the form of an animal or organism from which all its own organic substance has entirely disappeared, but which has kept its shape, because it has been filled up by some totally different substance. And even where something of value still remains, it is enveloped by other and harmful contents."

Thus it will be seen that he was strongly opposed to organised religion, if not to personal belief in religion. We do not know if Nehru would have revised his views in the light of contemporary re-emergence of religion on socio-political scene or these developments would have further confirmed him in his views. But one thing is sure; Nehru was far from being dogmatic. As pointed out before, he was fully aware of the hold the religion has on the minds of people. It is also interesting that Nehru personally felt closest to two profoundly religious personalities i.e. Mahatma Gandhi and Abul Kalam Azad. He held both of them in high regard and greatly valued their contribution to Indian nationalism. This shows that Nehru was not against religion *per se* but against misuse of religion for political ends.

He also clarifies his ideas about religion when he says, "Nor am I greatly interested in the after life, in what happens after death. I find the problems of this life sufficiently absorbing to fill my mind. The traditional Chinese outlook, fundamentally ethical and yet irreligious or tinged with religious scepticism, has an appeal for me, though in its application to life I may not agree. It is the *Tao,* the path to be followed and the way of life that interests me; how to understand life, not to reject it but to accept it, to confirm it and to improve it."

If anything can describe Nehru's attitude to religion it is the phrase used by him religious scepticism. Nehru was basically against dogmatism, the assertion that "this is the only truth". He was basically sceptic. He was more interested in questions pertaining to this life, affirmation of life here on earth rather than the dogmas pertaining to the life hereafter. This clearly reflects Nehru's idea of secularism in general. It was for this reason that he was greatly drawn towards Buddhism. Buddhism was more intellectually satisfying for him because Buddha rather than indulging in debates about metaphysical questions, concerned himself more with the question of removing *dukkha* i.e., suffering both in spiritual and material sense.

Nehru also maintains that "moral standards have no relation to social needs, but are based on a highly metaphysical doctrine of sin. And organised religion invariably becomes a vested interest and thus inevitably a reactionary force opposing change and progress."

Yet, it must be said that Nehru was profoundly religious in his attitude though not in terms of dogmas. Far from it, he was passionately committed to certain ideals like democracy, secularism and freedom of thought; he fought for these ideals with all the passions at his command. These were guiding principles of his life like religion to the faithful. He accepted the definition of religion given by the American philosopher John Dewey. He defined religion as "whatever introduces genuine perspective into the piecemeal and shifting episodes of existence"; and "any activity pursued in behalf of an ideal and against obstacles, and in spite of threats of personal loss, because of conviction of its general and enduring value, is religious in quality."

It is this definition of religion which described Nehru's idea of religion. He was, as pointed out, passionately committed to certain ideals, which he thought life-promoting, and fought passionately for them at the cost of his own personal loss. It is this idea of secularism which is still quite relevant to India. It promotes life-affirming values and it accepts change and progress. He also quotes French author Romain Rolland who sees true religiosity in "search for truth at all costs with single-minded sincerity prepared for any sacrifice." Such a religiosity presupposes faith in an human effort higher than the life of existing society, and even higher than the life of humanity as a whole.

Nehru's secularism was dubbed by the Bharatiya Janata Party (BJP) as "pseudo-secularism" during the mid-eighties. I think it as quite unfair to Nehru and it was nothing more than an attempt to exploit politically a half-truth that Nehru was very sympathetic to minorities. In fact Nehru was sympathetic to all the oppressed and weaker sections of society in keeping with his socialist convictions. He was not sympathetic to Muslims *per se* but as those belonging to the weaker sections. Nehru emphasises this when criticising the 14-point demand advocated by Jinnah and Mohd. Iqbal he says, "As he knows, my chief interest in politics is the raising of the masses and the removal of barriers of class and wealth and the equalization of society." And he criticised the fourteen-point demand of the Muslim League because "this point of view was apparently never considered by the framers of the fourteen points."

Nehru was sincere in condemning unyielding religious orthodoxy and communalism in all communities. He did not spare Muslim communalism though he maintained that the minority communalism is by and large defensive communalism while majority communalism besides being aggressive, is politically reactionary in character. Thus he criticises Sir Muhammad Iqbal and Aga Khan in *An Autobiography* (op.cit, p.294-95). He also severely criticises both Muslim and Hindu orthodoxy when they jointly opposed the Sarda Act on prevention of marriages of minor girls. Thus he writes satirically, "This was a joint protest by the orthodox of both religions against the Sarda Act... which prohibited marriages of girls under fourteen. The pious and the holy of both faiths had joined ranks and hands to declare that they would not submit to this outrage on their deepest convictions and most cherished rights. Were they going to be bullied by the threats of so-called reformers into giving up their right to marry child-wives? Never!"

He also writes,"... those Hindus and Muslims who are always looking backward, always clutching the things which are slipping away from their grasp, are a singularly pathetic sight. I do not wish to damn the past or to reject it, for there is so much which is singularly beautiful in our past. That will endure I have no doubt. But it is not the beautiful that these people clutch at, but something that is seldom worthwhile and is often harmful."

Criticising the Muslim communalists Nehru observes, "The British Government... gave every encouragement to the Muslim communal leaders who were politically thoroughly reactionary." But he also rightly points out, "Even so a very strong group of Muslim leaders remained throughout with the Congress." Then about the Hindu Mahasabha he writes, "Noting the success of these (Muslim) reactionaries the Hindu Mahasabha began to compete with them in reaction, thereby hoping to win the goodwill of the Government. Many of the progressive elements in the Mahasabha were driven out or left their own accord, and it inclined more and more towards the upper middle classes and especially the creditors and banker class."

He also tries to explain that the majority communalism wears the cloak of nationalism while the minority communalism appears to be separatist. "The Hindu Mahasabha", he writes, "is always laying stress on its own irreproachable nationalism when it criticises Muslim communalism. That the Muslim organisations have shown themselves to be quite extraordinarily communal has been patent to everybody. The Mahasabha's communalism has not been so obvious, as it masquerades under a nationalist cloak. The test comes when a national and democratic solution happens to injure upper class Hindu interests, and in this test the Mahasabha has repeatedly failed."

He demolishes all the claims of the communal organisations to be religious and cultural in nature. He says, "What are communal organisations? They are not religious although they confine themselves to religious groups and exploit the name of religion. They are not cultural and have done nothing for culture although they talk bravely of a past culture. They are not ethical or moral groups for their teachings are singularly devoid of all ethics and morality. They are certainly not economic groupings for there is no economic link binding their members and they have no shadow of an economic programme.

Some of them claim not to be political even." But Nehru points out, "As a matter of fact they function politically and their demands are political, but calling themselves non-political, they avoid the real issues and only succeed in obstructing the path of others."

It can be seen that Nehru was quite balanced in his condemnation of Hindu and Muslim communalism. But in post-Independence India he was more critical of Hindu communalism as it was more offensive and aggressive. However, it does not mean that he in any sense approved of Muslim communalism. Communalism, be it Hindu or Muslim, is dangerous for secular democracy and must be weeded out to maintain and strengthen its secular character. Nehru's secularism was far from fake or pseudo. He had many analytical insights into communal problem which his opponents did not have. However, Nehru's analysis of communal problem had its own limitations. He often tended to be reductionist. More-over many dimensions of communalism unfolded when democracy deepened in the Independent India. Nehru died before he could witness these aspects. He wrote on communalism more from his pre-Independence experiences rather than post-Independence ones. Also, his view that secularism will become stronger with spread of education, science and technology was also too mechanical to be true.

22

Gender Equality Through Women's Empowerment

V. Mohini Giri

THE NATIONAL COMMISSION for Women has as its main mandate the task of identifying factors and recommending measures to mitigate hardships and inadequacies to ensure equality and development of women and through it their empowerment.

Women all over the world are overwhelmingly concerned with the issue of gender equality through women's empowerment. During the past five decades that the United Nations has been in existence, many countries of the world, and the women's movement almost everywhere have organised in a systematic and sustained manner the strategies and approaches that would effectively enable women to be equal partners in progress and prosperity. The results are periodically assessed in world conferences, of which we have had four since the Mexico Conference, the last one was held in Beijing in July 1995. In the intervening period national and international conferences deliberated on women's issues including gender equality.

Since the days of Raja Rammohun Roy, we have brought in a great measure of social reform in the country. India's Constitution conferred equality before law, universal adult franchise and equal opportunities for men and women. We are on the eve of completion of our fiftieth year of Independence. It is opportune at this juncture, to briefly take stock of the process of women's empowerment. As a matter of fact the last five decades have been momentous for women's movement in India. In terms of constitutional, legal and administrative measures as well as enabling support to improve the working and living conditions of women, many initiatives were taken between 1947 and 1997. Prominent among them are the constitutional mandates for gender equality and justice, enactment of very many new laws and amendment of existing laws to protect and promote the interests of women, setting up of women specific administrative and economic structures like the separate Women and Child Development Department at the Union and State Government levels. Other measures include the constitution of the National Commission for Women, Commissions for Women in several States, State Women Development Corporations, orientation in plan strategy to include women specific and women related programmes, launching of special schemes like Rashtriya Mahila Kosh, Indira Mahila Yojana and Mahila Samridhi Yojana. The foremost among them are the provision to reserve for women one-third number of seats to be filled by direct election in Panchayats and Urban local bodies as also offices in specified rural and urban local self-Government institutions and introduction of 81st Constitution (Amendment) Bill for reservation of seats in Lok Sabha and State Legislatures.

Thus, we have enacted useful legislations to arrest indignities on women and provide safety and security and harmony in the family as well as society while some countries are still struggling for the emancipation of women. What we find is that these social legislations, such as those on dowry prohibition, equal remuneration and the like, lag behind in implementation because society has not kept pace with the rapidity of legislations and fast changing societal norms and dynamics of human behaviour and the needs of human rights prerogatives. Our culture accords a high position to women. We venerate women; we accord the highest place to the mother in the family, yet women are denied equality of status; contradictory and strange are the human motives. In this context, I am reminded of what A.C.Pigou said in his *Welfare Economics.* To quote, "When we elect to watch the play of human motives, that are ordinary, that are dismal and ignoble, our impulse is not the philosopher's impulse, knowledge for the sake of knowledge, but rather the physiologist's, knowledge for the healing that knowledge may help to bring". This is to remind all of us that the knowledge that we may gain through conferences and other means must be utilised to heal the ills of society and to bring about sober and sound systems that make the home, society and the country a place worth living.

Empowerment is an omnibus phrase. It encompasses social, political and economic empowerment. Gender equality, as in many other areas, is a relative term. While in a female headed household or matriarchal system, the women may have equality to a larger degree, when it comes to society, the social status varies considerably from community to community. In general, women lag behind the equality status. Society and the Government has not been able to shed its inhibitions and reservations in according an equal status to women, notwithstanding very many progressive elements found in many of the religions of the world as well as the Constitutions of the countries.

When it comes to economic empowerment, while women work along with men equally hard if not harder, their work is neither recognised nor taken into account in computing income. The statistics in our country, so also in very many others, show that the number of women in employment of a regular nature has been increasing and women are now to be found in a variety of jobs once considered to be preserves of men. It is a universal truth that if real empowerment is to be had, women must be economically independent. Many family discords occur mainly because of glaring unequal economic status of couples. It is also essential that the title of property owned should at least be, in the joint names of the couples if not exclusively in the name of female especially if the property was acquired through money brought from parental home. The role of women in taking decisions in the family affecting economic areas must also be a joint effort of husband and wife, father and mother, daughter and son, brother and sister and so on, involving equally the males and females. Then alone can harmony be built. As somebody put it, "a happy home is heaven in advance".

In our country, the main obstacle for empowerment is the dismal female educational level. It is a paradox that even after half a century of Independence, according to the 1991 literacy figures, there are States, where female literacy rate is a mere four percent and there are social groups among whom female literacy rate is even less than one or negligible. To put it mildly, illiteracy is the greatest casualty among girls and women in many countries like India and is the stumbling block towards empowerment. It requires no reiteration that the other major challenge towards gender equality and empowerment are the archaic social customs.

The gender disparity that vitiates the development process has its origin at the most vulnerable point in a women's life, girl-child growing up in a family. Education of the girl-child is the best remedy to correct the imbalance and no cost is too high to achieve it. In respect of girls' education, we may not be wanting too much in theoretical formulations and planning strategies, our major weakness seems to lie in the lack of sincerity in execution and vigour in implementation.

In the empowerment route, participation of women in decision making at all levels has special significance, especially in a democratic set-up. It is unfortunate that some countries in the world have yet to confer full voting rights to women. In our country, the process of political empowerment was well begun when we adopted our Constitution and gained momentum when the Constitution was amended reserving for women one-third of seats in local bodies, both rural and urban, as also specified post of office bearers. This process is being taken to the zenith with the introduction of 81st Amendment Bill providing for one-third reservation of seats for women in Lok Sabha (Lower House) and State Legislatures. Many State Governments have reserved specified quota, generally 30 per cent of posts in public services for women. The Government of India has also under its consideration a proposal to reserve 30 per cent posts in the Union Government services. It is to be expected that these measures should hasten the empowerment process in an adequate measure.

The empowerment of women and the achievement of equality should not be considered in isolation. The realisation of these goals is the only way to build a harmonious, just and balanced society. Let us pledge ourselves to actively pursue these essential requisites for the good of humanity.

23

Emancipation of Scheduled Castes and Scheduled Tribes

S. R. Sankaran

THE SOCIAL and economic position of the Scheduled Castes and Scheduled Tribes has been the concern of the Indian political and social movements even before Independence. Indeed to Gandhiji, the Father of the Nation, freedom was not a mere political objective but raising the masses of people from poverty and degradation. The mainstream political movements were profoundly influenced by the Gandhian approach which emphasised the need to uplift the economic and social status of the poorest of the poor, particularly the Scheduled Castes and Scheduled Tribes.

Independent India adopted its Constitution which came into force on the January 26, 1950. The Preamble to the Constitution of India placed 'Justice - Social, Economic and Political' as the first among the objectives of constituting India into a sovereign democratic republic. The Constitution contained a number of provisions for the elimination of the inequities and inequalities prevalent in the Indian society and for promoting equality and social justice. Article 14 of the Constitution guaranteed equality before law. Article 15 prohibited discrimination on the grounds of religion, caste, sex or place of birth as well as disabilities in regard to access to public places. Article 15 also specifically laid down that nothing shall prevent the State from making any special provision for the advancement of any socially and educationally backward classes of citizens or for the Scheduled Castes and the Scheduled Tribes. Article 16 provided for equality of opportunity in the matter of public employment. Article 17 abolished untouchability forbidding its practice in any form and making the enforcement of any disability arising out of untouchability a punishable offence. Article 23 prohibited forced labour and Article 24 barred the employment of children below fourteen years in any factory or mine or hazardous occupations. While these Articles formed part of the Fundamental Rights incorporated in Part III of the Constitution, the Directive Principles of State Policy in Part IV contained a large number of mandates to the State for policy measures in favour of the poor and downtrodden. Article 38 laid down that the State shall strive to promote the welfare of the people by securing and protecting a social order in which, justice — social, economic and political shall inform all institutions of the national life. Article 39 visualised the right to adequate means of livelihood. Article 45 envisaged provision of free and compulsory education for children below the age of fourteen years. Article 46 mandated that the State shall promote with special care the educational and economic interests of the weaker sections of the people and, in particular, of the Scheduled Castes and the Scheduled Tribes and shall protect them from social injustice and all forms of exploitation.

Article 330 and Article 332 provided for reservation of seats for the members of the Scheduled Castes and Scheduled Tribes in Parliament and in the Legislative Assemblies of the States. Article 335 enabled the reservation in appointments in services and posts under the Government for the Scheduled Castes and the Scheduled Tribes. Article 338 envisaged initially a Special Officer and later, after the amendment in 1990, the setting up of a National Commission for the Scheduled Castes and the Scheduled Tribes. Article 339 provided for the establishment of a Commission for the administration of the Scheduled Areas and the welfare of the Scheduled Tribes from time to time. Special provisions were also incorporated in the Constitution in regard to the administration of the tribal areas included in the Fifth Schedule and the Sixth Schedule of the Constitution. More recently Part IX and Part IXA of the Constitution based on the Seventythird and Seventyfourth amendments have, among other things, provided for the reservation of seats and posts of chairpersons in Panchayats at all levels and the urban local bodies in favour of the Scheduled Castes and the Scheduled Tribes.

The Founding Fathers of the Constitution, especially Babasaheb Dr.Bhim Rao Ambedkar, who was the Chairman of the Drafting Committee, were conscious of the iniquitous forces embedded in the social system, economic institutions and political organisations in relation to the weaker and vulnerable sections of society and therefore, considered it necessary to provide for specific safeguards in the Constitution in their favour. The safeguards for the members of the Scheduled Castes related to the removal of disabilities and positive measures to enable them to acquire a dignified position in the national life. The major concern about the members of the Scheduled Tribes has been that of safeguarding their command over the local natural resources and the best in their tradition. The Indian Constitution is a unique document which provides for a comprehensive framework for the socio-economic development of the Scheduled Castes and the Scheduled Tribes to achieve the objective of a just and humane society.

Development Approach

The Scheduled Castes and the Scheduled Tribes constitute a very large segment of the poorer sections of the Indian society. The term Scheduled Castes appeared for the first time in the Government of India Act 1935. After the Constitution of India was enacted, the list of Scheduled Castes and Scheduled Tribes was notified by the President of India in accordance with the provisions of Article 341 and Article 342 of the Constitution. The Scheduled Castes represent a collection of castes, communities or groups suffering from the traditional stigma of untouchability. The Scheduled Tribes were identified on the basis of certain well defined criteria including the traditional occupation of a definite geographical area, distinctive culture including shyness of contact, occupational traits such as preagricultural modes of cultivation and general lack of development.

The population of Scheduled Castes in India according to the 1991 Census is 13.82 crore which is about 16.48 per cent of the total population of the country. Eight States, namely Uttar Pradesh, West Bengal, Bihar, Tamil Nadu, Andhra Pradesh, Madhya Pradesh, Rajasthan and Karnataka, account for more than 75 per cent of the total Scheduled Castes population of the nation. The population of the Scheduled Tribes in 1991 was 6.78 crore which is around 8.08 per cent of the total population. Six States — Bihar, Gujarat, Madhya Pradesh, Maharashtra, Orissa and Rajasthan — account for about 75 per cent of the total tribal population.

The Scheduled Castes live mostly in rural areas, with only 14 per cent of them found living in urban agglomerates. The habitations of the Scheduled Castes are scattered allover the country generally in parts of villages or small villages. While some of them are small and marginal farmers, most of the Scheduled Caste families in rural areas work largely as agricultural labour. Almost all primary workers in the leather industry come from among the Scheduled Castes. Fishermen belonging to the Scheduled Castes are found in the eastern region of the country. There is a large concentration of weavers belonging to the Scheduled Castes in the western India. In the urban areas, a large proportion of unorganised workers including rickshaw pullers and civic sanitation workers are from the Scheduled Castes. The scavengers and sweepers constitute one of the most vulnerable sections among the Scheduled Castes. The Scheduled Castes suffer from the inhuman practice of untouchability, which is the most extreme form of the denial of human dignity and social oppression. The proportion of the Scheduled Castes among the poverty groups is high and they are among the poorest of those below the poverty line. Two-thirds of the bonded labourers identified in the country are from the Scheduled Castes and the Scheduled Tribes.The poignant observations of the Working Group on the Development of the Scheduled Castes (1980-85) are worth quoting:

> "Notwithstanding this extremely adverse situation, the Scheduled Castes contribute significantly to the sustenance and growth of the production systems of the country and the nation's economy. The largest single group among the agricultural labourers in the country are the Scheduled Castes. Footwear and other leather products are made by the Scheduled Castes. They have a considerable share in the fishing activity of the country. Moreover they are the people who keep the country clean. The Scheduled Castes constitute, in the main, the bedrock on which society and economy rest. Rarely has any section of a nation contributed so much for so long in return for so little. The Indian society owes to the Scheduled Castes a heavy moral and material debt yet to be discharged."

For the tribal population, there has always been a close traditional association with a territory or a tribal domain with the tribal community enjoying a collective command over the natural resources. There are certain States and Union Territories which are almost exclusively tribal such as Nagaland, Mizoram, Meghalaya or Lakshadweep. There are other areas or States where there is a substantial tribal population. The tribal areas are often hilly with a large forest cover, with poor infrastructure and sparsely populated. The tribal economy revolves largely around land and land-based resources; but land is more than a source of livelihood for the Scheduled Tribes. Many tribal groups practise shifting cultivation. A large number of tribal families dwell in the forests or live close to the forests and their economy is closely interlinked with the forest resources. The tribal tracts are often rich in minerals and natural resources.

Since Independence, a variety of initiatives have been undertaken by the State for the socio-economic development of the Scheduled Castes and the Scheduled Tribes. They include an array of constitutional commitments, enactment of special legislations, reservations in public employment and in elected representative bodies, planned development programmes, budgetary allocations and generally high priority in all Governmental programmes. The Protection of Civil Rights Act, 1955 and the Scheduled Castes and Scheduled Tribes (Prevention of Atrocities) Act 1989 are special legislations for social protection of the Scheduled Castes and the Scheduled Tribes. In addition to these special enactments, there are also other protective measures of special relevance to the Scheduled Castes and the Scheduled Tribes such as the Minimum Wages Act 1948, the Bonded Labour System (Abolition) Act 1976 and the Child Labour (Prohibition and Regulation) Act 1986. Protective legislations and regulations specifically for the Scheduled Tribes include laws and regulations under the Fifth Schedule of the Constitution prohibiting transfer of land to non-tribals, regulating and restricting money lending and trade and provision for monopoly rights in the collection and marketing of the tribal produce.

Initially, the development approach to the Scheduled Castes and the Scheduled Tribes took the form of only a few schemes of ameliorative nature by the Centre and the States. The most important step was the reservations in the public services and reservation in educational facilities along with the introduction of scholarships for studies in the post-matric courses. Reservation in the public services as well as the post-matric scholarship for the Scheduled Castes introduced as far back as in 1943 were strengthened, enlarged and continued after Independence. In the States, in the first quarter of Independence, schemes for the Scheduled Castes and Scheduled Tribes consisted largely of programmes of education, housing distribution of government wasteland/Gair Mazrua land and opening of hostels for the students. In some of the States, a part of the available land at the disposal of the Government was specifically reserved for the Scheduled Castes, who constitute the bulk of the agricultural labour.

A specific developmental sector termed as the Backward Classes sector was included in the First Five Year Plan (1951-56) to cater to the special needs of the Scheduled Castes and Scheduled Tribes. It was visualised that the general development programmes themselves should be able to take care of the needs of the Scheduled Castes and Scheduled Tribes adequately and the provisions in the Backward Classes sector would be only additive to be used for meeting the special development needs of these groups. However, the expectation that the general development programmes will meet the needs of the Scheduled Castes and Tribes was not realised and the provisions in the Backward Classes sector instead of supplementing the general sectors of development tended to substitute the general sector provisions. It was in this context that the concept of Tribal Sub-Plan and the Special Component Plan for Scheduled Castes were evolved. Thus, over the successive Five Year Plans, particularly from the beginning of the Fifth Five Year Plan (1974-79), the approach to the development of the Scheduled Castes and the Scheduled Tribes has undergone a basic change with the emphasis shifting to that of ensuring of adequate flow of benefits from all the sectors of development in favour of the Scheduled Castes and the Scheduled Tribes rather than confining the attention merely to the specific programmes in the Backward Classes sector.

A systematic institutionalised effort in planning for the development of the Scheduled Castes was initiated late in 1978 in the nature of Special Component Plan (SCP) for the Scheduled Castes. The SCP was designed to channelise the Plan outlays and benefits in all the sectors to the Scheduled Castes at least in proportion to their population to secure their integrated development. It is intended to be a plan for the development of the Scheduled Castes in relation to their resource endowments and their needs in all the areas of social and economic activity including agriculture, animal husbandry, poultry, fisheries, education including scholarships, hostels and mid-day meals, provision of drinking water, electrification of Scheduled Caste localities, development of sericulture, minor irrigation including construction and energisation of irrigation wells, programmes for specially vulnerable groups, housing and house sites, link roads, self-employment schemes, social forestry, allotment of land as well as schemes for development of lands and allotment of shops and stalls in the public places. The SCP is an important and integral part of the planning process intended to secure the rapid socio-economic development of the Scheduled Castes. In 1980, the Special Central Assistance was also introduced as an additive to the Special Component Plan. Thus, the strategy for the development of the Scheduled Castes is anchored on the Special Component Plan formulated and implemented by the Centre and States supported by the central scheme of Special Central Assistance.

The expenditure for the development of the Scheduled Castes in the Central Sector was only Rs.5.97 crore in the First Plan (1951-56). It rose to Rs.67.76 crore in the Fourth Plan (1969-74); Rs.842.82 crore in the Sixth Plan (1980-85); Rs. 1,234.15 crore in the Seventh Plan (1985-90) and about Rs. 2,291 crore in the Eighth Plan (1992-97). The flow of outlay to the Special Component Plan from various sectors of the State Plan was Rs.3,000 crore in the Sixth Plan, but it increased to Rs. 6,916 crore in the Seventh Plan and is expected to have reached about Rs. 19,000 crore in the Eight Plan. In terms of the proportion of the total Plan outlay, the outlay on the Special Component Plan increased from 6.32 per cent in the Sixth Plan to 7.74 per cent in the Seventh Plan and around 10.53 per cent in the Eighth Five Year Plan. The Special Central Assistance which was started with a token provision of Rs.5 crore in 1978-79 increased to Rs.600 crore in the Sixth Plan; Rs.876 crore in the Seventh Plan and Rs. 1,125 crore in the Eighth Plan.

It was only in the seventies that the State Governments created specific institutional mechanisms for providing assistance for economic development of the Scheduled Castes. The State Governments with substantial Scheduled Castes population have set up the Scheduled Castes Development Corporations (SCDCs) to enable the members of the Scheduled Castes to take up viable income generating activities. In 1979, the Government of India also introduced the centrally sponsored scheme of assistance to the State Governments for investing in the share capital of their corporations. The Government of India established the National Scheduled Caste Finance and Development Corporation (NSFDC) in 1989 to provide support to the economic development programmes for the Scheduled Castes. Since its inception, up to the end of 1995-96, the NSFDC has disbursed about Rs. 300 crore for schemes of agriculture, horticulture, animal husbandry, minor irrigation, small industries, trade and transport. The State Scheduled Castes Development Corporations have catered to about 87 lakh beneficiaries until 1994-95.

In order to achieve the objective of elimination of the dehumanising practice of manual scavenging, the National Scheme for Liberation and Rehabilitation of Scavengers and their dependents was launched in March 1992. The National Commission for Safai Karmacharis was also set up in August 1994 to monitor and oversee the programmes.

Following the stipulation in Article 17 of the Constitution, the Untouchability Offences Act enacted in 1955 was replaced by the comprehensive Protection of Civil Rights Act enacted in 1976. Untouchability was made a cognisable and non-compoundable offence and a minimum punishment was stipulated for enforcing the religious, social and other disabilities. A Centrally Sponsored Scheme of strengthening the machinery for implementation of the Protection of Civil Rights Act was introduced under which the States are provided with financial assistance for the purpose. The number of cases registered under the Protection of Civil Rights Act was 3406 in 1991, 3086 in 1992 and 1581 in 1993 showing a declining trend over the years.

The Scheduled Castes and Scheduled Tribes (Prevention of Atrocities) Act 1989 was promulgated to deal with the commission of crimes on the members of Scheduled Castes and Tribes. The Act sets out a series of offences covered by the term 'atrocities' against Scheduled Castes and Scheduled Tribes and provides for severe punishment, setting up of Special Courts and also effective measures for the prevention of atrocities including externment from the Scheduled Areas. The State Governments have specified the existing monetary relief and measures for the rehabilitation for the victims of atrocities.

Soon after Independence, the basic principles that should guide and provide approach to the development of the Scheduled Tribes were clearly set out by Pandit Jawaharlal Nehru in the form of five principles known as 'Tribal Panchsheel' which was later endorsed by the Scheduled Areas and Scheduled Tribe Commission i.e. Dhebar Commission (1961) and the Shilu Ao Committee (1969). The Panchsheel laid down specifically:

- the tribal people should develop along the lines of their own genius and we should avoid imposing anything on them but rather try to encourage in every way their own traditional arts and culture;
- tribal rights in lands and forests should be respected;
- we should try to train and build up a team of their own people to do administration and development;

- we should not over administer these areas or overwhelm them with multiplicity of schemes; we should rather work through and not in rivalry to their own social and cultural institutions; and
- we should judge the results not by statistics or the amount of money spent but by the quality of human character that is evolved.

The Dhebar Commission and Shilu Ao Committee made important recommendations in regard to the tribal development programmes. They pointed out that while the provisions of the Constitution were clear on the need to promote, with special care, the educational and economic interests of the weaker sections and in particular Scheduled Castes and Tribes and to protect them from social injustice and all forms of exploitation, the implementation of protective and anti-exploitation measures left much to be desired.

A programme of Community Development was launched in the First Plan and by the end of the Second the entire country was covered by the Community Development approach. While this approach applied equally to the tribal areas, the efforts in the tribal areas were supplemented in 1954 by the starting of special multipurpose tribal development projects covering a few blocks. The Special Multipurpose Tribal Development Blocks were reviewed in 1956 and a more general concept of a Tribal Development Block applicable to all tribal areas was evolved.

Till the Fourth Plan (1969-74), the socio-economic development of the Scheduled Tribes was accepted as a goal to be achieved through the implementation of the general sectoral programmes. In the Fourth Plan, when a series of special programmes were formulated for the specific target groups and areas such as for small farmers, agricultural labourers and drought prone areas, it was considered desirable to take up similar programmes for tribal areas on a pilot basis. Accordingly six (later increased to eight) Tribal Development Agencies were started in Andhra Pradesh, Orissa, Bihar and Madhya Pradesh. These agencies took over within their fold the implementation of protective measures, programmes of economic development, schemes of arterial road development and social services.

The tribal situation in the country was gone into in depth before the concept of Tribal Sub-Plan was evolved in 1974-75. The new Tribal Sub-Plan (TSP) strategy took note of the fact that a clearer approach to the tribal problems was necessary in terms of their geographic and demographic concentration if faster development was to take place. Accordingly, the tribal areas of the country were classified into three broad categories - first, the States and Union Territories having a majority Scheduled Tribes population; second, the States and Union Territories having a substantial tribal population with major tribal population concentrated in particular administrative units such as Blocks and Tehsils, and thirdly, the States and Union Territories having dispersed tribal population. In the light of this approach, it was considered that tribal majority States like Arunachal Pradesh, Meghalaya, Mizoram, Nagaland and Lakshadweep may not need a Tribal Sub-Plan as the entire Plan of these States was meant for the Scheduled Tribe population. For the second category of States and Union Territories, the Tribal Sub-Plan strategy was adopted after delineating areas of tribal concentration. A similar approach was adopted in the case of States and Union Territories having dispersed tribal population by focussing special attention on the pockets of tribal concentration keeping in view the nature of their dispersal. In order to effectively administer the programmes, the Tribal Sub-Plan strategy adopted the Integrated Tribal Development Projects (ITDP) for tribal areas with substantial tribal population. The Modified Tribal Development Approach (MADA) was for pockets of tribal concentration and special projects for Primitive Tribal Groups (PTG) along with administrative, financial and functional integration to eliminate exploitative relationships.

By the end of 1995-96, the Tribal Sub-Plan (TSP) strategy was being implemented through 194 Integrated Tribal Development Projects, 252 pockets of tribal concentration (MADA), 78 clusters and 75 primitive tribal group projects. There was substantial increase in the flow of funds for the development of Scheduled Tribes, resulting in the expansion of infrastructural facilities and enlargement of coverage of the tribal population.

A number of States have set up Tribal Marketing Corporations for securing a fair price for the minor forest produce and the agricultural products procured and sold by the tribals. The Government of India also set up the Tribal Cooperative Marketing Development Federation (TRIFED) in 1987 as the apex coordinating body for the State Tribal Marketing Corporations. The objective was to ensure remunerative prices for minor forest produce and agricultural items produced or collected by the tribals and to protect them against exploitation by private traders and middlemen.

The investments in tribal areas from the First Plan to the Sixth Plan showed that the developmental outlay in the tribal development sector as a proportion of the total Plan outlay went up from one per cent in the First Plan to about three per cent in the Fifth Plan. The flow of funds from the State Plan to the Tribal Sub-Plan (TSP) during the Fifth Plan, when it was first introduced, was Rs. 751.33 crore; it increased to Rs. 3,718.56 crore in Sixth Plan and Rs. 7,076 crore in the Seventh Plan. As a proportion of the total State Plan outlay, the outlay on the Tribal Sub-Plan increased from 4.25 per cent in the Fifth Plan to 8.77 per cent in the Sixth Plan and 9.57 per cent in the Seventh Plan i.e. Rs.485 crore in the Sixth Plan and Rs. 846 crore in the Seventh Plan. The allocation for Special Central Assistance in the Eighth Plan has been stepped up further to Rs. 1,125 crore.

The Government of India had also issued guidelines in 1975 in regard to excise policy in tribal areas emphasising the banning of commercial vending of liquor, while permitting the tribals to brew their own liquor for consumption at home and for religious and social occasions. The National Forest Policy 1988 reiterated the symbiotic relationship between the tribals and forests. It stressed the need for associating the tribal people closely in the protection, regeneration and the development of forests as well as providing gainful employment to the people living in and around the forests. The policy also provided for the full protection of the traditional rights and concessions enjoyed by the tribals.

A significant development in regard to the self-government in the Scheduled Areas is the recent Parliamentary legislation extending the provisions of Part IX of the Constitution to such Areas. This legislation is unique in requiring the States to confer larger powers and authority on the Gram Sabhas and also reserving the posts of Chairpersons exclusively to the Scheduled Tribes in Panchayats in the Scheduled Areas.

Empowerment Programmes

As the Scheduled Castes and the Scheduled Tribes constitute a large segment of those below the poverty line, an overriding priority has been accorded to their families in all the Poverty Alleviation Programmes, particularly in the field of rural development. In the Integrated Rural Development Programme (IRDP), the most important poverty alleviation programme which was extended to the entire country in the year 1980, 30 per cent of the outlay was earmarked for the Scheduled Castes and Scheduled Tribes in the initial years. Since

1990-91, a minimum of 50 per cent of the total outlay has been set aside for the Scheduled Castes and Scheduled Tribes. The Scheduled Caste as well as Scheduled Tribe beneficiaries are also eligible for a higher subsidy of 50 per cent as against 25 per cent for small farmers and 33 1/3 per cent for the marginal farmers and landless labourers. The number of Scheduled Caste and Scheduled Tribe families covered under IRDP all over the country since its inception until 1995-96 is about 200 lakhs.

Under the major rural wage employment programme of Jawahar Rozgar Yojana (JRY), an overall preference is given to the Scheduled Castes, Scheduled Tribes and freed bonded labourers. Weightage is also given to the population of the Scheduled Castes and Scheduled Tribes in allocating funds under the JRY at the district and Panchayat levels. At the district level, the District Rural Development Agency (DRDA)/Zilla Parishad is required to utilise 22.5 per cent of the funds for individual beneficiary schemes for the Scheduled Castes and Scheduled Tribes. A similar stipulation exists in regard to the Village Panchayats also.

The Million Wells Scheme (MWS) was launched in 1988 with the objective of providing open irrigation wells to the poor small and marginal farmers belonging to the Scheduled Castes and Scheduled Tribes and freed bonded labourers, and 20 per cent of the funds under the JRY is allocated for this scheme. By the year 1995-96, one million wells mostly for the Scheduled Castes and Scheduled Tribes, were constructed with an investment of about Rs. 3,500 crore. The Indira Awas Yojana (IAY) was started from 1985-86 as an important component of the Rural Labour Employment Guarantee Programme (RLEGP) and later became part of the Jawahar Rozgar Yojana (JRY) in 1989-90 with six per cent of the funds being set aside for the construction of houses for the Scheduled Castes and Scheduled Tribes and freed bonded labour. About three million houses have been constructed for the Scheduled Castes and the Scheduled Tribes until 1995-96 involving an outlay of about Rs. 3,600 crore.

Under the Accelerated Rural Water Supply Scheme of providing drinking water to rural habitations, there is earmarking of 25 per cent of the funds for the Scheduled Castes and 10 per cent of the funds for the Scheduled Tribes. It has also been laid down that the first source of drinking water in any village should be located in their localities.

In sum, a policy of preference and exclusive allocation of funds under various poverty alleviation programmes has been one of the significant features of the efforts made for the development of the Scheduled Castes and Scheduled Tribes in the last few decades.

Reservations of Posts

An important measure which has its origin in pre-Independence days but pursued with greater vigour in Independent India is the reservation in appointments in the public services in favour of the Scheduled Castes and Scheduled Tribes. Though only a small proportion of the Scheduled Castes and Tribes have been able to secure employment in government and other public sector organisations, however those who secured employment have been able to cross the line of economic freedom and of self-respect. The representation of the Scheduled Castes and Scheduled Tribes in the Central government services has shown a substantial improvement over a period of years since Independence as would be seen from the following table.

It may be seen that in the case of Scheduled Castes the representation, in overall terms, has reached the same level as the proportion of the population though there is still a significant shortfall in Group A and Group B posts. The position in regard to the Scheduled

Percentage of SC and ST Representation in Central Government Services as on 1 January 1994. (Figures in brackets as on 1 January 1965)

	Scheduled Castes	Scheduled Tribes
Group A	10.25(1.64)	2.92 (0.27)
Group B	12.06(2.82)	2.81 (0.34)
Group C	15.73(8.88)	5.38 (1.14)
Group D (excluding sweepers)	20.46(17.75)	6.15 (3.39)
Total	16.90(13.17)	5.48 (2.25)

(*Source* :Annual Report 1995-96, Ministry of Personnel, Government of India)

Tribes however shows shortfalls in all categories. While this reflects the position only in respect of the posts under the Central Government, there have been improvement in regard to the posts under the State Governments as well as in the public undertakings. A number of pre-examination training centres have also been set up for coaching the candidates in order to enhance the competitive ability of the Scheduled Caste and Scheduled Tribe students appearing in the examinations for entry into public services.

One of the earliest efforts of the State in regard to the development of the Scheduled Castes and Scheduled Tribes has been in the field of education. The schemes include scholarships for pre-matric studies and post-matric studies, free supply of school uniforms, stationery and text books, opening of hostels, establishment of residential schools as well as the setting up of Ashram Schools. The number of Scheduled Caste and Scheduled Tribe students availing of the post-matric scholarships in 1995-96 was around 20 lakhs. These scholarships were given for courses of study in arts, science, commerce as well as professional and technical degrees and diplomas. The scheme and pattern of scholarships are intended to ensure that both at pre-matric and post-matric stages, problems like high dropout rates, stagnation, non-enrolment of girl students and uneven growth are effectively tackled. The Post-Matric Scholarship Scheme is particularly noteworthy because of its open ended nature making all the eligible Scheduled Caste and the Scheduled Tribe students entitled to scholarship at all levels of post-matric education. The scheme has contributed significantly to the access and retention of Scheduled Caste and the Scheduled Tribe students in higher education. A scheme of book bank was introduced for Scheduled Caste and Scheduled Tribe students studying in engineering and medical colleges. Hostel facilities for the Scheduled Caste and Scheduled Tribe students were considerably expanded. In addition to the efforts of the State Governments, the Government of India introduced a Centrally Sponsored Scheme of establishment of hostels for Scheduled Caste girls during the Third Five Year Plan (1961-66) and this was extended to Scheduled Caste boys in 1989-90. A scheme of scholarships for pre-matric classes for the children of those engaged in unclean occupation was also introduced by the Government of India in 1977-78.

The National Policy on Education 1986 laid special emphasis on the removal of disparities and equalisation of educational opportunities. The policy laid down that the central focus in the educational development of the Scheduled Castes is their equalisation with the non-Scheduled Caste population at all levels and stages of education in all areas in all the four dimensions — rural male, rural female, urban male and urban female. The Programme of Action (POA) 1992 accorded priority to the opening of primary and upper primary schools to meet the needs of the Scheduled Caste habitations and hamlets; provision of non-formal distance education; adequate incentives; coverage of the Scheduled Caste localities and tribal areas under the Operation Black Board and the programme of universalisation of elementary education.

The following table will show the position in regard to literacy among the Scheduled Castes and Scheduled Tribes.

(Percentage to total population)

	SCs	STs	non-SCs/STs	General
1961	10.27	8.54	27.86	24.00
1971	14.67	11.30	33.80	29.45
1981	21.68	16.35	41.30	36.23
1991	37.41	29.60	57.40	52.21

It will be observed that while significant progress has been made and there has been an increase in the percentage of literacy among the Scheduled Castes and Scheduled Tribes from 10.27 per cent in 1961 to 37.41 per cent in 1991 and 8.54 per cent in 1961 to 29.60 per cent in 1991 respectively, there is a need for intensive efforts to remove the disparity in the levels of literacy and to achieve a reasonably high rate of literacy.

Land Distribution

As a majority of the Scheduled Castes and Scheduled Tribes lives in rural areas, and land is one of the most critical assets giving them economic and social status, it is necessary to refer to the measures of land reforms taken up since Independence. The first phase of land reforms soon after Independence consisted of the abolition of intermediaries and this brought about 20 million peasants, many of them belonging to the Scheduled Castes and Scheduled Tribes, in direct relationship with the State. Under the land ceiling laws enacted by various States, about 51.6 lakh acres of land have been distributed by the end of 1995 to 50.33 lakh beneficiaries; of this 17.87 lakh acres were allotted to 18 lakh beneficiaries belonging to the Scheduled Castes and 7.22 lakh acres were assigned to 7.13 lakh beneficiaries belonging to the Scheduled Tribes. In addition, in a number of States efforts were made to allot lands available at the disposal of Government to the Scheduled Castes and the Scheduled Tribes on a preferential basis. The tenancy reforms also resulted in the conferment of ownership rights on about 110.42 lakh cultivators in respect of 144.9 lakh acres of land and the tenants belonging to the Scheduled Castes and Scheduled Tribes benefited from this measure. The extent of alienated tribal land restored is about 4.04 lakh acres.

A large number of people belonging to the Scheduled Castes and Scheduled Tribes work as bonded labourers and most of the child labourers are also from these communities. There are innumerable variants of the bonded labour system in the country and apart from bonded labour in agriculture, there are also large number of bonded labourers in brick kilns, stone quarries, limestone mines, match factories, carpet weaving, irrigation works and a variety of other occupations. The distinction between child labour, bonded labour and migrant labour is indeed very thin and is a part of the wide spectrum of the slavery of labour. There has been some relief to the Scheduled Castes and Scheduled Tribes wherever the Bonded Labour (Abolition) Act and the Child Labour (Prohibition and Regulation) Act have been effectively implemented.

The Eighth Plan (1992-97) which has just been completed visualised an intensification of efforts to bridge the gap in levels of development of the Scheduled Castes and Tribes in relation to the others so that by the turn of the century these disadvantaged sections of the people are brought on par with the rest of the Indian society. The most recent policy pronouncement in regard to the development of the Scheduled Castes and the Scheduled Tribes is the document on the Approach to the Ninth Plan (1997-2002) which reaffirms the constitutional commitment of removing the economic and social disabilities of the Scheduled Castes and the Scheduled Tribes. In the Ninth Plan, a high priority is proposed to be accorded to empowering these special groups economically and socially to enable them to join the mainstream of the national development at the earliest. As the Scheduled Castes have been subjected to social discrimination since long, all programmes meant for them are to be so designed as to empower them and provide them with both social and economic mobility. On the social side, priority is to be given to the elimination of the pernicious practice of untouchability through legislative and socio-economic measures. Endowing every landless Scheduled Caste family with a minimum piece of land, preservation and restoration of land ownership and implementation of existing legislations to protect the agricultural land being appropriated by others are some of the important steps that are intended to be taken up in the Ninth Plan. A national policy for Tribal Development will be formulated during the Ninth Plan and it will be ensured that the tribal economy is protected and supported against threats from external markets. An Action Plan will be drawn up and implemented for the Primitive Tribal Groups incorporating total food and nutrition security, health coverage and education facilities with inbuilt flexibility to cater to the needs of each tribe and their environment.

Notwithstanding many shortcomings, it is to be recognised that there has been a significant progress in regard to the socio-economic development of the Scheduled Castes and Scheduled Tribes in the five decades since Independence. Commencing with the constitutional commitments and the special legislations to secure equality and human dignity, a large variety of measures have been taken up both as policy measures and developmental programmes in all the fields of development and welfare. There is no doubt a vast ground is yet to be traversed, given the historical situation at the time of Independence and the heterogeneous nature of the Indian society itself. The development of the members of the Scheduled Castes and Scheduled Tribes has to be viewed at not only in absolute terms but also in relation to the development of the rest of the Indian society. The progress in relative terms requires that there is not only a positive change in their socio-economic situation but also that the rate of change is fast enough to ensure that the disparity is progressively minimised and ultimately eliminated altogether. The development of the Scheduled Castes and Scheduled Tribes is thus a part of the quest for equality and social justice, the objectives enshrined in the Constitution and pursued since Independence in free India.

24

Welfare of Backward Classes

P. S. Krishnan

THE BACKWARD Classes (BCs), referred to variously as the Socially and Educationally Backward Classes (SEBCs) or Other Backward Classes (OBCs), can be meaningfully understood only against the background of the Indian caste system and in conjunction with the Scheduled Castes (SCs) and Scheduled Tribes (STs). These three together constitute the exploited and deprived social categories of the Indian population.

The Indian caste system is the protoplasm and gene of the Indian society. It has been supplying, and still supplies, the building blocks of Indian society. It permeates every aspect of Indian life -- its economy, its polity, its social relations, its culture, its linguistic behaviour in social contexts, its psyche, its ethos.

The Indian Caste System

According to the classical theory, propounded and propagated by the beneficiaries of the Indian caste system and others influenced by the world-view of its beneficiaries, the origin of Indian castes running into a few thousands, is traced to an original four *Varnas*, the Brahmins or the category of priests and teachers, *Kshatriyas* or temporal rulers and warriors, *Vaishyas* or traders and *Shudras* or the category of servants and labourers. These *Varnas* and the resultant numerous castes are supposed to be graded and ranked hierarchically on the basis of the Principle of Purity and Impurity -- purity and impurity understood not in the ordinary sense but in some sort of transcendental, mystic sense. Entry into *Varna* and caste is determined by birth; such birth in turn is attributed to *Karma,* literally action or deeds -- the deeds in question being those done in prior births i.e., in previous lives. Thereafter one's position, station and function in community life is determined by *Dharma,* interpreted and understood in this context as a code of moral duty appropriate to each *Varna*/caste. Since *Varna* in Sanskrit literally means colour, efforts have also been made to trace the *Varna* system and caste system to some sort of racial origin and the necessity of maintenance of "racial purity".

In order to be able to perceive the essence of the nature and functions of the Indian caste system, it is necessary to study it from the point of the large majority of the Indian people, who have been its victims in various forms and degrees, and to understand how the Indian caste system works in relation to the SCs, the STs and the BCs.

Ambedkar was the earliest thinker to bring a fresh approach to the examination of the caste system. More than three quarters of a century back, he made a four-fold formulation of the origin of caste in India, of which two are relevant here:

> "... (1) that caste is a parcelling into bits of a larger cultural unit;
>
> (2) that there was one caste to start with..."

Ambedkar pursued his theme of the non-racial basis of caste differentiation in his book *Annihilation of Caste.*

Contrary to earlier and later practice, he focussed attention on labourers in relation to the caste system. He identifies one of its important features by characterising it as "a division of labourers" into watertight compartments and as "an hierarchy in which the divisions of labourers are graded one above the other." He refers to this as a "stratification of occupations".

He further developed his view in his inquiry into the origin of Shudras, in which, from a study of Avestan, Vedic and other scriptural sources, he establishes that "Varna" has nothing to do with colour or complexion. His thesis is that the Shudras were Kshatriyas who were degraded. Some of his pioneering initiatives and insights have found echoes in recent scholarship. Thus, Morton Klass has also come to the same conclusion as Ambedkar -- apparently without knowledge of Ambedkar's analysis -- that *Varna* cannot have anything to do with colour or racial attributes. His conclusion that, from the evidence of skeletal material and representations of human beings in ancient art, the population in South Asia 5000 years ago was similar in its range of physical types to the present population, chimes with Ambedkar's path-breaking formulations regarding a common stratum of population in each region of India, subsequently divided by caste into castes.

Looking at the Indian society in relation to the socio-economic frame of India, from the viewpoint of SCs, STs and BCs, I consider it realistic and enlightening to distinguish four layers of castes -- very different from the traditional four *Varna* model.

The topmost layer is the layer of privilege and prestige. It consists of castes, to which all — a disproportionately large number of persons in prestigious and privileged positions and occupations traditionally belong. Such traditional positions and occupations include religious/spiritual authority, State governance and public administration, control over agricultural land (irrespective of whether and when individual ownership came into existence in a region), military professions, commerce and the like. The second layer consists of cultivating peasant castes. In relation to land, their traditional position was between land-controlling castes and agricultural labour castes. But, as a result of post-Independence land reforms, they have recently become land-controlling castes in some parts. Some of these are also castes of herders of cattle, sheep, goats. The third layer consists of two or three sub-layers -- the castes of traditional artisans and of other artisanal producers, the castes providing various personal services and pastoral castes. The lowest layer consists essentially of castes of agricultural labourers. The castes of the three lower layers have traditionally been producing primary and secondary goods and rendering various types of services and labour mainly for the top layer, on unequal terms adverse to the former, in varying degrees and forms, and involving exploitation in varying degrees and of different forms. This has been facilitated by the economic power of the top layer aided by the ideology of "Caste-with-Untouchability", the latter part directed against the castes in the lower layer.

The British period and the post-Independence decades have no doubt introduced changes, but have not fundamentally altered the four-layer profile of the socio-economic frame of non-tribal India.

The continuity of the caste-occupation-social-status nexus can be illustrated with the following percipient observations of the Supreme Court of India in its majority judgement in the Mandal case -- "... a caste is nothing but a social class -- a socially homogeneous class. It is also an occupational grouping, with this difference that its membership is hereditary. One is born into it.... Even if one ceases to follow that occupation, still he remains and continues as member of that group... it is a socially and occupationally homogeneous class. Endogamy is its main characteristic. Its social status and standing depends upon the nature of the occupation followed by it. Lowlier the occupation, lowlier the social standing of the class in the graded hierarchy. In rural India, the occupation-caste nexus is true even today... Urbanisation has to some extent broken this caste-occupation nexus but not wholly.... in the case of an overwhelming majority, the caste-occupation nexus subsists. There may be exceptions here and there, but we are concerned with generality of the scene and not with exceptions or aberrations. Lowly occupation results not only in low social position but also in poverty; it generates poverty. 'Caste-occupation-poverty' cycle is thus an ever present reality. In rural India, it is strikingly apparent; in urban centres, there may be some dilution. But since rural India and rural population is still the predominant fact of life in India, the reality remains. All the decisions since Balaji speak of this caste-occupation-poverty nexus... This is the stark reality notwithstanding all our protestations and abhorrence and all attempts at weeding out this phenomenon."

In arriving at these findings, the 9-member Constitutional bench had the benefit of referring to the extensive sociological literature on caste and to 78 Indian cases including the two decisions on BCs delivered by the Supreme Court soon after the Constitution of India came into force, viz., State of Madras Vs Champakam Dorairajan and Venkataramana Vs State of Madras; 21 foreign cases mainly pertaining to Blacks in the USA, beginning with Dred Scott Vs Sanford, which held that Blacks were the lawful property of their masters and were not entitled to be treated as citizens, and Plessey Vs Fergusson, in which the doctrine of 'separate but equal' was evolved -- a judgement which recalls to mind the Privy Council's ruling, in a case relating to the struggle of the Nadar, a BCs Caste of Tamil Nadu, which was earlier subjected to "untouchability", for equal right of worship in Hindu temple (in the town of Kamudi, which they forcibly entered on 14.05.1897), that they should have separate but equal religious facilities.

Broadly speaking, most of the castes in the lowest layer have been classified as SCs, for the purpose of measures of special protection and safeguards since 1935 (i.e., even prior to India's Independence) and also after Independence, under a series of Presidential orders issued in terms of Article 341 of the Constitution. They have been so classified on the basis of the criterion of "untouchability". To clarify, castes of those who have been the victims of "untouchability" have been classified as SCs. The educated sections of SCs have assertively and defiantly adopted the appellation of Dalit, which means the Oppressed. While the numerically large castes in this layer are typically agricultural labour castes (ALCs), to this layer should also be assigned a number of numerically small castes which are nomadic (N), semi-nomadic(SN) or "Vimukta Jati" (VJ) or "ex-criminal". Some of them have also been classified as SCs, on account of their being found to be the victims of "untouchability".

To this layer also belong a number of STs which live outside tribal areas or tribal homelands. Some of them represent tribes which have been sucked out of their homelands and have virtually become ALCs like the typical SCs. Some others represent tribes which never had a homeland and still others may be representatives of those submerged by the inexorably advancing caste-based agricultural civilisation of India. Most of these live in style and circumstances which are little different from those of the SCs. Some of the N, SN and VJ categories have been included in the lists of STs, issued under a series of Presidential orders in terms of Article 342, on account of their possession of tribal characteristics.

Castes in the layer above the lowest i.e., the Lower Mid Layer are almost invariably found included in the lists of BCs of the 14 States where such lists existed prior to the Government of India's historic Memorandum of 13 August.1990, for the first time providing for the BCs reservation in Government and public sector jobs as well as prior to the Supreme Court's Mandal Judgement of 16 November, 1992, upholding that Memorandum, and in the lists of the 11 other States issued by the respective State Governments in 1993, 1994 and 1995. They are also found in the Central Lists of BCs for the first 14 States prepared initially and partly in August-October 1990 and finally and completely in June 1993 by the Expert Committee on BCs appointed in February 1993, based on the principles of "commonality" between the respective State lists and the Mandal lists for each of those States, and issued by the Government of India on 13 September, 1993, and also in the Central Lists of Backward Classes issued by the Government of India in 1994 and 1995 in respect of the 11 other States/UTs, though a few castes/sub-castes/synonyms are not included in the common (Central) lists as they are missing in the Mandal list while being included in the State list and vice versa.

The castes in the second layer i.e., the Mid Layer are generally found in the lists of BCs. Presence of any caste of the top layer in the lists of BCs is exceptional.

Mention must also be made of a layer broadly parallel to the lowest layer and partly jutting above vaguely, consisting of STs of Tribal areas -- accounting for two-thirds to three-fourths of the STs population of India. This fifth or the *Panchama* has nothing to do with the *Panchama* of/outside the four-*varna* pseudo-model.

A diagrammatic representation of the above picture of the Indian social situation is given on the following page.

It is now possible to see the design, pattern, purpose and function of the Indian caste system or the socio-economic structure of India as one of gradation, degradation, deprivation and exploitation. Specifically in the present context, the BCs consist of castes of artisans and artisanal/artisan-like producers, castes of those rendering various personal services held in general esteem to be lowly and inferior, pastoral castes, many of the castes of peasants and also those of the nomadic, semi-nomadic and Vimukta Jati communities, and labour-providing castes which are not classified as SCs or STs. The terms of their economic relations with the castes of privilege and prestige have been adverse and oppressive to the former in varying forms and degrees.

The functioning of the Indian caste system also meant denial, to the castes of the lower layers -- the SCs, the STs and the BCs -- of opportunities of education and advancement into the top layer. Symbolic of this, in the pre-historic period, is the legend of Ekalavya and, in the modern period, the boycott of a Government School by upper caste parents in 1853 when the first boy of the Mahar caste (an SCs) was admitted to the school in Dharwar, then in Bombay Presidency and now in Karnataka.

The most telling evidence and illustration of the design, purpose and function of the Indian caste system would be a quantitative, contrastive existential analysis of the SCs, who constitute the bulk of the bottom layer vis-a-vis the castes constituting the top layer or the Advanced non-SCs and non-STs (ANSCT) population. Such quantitative data are available for SCs and STs as a whole, but are not available for ANSCT in the country as a whole or in any region as a whole. The next best available are data for the "General Population" which consists of ANSCT+SCs+STs+BCs populations. Extracting therefrom data for the Non-SCs, Non-STs (NSCT) population (=ANSCT+BCs) as a whole and collating quantitative data from different sources, I have elsewhere analysed contrasts between SCs and NSCT along different significant parameters of nation-wide relevance and parameters or region-wide relevance to bring about the nature and extent of the exploitation and deprivation of SCs and to highlight therefrom the true nature and function of the Indian caste system. Such data for BCs are available only at village level or local level from individual studies and in a few States at State-level limited to a few parameters. I shall here present some of those data, falling back for the present on observations from my visits to a large number of villages and towns in all regions/States of India and referring to some data available in reports of various commissions in India and the States. Before doing so, it will be useful to focus on the growth of what may be called the BCs movements for justice, the evolution of reservation in governmental jobs and educational seats for them, and in some detail on the profile of the BCs.

Backward Class Movements

The significance of BCs movements in the context of the welfare of BCs is that measures for their welfare, encompassing community efforts of the people and State interventions, were essentially responses to movements which can be characterised as BCs movements -- covering mainly movements of BCs and also, in a way, movements on their behalf.

Contrary to the erroneous impression that till the arrival of Western education and modern ideologies of the West, all was quiet on the caste front in India, there are indications that the castes belonging to the layers below the top layer have always been straining at the leash, however much they were lulled by the *Karma-Dharma* ideology, whenever there was opportunity, though it is true that the widest and most sustained opportunities arrived with the appearance of Europeans in India, the consequent shake-up of the traditional Indian polity and the growth of the ideologies of humanism, egalitarianism, nationalism and democracy.

A Diagrammatic Representation of India's Socio-Economic Structure

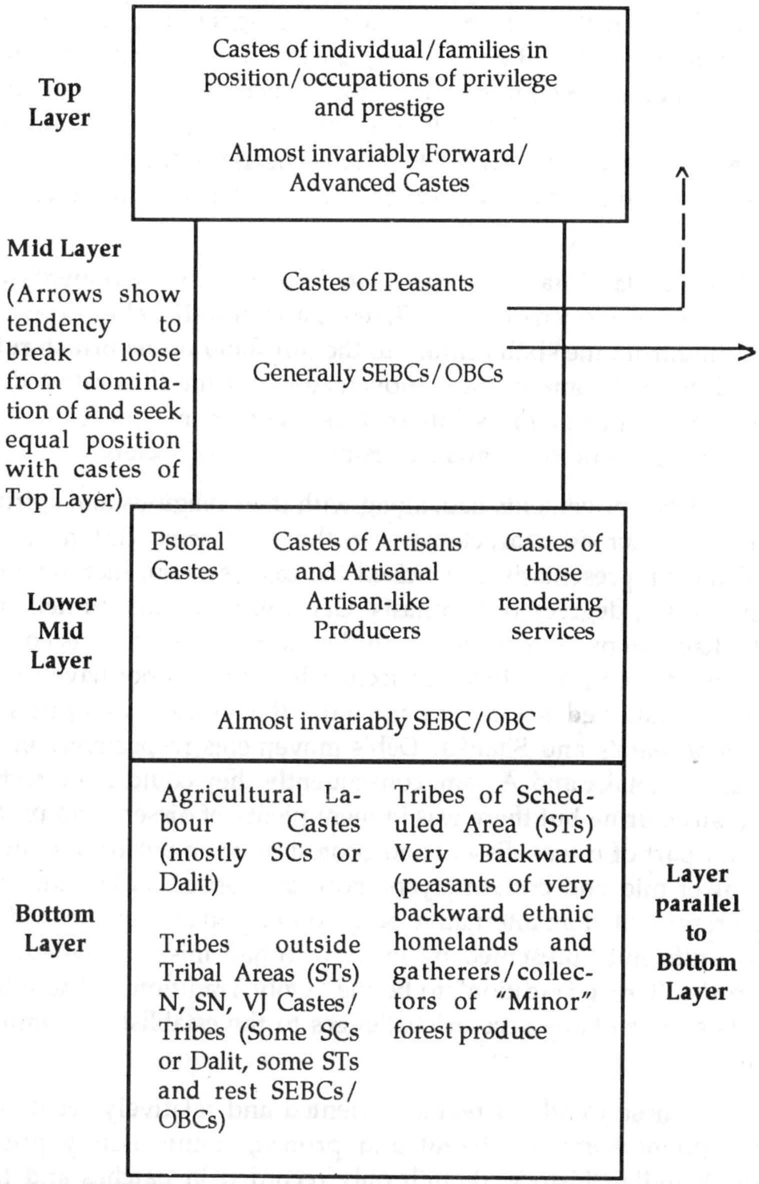

In keeping with the prevalent contemporaneous context, the earlier glimmerings, we have of resistance to the caste-based rigidities, are linked with religion. Buddhism has been considered to be a counterpoint to Brahminist theories of caste. It is associated with a socially egalitarian character, which has made it a magnet of attraction for all those who have cherished social equality as a value and condemned the Indian caste system, the latest of them being Dr. B. R. Ambedkar. Buddhism and also Jainism had a practical egalitarian significance for those who did not want to accept the rigid caste-based socio-ideological frame which was advancing with the agricultural civilization.

Another landmark is represented by Bhakti movements and Bhakti-related movements in different parts of India, chronologically extending from the sixth century to the threshold of the British rule. I have described some of these movements in some illustrative detail elsewhere. Many of the saints of these movements themselves belonged to castes of lower mid and bottom layers of society.

All these movements had, along with their religious and spiritual aspects, two broad characteristics in the social context. On the one hand their representatives criticised the caste system, hierarchy etc., with varying degrees of emphasis. Generally they discountenanced caste distinctions among saints and devotees in the religious context. But they did not carry this into secular life and did not have significant or sustained social impact with the limited exceptions of Basaveraswara's and Shankar Deb's movements respectively in medieval Karnataka and Assam; consequently they could not effect social restructuring but there was in them plenty of dissent and protest. A good part of it was dissent and protest of or on behalf of castes of the lower mid and bottom layers, now categorised as BCs and SCs. They represented an alternative pole, contrary to the picture of deadened uniformity presented by those who had misrepresented/mistaken the "Great Tradition" to be the "Only Tradition". There have also been essentially secular challenges to the established dominant order.

Both these trends of religion-oriented and relatively secular-oriented phenomena of dissent and protest, unmistakably present through Indian history, though only recorded in patches and fragments, had features of incipient movements which in today's terminology can be termed as BCs or SCs movements. Later, under more favourable circumstances, brought about positively as well as negatively by the British Rule and catalysed by factors positive as well as negative introduced by the British Rule, these seeds sprouted and luxuriantly and naturally grew into the BCs movements associated with men like Mahatma Phule, Narayana Guru, Periyar E.V.Ramaswamy and Ambedkar in Peninsular India and the more recent backward class movements in North India. Gandhiji's movement against untouchability, though not categorised as a BCs movement in the Twentieth century context, is traceable to the same indigenous source of dissent and protest. So are Swami Vivekananda's and Dr. Ram Manohar Lohia's attacks on caste-based oppression of and discrimination against lower castes. Christian missionary activity and Marxist revolutionary movements also drew their social sustenance from the same indigenous source of dissent and protest and in turn imparted some strength to them.

The establishment of the British rule deprived the top layer castes - Brahmin as well as non-Brahmin -- of the benefit of direct and interested maintenance of the Indian caste system. The opening of formal, modern education to castes other than of the top layer slowly built up an educated elite in some of the castes of these layers. They were sensitive to the monopoly of the services under the British by one or more of the castes of the top layer. They, especially those of numerically strong peasant communities established in land, were sensitive to caste-based pretences to superiority of Brahmins and other dominant top layer castes.

Movements grew round two foci -- opposition to caste-basted monopolies in the services of the colonial State and the princely "native" States and resistance to traditional caste-based humiliations. As monopolies and deprivations, arrogance and humiliations were based on caste, the movements and mobilisation were also based on caste -- but for the students of India's social history, mobilisation and movements based on caste are not a novelty, only the scale and level of organisation was new but a logical growth of what was indigenous catalysed by new elements in the polity.

I have elsewhere illustratively described some of the BCs and SCs movements in the Nineteenth and Twentieth centuries, associated with Mahatma Phule (1827-1890), Shri Narayana Guru (1856-1928), Ayyankali (1863-1941), Periyar EV Ramaswamy and the contributions of Chhatrapati Shahu of Kolhapur (1874-1922) and Maharaja Sajai Rao Gaekwad of Baroda (1863-1939) in different regions of India. The numerous movements of many castes/communities and tribes in different parts of the country of varying strength and effectiveness during this period await full description.

Dr. Babasaheb Ambedkar's (1891-1956) movement was national in sweep and comprehensive in nature, as it covered all aspects of public life -- social, educational, constitutional, economic -- and created permanent institutions and structures within the State and outside to carry forward, uninterrupted by his death, the changes initiated by him. It represented the peak of social revolution so far experienced in India. While focussed on the SCs, his movement had its relevance to the BCs also. While he resisted the efforts of some BCs leaders to get the BCs included in the lists of SCs, on the objectively correct ground that BCs were not "untouchable" while "untouchability" was the touchstone for inclusion in the SCs lists, he supported reservation or quotas for the BCs separately on the ground of social backwardness. In fact, in upholding the constitutionality of the principle of reservation or quotas for BCs on the basis of castes and caste-like communities as units, the Supreme Court, in the Mandal judgement, relied on Ambedkar's formulations in his paper of 1916. It also took note of his speech in the Constituent Assembly as Chairman of the Drafting Committee of the Constitution to clarify draft Article 10(3) --- since renumbered as Article 16(4) -- and piloting that Article since the Drafting Committee, and he in particular, was responsible for introducing in that Article the word "backward" which was not there in the original draft. His speech in Parliament when it was enacting the Cons-titution (First Amendment) Bill in 1951, by which Article 15(4) was inserted, in the aftermath of the Supreme Court's judgement in the Champakam Dorairajan and Venkataramana cases in 1951 was also considered.

Before taking leave of movements of/for BCs, mention must be made of one type of BCs movement -- a movement in the literal sense of the term -- a movement whereby the BCs along with the SCs and STs "voted" with their feet against the Indian caste system, i.e., by leaving the Hindu fold in large numbers wherever circumstances favoured. The affiliation of urban artisan to Buddhism and Jainism in ancient times, is evidenced for example in Burton Stein's study of medieval South Indian State and Society. In the medieval period large numbers belonging to artisan and untouchable castes turned to Islam. As a result, in North India, especially in the States of Uttar Pradesh and Bihar, the proportion of BCs among adherents of Islam is higher than the proportion of BCs among adherents of Hinduism. A good number of weavers of Bengal are also Muslims. A major proportion of the population of artisan castes in UP and Bihar are Muslims. In Punjab, a large proportion of the population of artisan castes became Sikhs. In South India, in the medieval and modern periods a good part of the population of "Untouchable" and other "lower" castes became Muslims. In the modern period another good number in South India, especially Kerala, Tamil Nadu and Andhra Pradesh, became Christians as also did the Scheduled Tribes in the Jharkhand region of Bihar and adjoining States. The post-Independence wave of conversion to Buddhism under Dr. Ambedkar's leadership in 1956 and afterwards was a phenomenon limited to the SCs/ Dalits and has not so far extended to the BCs.

While these conversions were substantial and their social import must be clearly understood, the bulk of the BCs remained Hindus. One of the results of this is that among the BCs are adherents of different religions, Hinduism, Islam, Christianity and Sikhism, the first constituting the majority and the latter three also being numerically substantial.

Reservation in Services

It is in response to these movements of BCs and other non-Brahmin castes that job-reservation and other programmes of development and welfare were introduced for the BCs by many provincial/State governments before and after India's Independence in 1947 and recently by the Government of India in 1990 and afterwards. To put matters in the correct perspective, State intervention for the development and welfare of BCs followed popular movements and community efforts for self-improvement and community movements of assertion of human dignity and socio-economic rights. The community efforts and movements included particularly efforts and movements to acquire modern education perceived as the only vehicle for upward mobility, through agitations for admission of their children to educational institutions of the Government; and in the case of the limited number of communities, which had relatively grater economic capability, through private educational institutions set up by themselves -- the last avenue was not available to most of the communities of the BCs for want of economic capability.

I have elsewhere outlined the introduction of reservation of posts in the services of the State, beginning with the small princely State of Kolhapur in 1902, followed by the much larger princely State of Mysore on the basis of the Report (1921) of the Miller Committee appointed in 1919 -- the first Committee/ Commission on BCs appointed in India; and immediately thereafter the sprawling Madras Presidency also in 1921; the large Bombay Presidency in 1931 following the Report of the State Committee; and the princely State of Travancore in 1935.

Thus, prior to Independence, reservation for BCs or for all/ almost all non-Brahmin castes including those who were later recognised as BCs covered the whole of the Peninsula. But the Vindhyas seemed to be barrier beyond which reservation for BCs did not proceed before Independence or even well after Independence. There are obvious explanations for this. Nor did a central policy emerge before Independence regarding the BCs unlike the position regarding the SCs, thanks largely to Dr. Ambedkar.

Along with, and in fact anterior to reservation in jobs, the provinces and princely States of the Peninsula, especially Madras, Mysore, Kolhapur had instituted measures for promotion of education among the BCs and SCs (often referred to then as the Depressed Classes).

The Constitution of India, 1950, was an important marker. An important feature of it is a series of provisions to eliminate the traditional caste-based iniquities, discriminations and exploitation and oppression and provisions for advancing the social, educational and economic interests of the victims of the Indian caste system, including the BCs. I have elsewhere detailed this edifice of integrated egalitarian provisions within the larger edifice of the Constitution. Briefly, among these provisions mention must be made of Articles 16(4), 15(4) and 340. Article 16(4) provides for reservation of appointments/ posts in favour of any backward class of citizens which is not adequately represented in the services under the State. Article 15(4) provides for special provisions for the advancement of the Socially and Educationally Backward Classes (SEBCs) and the SCs and STs. Articles 340(1) provides for the appointment of a Commission by the President of India to investigate the conditions of SEBCs within the territory of India, the difficulties under which they labour and to make remedial recommendations of steps required of the Union or any State. The task of this Commission, by necessary implication and reading this Article with Clause (10) of Article 338, includes the identification of BCs.

Confining ourselves in the present context only to BCs (other than SCs and STs), the first step taken by the Government of India, pursuant to the above Constitutional mandate, was to appoint the Backward Classes Commission known as the Kaka Kalelkar Commission on the 29th January, 1953, under Article 340(1) of the Constitution in order to identify the Backward Classes, examine their conditions and propose ameliorative actions. This Commission submitted its Report on the 30th March, 1955.

Here was an opportunity for the Government of India to provide an integrated framework for the whole of the country for identifying the Backward Classes in a rational, socially realistic and consistent manner as had been done before Independence in respect of the SCs and STs, and provide for meaningful State intervention by the Central as well as the State Governments to remedy the historically inherited iniquitous situation. Unfortunately, this responsibility, cast on it by Article 340(1), was stalled and was ultimately abdicated when the Central Government by its letter of 14 August, 1961, to State Governments "disposed" of the Report after five years of "motion". The observations of the Supreme Court in its Mandal judgement on this constitute an indictment of the Government of India for this.

In view of the Centre's failure to play its Constitutional role, the States were left to decide for themselves and the BCs were left to whatever steam they possessed in each region. The resultant lists of BCs have been the product of State-level Committees within the executive and Committees and Commissions appointed by the respective State Governments under the Commissions of Inquiry Act 1952. The percentage of reservation has been varied from time to time and the lists have also been modified from time to time. Similar orders have been passed with regard to reservation in educational institutions also.

After the Constitution, action in the States south of the Vindhyas consisted mainly of revising the then existing BCs lists and the then existing scheme of reservation in line with the Constitution, especially after the judgement of the Supreme Court in the Balaji case. The States north of the Vindhyas slowly began to introduce reservation. They were in no hurry because there BCs mobilisation was slow, poor and weak despite the strong support of Ram Manohar Lohia who was one of the few persons who had a deep perception of the interlink between the caste-based social classes of India and economic classes in the Marxist sense. However implementation of reservation in the North Indian States remained slow and half-hearted and devoid of the advantage of central pressure as was available, thanks to the systems instituted primarily by Dr. Ambedkar, in respect of the SCs and STs. At the beginning of this decade four major

States still remained without listing of BCs and consequently without any reservation or other special measure for BCs.

Some States have taken note of the different levels of backwardness among the BCs and have sought to meet this situation and preclude or minimise unequal competition among them by providing for compartmental groups and sub-quotas or sub-rotations. In fact, south of the Vindhyas, compartmentalisation and sub-quotas are a normal pattern. Among the States north of the Vindhyas which entered the field of reservation for OBCs recently, only one namely Bihar has this feature.

Various orders passed by the State governments have been challenged in the High Courts and Supreme Courts. The issues of challenge are broadly the following :

1. The constitutionality of caste-based reservation.
2. Correctness of inclusion of one or more castes in the list or exclusion of one or the other castes from it or sometimes, arising from this, the validity of the methodology followed.
3. The constitutionality and reasonableness of the quantum of reservation provided.

Of the three major issues, which have been settled, initially with reference to Tamil Nadu, Andhra Pradesh and Karnataka and finally by the Mandal judgement in relation to the Centre and for the country as a whole that caste is a class -- not in the Marxist sense of the term but in the sociological sense of the term -- and in fact, castes constitute the most important social classes of India, and that it is constitutional to examine which of them are backward in terms of the criteria or backwardness followed and to designate backward classes in terms of castes. It is also permissible and necessary to similarly examine social groups other than castes. Reports of some of the Commissions like those of Karnataka and Kerala and some of the judgements like the one by the High Court of Kerala in Hariharan Pillai Vs State of Kerala and others (1967) and the Mandal judgement itself have held that socially advanced persons and sections (SAP/S), born in castes identified and designated as backward, cannot be part of the Backward Classes for the purpose of reservation -- in the case of the Mandal judgement, it applies only to reservation in services. In other words, the Supreme Court formula can be summarised as Backward Caste Minus SAP/S=Backward Class.

Mandal Commission

Regarding appropriateness of inclusion, the Mandal judgement has recognised the fact that there can be genuine claims and counter-claims with regard to inclusions and exclusions, and has created a potentially effective mechanism by ordering the creation of a permanent body in the nature of a Commission or Tribunal to which complaints of wrong inclusion or non-inclusion of groups, classes and sections in the lists of BCs can be made. Its advice shall ordinarily be binding upon the Government. If the Government does not agree with it, reasons should be recorded. Before any new class or group is proposed to be included, the recommendation of this body should be taken first. Periodic revisions of the Lists should be made at least once in 10 years in consultation with such body. Such bodies should be constituted one at the Central level and one each in each State. The Supreme Court has also turned its attention to the composition of these bodies and has laid down that their members, both official and non-official, must be experts in the field. Parliament as well as some of the State legislatures have made legislative enactments incorporating these directions; other State governments have issued executive orders instead, setting up such commissions and in a few cases committees. Once these commissions are set up and if by democratic vigilance of the people and judicial vigilance of the Supreme Court and High Courts, the principle laid down by the Supreme Court with regard to the composition of the Commissions/ Tribunals is ensured or enforced continuously, the issues regarding correctness of lists and correctness of inclusion and omissions can be settled in a reasonable time frame and in an objectively satisfactory manner, free from political or executive arbitrariness or "discretion".

On the third issue, earlier judgements have indicated and the Mandal judgement has laid down that the total ceiling for all "vertical" reservations under Article 16(4) should not exceed 50 per cent.

Meanwhile the movement of the backward classes at the supra-regional level, especially in North India, gradually gathered strength. This led to the establishment of the Second Backward Classes (Mandal) Commission on the 1st January, 1979, to determine the criteria for defining the SEBCs, recommending steps for the advancement of SEBCs so identified and to examine the desirability or otherwise of making provisions for the reservation of appointments and posts in public services under the Union and States in favour of BCs not adequately represented in the public services.

The Mandal Commission gave its report on the 31st December, 1980. Thereafter, it took another 10 years of "motions" before the Gordian knot was cut in 1990, with the decision of the Government of India on the 6th August, and announcement in Parliament on the 7th August, and issue of its formal order dated 13th August, 1990, providing for reservation of 27 per cent in civil posts and services under the Government of India and in the central public sector undertakings and financial institutions for the BCs. Its implementation was however held up by ill-informed agitations mainly in North Indian cities and the spate of writ petitions on account of which the Supreme Court stayed the implementation of the order till November 16, 1992. The way in which and the grounds on which the historic decision of 1990 was made, the facts that were marshalled in the Government's affidavits to effectively meet the pettifogging and the pinpricks of those who attacked this constitutionally mandatory and long overdue step and ultimately the judgement of the Supreme Court and the subsequent actions of Government of India in 1993 all go to show that the delays of the eighth decade and the entire inaction from 1956 till 1990 were on flimsy, untenable and un-constitutional grounds.

Pursuant to the specific directions of the Supreme Court in its Mandal judgement, the Government of India took the following steps :

i) An Expert Committee on BCs was appointed on 22 February, 1993, initially to determine the basis i.e., criteria for the identification of the SAP/S, which it furnished to the Government of India on the 10th March, 1993, and subsequently to prepare the first phase Central list of BCs consisting of those castes/communities found in both the respective State lists of the 14 States and the Mandal lists for these States, which it furnished on the 26th June, 1993.

ii) Based on the recommendations of the Expert Committee, the Government of India issued formal orders on 8 September, 1993, actually commencing and enforcing 27 per cent reservation for BCs and issued orders two days after formally notifying the first phase of Central List of BCs.

iii) It moved a bill in Parliament which enacted the National Commission for Backward Classes Act, 1993 (No.27 of 1993) on the 2nd April, 1993, effective from 1st February, 1993.

iv) It notified the first 5-member team of the Commission on 14 August, 1993.

Thus, the reservation for BCs actually commenced more than 43 years after the Constitution came into force and the National Commission for Backward Classes (NCBCs) came into existence on the 33rd anniversary of the rejection of the Kaka Kalelkar Commission's Report. Indian society took a decisive and irreversible turn after the series of events in the momentous three year period from September 1990 to September 1993. Its effect on the Indian society, economy and polity is unfolding itself with increasing tempo.

The inevitable, the Constitutional imperative (which to nation-builders is no less a Moral Imperative than Kant's Categorical Imperative) was grossly delayed but could not be averted. But in the process serious harm was done to the legitimate interests not only of the BCs but also of the nation as a whole by widening the credibility gap. Unfortunately, the mass media and most of the middle class intellectuals outside the State and the establishment also contributed their mite to widening the credibility gap.

Now the stage has come for implementation of reservation in the Central Government and related services sincerely and effectively without any shortfalls of the type which has been occurring in the past in respect of SCs and STs. It is the duty of the intellectuals within and outside the government and establishment to continuously apply the vigilance and moral pressure required to ensure that there is no shortfall in sincerity or professional efficiency in implementation.

The stage has also come to go beyond job reservations in order to find a permanent solution to the traditional fracturing of Indian society by eliminating the social, educational and economic backwardness of the backward classes related to historically inherited but currently still alive birth-based iniquitous social structures. Unfortunately in this regard even after recognition was at last accorded to the Backward Classes in 1990 and 93, only two plan schemes have been introduced for them at the national level till now; one, a poorly funded, defectively conceived and weakly administered Pre-Examination Coaching Scheme for Weaker Sections including particularly the BCs and, second, the National Backward Classes Finance & Development Corporation, which can only provide loans for schemes of economic development for the BCs (as though the only remedy required for backwardness is loans and oblivious of the fact that economic infrastructure provided by the State is no less the need of BCs for their economic advancement than that of the large-industrial investor-class for their profit). While it is a matter for appreciation that the Welfare Ministry had initiated preparatory steps early in 1992 by setting up this Corporation as a non-profit company under Section 23 of the Companies Act, with an authorised capital of Rs.200 crore and a paid up capital of Rs. 156.90 crore, so that it became possible for the Corporation to make disbursement from the financial year 1992-93, severe constraints have been imposed on the outcome *ab initio*, on account of the severe conceptual limitations in understanding and appreciating the dimensions of development of Backward Classes.

It is now necessary to understand the full dimension and magnitude of the development of Backward Classes and for this purpose have an idea of the profile of the Backward Classes as obtaining today.

Profile of Backward Classes and Tasks Ahead

The largest number of Backward Classes are castes linked with traditional crafts, artisanal/artisan-like production, and various service occupations. Another number are indigent beggar castes, nomadic and semi-nomadic communities and communities which had earlier been stigmatised as criminal. Another group of backward classes are peasant castes and pastoral castes.

Of the traditional craft-persons, weavers and potters are a typical example. Of artisanal and artisan-like producers, fisher-people and stone-cutters are typical example. The condition of those engaged in these traditional occupations often poignantly come to notice. Generally they have no control over the resources of their raw materials, and they get them on terms disadvantageous to themselves; they have little access to relevant modern technology and to sources of finance; and they are at the mercy of the market forces which are not friendly to them. While the accepted macro-economic policies of the past did not meet their needs, there is a danger of the new macro-economic trends undermining these traditional producers. This is true also of artisanal/artisan-like producers like fisher folk.

The programmes of the past have, even where they have succeeded, not been more than tokenism. But there have been instances of success, whether on account of efforts of individuals in the establishment or on account of non-governmental activists, enough to give confidence that their economy is not beyond redemption if this is taken up seriously and consistently by re-orienting the governmental machinery and institutions, empowering the producers for their own development and advancement and securing the cooperation of non-governmental activities and experts.

Education is another weak area. For example, Shantha Krishnan's study of potters of Delhi, based on a complete census shows that their literacy (54.18 per cent in 1986) is midway between that of Delhi's non-SCs urban population (67.51 per cent in 1981) and Delhi's SCs population (39.91 per cent in 1981).

In the field of education, it is not only necessary to improve general education and literacy but it is also necessary to make it possible for them to secure the benefits of technical and professional education to enable and empower the backward classes to compete in the market on their own whether in their traditional areas or in new areas of the economy.

So far as reservation is concerned, many of the indigent castes and castes of N, SN and VJ have not had any benefit from reservation. No pointed efforts have been made to make it possible for them to have the benefit of reservation. Many other communities have also not had their due share of employment even after decades of reservation. These are areas not only for quantitative fulfilment but also for bridging the credibility gap.

Some of the macro-agricultural policies as well as individual-oriented programmes have been of benefit to peasant castes in irrigated areas, but many of the peasant castes still remain backward on account of the hang-over of the past disadvantages and/or current disadvantages especially in unirrigated or rain-fed areas. Dryland cultivators, a large number of whom belong to the backward peasant castes, need irrigation wherever possible and better dryland farming where irrigation is not possible. The impact of new macro-economic policies are a source of anxiety to peasants and it needs to be watched carefully so as to take timely protective, preventive and corrective actions.

A careful look at various categories of BCs show the occupations they are associated with -- like washing of clothes, pottery, hair-cutting, blacksmithy, weaving, shepherding and other cattle-herding, stone-cutting, fishing, boating, distilling of liquor, milk-vending, toddy-tapping, begging and entertainment through acrobatics. Attention will have to be given to each of these professions to enable their resources and factors of production on fair terms and choices whether in the traditional or modern sectors. In fact, the traditional sectors themselves have to be modernised without their losing control over these sectors as has been happening, for example, in leather and fishing. In case of occupations like professional begging, diversification into alternative economic fields cannot wait for the next generation.

A large number of people belonging to the castes connected with the above type of occupations have been/are being reduced to landless wage labourers. This underlines the importance of the deliberately and intentionally neglected areas of land distribution and redistribution and enforcement of statutory minimum wages.

A few States have set up Backward Classes Finance & Development Corporations. The Government of India has also recently set up a National Backward Classes Finance & Development Corporation. Unless these Corporations take up their work keeping in view the above aspects and in large magnitudes, and their activity covers micro-lending as well as micro-infrastructure, the results may at best be patchy and make no significant difference to the conditions of BCs engaged in these occupations.

From the point of view of a fresh and meaningful approach to the development of Backward Classes, two important initiatives occurred in 1996 -- partly by the non-governmental sector and partly by the Government. The first was the formulation of the Dalit Manifesto by the present author under the auspices of the National Action Forum for Social Justice. Its Part-III deals with various measures required for the educational and economic advancement of the BCs and a thorough implementation of job reservations and actively commended to various political parties in the months before the General Elections of 1996 to the Lok Sabha (House of People of the Indian Parliament). It was accepted by the coalition Government and the parties constituting it and supporting in June 1996 and incorporated as part of the Common Minimum Programme of the United Front Government. But almost all of it is yet to be implemented. It is hoped that the Government of India will settle down to implementation of each of these items thoroughly and without further delay.

The second important step was the setting up of the Working Group for the Development and Welfare of Backward Classes during the Ninth Plan by the Planning Commission in consultation with the Ministry of Welfare with the present author as its Chairman. This is a historical step and a long overdue step in Indian planning because it is for the first time after five decades of India's Independence and

Eight Plans of development that, so far as the Centre is concerned, a working group for the backward vlasses has been thought of. Departing from the usual pattern of having only members from Departments and Ministries, the Working Group co-opted four non-official members with wide experience of BCs and also belonging to the BCs of their respective States. Two of them are members of minorities and two of artisan and artisan-like communities. This would impart to the conclusions and recommendations of the Working Group a touch of the life experience of BCs.

In its first interim report of May 1996, the Working Group has outlined the approach for the development of Backward Classes required to replace the limited, truncated and ad hoc measures hitherto. To facilitate meaningful planning, it has grouped them under the following categories :

(a) Communities without resources or skills -- a good number of castes/communities are indigent and their traditional occupation has been and still is begging, sometimes with religious overtones. Many of them are nomadic or semi-nomadic.

(b) Artisan castes/communities with traditional skills engaged in various traditional crafts providing a variety of goods at family/ cottage scale like weavers, potters, blacksmiths, carpenter etc., - these are the original and true manufacturing classes of Indian society who were engaged in secondary production even at a time when many of the major industrial houses of today were moneylenders and *hundi* operators. [Their traditional occupations have been and are under different forms of threat, while entry into modern sectors and facilities for upward mobility denied.]

(c) Castes/communities of artisanal producers like fisher folk, toddy tappers, stone-cutters, earth workers, etc.

(d) Castes/communities providing traditional services like haircutting and grooming, washing of clothes, safai ("scavenging").

(e) Castes/communities of poor peasantry including tenant peasantry of the former zamindari and other intermediary tenures.

These communities include people who follow different religions sharing the same traditional occupations. But difference of religion does not make any significant difference in their objective socio-economic conditions.

The basic principle pointed by the Working Group is that a free society of equal individuals, enjoying human dignity in the same measure, is not possible unless the harsh conditions in which the BCs live and work are altered to secure economic self-reliance in their traditional or in other diverse activities, according to their choice (which may have generational differences). For this, the full benefit of modern technology, access to finance, control over raw material resources, marketing facilities etc., on terms which are fair, affordable and viable to them are required to be made available. Also the facilities for education, health, housing etc., so that they cease to be placed at a disadvantage in the process of development. They need to have what is currently often referred to as a truly "level playing field" -- a concept often urged for the large-scale industrial and business class, but ignored in the case of SCs, STs and BCs.

Developmental planning meaningful to the Backward Classes must subsume all these aspects and have as its objective removal of the conditions under which they are distinguishable as socially and educationally backward. In other words removal of their social and educational backwardness (this necessarily requires creation of economic self-reliance), as experienced by them, would lead to the destruction of caste and caste-like barriers and annihilation of caste and similar manifestations in the Indian society.

In order to ensure that hereafter their development is undertaken along sound lines and in a comprehensive and integrated manner, both from the point of view of maintaining and promoting their hold and growth in their traditional occupational areas and facilitating their diversification into new and modern occupational areas, the Working Group has suggested the following steps:

1. This Working Group will, after the Interim Report is furnished to the Planning Commission, inter alia, associate other persons of experience and expertise belonging to the Backward Classes of different categories especially those mentioned above. Also those who have empathy for the Backward Classes and have knowledge and expertise pertaining to different areas of economic activities and planned development of Backward Classes. They would work out meaningful, comprehensive and integrated models for the development of Backward Classes well in time for the formulation of the Ninth Plan;

2. The conclusions arrived at by Working Group should be taken seriously in terms of content and magnitude including invest-

ment, by the Planning Commission and the Central and State Governments. Decisions should be taken and implemented expeditiously, without resorting to the usual nit-picking and hair-splitting (often an alibi or cover for unwillingness to provide outlays required to the long-neglected development of weaker sections including Backward Classes).

3. The usual gross gaps between need and plan outlay, between Five-Year Plan and Annual Plan outlays, between the Annual Plan outlays and annual budgets, should be strictly eschewed in the case of BCs, especially in view of the 45-year lag in making a beginning in planning for the BCs.

While this process was on in order to facilitate the preparation of the Approach Document for the Ninth Plan, it has suggested some directions and aspects of economic and educational development of BCs and implementation of reservation. It has also indicated the new empirical initiatives required for this purpose and a new personnel policy of the Government related to the Backward Classes. Subsequently in September 1996, it has worked out outlays that obviously will be required in the Ninth Pan for the BCs in matters like post-matric scholarships, residential schools, hostels, coaching programmes, economic development including provision of local micro-infrastructure (which cannot be in the shape of loans, but to which loans can be meaningfully superadded). The Ministry of Welfare has furnished this requirement to the Planning Commission.

The Working Group has to be facilitated by the Government of India and the Planning Commission to continue its work in order to provide guidelines for the planning process. It is hoped that the Ninth Plan, both in the Central Plan as well as in the State Plan sectors, will draw upon the knowledge available and potentially available, in order to formulate a comprehensive programme of development for the Backward Classes.

These steps, of which reservation in government jobs is only one item, are necessary not only to ensure that they get their due share but also to lay a secure social foundation for nation building in a plural multi-ethnic, multi-layered society that India is. The "ethnic" aspect here does not relate to the BCs and SCs but to the STs. As explained earlier, the dividing lines between the different castes, the different layers of castes, and between the advanced castes, the SCs and the BCs of each region are not ethnic. They are social divisions of the same ethnic group. The antagonisms between them and among them are not deep. There are many factors that bind them together like common language, common customs, common traditions. They live in every village together though in separate portions/streets and in the case of SCs in nearby ghettos. The present tensions are not only manageable but curable. These are caused by the unfair distribution of advantages and burdens shared by members belonging to these different castes and layers of castes. To illustrate, the object of antagonism of all or most castes varies from region to region and period to period. Where one particular caste is found to have a disproportionately large share of advantages in coveted areas/sectors, that caste attracts general hostility and odium. In some places and times, it may be the Brahmins alone. At others, it may be the Brahmins along with one or two other castes of the same region. At still others, it may be one or two other non-Brahmin castes. When the disparity is reduced, the temperature falls. When the disparity is shifted, the object of hostility also shifts. Fairness and equitability in the distribution of advantages and opportunities without any perceivable significant advantages or disadvantages of being born in any particular caste, or in other words the snapping of the link between backwardness and any caste, will not only remove hostilities in general but will also lay the foundation for the elimination of the caste system itself. It will help creation of a larger society co-terminus with the nation or at least with each region of the nation, unfractured by inter-generational continuity, "programmed" by means of birth-group-based endogamy. In achieving these tasks, the large number of intellectuals and those in responsible positions, most of whom still belong to the castes of the top layer, have an extraordinary responsibility, especially in the context of the severe erosion of their credibility in the past four or five post-Independence decades. This in conjunction with reform-cum-developmental mobilisation of the BCs, along with the SCs and STs, is essential to enable India to leave behind what has been and still is the morally and materially debilitating part of its legacy.

25

Minorities in Free India

Dr. Asghar Ali Engineer

MINORITIES, RELIGIOUS or linguistic, always face some problems vis-a-vis a majority. The problem of a minority is a universal problem. It exists in all modern nation States, Western or Eastern, Asian or African. It also often explodes if not handled carefully and with due sensitivity. We are completing fifty years of our secular democracy and various organizations are arranging seminars and conferences to take stock of the minority situation after fifty years of our nationhood. The Rajiv Gandhi Foundation (RGF) which is deeply interested in this area organised a one-day seminar recently in Delhi on "Minorities in India". Noted intellectuals, academics, bureaucrats and social activists were present. I had the privilege of participating in the same. Views expressed in the seminar by eminent Indians deserve serious consideration by all of us. Excerpts are below:

Dr.Abid Hussain, Vice-Chairman, RGF, felt that the question of minorities is quite important, not only for India but also for our neighbours. The question of democracy and minority, he said, is of special interest. In a democratic society dissimilarities and diversity are tremendously important. The American experiment of melting pot has failed. Dictatorships also did not succeed in this matter. Thus, democracy and diversity both are integrally related. Those who want to do away with differences have pushed society to dangerous limits. Even Gorbachev felt that diversity is most fundamental. But a question troubles us: was it right to create Pakistan on the basis of diversity?

Prof. Akil Bilgrami, who teaches philosophy in Columbia University, New York, stated that all discussions on minority begins with a foolhardy efforts of defining it. It is difficult to define minority. Socrates at the end of his life said that only concept he has succeeded in defining is mud. Numerical strength, Prof.Bilgrami said, and socio-economic condition are bare minimum to define minority. But it is not enough. Minority is an extremely relative term, crisscrossing with different concepts. Even the Congress was aware of this problem right from the Nehru Report in 1928 to the Constituent Assembly.

According to Bilgrami, Ambedkar said that both majority and minority are wrong; majority because it wants to deny existence of minority and minority because it wants to perpetuate itself. Again, majority denying existence of minority has two aspects: (i) exclusionary and (ii) inclusionary. Exclusionary, when majority denies its rights to minority, and inclusionary when majority wants to assimilate it with itself. Dalits have been excluded and Muslims are under pressure to give up personal laws and adopt common civil code. He said a community can be defined in normative or in descriptive way also. Normatively speaking, it is a depository of traditions and certain values. A community can be hijacked by communalists so some tend to define it descriptively. Again, if we talk of minority rights, community becomes focus of rights, not an individual. The problem is to safeguard community rights as well as to bring about non-coercive change in personal laws to promote gender justice.

Prof. Iqbal Ansari of Aligarh Muslim University (AMU) disagreeing with Bilgrami felt that the concept of minority has been defined by the UN declaration. Minority could be either dominant or dominated. If it is dominated, it has a different problem. Identity for minorities could be negative in certain situations like for the blacks in America and dalits in India. The dalits want to throw away their negative identity imposed on them. So the idea of minorities perpetuating themselves is more complex. Again identities are changeable and changing. Some identities are cherished and some loathed. The UN declaration also talks of promoting some cherished identities. Even tribal identities are cherished ones and must be promoted. Similarly cultural, linguistic and religious identities are cherished and will perpetuate themselves.

Archbishop Angelo Fernandes was of the opinion that while discussing minority problem we have to keep two principles in mind: one is of basic human dignity and unity of all human beings. Second principle is of minority identity which should also be judged by the contribution it makes to make the life more human. Fraternity cannot be overlooked while talking of majority-minority. He felt that the concept of human rights is too legalistic. It is human person which is more important. Our objective should be to make our life more human. If one injects the idea of injustice in the minds of majority, it may lead to great trouble. We have to create a balanced society.

Syed Shahabuddin on the other hand said that he considers the concept of minority a valid concept. In democracy there are no dominant minorities. There are resurgent ethnicities everywhere. There is no homogeneous society in the world except perhaps Alaska where perhaps only Eskimos live. India is a country of all types of diversities. Not only this, in every identifiable community there are sub-identities. We must, therefore, talk of social groups and all social groups are in minority. We have to keep in mind the legitimate uses of identities. People want just share in the fruits of development. There may be some minorities which desire to be assimilated. Therefore, integration or assimilation is a voluntary process.

S.S.Gill thought that minority can be defined in a particular context. Today Muslims are, he thought, a genuine and authentic minority. But the Muslims did not consider themselves as a minority during the medieval period. Sikhs in Delhi never considered themselves as minority before. But 1984 violence against them changed the situation. In fact it is discrimination which creates the feeling of minority. Mr.Gill felt that the minorities should give up their rights as they are not substantial anyway. It will take away sting from majoritarian propaganda.

Prof. Zoya Hasan of Jawaharlal Nehru University (JNU) was of the opinion that the problem is that democratization of Muslims has not taken place due mainly to the Congress. Though after Independence there has been descriptive acknowledgement of minorities but there has not been democratization of Muslims. The State, according to her, has abdicated its role. Indian State has created public-private domain. So personal law cannot be reformed as it belongs to the private domain. Thus, this duality is the problem.

Virendra Dayal of the National Human Rights Commission said that the question of definition (of minority) takes us no where. What is important is the perspective. We often talk of human rights and minority rights. The League of Nations and the United Nations adopted different perspective i.e., universal declaration of human rights was given primacy. Minority rights came last. Minority rights should be seen within a wider perspective of human rights. We not only belong to a minority but we also function within certain context. As a State cannot be given right to torture people in the name of sovereignty, minorities also cannot be allowed to persecute and oppress its own groups.

Virendra Trehan, an industrialist, felt that minorities are not always weaker. Take Parsis, for example. Tatas or Manekshaws or Zakir Hussain for that matter, they all belong to the minority and yet they were so powerful. Thus minorities do not always suffer.

Syed Hamid, former Vice-Chancellor, AMU, however, had a different view. The ground situation, he said, was more important than academic expertise. It is not true that minority and minority identity are not important. It is also not true that minorities are not democratic or have not been democratised. They are very much the part of democratic process. But there is no honesty and transparency in dealing with them. Take 15-point programme for instance. It is meant for uplift of minorities. But education was not included in it at all. Even the document on the new Education Policy had acknowledged that the two minorities i.e., Muslims and neo-Buddhists are quite backward in educational field. Also there are government documents which clearly bring out that the Muslims have slid back and yet much is not being done to remedy the situation. These minorities can justifiably ask why they have been left out?

K.F.Rustomjee, the ex-director general of police, said that though he belongs to minority he hates to call himself a minority. He had never suffered as a minority. He hoped and desired that all minorities feel that way. Then he posed a question how did we allow Babri Masjid to be destroyed? Why did we descend to that level? Could we not have prevented that? Who creates minority problem? If we look deeper, minority problem was created by the British, and the Muslims like Jinnah exploited it. Then the Kashmir conflict was exploited by Pakistan further accentuating it. Democracy essentially means dialogue. Babri Masjid could also have been saved by dialogue, concessions and compromise. But we violated the democratic norms. Rustomjee also referred to the problem of communal riots and communalisation of police. It is a dangerous situation. Police force must be secular and devoid of the feeling of minority, majority.

Prof. Bhargava said that it is only a propaganda that minorities are pampered. One must see in proper perspective as to why minorities have been given certain rights. The answer is that our social, cultural and economic structures are so built that benefits only go to majority. Thus, the idea that the minorities should give up their rights is a dangerous idea. Mr. N.N.Tandon also thought that the life lived in the raw by Muslims in towns and mohallahs should be taken into account to understand their problem. The State has been partial; it could not stop destruction of Babri Masjid. He pointed out the problems of poor administration of law and communalisation of police.

Mohit Sen felt that we have remained democratic and secular but our secularism should not be elitist under democracy. There are tensions between democracy and secularism. Democracy can also lead to majority communalism. Also, a nation State should not be homogeneous. Its strength lies in its heterogeneity. Also, India is a nation in making and is facing problems as such.

Prof. Imtiaz Ahmed was of the view that the Hindu-Muslim problem alone should not be focussed. It will amount to being dishonest to other minorities. It is true that Hindus and Muslims have quite a convoluted concept of each other. He also felt that over the years there has been erosion and devaluation of the constitutional rights of minorities. He has pointed out that minorities resent homogenization but it is dominant trend today and market processes and globalisation is also leading towards homogenisation. Also, there should be negotiation as to what minorities would like to preserve and what they would like to give up. Prof. Imtiaz also said that the State has tendency to be an instrument of majority. So it is in India. The minorities should have right to their religious and cultural identities provided they do not violate rights of their sub-groups.

Varadarajan, ex-member, Minority Commission, focussed on the actual problem of minorities, specially the Muslims and how they have been denied access to the fruits of development. He substantiated his assertion through available data on Muslims. What rights are we talking about, he asked and said they have not been conferred any great rights. He even maintained that Article 25 is not very special as it is not only for minorities but for all. The question of minority will remain as long as they are disadvantaged.

Prof. Roy Burman focussed on the tribal problem and felt they should not be equated with minorities. If they are equated the world order will be distorted. Tribals are fighting to preserve their culture.

Rights of tribals and minorities should not be mixed up. He felt that human rights discourse can be misleading. Collective rights should be respected.

In my submission to the seminar, I stressed that sub-groups within minorities sometimes suffer acutely. They suffer because minority rights are grossly misused to perpetuate iniquitous order. I gave example of the struggle of reformist Bohras who are a tiny minority within a minority. The religious head often invokes minority rights like Article 25 of the Indian Constitution to claim privileges which result in suppression of rights of reforms of Bohras. By invoking minority rights the Bohra high priest has caused acute agony to hundreds of divided families. While collective rights are important, individual rights and rights of sub-groups should not be overlooked.

Even after 50 years of liberal democracy, we are yet to crystallize our views on how to handle the sensitive issue of minorities in a vast country like India. We have been looking at the issue of minorities as a Hindu-Muslim problem. Nothing can be farther from the truth. Unless the nation develops a healthy policy of welfare of minorities with a liberal outlook, dissonance and violence in our society cannot be avoided.

PART V
Public Order

- Intelligence Services in India
- Fifty Years of Policing: Urgent Need for Reforms
- Central Reserve Police Force: Peace Keepers of the Nation

26

Intelligence Services in India

T. V. Rajeswar

INTELLIGENCE IS an indispensable function of the State and no one dealt with it in greater detail than Kautilya. Under his guidance the Mauryas had a secret service department, organised in the most uninhibited manner. The Mauryan rule was threatened constantly by foreign aggressors and internal dissensions and it was able to meet the challenges by implementing the instructions laid down by Kautilya. Techniques of espionage were detailed by Kautilya which included employing of double agents, capturing enemies' wives and children as hostages, using courtesans for trapping men, etc. Kautilya prescribed that when the report of a spy was corroborated by two others it should be believed. Around the same time, in the deep South, Thiruvalluvar, the celebrated Tamil scholar of Sangam age laid down that the report of a secret agent should be checked and cross-checked by at least two other independent sources before accepting it.

Fundamentals of statecraft, whether in the field of police administration or that of intelligence, were the same and it goes to the credit of Indian genius that these were known and practised from the most ancient times. Skipping the middle ages and the Mughal era, we may proceed to the British era in the mid-Nineteenth century when the British were settling down after the Sepoy Mutiny to administer the country in an organised manner. The British found the country almost in an anarchical condition and chaos prevailed extensively. The earliest efforts of the British were directed towards putting down '*thuggery*', human sacrifices, slavery, *sati*, infanticide, etc. They built up a police force, courts, jails, etc., and introduced administration of justice which was fair and unknown in earlier times. It was by putting down the terrible pestilence of *thuggery* throughout India that the British succeeded in bringing about certain amount of order. William Sleeman, who rose to the rank of Major General later, did yeoman service in suppressing *thuggery*. The origin of an organised police force under the British rule is traced to the resolution of the Government of India dated January 10, 1835, setting up the anti-*thuggery* department with Sleeman as its General Superintendent. Subsequently, this department was expanded to include special operations to deal with intelligence gathering, and a Central Special Branch emerged as part of the *Thuggery* Department. It was this unit which later in 1888 emerged as the Intelligence Bureau.

In 1860, the Government of India appointed a commission of enquiry into the entire gamut of police administration in India and it recommended the setting up of a single homogeneous force of civil constabulary for performing all police duties. To secure unity of action and identity of system, the general management of the force in each province was entrusted to an Inspector General and each district was to be placed under a District Superintendent. The Police Act of 1861 which was enacted still forms the basis of police administration in India. There have been constant demands and representations for a drastic revision of the Act in keeping with the needs of modern times. A Police Commission headed by Dharma Vira was appointed in 1977, and it submitted its report in 1979-80, but much of what he recommended is yet to be implemented.

The Indian Constitution places law and order in the State List but the Centre has its own responsibilities as mentioned in Articles 246, 256 and 355. In particular, Article 355 states that it shall be of the duty of the Union to protect every State against external aggression and internal disturbance and to ensure that the Government of every State is carried on in accordance with the provisions of the Constitution. The Seventh Schedule of the Constitution under Article 246, provides for item 8 — "Central Bureau of Intelligence and Investigation". The evolution of the Central organisations such as the Intelligence Bureau, the Central Bureau of Investigation and the several paramilitary forces like the Central Reserve Police Force, the Border Security Force, the Indo-Tibetan Border Police, the Central Industrial Security Force, the Railway Protection Force, etc., were all set up in pursuance of these constitutional provisions. There has been no dispute on their functioning in various States including Kashmir.

The Intelligence Bureau is entrusted with the responsibi-lity of collecting information from various sources pertaining to the security of the State, maintenance of law and order and keeping a watch on the activities of people and organizations which would have an impact on administration. India has gone through several big turmoils during the past fifty years from the eve of Independence such as the pre-partition communal riots; the partition and the great exodus of people between India and Pakistan and vice versa; the reorganisation of the States, the emergence of the Kashmir problem; the Sino-Indian clashes of 1962, the Bangladesh war of 1971; the imposition of emergency and its aftermath in 1975-1977; the growth of militancy in Punjab followed by Operation Blue Star in 1984; the assassination of Indira Gandhi; growth of militant and insurgent groups in the north-east assisted by ISI of Pakistan in the 1980s and thereafter; disclosures of large scale corruption on the part of Ministers and highly placed officials in recent years. The list is not exhaustive and there were no doubt several other matters of national importance during this period.

In the north-east, practically every State has active militancy if not insurgency going on. Assam, Nagaland, Manipur and Tripura are highly disturbed. The United Liberation Front of Assam (ULFA) emerged immediately after the erstwhile agitators came to power under the Asom Gana Parishad's banner in 1986. The orgy of murder, kidnapping and loot indulged in by the ULFA extremists was abetted and aided by Pakistan's ISI with its base in Bangladesh. Regretfully, the Bangladesh government had been extending full cooperation all these years, and it is hoped, as indeed promised by Prime Minister Sheik Hasina recently, that the ISI activities in Bangladesh would cease and the free run that various militant groups from the north-east had in that country would now end.

The external intelligence is looked after by the Research and Analysis Wing (R&AW) which came into being in 1967. it did remarkable work prior to and during the Bangladesh war. It has a difficult task on its hands in maintaining a close watch on the activities of various militant groups visiting the neighbouring countries like Pakistan, Bangladesh, Myanmar, etc., and also the activities of hostile foreign groups like the ISI.

Due to India's independent stand in the matter of Non-Proliferation Treaty (NPT), Comprehensive Test Ban Treaty (CTBT) and the Missile Control Regime (MCR), as well as the highly sophisticated technical establishments, the missile test centres in Andhra, Orissa and Kerala are all inevitable targets for infiltration and intelligence gathering by the foreign intelligence agencies. In the game of intelligence gathering, there is no distinction between friends and foes and every foreign country is deemed to have a hostile interest in the matter. Consequently the Intelligence Bureau and its various allied agencies have to maintain round the clock watch on them. They have been able to unearth a large number of cases leading to expulsion of several foreign diplomats involved and jailing of Indian agents. Pakistan's agents are the largest single constituent in these activities and consequently, of all the agents prosecuted successfully and jailed, Pakistanis and their contacts account for most.

There are many areas in which the intelligence efforts have to be strengthened. For example, the case of large scale arms dropped over Purulia in December 1995, is not yet fully worked out and the persons behind the operation are yet to be traced. The traffic of militants from across the border, infiltration of arms, ammunition and explosives have not been stopped effectively. The activities of the north-eastern militants are yet to be checkmated. The migration from Bangladesh which has already brought about a crore of illegal immigrants to this country is yet to be stopped effectively. The militancy in Kashmir and Punjab has not been halted though its intensity has come down. The efforts of the security services in these areas have to continue with even greater efforts.

As India nears the twenty-first century, the political and social scene within the country is almost chaotic. The economic scene is not very bright either. The extensive corruption at high levels and the widespread publicity by the media have led to loss of faith on the part of the people at large in those who govern the country. This will inevitably percolate to people's loss of faith in the limbs of the State viz. administrative machinery, the police, the judiciary and so on. The overall condition of the country could at best be described as unstable requiring close monitoring.

27

Fifty Years of Policing

The Urgent Need for Reforms

K. F. Rustamji

NO GOVERNMENT at the Centre or in the States has been able to remove the taint which centuries of feudalism have stamped on us. We still want a rule which is only meant for the benefit of the ruler and his robber barons. That is the essence of fuedalism — the relationship between the ruler and his vassals, which today are all the agencies of the State. Politicians do not want to change that. They swear by democracy but it has to be only for their benefit, to satisfy their greed and lust for power. The manner in which the police forces of India have been used to serve politicians of the ruling party is a crime against democracy, but it is skillfully concealed, and is seldom noticed by the judiciary, the media or the scholars who keep a tab on the health of the nation.

The National Police Commission (NPC) had proposed a method of reducing, if not eliminating, the grip of the party in power on the police which is exercised by the unabashed use of transfers, promotions or protection of those who help them in corruption, and transfer to oblivion posts of those who show an inclination to be subservient to the law and not to them. The NPC proposed that a State Security Commission presided over by the State Minister in charge of police with one member from the Government and one from the opposition, and four others unconnected with politics, should give the direction for police performance and discipline. There were many other safeguards for the protection of the public in the report such as a mandatory judicial enquiry in cases of alleged rape, or death in custody, or deaths of two or more persons in police firing. The NPC had also suggested a method of redressal of grievances which has special significance today when all the forces are agitated over the recommendations of the Fifth Pay Commission. It is a strange feature of the Government that they want to push down the police, but keep on asking and expecting more and more from them in performance. Thanks to Prakash Singh and others, a writ is shortly to be decided in the Supreme Court on the implementation of the Police Commission's report.

The question often put to me in meetings is, "Why is the image of the police so poor?". When I ask them whether the image of the politician and lawyer is better, they say, "It is the same". Yet it is the politicians, mostly lawyers, who took up the question of freedom, worked for it, suffered and sacrificed for it, and finally succeeded in securing it from a well-entrenched British government. Also what is not known is the work done by many police officers in preventing the Government from taking harsh measures against the freedom movement. The work of the Indian Civil Services (I.C.S.) and Indian Police (I.P.) in this regard has seldom been mentioned, but it did have an impact on the rulers. The officers of the Armed Forces, fresh from the Second World War, also told the British in no uncertain terms that the time had come for them to leave.

For fifty years we have all worked for democracy — judge, soldier, police, politician, lawyer and common citizen — all have done their best to sustain and preserve democracy. Each has played his part. If we are often sceptical about the future, it is because democracy itself has shown some defects which we must correct. What I would like to sketch out here is the part played by the police in the consolidation of Independent India, the defects which have appeared in policing in the last fifty years, and the measures which need to be taken to improve performance in the future.

To talk of police failures is easy. There are the blindings, the custodial deaths, the rapes in custody, the delays in investigation, the outbreaks of crime, the nexus with politicians and criminals, the rudeness and lack of courtesy in police stations. All this can be corrected. What passes unnoticed is that in this vast land which suffered a traumatic partition in 1947, in which millions were uprooted and millions perished, and in which millions live below the poverty line, we were able to settle down in 10 years, and have had elections after elections peacefully. We have had waves of disorder like the States' re-organisation, massive waves of communal unrest, wars and terrorism, famine and food shortage, and all of them have been dealt with successfully.

We have had communal riots. In the majority of them the role of the police has been commendable. What is not known is that on thousands of occasions serious rioting could have taken place and was prevented by firm and impartial action, often by two officers (the Collector and the Suprintendent of Police) who had the ability to foresee and lead their men with courage and conviction. Where the police failed, the army was able to come to their help and order was restored. The only blot was Ayodhya. That was mainly owing to political blunders. All the same secularism has been preserved. The Flag is flying high in Kashmir.

We still have a few areas that are subject to dacoity but let us look back to the fifties when the dacoit gang of Mansingh ruled over a part of the Chambal basin as if it was a new native state. Let us give credit to a brave politician — Narsingh Rao Dikshit — who succeeded in his promise in the Madhya Bharat Assembly to bring the dacoity down or resign from the office. After that, in the fifties and the sixties a large number of gangs arose in the border area of Uttar Pradesh, Madhya Pradesh and Rajasthan — Rupa, Lakhan Singh, Gabbar and others. All these gangs were removed one by one by a combination of intelligence and brave armed police work. More than a hundred officers lost their lives in these operations.

The police had also to bear the brunt of terrorism, first in Assam, Nagaland and Mizoram and then in Punjab and Kashmir. The main credit undoubtedly goes to the army but in each place after the first few months of ambush and encounter, the place had to be kept under control by the police and paramilitary. We cannot say that no mistakes were made. Unfortunately there are some officers in the police who have their own distorted ideas about minimum force and human rights. They attract a lot of political support because they promise a quick result. In the end it is the day-to-day routine of thana work, and police and paramilitary integration in operations, and steady flow of intelligence that was able to defeat the plans of the estranged neighbour. The battle still goes on in the Naxalite areas where land mines have maimed many police officers.

Equally important was the part played by the police in assisting the army in the wars with Pakistan. In the last one in 1971, the Border Security Force (BSF) manfully conducted operations for many months before handing over to the army. If there is any future war, the police will play a more significant part.

While there have been many successes, it cannot be denied that steadily the work of the police has been deteriorating. Whichever way we turn for a new look at policing, we come back to the National Police Commission Report, which even if it is dated, shows what a lot of changes are required. There is need to reorganise policing from the thana level because it is there that a serious decline has set in. It all began with senior officers neglecting the thana and spending their time in genuflections to politicians. At the same time some of them put across the pernicious doctrine that policing without violence is impossible. They had to be corrected. Training has been seriously neglected. One by one all the supports of good policing are being withdrawn. It began with the indiscriminate posting of guards during the terrorist phase. Security gradually became a farce - the protection of a few, and neglect of the many. The role of the police in patrolling was given up. Street presence was no longer considered necessary. Knowledge of criminals is weak because of frequent transfers. Grassroots intelligence is almost nil. Registration of crime is selective. Worst of all the sanctity of thana records is fast getting lost. No officer takes the trouble to inspect the thana in detail.

When bad policing is combined with laxity in trials and congestion in courts, we reach the stage when there is no deterrence of the type required. You have only to see the large number of scams that have broken out like a rash, or extortions, kidnappings and day-light killings, or the new types of crimes that are appearing in banks for instance, all because we have made the criminal justice system totally ineffective.

It would be absurd to put all the blame on politicians or lawyers or the police or the judiciary. The truth is that we have not learnt how to work together, for the benefit of the people. There were some resolute men in the police — who stood up for correct methods, but all the officers of the I.P.S. did not support them. If they had, the country would not have had to face the next century with the type of decay that has occurred in policing.

28

Central Reserve Police Force

Peace Keepers of the Nation

M. B. Kaushal

THE CENTRAL RESERVE POLICE FORCE (CRPF) is an epitome of bravery, courage and dedication. With its dedicated service for the unity and integrity of the country, the Force has carved out a niche for itself in the minds and hearts of the people of India. The sight of the CRPF is very reassuring to the people and also to the State Governments. It is the most versatile of the central police force today. Its capacity to switch over from one role to another is amazing. In all its assigned tasks, whether within or outside the country, the Force has acquitted itself creditably. Its contribution in bringing normalcy in Punjab is well known. The significant contribution made by the CRPF in restoration of democratic process in Jammu and Kashmir would remain a landmark in the history of the country. The invaluable assistance of the CRPF to the States in the North-East in day to day administration and to keep fissiparous elements at bay has been appreciated. It has the distinction to participate in peace keeping operations alongwith the Indian Army in Sri Lanka and under the flag of United Nations at Haiti. The presence of a separate Mahila Battalion component and an elite Rapid Action Force under its umbrella has made the CRPF unique amongst the central police forces.

The internal security management in a multi-lingual, multi-religious and multi-caste democratic country of the size of India is a daunting task. In the federal set up under the Indian Constitution, the basic responsibility of maintenance of law and order is of the State. Hence, there is need of a central force, comprising people from different religions, from different States speaking different languages and still working under one flag, to assist the States in maintenance of law and order. By ensuring unity and integrity of the country and also secular fabric of the Indian society, CRPF fulfills this essential need and act as the healing arm of the Union of India.

The Central Reserve Police Force is the premier central force for internal security management. It is one of the oldest central para military force. The one lakh and sixty thousand strong Force has an all India character; both in organization and in deployment.

The salient characteristics of the CRPF are mobility and adaptability. It keeps on moving across the length and breadth of the country at very short notice to deal with internal security problems. No other central para military force in the world could be so mobile with the limited resources. Due to high adaptability, whenever the Force is sent on duty to various States, they get tuned to local conditions promptly and start functioning effectively. Due to these characteristics, the demand for it from the States is incessant.

Right from its inception, the CRPF has made a historic contribution to maintain the unity and integrity of the country. There has not been even a single instance when there may be serious threat to unity and integrity of the country from internal or external sources and within the country or on borders and the CRPF was not deployed. In his address on CRPF Day, 1996, the then Prime Minister said "This Force of one lakh sixty thousand represents the will of the Government to uphold the unity and integrity of the country and to maintain the secular character of Indian Society".

The primary duty of the CRPF is to assist States in maintenance of law and order. The strength of the Force is that it can work in perfect harmony with the State Police and at the same time, with its professionalism, act as catalyst for its upgradation in the efficiency in meeting difficult internal security problems. The CRPF could justifiably claim credit for rejuvenating Punjab Police and Jammu and Kashmir Police to enable them to stand on their own to fight the menace of militancy.

It is the only general purpose reserve force trained to perform a wide gamut of duties from crowd control, VIP security, riot handling to counter insurgency and militancy. Recently the Force played a pivotal role in peaceful conduct of Parliamentary and Assembly elections in Jammu and Kashmir by coordinating movement, deployment and utilization of all central forces and polling personnel sent from outside for election duty.

The Central Reserve Police Force had its origin in 1939 at Neemuch as the Crown Representative Police. After independence, the Force was renamed as Central Reserve Police Force by an act of Parliament on 28th December, 1949. This Act constituted CRPF as an Armed Force of the Union. Sardar Vallabhbhai Patel, the then Home Minister, visualized a multi-dimensional role for it in tune with the changing needs of a newly independent nation. Speaking in Parliament, he described the Central Reserve Police as a stabilizing influence whenever any threat to the security manifested itself.

In the CRPF, there are 136 Battalions including 10 RAF Bns and two Mahila Bns, five Signal Bns and one Special Duty Group. There are 13 sectors including 3 operational sectors, 28 ranges including six operational ranges and 30 Group Centers including one Signal Group Centre.

In view of the impeccable record of the CRPF in maintaining communal harmony, 10 CRPF Battalions were converted into Rapid Action Force in 1992. Two Mahila Bns have also been raised as a part of the CRPF for dealing with women and children with dignity and compassion.

After its basic training in 1941, the Central Reserve Police detachments were sent to Charkhari State, Mhow and Indore to preserve peace, and later to Abu and Deoli to guard the important political detenues of German and Italian descent. In March 1942, a detachment of CRP dealt with Hur menace at Khairpur State of Sindh and captured a large number of notorious Hur outlaws and recovered arms and ammunitions. In 1942 the first medal George Cross (G) was awarded to Naik Barkat Singh of 1 Bn. From 1943 to 1946 CRP contingents participated in anti-dacoity operations in Balasisnor and Kishangarh States.

During early 1950s, the work of the CRPF detachment at Bhuj, Pepsu and Chambal ravines against dacoits earned appreciation from all quarters. The Force played a significant role during the amalgamation of princely States into the Indian Union. It helped the Union Government to discipline the rebellious princely State of Junagarh and the small principalities of Kathiawar which had resisted to join the Indian Union.

Soon after independence, the CRPF contingents were sent to Kutch, Bhuj, Rajasthan and Sind borders to check infiltration and trans-border crimes. They were subsequently deployed on Jammu and Kashmir border with Pakistan against planned attacks launched by Pakistani infiltrators and other anti-national elements. In 1956, at Chhabbet Island on Kutch border, the Force gave an excellent account of itself by assisting the Army in recapturing the Island against very stiff resistance put up by the Pakistan Army. In 1957, CRPF contingents were deployed in Ladakh region of Indo-Tibetan border. During late 50s, the CRPF was inducted in North East for the first time in Nagaland and Mizoram to control insurgency.

The CRPF bore the brunt of the first onslaught of the Chinese at Hot Springs(Ladakh) on October 21, 1959. A small CRPF patrol was ambushed by the Chinese. Ten CRPF men laid down their lives for the motherland. Their martyrdom on October 21 is remembered throughout the country as the Police Commemoration Day every year.

During 1962 Chinese aggression, the Force once again assisted the Indian Army in the NEFA region; eight CRPF personnel made the supreme sacrifice at the alter of duty in this war.

In 1965, four companies of CRPF defended Sardar Post and Tak Post in Rann of Kutch against the fierce attack of a Pakistani Infantry Brigade. The CRPF inflicted heavy casualties on the enemy forcing them to retreat leaving many dead and injured. In 1971 war also, the Force fought shoulder to shoulder with the Indian Army, both on the western and eastern border. During the liberation of Bangladesh, two CRPF contingents operated inside Bangladesh territory alongwith the Army. Subsequently, the task of guarding thousands of Pakistani prisoners of war was performed by the CRPF with credit.

For the first time in the history of para-military Forces in India, 13 companies of CRPF including one Mahila Company were airlifted to join the Indian Peace Keeping Force in Sri Lanka to fight Tamil militants. As many as 14 men sacrificed their lives and several were injured in fight against LTTE elements. One gallant jawan was decorated with Vir Chakra posthumously and an officer was honoured with the Yudh Sena Medal. Two others, one of them a Mahila constable, were awarded the Sena Medal. The woman constable, thus, became the first police woman of the country to be honoured with a Sena Medal.

In the late seventies, when extremist elements disturbed peace in Tripura and Manipur, the CRPF battalions had to be deployed in strength. During those years, a great turmoil erupted in the otherwise tranquil Brahmaputra Valley. The students and youth of Assam launched agitations against the State on the so called foreign national issue. The agitation which started on a low key gradually assumed massive proportions and spread far and wide encompassing the entire State of Assam. The CRPF had to be inducted in strength not only to maintain law and order but also to keep lines of communication free from disruption. The commitment of the Force continues to be very high in the North-East to deal with the internal security in the region. The CRPF has made major contribution in checking insurgency in the North-East.

In North-East, about 8000 insurgents have been apprehended while 131 were killed during the period 1988-1997. The Force also recovered 1910 arms and 18393 rounds of ammunition from insurgents. But the CRPF also had to pay very heavy price with 215 Force personnel having been killed and 383 wounded.

The simmering discontent brewing up in Punjab manifested in the ugly shape of terrorism in the early eighties. The misguided youth of Punjab were misled into believing the possible formation of a sovereign State called "Khalistan". As the State administration could not control the deteriorating law and order situation, a large scale induction of CRPF personnel was sought by the State. Be it "Operation Blue Star" or "Operation Black Thunder" or round the clock patrolling all over the State or establishing *nakas* along the highways, it was the CRPF which faced the terrorist challenge in full strength suffered heavy casualties.

Initially in 1981, 50 companies were inducted and this figure gradually went up to a peak figure of 336 companies, i.e. about 56 bns. With vast deployment, the CRPF was able to help State Police and administration to bring the situation under control and make the people there realise the futility of resorting to violence.

The CRPF killed 2,551 terrorists and apprehended 12,997 during the period 1983 and 1995. As many as 5,694 sophisticated arms and 2,06,012 rounds/ammunition were also recovered. Some 192 Force personnel sacrificed their lives and 500 were injured while fighting the terrorists and secessionist elements in Punjab.

The first major bomb blast around October '88 in Jammu and Kashmir signalled the return of militancy in the State. Thousands of people organised pro-Azadi demonstration. The CRPF Bns/Coys had to be rushed by air to deal with the deteriorating situation in December 1989. The CRPF bore the major brunt of militancy in the state from 1990 to 1992. Its contribution in dealing with post Charar-e-Sharif scenario was appreciated by all quarters. The CRPF is also assisting the State Police in directly fighting militancy with the help of Special Task Force so that it may stand on its feet. At present the CRPF is deployed mainly to deal with law and order situation with the revival of political process and to ensure security of important persons and vital installations.

Since 1988, 323 militants were killed in various operations undertaken by CRPF in J & K and 3,412 were apprehended. Over 1,700 sophisticated arms and 75,058 rounds of ammunition were recovered. During the course of their duty, 157 Force personnel laid down their lives and 1,539 were injured.

Rapid Action Force

Rapid Action Force (RAF) was formed in October 1992 to deal with communal riots and riot like situation by converting 10 battalions of CRPF. Since its raising RAF has promptly quelled communal disturbances and defused tension in various parts of the country. With the growing public confidence in professionalism, impartiality and effectiveness of the RAF, it has become the symbol of the nation's determination to maintain secular character of the country. Blue dangree and white gypsy of the RAF have become the harbinger of communal harmony and peace to the common man. They have been successful in restoring minorities' confidence in the Government by handling communal elements firmly with promptitude and thereby reducing communal tension.

The RAF has succeeded in projecting human face of the Union of India and build bridges with the public by carrying out prompt rescue and relief operations during floods, earthquake, cyclone, outbreak of dengue fever and plague etc., in various parts of the country.

Mahila Battalion

The CRPF is the only para military force in the country which has two Mahila battalions. The Mahila CRPF personnel won laurels for their outstanding work in communal and militancy/insurgency situations and also in Sri Lanka.

The Environment Protection

The CRPF has undertaken programmes for massive tree plantation all over the country. Over 1.5 lakhs trees have been planted by the CRPF in 1996 alone. In Orissa, Barbera Forest (approximately 24,000 hectares) was adopted by CRPF for preservation and protection of flora and fauna since 1994. The Force has been able to check effectively environmental degradation and ensured regeneration of local flora and fauna. The Force also recovered valuable forest produce from miscreants during the last one and half year.

Humane Face of CRPF

The CRPF extended assistance to the Government of India and Rotary International in 'Pulse Polio' programme all over the country including J & K and North Eastern States in December 96 - January 97, and thus, succeeded in getting inoculated over 13.5 lakh children in the country. The Force also organised community welfare programmes in disturbed areas of Jammu & Kashmir and Assam and earned appreciations.

Since its inception in July 1939, the CRPF has earned 1 George Cross(G), 1 Vir Chakra, 1 Padmashri, 3 King's Police Medal for Gallantry, 49 President's Police and Fire Service Medal for Gallantry, 86 President's Police Medal for Gallantry, 418 Police Medal for Gallantry, 4 Vishist Seva Medal, 1 Yudh Seva Medal, 5 Sena Medal, 75 Prime Minister's Life Saving Medal and one Jeevan Raksha Padak.

The Central Reserve Police Force has made significant contribution in promoting games and sports. It has given outstanding sports persons of national and international level like G.S. Randhawa, Hari Chand, Ishwar Singh, Khazan Singh, Bhanu Singh, Sukhwant Singh, Suresh Chand, R.S. Bal, Ms. N. Kunjarani Devi, Jeevan Jyothi, N. Lakshmi, Raja Ram Tokas, Tilak Thapa, Paramjeet Singh and Rigzen Angma. G.S. Randhawa was the first ever athelete to win 'Arjuna Award' and Hari Chand, Khazan Singh, Ms. Kunjarani Devi and R.S. Bal followed suit. The CRPF has the rare honour of winning all India Police Athletics Championship for 11 consecutive years from 1979 to 1989. Five athletes and swimmers and 3 weightlifters have been selected to represent India in World Police and Fire Games 1997 held at Calgary, Canada, and at Yangzhou, China, respectively.

In addition to the sports and games, the Force has also entered into the field of adventure sports. "Abhiyan Ganga Sagar", a rowing expedition, was organised on river Ganga from Haridwar to Calcutta in 1994. The CRPF mountaineers have successfully climbed the peaks Jogin-1 and III in 1995. The CRPF Mahila personnel organised All Women White Water River Rafting Expedition from Srinagar (Garhwal) to Rishikesh in 1996. The Force is now planning to organise All Women Mountain Biking Expedition from Sarhan, Himachal Pradesh, to Chandigarh 1997.

With its dedicated service for maintaining unity and integrity of the country, the Force has come to be reckoned as an important embodiment for ensuring internal security, peace and national integration of the country. It has done justice to the confidence reposed by the Government and the people and to its motto "Service and Loyalty".

The country is passing through a critical period. The problems of our multi-ethnic and multi-racial society are escalating to critical levels, sometimes threatening the very integrity and the social fabric of the nation. In the recent past, we have had serious disorder over issues involving caste, creed, religion and social and economic disparities. The strains of sub-nationalism and terrorism have also spread to many parts of the country. Therefore, the CRPF is now facing a challenging situation to contain violence unleashed by these Forces. In this scenario, the CRPF has to achieve operational excellence to uphold the faith bestowed by the people in the Force as 'Peace Keepers of the Nation'.

PART VI
Human Rights

- Human Rights : An Overview
- Human Rights in Indian Armed Forces
- Prevention of Deaths in Police Custody

29

Human Rights

An Overview

Dr. S. Subramanian

ALL HUMAN RIGHTS derive from the dignity and worth inherent in the human person and that the human person is the central subject of Human Rights and Fundamental Freedoms. In simple terms, whatever adds to the dignified and free existence of a human being should be regarded as Human Right. Evolution and crystallisation of the concept took a long time. Initially there was confusion between the Natural Rights propounded by political philosophers in the bygone ages and the concept of Human Rights. The latter is an all encompassing one.

In recorded history and ancient scriptures, there have been references to the basic Human Rights, though they were not referred to by that name. Modern historians credit the origin of the concept to Magna Carta. On close examination, it will be seen that Magna Carta was a petition urging the King to concede certain rights to particular sections of the people. Its contents neither had the universality of application nor direct relevance to common man's basic freedoms.

The term Human Rights was introduced in the United States Declaration of Independence in 1776 and the US Constitution embodied a Bill of Rights. The French Revolution gave birth to the Declaration of Rights of Man and Citizen in 1789. In 1929, the Institute of International Law, New York, U.S.A. prepared a Declaration of Human

Rights and Duties. In 1945, the Inter-American Conference passed a resolution seeking establishment of an international forum for the furtherance of Human Rights of Mankind.

The unspeakable atrocities committed on political and ethnic minorities by the Axis Powers, shocked the conscience of the world, and the Allied Powers vowed to usher in a world order for promoting respect for and observance of Human Rights and Fundamental Freedoms. The Charter of the United Nations Organisation in its preamble declared 'We the Peoples of the United Nations determined .... to reaffirm faith in the fundamental human rights, in the dignity and worth of human person, in the equal rights of men and women and of the Nations large and small............. . The Charter also declared that the purpose of the United Nations is 'to achieve international cooperation in solving international problems of an economic, social, cultural or humanitarian character and in promoting and encouraging respect for Human Rights and for Fundamental Freedoms for all without distinction as to race, sex, language or religion.' The United Nations also proclaimed the Universal Declaration of Human Rights in 1948.

International Endeavours

In keeping with its charter to promote and encourage respect for Human Rights and Fundamental Freedoms for all without distinction, the U.N.O. came out with an International Bill of Human Rights consisting of the following documents:

1. Universal Declaration of Human Rights (1948);
2. The International Covenant on Civil and Political Rights (1966);
3. The International Covenant of Economic, Social and Cultural Rights (1966); and
4. The Optional Protocol (1966) providing for the right of an individual to petition an international agency.

The principles on which the above are based are :

(a) All human beings, without distinction, have been brought within the scope of human rights instruments.

(b) Equality of application without distinction of race, sex, language or religion.

(c) Emphasis was on international cooperation for implementation.

The United Nations Organisation held that all human rights and fundamental freedoms are indivisible and interdependent; equal attention and urgent consideration should be given to the implementation, promotion and protection of civil, political, economic, social and cultural rights.

Human Rights can be broadly classified in different categories. These are detailed as follows:

Civil and Political Rights

The rights pertaining to the life, integrity, liberty and security of human person; the rights with respect to administration of justice; the right to privacy; the rights to freedom of religion or belief and to freedom of opinion and expression, freedom of movement; the right to assembly and association; and the right to political participation are among the civil and political rights.

Economic, Social and Cultural Rights

The right to work; trade union freedoms; the right to adequate standard of living, including food, clothing and housing; the right to health care; the right to education; and the right to take part in cultural life are among the economic, social and cultural rights.

The United Nations Organisation has been endeavouring to relate human rights to global issues and strenuously working to find solutions for human rights concerns affecting the millions of deprived, dispossessed, discriminated against and marginalised people. This approach of the United Nations was formalised in the Proclamation of Teheran (1968), known as the 'structural approach'. Its salient features are:

1. To link human rights to major worldwide patterns and issues.
2. To identify the root causes of human rights violations.
3. To assess human rights in the light of concrete contexts, situations.
4. To recognise the diversity of political and social systems, cultural and religious differences and varying levels of development.

This 'approach' also recognises the central position of the human person in the development process, and links human rights with development.

The ceaseless efforts of the United Nations in the human rights area can be understood from the fact that there are nearly 90 international covenants, declarations and other documents. These are known as 'Instruments of Human Rights' and fall under the categories of general instruments, special instruments and legal instruments (treatise etc.). All these embody political commitments by member-States and also provide for the conduct of international relations in the field of human rights and bring the domestic policies in line with international code of ethics.

There are elaborate international implementation procedures in the field of Human Rights. Broadly these procedures serve advisory, assistance, correction, relief and remedy and preventive functions. At times, to deal with an individual country and special situations, special procedures are also adopted. It may be borne in mind that the actual realisation of human rights by the people would depend upon the commitment of the member-States to the cause of Human Rights. The role of U.N.O. is moral in nature. In the ultimate analysis, Human Rights implementation is to be done at local and national levels.

The Republic of India ratified the International Covenants on Civil and Political Rights and on Economic, Social and Cultural Rights with certain declarations (reservations).

A careful reading of these instruments would reveal the concern of the United Nations for Human Rights. All ratifying member-States including the Republic of India have accepted the values propounded in these covenants and are duty bound to bring their national policies and procedures in line with these covenants as required under the International Law and Treaty.

From the conceptual stage, the U.N.O. had marched to the operational stage with great vigour. An elected Human Rights Committee of the U.N.O. functions to consider communications from a State party alleging non-fulfillment of covenant obligations by another member-State. Citizens of those member-States, who are a party to the Optional Protocol, can directly petition the Human Rights Committee, if they have exhausted all available domestic remedies.

International covenants and instruments are beacon lights showing the path of justice and humanity to the nations. The urge to implement and uphold Human Rights should come from within a nation. The international endeavours have not been in vain. It takes time to transform international good intentions into national norms. In the meantime, these give the national judiciary an opportunity to interpret national laws in the light of international obligations of the nation.

Development of Human Rights Concept in India

It is interesting to note that the concept of Rights of human beings is neither entirely Western nor modern. *The Rig Veda* cites three Civil Rights, that of *Tana* (Body), *Skridhi* (Dwelling place) and *Jibhasi* (Life). *The Mahabharata* tells about the importance of the freedoms of the individual (civil liberties) in a State. Concept of *Dharma* rights and duties of individuals, classes, communities and castes have been delineated in our scriptures. Before the second century B.C., Indian states could boast of elected kings. *The Arthasastra* elaborates on civil and legal rights first formulated by Manu which also included economic rights. When the British ruled India, resistance to foreign rule manifested in the form of demand for fundamental freedoms and civil and political rights for the people. The Indian National Congress, which was in the vanguard of the freedom struggle, took the lead in this matter.

The Constitution of India Bill 1895 prepared by the Indian National Congress also known as the 'Home Rule Document' talked about a constitution guaranteeing everyone of the citizens basic Human Rights like freedom of expression, inviolability of one's own home, right to property, equality before law, etc.

In August 1918, the Indian National Congress demanded incorporation of a Declaration of the Rights of the People of India as British Citizens! It demanded, *inter alia,* guarantees of Equality before Law, Protection in respect of Liberty, Life and Property, Freedom of Speech and Press and the Right of Association. In the Delhi Session of December 1918, the Indian National Congress included the Principles of Self Determination as one of the basic rights.

The Constitution of the Irish Free State 1921 included a List of Fundamental Rights. This had profound influence on the thinking of the Indian National Congress, which in 1925 finalised the draft of 'Commonwealth of India Bill' embodying a Declaration of Rights. The Madras Congress of the Indian National Congress in 1927 demanded incorporation of a Declaration of Fundamental Rights in any future constitutional framework. A committee under Motilal Nehru was appointed. Reporting in 1928, this committee, declared that the first concern of the people of India is to secure fundamental rights. It is interesting to note that the Constitution of the Republic of India enacted in 1950, incorporated ten of the nineteen Rights enumerated in the Motilal Nehru Committee Report.

The Rights emphasized by the Motilal Committee Report are:

1. Personal Liberty, Inviolability of dwelling place and property;
2. Freedom of conscience and of profession and practice of religion subject to public order and morality;
3. Right of free expression of opinion and to assemble peaceably and without arms and to form association and unions subject to public order and morality;
4. Right to free elementary education and in the matter of admission into any educational institution maintained and aided by the State without distinction of caste or creed;
5. Equality for all citizens before the law and in civil rights;
6. Right to every citizen to the writ of Habeas Corpus;
7. Protection of respect of punishment under *ex-post facto* law;
8. Non-discrimination against any person on grounds of religion, caste or creed in the matter of public employment, office or power or honour and in the exercise of any trade or calling;
9. Equality of Right to all citizens in the matter of access to, and use of public roads, wells and other places of public resort;
10. Freedom of combination and association for the maintenance and implementation of labour and economic conditions;
11. The Right to keep and bear arms in accordance with Regulations; and
12. Equality of Rights to men and women as citizens.

The Lahore Congress of 1930 declared Freedom from the Foreign Rule as a Fundamental Right. the Karachi Congress passed a Resolution in 1931 on 'Fundamental Rights and Social Change', in three parts; (a) Fundamental Rights and Duties; (b) Labour and (c) Economic and Social Programme.

The Government of India Act, 1935 - Sections 297-300 incorporated certain rights with built-in exceptions. The Sapru Committee in 1945 stressed on the need for a Written Code of Fundamental Rights. In the Constituent Assembly (1946) also a demand for Declaration of Fundamental Rights was raised.

Promulgation of the Constitution by the People of India in January 1950 is a watershed in the history of Development of the Concept of Human Rights in India. The Preamble, Fundamental Rights and the Directive Principles of State Policy together provide the basic Human Rights for the people of India. Democratic socialism spelt out in the Preamble and the Directive Principles is meant to provide the context in which the fulfilment of the Fundamental Rights has to be achieved. While the Fundamental Rights stress on the existing rights, the Directive Principles provide the dynamic movement towards the goal of providing Human Rights for all.

The Preamble of the Constitution of India declares that the People of India have solemnly resolved to constitute India into a Sovereign Socialistic Secular Democratic Republic and to secure to all its citizens:

JUSTICE	:	social, economic and political;
LIBERTY	:	of thought, expression, belief, faith and worship;
EQUALITY	:	of status and opportunity; and to promote among them all;
FRATERNITY	:	assuring the dignity of the individual and the unity and integrity of the nation.

The Fundamental Rights are enumerated in Part III of the Constitution. They in short are:

I. Right to Equality

Article 14	-	Equality before Law.
Article 15	-	Prohibition of discrimination on grounds of religion, race, caste, sex or place of birth.
Article 16	-	Equality of opportunity in matters of public employment.
Article 17	-	Abolition of untouchability.
Article 18	-	Abolition of titles.

II. Right to Freedom

Article 19	-	Protection of certain rights regarding freedom of speech, etc.

Article 20	-	Protection in respect of conviction for offences.
Article 21	-	Protection of life in personal liberty.
Article 22	-	Protection against detention in certain cases.

III. Right against Exploitation

Article 23	-	Prohibition of traffic in human beings and forced labour.
Article 24	-	Prohibition of employment of children in factories, etc.

IV. Right to Freedom of Religion

Article 25	-	Freedom of conscience and free pursuit of profession, practice and propagation of religion.
Article 26	-	Freedom to manage religious affairs.
Article 27	-	Freedom as to payment of taxes for promotion of any particular religion.
Article 28	-	Freedom as to attendance at religious instruction or religious worship in certain educational institutions.

V. Cultural and Educational Rights

Article 29	-	Protection of interests of minorities.
Article 30	-	Right of minorities to establish and administer educational institutions.

VI. Right to Constitutional Remedies

Article 32	-	Right to Constitutional remedies.

As stated by Jeremy Benthem, 'Right is a child of Law. From Real Laws Come Real Rights'. Keeping this maxim in view, to enable the citizens to enjoy all the Rights enumerated, many pieces of social legislation have been enacted in the past 50 years in India. Added to these, the Supreme Court of India, through judicial interpretation has widened the horizon of Human Rights in India.

30

Human Rights in Indian Armed Forces

Air Cmde R. V. Kumar, AVSM

A period of fifty years is a long period to do an introspection on important issues concerning the nation. One of the most important issues, concerning the comity of nations and the humanity, today is the issue of human rights.

Human rights, in simple language mean those rights which every human being is entitled to enjoy and to have protected. In other words, these are those rights which every human being is entitled to enjoy by virtue of being a member of the human species.

The fact that the human rights in one form or the other have always been a part of Indian ethos would be stating the obvious. We may use any terminology but the fact remains that Indian ethos is interwoven with all facts of so-called contemporary human rights since times immemorial. Even a cursory peep in the Indian scriptures, be it Vedas or Upanishads or any other scripture, would bring out a universality of this truth.

For example in Rig Veda it is enjoined that there is one race of human beings, which shows the spirit of humanity and universality in the Indian tradition. It will be useful to see the beautiful *shanti path* in the Vedas, a prayer for peace which was written thousands of years ago and which articulates the yearnings for the universal harmony and peace.

Even in the contemporary times one man's ambulance brigade of Bhai Kanihaya, whose sole religion was to look after the sick and wounded in the battlefield specially the enemy troops during the anti-tyranny wars between Aurangzeb and Guru Govind Singh, is an outstanding example. Even as late as the recent times Mahatma Gandhi wrote, "I learnt from my illiterate but wise mother that all rights to be deserved, come from duty well done. Every right is co-related to some corresponding duty to be first performed. Any other right can be said to be a usurpation, hardly worth fighting for."

The present set of contemporary human rights are contained in the Universal Declaration of Human Rights which was proclaimed and adopted by the General Assembly of the United Nations on 10th December, 1948, which has 30 Articles. The declaration elaborates the common minimum standard of achievments for all people of all nations. They are supplemented by an international covenant of civil and political rights and a covenant of economic, social and cultural rights. Subsequently there are many other covenants, protocols and declarations on various specific aspects of concern to Human Rights.

As early as in 1931 at the Karachi Session of the National Congress, Mahatma Gandhi moved the famous resolution on fundamental rights which included the freedom of association, freedom of speech, freedom of conscience, equalilty, freedom of liberty from serfdom, adult suffrage and free primary education. It was against this background that in the Independent India the pride of place was provided in our Constitution to the Chapter of Fundamental Rights. In the historic objective resolution in the Constituent Assembly which was drafted by Pandit Jawaharlal Nehru, it was clearly provided "wherein shall be guaranteed and secured to all the people of India, justice — social, economic and political - equality of status and opportunity before law, freedom of thought and expression, belief, faith, worship, association and action subject of course to the law and public morality." Even the Preamble of the Indian Constitution solemnly resolved to secure for all its citizens justice — social, economic and political, liberty of thought, expression, belief, faith and worship, equality of status of opportunity and to promote amongst them all fraternity assuring the dignity of the individual and unity and integrity of the nation.

Human Rights and Indian Armed Forces

The Indian Armed Forces like any other segment of society have not remained isolated from this thought of human rights. Notwithstanding the motivated and perhaps inspired propaganda, for the so-called violation of human rights by the Indian Armed Forces particularly during counter-insurgency operations, either in NEFA or Punjab or Jammu & Kashmir, a close scrutiny of the records of the Indian Army for respecting and protecting the human rights would make it clear that the record of the Indian Armed Forces has perhaps been the best in the whole world.

We will briefly come to the facts and figures little later but in evaluating the human rights records of the Armed Forces one must take into account the unusual circumstances and the hostile terrain in which they had to operate. They operated against the terrorists, snippers and the mercenaries who have no code of conduct or moral principles of warfare. Another aspect which needs to be kept in mind is the psychological situation of a fatigued soldier operating in a far away place away from his family for months and years and operating in war like situation with a stengun in front and a bomber overhead. While reconstructing the human rights record of such a soldier in such a situation, it will be incorrect to sit back in an airconditioned office and in an easy armchair and blame that the soldier ought to have done this or ought not to have done that. One must put oneself in the situation under those acute circumstances in which he was, to determine whether a reasonably well-trained soldier ought to have done or ought not to have done. The psychology of the Indian soldier and the spirit of comradeship between a soldier and another soldier; and a soldier and an officer must also be taken into consideration.

It is not the question of fear of public reaction, in counter - insurgency operations or the pressure of the human rights activitist organisations, but it is a part of Indian ethos which have bound the Indian Armed Forces to the ethos of human rights.

As early as December 1961 after the military operation in Goa, the then Chief of the Army Staff in a message to the troops had said, "you will now enter Goa not as a conqueror of a foreign land but as a part of the Indian defence forces. In Goa you are with the compatriots, go defend and protect the people and let no one suffer violence." Even at the end of the 1971 war, when nearly 93,000 Pakistani officers and soldiers surrendered to the Indian Army, Lt. Gen. Jagjit Singh

Arora gave a solemn assurance that "the personnel who surrendered shall be treated with dignity and respect that soldiers are entitled to in accordance with the Geneva Conventions and protection will be provided to the foreign nationals, ethnic minorities and the personnel of West Pakistan origin."

A lot is being made out of the violation of human rights by the Indian troops while operating in Jammu & Kashmir, North - Eastern States and Punjab. It may, however, be news to many that even before the National Human Rights Commission was established, the Indian Army had created a separate cell for Human Rights at Army Hqrs. headed by a Major General, a full colonel and the other staff at work from its own resources without a separate established strength and this extended to the operating commands and right upto the batallion level.

The charter of these cells is to regularly receive, monitor, investigate and submit reports on the human rights violations by the Army personnel. It may, however, be noted that Human Rights violations in the troops itself is outside the purview of these cells and are treated like normal disciplinary matters.

Investigations by the Army Hqrs. cell have revealed that over 95 percent of the human rights violation cases alleged against the army were found to be false or bogus. About 5 per cent excesses did exist but they were mostly of technical nature. With serious violation being negligible, those found guilty were given exemplary punishment. During 1990-95, a total of 471 complaints were received and as stated earlier more than 95 per cent were found to be false. Where found true, army personnel were awarded punishments ranging from reprimand to dismissal, the number of such personnel were over forty.

Even the National Human Rights Commission of India received a total of 174 cases in 1994-95, out of which 10 were alleged excesses by the Armed Forces. Here it must also be noted that the term "armed forces", in this context, include not only the Army but also the para-military forces like BSF, CRPF, ITBP, etc. The fact that under the Indian system, Army is called out against counter-insurgency operations in rare cases where others have not worked effectively would mean that not even 0.5 per cent complaints were against the Indian Army. Even as recently as June 1997, Gen. Padmanabhan, GOC-in-C, Northern Command, stated that a total of 584 cases of human rights abuse were received. Out of these, 578 cases were investigated and

556 were found false or baseless. For 22 human rights abuse cases which were justified 52 army personnel were punished.

Having seen in brief the human rights record of the Indian Army in some detail, it will be of interest to know that in 1993, the then Chief of the Army Staff had issued 10 Commandments on human rights for strict compliance which specifically prohibited rape, molestation, torture, military disgrace, etc. As a corollary to the 10 commandments of the Chief of Army Staff, the Corps Commanders have further issued 10 directions for strict compliance which prohibit amongst others any harm to the children or repraisals and specifically includes respect for local customs, traditions and concern even for the apprehendees.

Human rights awareness in Indian Army is promoted not only by various training courses at various levels but also situational courses to the units which are assigned the task of supporting internal security and counter-insurgency operations. Detailed training notes have also been issued and respect for human rights is inculcated everyday during roll calls through a periodical *sainik sammalen,* etc. Since bulk of the human rights violations against the Army relate to the conduct of search operations without full compliance with legal formalities or illegal arrests, this aspect is also fully explained, and even a set of Do's and Dont's, before, during and after such operations have also been issued. The troops which are assigned for international peace keeping operations like Congo, Katanga, Somalia, Bosnia, etc., have to undergo a regular human rights training before being despatched for deployment. A list of likely situations and desirable responses are also brought home to all engaged in internal security or counter-insurgency operations. Even the National Human Rights Commission in its report of 1993-94 regarding human rights in the Armed Forces has observed, "contacts have been instituted with the armed forces amongst whom there is notably heightened appreciation of the necessity and value of imparting training in human rights. Indeed at the seniormost level of the armed forces the Commission has recently noted a sensitivity towards and recognition of the need to develop a culture of human rights." In its report of 1994-95, it further observed, "the Commission welcomes these instructions (instructions of the Chief of the Army Staff and Corps Commanders) as evidence of growing sensitivity amongst armed forces personnel to human rights matters. The example of armed forces leadership need to be followed at all levels. Apart from observing and respecting the human rights during operations, the Indian armed forces have greatly involved themselves in humanitarian work such as providing free medical aid to the sick and wounded civilians, establishing schools for local children, building roads and distributing ration from its own resources. Same goes for the BSF and other para military forces."

Humanitarian Work

Apart from observing and promoting human rights in the country during internal and counter-insurgency operations in the country, the armed forces of India have significantly contributed in humanitarian work in various international peace keeping operations. Whether it was in Korea, Indo-China, Gaza, Lebanon, Congo, Cyprus or in the UN Iran-Iraq Military Observer Group, Namibia or Iran-Kuwait Observers Mission or Yugoslavia, it has covered itself with glory and won laurels for its humanitarian work from the countries concerned and even the United Nations.

The BSF which is the largest paramilitary force in the world has also an excellent track record of human rights whilst dealing with counter-insurgency operations. It promotes the human rights culture amongst the force by various courses of training, seminars, workshops and discussions at all levels. For the constabulary it has issued a set of code of conduct in the form of Do's and Dont's in simple varnacular language for strict observance. For the period 1990-95, it had received a total of 259 complaints, out of which 248 were found false and 36 personnel were punished for violation of human rights, even as a result of suo moto action when even no complaint was received.

The Indian Navy and the Air Force though not directly involved in eyeball to eyeball situation have also indoctrinated their officers and men in human rights and humanitarian laws through various courses and training institutions, a peep into their record of 1971 operations would clearly establish that even during the war they had strictly observed the international humanitarian laws and acted according to international priniciples whether in operation or otherwise. It can therefore safely be stated that since Independence, the armed forces of India have not lagged behind any other institution in observing and enforcing the human rights.

31

Prevention of Deaths in Police Custody

Dr. S. Subramanian

DEATHS IN POLICE 'lock-ups' and in 'encounters' occur frequently and the fact that majority of the victims are from the weaker sections of society and these deaths are the outcome of the 'third degree methods' and flagrant violation of Human Rights of the citizens, are causing concern to all right thinking citizens of India. They not only sully the image of India as a liberal democracy but are also providing grist to anti-India propaganda by vested interests. Mere denunciation of police will not make this evil disappear. We should calmly analyse the root causes and take appropriate remedial measures.

In India, every year, lakhs of people are taken into custody by the police and majority of them are suspected of having committed property crime. They are generally from the poorer sections of society, illiterate, lack financial resources to afford legal aid and are unaware of their rights. Bulk of these arrests are made in the cities and towns where property crime occur in good number. To solve property crime, police resort to third degree due to: (a) tacit approval of society for the use of force against a suspect to detect the crime; (b) psychological factors including fear psychosis in the minds of suspects and to exaggerated stories of police brutality; (c) lack of adequate time and pressure to produce quick results which preclude the use of time consuming and painstaking modern methods of crime detection; and finally (d) legal impediments which deny police adequate time to interrogate the suspect.

Police are not psychopaths given to murdering people. What happens in the field is when the police start applying third degree to the suspects, many of them die due to the fact that they are generally undernourished, of poor health with serious medical problems and the existence of fear psychosis generated due to the trauma of custody and stories of police brutality.

'Encounters' occur due to the legal problems faced by the police. Notwithstanding the presence of much publicised 'Draconian Laws' on the statute book, it is a dismal fact that our courts have not been able to deal with terrorists and their ilk severely. No sane citizen will place himself in jeopardy by giving evidence against terrorists in a court of law.They cannot be saved by the police from reprisals. Police cannot produce the intelligence at their disposal as evidence, as much of it will be hearsay and inadmissable in evidence. The pressure to put down political violence and terrorism by the State authorities and the public drive the police to take recourse to 'encounters' to gain respite from the pressures of the State, public and the terrorists.

It is not our intention to justify or condone these deaths. Unless we know the realities on the ground and know why these occur, we cannot possibly devise measures to prevent them.

In the first place, we have to ensure that all arrested persons are accounted for and given proper treatment. To do so, there is need to establish the central reception facilities at towns and cities to handle all arrestees. All persons taken into custody in a city or town should be brought to a central reception facility, which should be under the direct charge of a senior gazetted police officer. All arrestees should be subjected to a thorough medical examination and a record of the same should be kept. Further, every arrestee should be given a pamphlet in vernacular listing out his rights and his acknowledgement obtained. If the arrestee is an illiterate, the same should be read over to him and the official doing so should make a record to this effect. In case of the arrestees suffering from custodial shock, trauma and depression, the assistance of a psychiatrist should be made available. The arrestees should be held over in the central reception facility till produced in the court or when they are remanded to police custody by the courts.

Special investigation rooms with modern facilities should be available to enable the investigating officers to carry on further interrogation of the arrestees. All movements of the arrestees during their stay in the central reception facility should be recorded. Separate accommodation for women and juveniles should be provided and an adequate number of women police officers should be available to take charge of them. Consequent on the establishment of a central reception facility, there would be no need for lock-ups in police stations and the holding of prisoners in police stations should be prohibited.

A judicial magistrate should be available round the clock at a designated place in the city or town to attend to the judicial needs of the arrestees. He should be vested with all powers to grant bail, record confessions, issue judicial processes, etc. His presence and availability will automatically reduce the need for the police to hold the arrestees overnight or when the courts are closed.

With the enactment of a plethora of social, fiscal and other laws, the powers of the police to arrest have widened beyond imagination. This gives scope for misbehaviour and avoidable custody. A review of these powers of arrest is called for and suitable corrective steps are to be taken.

Law should be amended to make it mandatory to have a judicial enquiry by a First Class Judicial Magistrate into all deaths in the police custody. The present practice of enquiries by Executive Magistrates have not yielded the desired results. Where it is proved that the death had in fact occurred in the police custody, the presumption of guilt that the death was due to police violence should be invoked in the trial. Similar provisions exist in respect of the custodial rape.

To look into and verify the complaints of the custodial deaths, a police complaint board consisting of a retired district and sessions judge (chairman) and a retired police officer of the rank of Superintendent of Police and a prominent senior citizen with administrative background as members should be constituted. On receipt of complaints of custodial violence, the board should visit the scene and ascertain the facts. If, in its opinion, a prima facie case exists, a direction should be issued to the local chief of police to register a criminal case against the police personnel concerned and hand over the case to the Crime Branch, CID, for further investigation.

A sustained publicity campaign to educate the public and police about the sanctity of Human Rights should be undertaken. This should be a positive campaign and not to denigrate the police. Instead of concentrating on custodial violence only, this campaign should speak in terms of rights of women, children, Scheduled Castes and Scheduled Tribes and the others. Protection from unlawful custody and violence while under custody should be brought in as part of the general picture. This is to ensure that the police do not feel that they have been singled out for denigration in public. In all police publications, an advertisement regarding Human Rights should be carried. The electronic media should also be used extensively. Such a campaign is necessary as the police force, with a strength of about ten lakhs, is spread out, in small groups all over the country and it is not possible to reach them otherwise to sensitise them on this issue.

It is necessary to make a beginning to implement these suggestions in cities and towns. Except for legal provisions, all others could be ushered in through administrative orders. Custodial deaths can be prevented with the support of enlightened police leadership, a proactive judiciary, a vigilant media and a socially conscious and well articulated public opinion. It should be borne in mind that what is called for is positive action and not a campaign to denounce police as an organisation.

PART VII
Education and Sports

- Elementary Education for Empowerment
- Sporting Achievements in India: Bright Spots in a Bleak Scenario

32

Elementary Education for Empowerment

S. R. Bommai

THIS YEAR we would be celebrating the 50th anniversary of our Independence. This is time for us to critically reflect on how far we could translate into reality the aspirations and goals of the Founding Fathers of our nation and extent to which we could accomplish the social and economic transformation envisaged in our Constitution. We have to be candid, objective and self-critical so that we can hasten the achievement of national goals which transcend the social and political divides.

Among the precious legacies of the freedom struggle are the goals of universal elementary education and universal literacy. As early as 1911, Gopal Krishan Gokhale moved in the Imperial Council a Bill for compulsory elementary education. Even in the midst of leading the titanic struggle Mahatma Gandhi was engrossed in developing basic education for masses. The Framers of the Constitution had dreamt of an educated India and they enshrined this hope and concern in the Constitution itself wherein the Directive Principles of the State Policy spoke of free and compulsory education to all children up to 14 years of age.

From the speech of the Union Minister, Human Resources Development, at the National Conference of State Ministers of Education, New Delhi on August 10, 1996.

I need not elaborate the dimensions of what has been accomplished and what we have not been able to. The number of institutions, both primary and upper primary, which stood at 2.23 lakhs in 1950-51 has risen to 7.44 lakhs in 1994-95. The number of teachers has increased from 6.24 lakhs in 1950-51 to 28.36 lakhs in 1994-95. The gross enrolment at the primary stage has risen from 19.2 million in 1950-51 to 109.1 million in 1994-95. The enrolment at the upper-primary stage has risen from 3.1 million in 1950-51 to 40.03 million in 1994-95. The elementary education system in India has succeeded in the gigantic task of providing access within a one-kilometer walking distance to 8.25 lakh habitations covering 94 per cent of its population. The growth in its enrolment has come close to 100 per cent at the primary level. To make education affordable, all State Governments have abolished tution fees in the government, local bodies and the aided schools upto the upper-primary level. Yet these statistics disguise regional and gender imbalances. While Kerala, in terms of enrolment, could match the very best among the third world countries, if not the Scandinavian countries, the enrolment rates in some other States are as low as those of some of the countries of the Sub-Saharan Africa. Regional imbalances are equally visible in the case of dropouts. And all over the country quality is a critical issue.

The greatest contribution we can collectively make to the celebration of the 50th anniversary of our Independence is to address the unfinished tasks of universalisation with despatch and resolve. Education, we all know, is a concurrent subject. The National Policy on Education (NPE), 1986, has defined concurrency as a meaningful and challenging partnership between the Centre and the States. For the first time since Independence, a real federal and democratic polity has come into existence. As equal partners in the enterprise of the social and economic transformation I seek cooperation of all the states.

The Common Minimum Programme of the Central Government envisages amendment of the Constitution to make universal elementary education a justiciable fundamental right. This amendment would be a fitting re-affirmation of our national resolve. It casts a heavy responsibility on all of us, on the nation as a whole, but it is a responsibility, which I am sure, we would not shudder from. We need meticulous planning and preparation with any eye for the detail to discharge this responsibility. In this context a number of questions spring to our minds. How many habitations have no school? How soon do we provide them? What draws children to schools? And what factors impede them from going to schools? Why is there a high dropout specially among the girls? Why has the joy gone out from learning? Why are children crushed under the burden of the school bag? How can elementary education be made more attractive? How can we draw more teachers into schools? How can we improve the motivation and competence of teachers who have a key role in educational transformation? These are some of the issues we have been addressing to over the years but which we now need to attend to more rigourously.

We need to address to the nuts and bolts of the implementation. Why, in spite of our best intentions and provisions of resources, is implementation poor? Why do programmes fail to deliver the expected results? We need to strengthen the mechanism for monitoring and supervison.

In this context I cannot emphasise enough, on democratic decentralisation of education. We need to coopt the local governments, panchayats and municipal bodies in our partnership of furthering the cause of education. The 73rd and 74th Constitution amendments have legitimised the status of Panchayats and urban local bodies as a tier of our federal system. We need to ensure that the provisions of these amendments are implemented in letter and spirit. The local bodies should be vested with power, responsibility and adequate resources to manage school education. It is only the supervision and owning of education by the local community that ensures achievement of our national goals and proper deliveries of programmes. Experience in my own state, Karnataka, had demonstrated the efficacy of decentralisation and the remarkable impact it had on the enrolment in schools and their performance.

The task of universalizing elementary education cannot be accomplished unless we pay particular attention to girls, children from the scheduled castes, scheduled tribes, minorities and other disadvantaged groups.

Another concern is the education of the disabled. We have imposed an obligation on ourselves by enacting the Persons with Disabilities (Equal Opportunities, Protection of Rights and Full Participation) Act, 1995. This Act confers on every child with a disability access to free education in an appropriate environment till he attains the age of 18 years. We need to work out together the modalities for ensuring that this right is available.

The task of universalizing elementary education cannot be accomplished if we confine our attention to schooling and do not earnestly attempt to provide effective non-formal education to children who, in spite of our best efforts and intentions, cannot reach our schools. ·We need to move away from the elitist concept of non-formal education as inferior education, and the practice of treating it as yet another scheme. We need to come up with a variety of alternatives which cater to the varying needs of out-of-school children who should be facilitated to learn at their own pace. The importance of enlisting communities and NGOs cannot be emphasised enough.

We are now engaged in the implementation of the programme of Nutritional Support to Primary Education. Soon all the government, local body and private aided schools would be covered. Close monitoring of the implementation of the scheme and removal of the problems of logistics and coordination is necessary. We have to ensure that the intended benefits reach the intended beneficiaries.

We cannot neglect the issues of quality and learning achievements. Universalization would be incomplete if our schools, particularly the government schools in rural areas, do not provide education of satisfactory quality. I, for one, do not believe that the masses are ill-informed; it is their political maturity and wisdom which is a source of strength for our democracy. If many parents are not inclined to send their children to school, the reason perhaps lies in the poor content and process of education. Here again, we need to strengthen and build upon various programmes like Operation Blackboard, District Institutes of Education and Training, Minimum Levels of Learning and District Primary Education Programme.

Our concern for elementary education is matched by our concern for universal literacy. For the young, we can provide access to schools, but what of those who have remained outside the school system, who have been denied education due to societal and economic constraints? They have to be brought under the ambit of literacy campaigns so that they can be imparted literacy skills and provided avenues of continuing education. Our vision is to make the whole of India literate by 2005. We need to translate our goals into action. We need to concretise our action plans and we need to pursue them with missionary zeal. We must remember that adult literacy is for the 15-35 age group, the productive age group, whose participation can make all the difference in the success and failure of our development programmes. We are proud of our achievement of having made 56 million non-literates literate under the adult education programmes of the National Literacy Mission (NLM) and of having brought 22 States and 4 Union Territories within the pale of literacy campaigns. But we are still far away from our objective. Forty-four million non-literates need to be made literate in a year or so. As we move into the States with low levels of literacy, we realise that a gigantic task awaits us. But tackle this problem we must. For, women's literacy is the key to women's empowerment. And women's empowerment is crucial to ensure that gender equity does not remain a mere platitude. Given the coverage of the campaign, we need to decentralise the decision making process and, as with elementary education, fully associate the local bodies and communities. We need to pay more attention to the quality of achievement and give coherence to post-literacy and continuing education so that the neo-literates do not relapse into illiteracy.

Vocationalization of education is also a thrust area of ours. Here again we need to have a broader vision and not restrict vocationalization to a scheme. Our success hinges on the ability to match the demand with the design of course and make vocational courses more flexible and focus on imparting skills rather than bookish knowledge. Ingenuity and innovation are called for to bring the world of learning and the world of work in harmony and to turn out more employable and self-employed youths.

We are resolved to augment the resources for education so that they do not constraint the accomplishment of our national goals. Right from 1968 our aspiration has been to invest 6 per cent of the Gross Domestic Product, as public expenditure, in education. We wish to achieve this objective by the year 2000 and ensure that 50 per cent of these funds are spent on primary education. The steep enhancement on the budgetary support for education is a concrete manifestation of our intentions. The 6 per cent norm can be achieved only if the Centre and the States together step up resources for education and ensure that the resources are effectively and efficiently utilised. It was decided at a meeting of the Chief Ministers held in July 1996, to transfer to the States all centrally sponsored schemes except in priority areas like elementary education and literacy. It was also decided to impart greater involvement, freedom and flexibility in the implementation of the programmes that would continue as centrally sponsored schemes. We should, in the true spirit of federalism, come up with a national plan of action on the achievement of our goals and aspiration. Time is the essence.

33

Sporting Achievements in India

Bright Spots In A Bleak Scenario

D. K. Bharadwaj

IT MAY sound somewhat banal to some that the fiftieth anniversary of our Independence is a historic occasion of great pride and joy for all Indians. However, the solemnness of the occasion dawns on us, the moment we realise that we were able to break the shackles of the cruel foreign yoke only after a very long, hard struggle and monumental sacrifices made by the millions of our countrymen. Today all this may appear merely a fairytale saga of serifice and valour, but it was a truly unique freedom movement of which we can be justifiably proud of. At the time of attainment of Independence our national leaders had resolved to make allout efforts to transform India into a strong and prosperous nation as well as to miligate the problems of the common man. Perhaps it would be appropriate at this juncture if we take stock of our achievements in various fields. Undeniably a lot has been done since Independence, but much more has still to be accomplished to attain our charished objective.

The situation in sports is no different from the other spheres. No doubt there have been many spectacular feats, but the failures and mediocre performances far outweigh our achievements at the international level. For a realistic assessment, however, we have to keep in mind that a sizeable portion of our ever growing population is still living below the poverty-line and our topmost priority as such is to provide adequate food, shelter and other basic necessities of life to it. Even then sports were not neglected, though what has been done in this field may look totally inadequate when compared with the rich countries. At the same time, no developing country and for that matter only a few developed countries can boast of such a wide sports base as we do have which ranges from as different games as cricket to carrom, from polo to billiards, from hockey to chess besides traditional indigenous games like kho-kho and kabaddi. It would be proper to recall that all major genuine efforts for sports promotion were made only during the post-Independence era.

Governmental Efforts

it is worth while to point out that sports being a State subject under the Consitution, the role of the Central Government has been primarily promotional, which included *inter alia* laying down the guidelines for the national sports federations and also doling out the financial assistance to them. The first notable national level promotional programme was the Rajkumari Amrit Kaur Sports Coaching Scheme which was launched just six year after Independence. However, with the establishment of Netaji Subhas National Institute of Sports at Patiala in 1961 this scheme lost its utility and became redundant. The same year Arjun Awards were instituted to honour the outstanding sports-persons followed by the Dronacharya Award meant for the eminent coaches in 1985.

Another notable governmental effort was the establishment of the Sports Authority of India (SAI) in January 1984, which was set up primarily with a view to looking after the infrastructure created in Delhi for the Ninth Asiad in 1982. SAI is now the nodal national agency for broadbasing the sports including training of the sports-persons. Subsequently, the Netaji Subhas National Institute of Sports and its allied centres at Bangalore, Calcutta and Gandhinagar as well as Lakshmibai Colleges of Physical Education at Gwalior and Thiruvananthapuram were placed under SAI, which is presently engaged in a number of schemes to scout and nurture sporting talent through its six regional centres at Bangalore, Calcutta, Delhi, Gandhinagar, Chandigarh and Imphal. Whether SAI has been able to deliver the goods as planned is another matter, but certainly a beginning in the right direction was made. Several States too have introduced sports as a compulsary subject and some of them are running even sports schools and sports hostels.

Reasons For Failure

The irony of situation is all these developments though paint a rosy picture, yet except at the SAARC level Indian sports-persons' performance at the international level has been by and large dismal. Not one or two but a combination of several factors are responsible for it including among others lack of adequate knowledge about latest developments in the sports-medicine and technology, non-availability of modern sports equipment at affordable prices, absence of killer instinct, lack of innovative coaching methods, poor stamina etc. One should not, however, lose sight of the fact that sports are no longer a pastime they used to be, they have become pure commercial ventures with a lot of money at stake for all those involved in them. Also, some countries take sporting achievements as a matter of national prestige and accord a very high priority to sports. Naturally today sporting competitions are fiercely contested with no holds barred and as such only the very best excel in them.

However, there is no room for despondency. There have been many bright spots in the somewhat bleak sports scenario and hopefully there would be many more in the future too. Significantly, all the major sporting achievements of India, barring the first three Olympic hockey golds, have been accomplished in the post-Independence era. Apart from organising several world championships and a horde of major international tournaments, India has the honour of hosting the Asian Games twice including the inaugural one as early as 1951.

Medal-wise Performance

Though India's achievements in the Olympic Games are meagre, even then we were able to claim 5 gold, 1 silver and 2 bronze medals in the hockey competition of the Olympics after Independence, a feat no other country can boast of in the game. Kishan Lal, Kunwar Digvijay Singh "Babu", Balbir Singh Sr., Charanjit Singh and Vasudevan Bhaskaran were the hockey captains who brought golden glory to the country. Besides, two more Olympic bronze medals one each in wrestling and tennis were bagged by K.D. Jadhav and Leander Paes respectively. In twelve Asian Games held so far, Indian sports-persons captured 87 golds, 111 silvers and 159 bronzes. In the Commonwealth Games, Indian players won 43 gold, 47 silver and 38 bronze medals and India generally figured among the first six in the medals tally.

Impressive Record

India's performance in cricket, the most popular game in the Commonwealth countries has been rather impressive. All the 57 Test victories so far including 13 wins abroad were secured in the post-Independence period. Though India won only five Test series abroad including series wins against West Indies, England, New Zealand and Sri Lanka, we were quite formidable on the home grounds. We have also won a number of trophies in one-day cricket including the Asia Cup which we have won four times, but the victory in the third World Cup in 1983 in England under Kapil Dev's inspiring leadership was the most fabulous achievement.

During the last fifty years, India has produced a large number of outstanding cricketers including such glorious names as Sunil Gavaskar, Gundappa Viswanath, Kapil Dev, Dilip Vengsarkar, Polly Umrigar, Vijay Manjrekar, Mohinder Amarnath, Mansur Ali Khan Pataudi, Farokh Engineer, Syed Kirmani, Bishen Singh Bedi, Bhagwat Chandrasekhar, Erapalli Prasanna, Srinivas Venkatraghvan, Dilip Sardesai, Ravi Shastri, Mohammad Azharuddin and Sachin Tendulkar to name a few, who thrilled the cricket fans world over by their dazzling performances. Many Indians were good enough to play in the county cricket in England and several became Oxford and Cambridge "Blues". As many as eight Indian players were honoured by Wisden, the bible of cricket, as cricketers of the year. An Indian Jagmohan Dalmiya, has been appointed President of the International Cricket Council (ICC), a rare honour indeed!

A few Indians have become part of the cricket lore by creating world records. The magnificant partnership of 413 runs for the first wicket by Vinoo Mankad and Pankaj Roy against New Zealand in the Madras Test in 1955-56 is still a world record. The "Little Master" Sunil Gavaskar was the first batsman to cross the 10,000- run barrier in the Test cricket. Though his world record of 10,122 runs in 125 Tests was later broken by Allan Border of Australia, Gavaskar still holds the world record of 34 centuries in Tests. Kapil Dev's mind-boggling haul of 434 wickets in Test cricket is the current world record, Azharuddin's three consecutive centuries in his first three Tests is another world record.

Triumph In World Cup Hockey

May be Indian hockey, though very artistic and pleasing to view, is passing through a lean phase nowadays, Indian team had won the third World Cup hockey tournament held in Kuala Lumpur in 1975 under the captaincy of famous centre-half Ajitpal Singh. India was runner-up in the second World Cup at Amsterdam in 1973 and was placed third in the inaugural World Cup at Barcelona in 1971. However, in the Asian Games we could win the hockey gold only once that too three decades ago at Bangkok in 1966. In women's hockey, India's biggest triumph was in the Ninth Asiad in Delhi in 1982, when our women's team led by Eliza Nelson won the gold in a splendid way.

Baffling Mystery

It is really baffling as well as distressing to note why Indian soccer has not been able to extricate itself from the quicksands of mediocrity and stagnancy? The fifties and early sixties were golden years of Indian soccer, when we won the soccer gold twice in the Asian Games and were placed fourth in the soccer competiton at the Melbourne Olympiad, otherwise despite various promotional efforts India's performance in football at the international level has been thoroughly disappointing. Hopefully the recent introduction of the national football league for the leading clubs of the country will give the Indian soccer a much needed impetus.

Some Fine Performances

India has produced a number of talented athletes since Independence. Though none of them could win a medal in the Olympics, yet the "Flying Sikh" Milkha Singh, hurdler Gurbachan Singh, middle-distance runner Sriram Singh and the "Payolli Express" P.T. Usha did the country proud by their sterling performances. At the Asian level, however, Indian athletes performed creditably winning as many as 54 golds in the Asian Games, though in the last two games they drew a blank. P.T. Usha's performance at Seoul Games in 1986 was simply outstanding as she won four golds and a silver. Unfortunately, unlike the past the present Indian athletics scene is devoid of star attraction.

Commendable Performance

India's performance in the glamourous game of tennis has been quite impressive if not spectacular. Undoubtedly no Asian nation can match India's achievements in tennis. In the men's international team competion Davis Cup, the symbol of supremacy in tennis, India has reached the final(previously known as the Challenge Round) thrice — in 1966, 1974 and 1987 — which is a commendable feat! Not many countries in the world have such an impressive record in the Davis Cup. Barring a few countries like the USA and Sweden, India has defeated almost all the leading tennis playing nations at one time or the other in the Davis Cup. The great players like Ramanathan Krishnan, his son Ramesh Krishnan and Amritraj brothers Vijay and Anand have done the country proud by their superb displays and now their mantle has fallen on Leander Paes and Mahesh Bhupathi who are serving the nation well.

Four-time Asian champion Ramanathan Krishnan, once ranked as high as world No.3, reached the semifinals at Wimbledon twice in 1960 and 1961 bowing out both times to the ultimate winners Neale Fraser and Rod Laver respectively. Winner of four grand prix tournaments held in India, Vijay Amritraj reached the quarterfinals at Wimbledon twice in 1973 and 1981 and Ramesh Krishnan accomplished this feat in 1986. Recently Mahesh Bhupathi in tandem with Rika Hiraki of Japan won the mixed doubles crown in the French Open and became the first Indian to win a grand slam event.

At the junior level, however, three Indians — Ramanathan Krishnan, Ramesh Krishnan and Leander Paes — have won great laurels. Ramanathan Krishnan won the Wimbledon junior title in 1954. Ramesh Krishnan's great year was 1979 when he won the junior titles at the French Open and Wimbledon. Leander Paes won the Wimbledon junior title in 1990 and the US Open junior title next year.

Apart from Ramanathan Krishnan, two other Indians Jaideep Mukherjea (1966 and 1969) and Dilip Bose (1949) won the Asian crown. Vijay Amritraj also won the prestigious WCT doubles title in 1977 in partnership with Dick Stockton of the USA.

Some Fine Shooters

As a sport shooting became popular in the country only after Independence. Dr. Karni Singh of Bikaner, who was arguably the best shooter produced by the country, claimed a silver medal in the world Clay Pigeon (trap shooting) event held in Cairo in 1962. In fact, Dr. Karni Singh and Vladimir Zimenko of the USSR had tied for the top spot, but in the shoot-off Zimenko won the gold by the narrowest margin of only one point. Rajkumar Randhir Singh of Patiala, Ashok Pandit of Maharashtra and in recent times Mansher Singh and young Jaspal Rana brought glory to the nation through their superb performances at the international level.

Kings' Game

Just like hockey, polo popularly known as the Kings' game, brought glory to the country both before and after Independence. The greatest moment in the history of Indian polo, however, was in 1957, when the Indian polo team led by Maharaja Swai Man Singh of Jaipur won the world polo championship held at Deauville, France warding off the spirited challenge of strong contenders like Argentina, England, Spain and the hosts France. The other members of the victorious Indian team included such legends as Rao Raja Hanut Singh, his talented son Kanwar Bijey Singh and Lt. Col. Thakur Kishen Singh.

After a long slumber of nearly three decades, the fortunes of Indian polo were revived again in 1995, when the young Indian polo team under the distinguished leadership of non-playing Captain Col. Kuldeep Singh Garcha, himself a player of great repute, qualified for the World Cup polo finals held at St Moritz, Switzerland in July 1995 - after beating Pakistan and the African Champions fancied Zimbabwe. The young Indian team finished only fifth in the World Cup beating the hosts Switzerland twice in the elite six-nation tournament which was eventually won by Brazil. However, India''s Manupal Godara had the distinction of being the top scorer with 11 goals alongside Diego Pando of Switzerland.

A Few Successes

Though wrestling has a glorious tradition in the country and this ancient sport is played and practised at the grassroots level, yet our successes at the highest competitions have been few and far between with only one bronze in the Helsinki Olympiad in 1952 by flyweight K.D. Jadhav and one silver and one bronze in the world wrestling championships by Bisambhar Singh and Uday Chand respectively. Indian wrestlers, however, have shown much better performances in the Commonwealth and Asian Games.

Prakash Best Shuttler

Of late our performances in badminton and table tennis have been rather indifferent. Nine-time national badminton champion Prakash Padukone of Karnataka has been our outstanding shuttler who won the prestigious Masters tournament and All-England badminton championships in London in 1979 and 1980 respectively besides a number of other prominent international tournaments. Prakash has to his credit fabulous victories over his almost all great Chinese, Indonesian and Danish rivals. Nandu Natekar, Dinesh Khanna, Suresh Goyal and Syed Modi are other prominent Indian shuttlers who have won laurels for the country at the international level. The fifties were the golden years for Indian badminton, when India had fared quite creditably in the Thomas Cup and Uber Cup, the symbol of supremacy in the men's and women's team competitions respectively, but the story is quite different nowadays. Aparna Popat among girls and P. Gopi Chand among men have given heartwarming performances in recent times.

The Golden Fifties

Like badminton, the fifties were the golden years for the Indian table tennis. This was the decade when Gool Nasikwala won the triple crown at the inaugural Asian table tennis championships in Singapore in 1952; Krishna Nagaraj reached the quarterfinals in the world championships in Tokyo in 1956; Sudheer Thakersey was declared the best player in Asia in 1957 and the Indian men's team secured tenth place in the Swaythling Cup in the world championships in Dortmund, Germany in 1959, which is India's best ever ranking in the world table tennis. Though India produced a number of excellent table tennis players since then, but none could win a significant title. In April 1997, however, India's doubles pair of Chetan Baboor and Subramanian Raman won a gold in the Commonwealth table tennis meet at Glasgow. Never before in the 26 year history of the Commonwealth table tennis had India won a title.

Other Sports

Boxing, weightlifting, swimming, basketball, volleyball and golf are some other sports in which our achievements are not at all commonsurate with the size and status of our great nation. Our pugilists have performed well at the Asian level and to some extent in the Commonwealth Games. Padam Bahadur Mall, Hawa Singh, Kaur Singh, Mehtab Singh, Badri Singh and Chandra Narayan are our golden boxers who brought glory to the nation at the Asian level.

Our weightlifters have done well only in the Commonwealth Games, otherwise their performance have been quite mediocre. However, the welcome emergence of a few truely outstanding women weightlifters in the recent times have brightened up the otherwise bleak scenario. Prominent among these amazons are N. Kunjarani Devi, Karnam Malleswari, Neelam Lakshmi, Sumita Laha,

Chaya Adak and Bharati Singh. With their scintillating performances, Malleswari and Kunjarani have really done the country proud.

Sea Swimming Marvels

Though India is a land of rivers, even then our performance in the competitive swimming at the international level is simply poor. Barring the inaugural Asian Games in New Delhi in 1951, our performance even at the Asian Games has been disappointing. Khazan Singh is the lone Indian swimmer who won a silver in 200 M butterfly event in the Seoul Games in 1986. However, in the non-competitive long distance swimming, several Indians distinguished themselves. Mihir Sen was the first Indian to earn accolades throughout the world for his heroic feats in the long distance sea swimming. He first swam the English Channel in less than 15 hours in 1958. Eight years later this legendary Indian swimmer crossed all the major straits in the world including the Palk straits, the straits of Gibralter, Dardanelles and Bosphorus and the Panama Canal. It was a hazardous feat unparalleled in the history of long distance swimming till then. Arati Saha became the first Asian woman to swim the English Channel. Subsequently several Indians brought glory to the country in long distance swimming. The child prodigies Kutraleeswaran, Chhavi Madan and Rupali Repale have sensational feats in long distance swimming to their credit. Kutraleeswaran crossed six seaways in 1994 at the precocious age of thirteen. Chhavi was even younger when she crossed several straits and channels a year later. Rupali Repale at the age of 14 became the youngest swimmer to crosss the gruellling 65-Km stretch across the Port Philipbay in Australia.

Though volleyball is played throughout India at the grassroots level, we failed to make the desired impact at the international level. India's biggest achievement in this sport was the magnificent title triumph in the inaugural Asian volleyball championship held in Tokyo in 1955. But subsequently like several other sports our standard in volleyball stagnated. Fortunately in recent years, our junior teams have performed fairly well at the Asian level giving a welcome hint of surging further ahead. Very poor is our performace in cycling, squash and gymnastics. Our archers too after initial successes failed to make any headway as yet. These are the games in which we are bracketted with the minnows. The situation is somewhat better in golf and yachting.

The country has produced a number of good amateur golfers such as P.G. "Biloo" Sethi, R.K. Pitamber, Ashok Malik, Vikramjit

Singh etc. in the post-Independence era. The best ever performance by the Indian golfers at the amateur level was in the Ninth Asiad in Delhi in 1982, when Lakshman Singh and Rajiv Mohta won a gold and a silver respectively in the individual event besides capturing a gold in the team competition. It is heartening to note that a new crop of talented young pros like Chiranjeev Milkha Singh, Gaurav Ghei, Arjun Atwal, Jyoti Randhawa, Ali Sher, Amritinder Singh, to name a few, is doing well in the Asian PGA tour. Among ladies, Simi Mehra is trying to break new grounds as a professional in the USA. The young Shivin Kwatra is also performing exceeding well in the international junior events. India's greatest performance in golf was a dream triumph over highly-rated Scotland in the prestigious Alfred Dunhill Cup in 1996.

India's performance in yachting has been satisfactory only at the Asian level. Our leading yachtsmen Soli Contractor, Afsar Hussain, Fali Unwalla, Commander S.K. Mongia etc. have served the country well. Indian yachtsmen have traditionally dominated the Southern Asia Yachting regatta and also won several medals in the Asian Games including a gold in the Ninth Asiad which was won by Farokh Tarapore and Zarir Karanjia in Fireball catagory. In the Ninth Asiad, India won three golds in equestrian events. Apart from a gold in Three-Day Event (team), Dafadar Raghubir Singh in Three-Day Event (individual) and Major R.S. Brar in tent-pegging won the golds.

Emulating the example of the "Pocket Hercules" Manohar Aich in bodybuilding, Prem Chand Degra has done the country proud by winning the coveted title of Mr. Universe. In the first Asian Games in New Delhi in 1951, Parimal Roy was declared "Mr. Asia".

Indoor Games

However, in indoor games like billiards, snooker, chess and carrom India has done particularly well. Billiards has the unique distinction of giving India three world champions in Wilson Jones, Michael Ferreira and Geet Sethi. Wilson Jones twice won the world amateur billiards championships in 1958 and 1964. His successors Michael Ferreira and Geet Sethi went a step further and accomplished a rare billiards "double" capturing both the amateur and professional world titles. Satish Mohan and Subhash Agrawal were India's other prominent cueists who though excelled at the international level but were distinctly unlucky not to win a world title. Om Agrawal was the lone Indian to win a world title in snooker.

Though chess originated in India and is truly a grassroots game, the organised activities in this cerebral game started only after Independence. Thanks mainly to the two trail-blazers Manuel Aaron and Viswanathan Anand, today chess is flourishing in the country as never before. Manuel Aaron was the first Indian to win the coveted title of International Master and Viswanathan ascended unprecedented heights for an Indian to become a Grandmaster. Anand is the first Asian to win the world junior chess title in 1987 and one of the elite few to become a runner-up in the world chess championship in 1995. Anand with the Elo rating of 2765 is currently ranked among the top three chess players in the world. A chess megastar, Anand has inspired a whole generation of chess players in the country by his exemplary deeds. Another Indian, a child prodigy P. Harikrishna from a small village in Andhra Pradesh, has done the country proud by winning the U-10 championship at Menorca, Spain in 1996. Before Independence there was not a single titled chess player in the country, today we have two Grandmasters in Viswanathan Anand and Dibyendu Barua, more than 20 International Masters and nine International Woman Masters. Among the Indian women chess players, Rohini Khadilkar, Bhagyashree Thipsay and Anupama Gokhle have dominated the Asian women's chess championships.

For a long time considered as a family pastime, carrom is steadily gaining popularity as a competitive sport not only in India but in other countries also. India has shown complete dominance over this new competitive indoor game at the international level by winning all the international competitions including the World Cup in which it has taken part. No Asian or western country has been able to match India's prowess in this game.

The indigenous game of kabaddi came to our rescue in the last two Asian Games. In fact, at the Beijing Games in 1990, kabaddi was the only game which gave us a gold medal under the captaincy of Ashok Shinde, while S. Rajaratnam led the Indian kabaddi team to fetch another gold four years later at Hiroshima. Earlier India had won the first Asian kabaddi championship at Calcutta in 1980.

Realistically speaking our achievements in various sports do not match either with the size, population or status of our great motherland, but there is no need to despair as despondency is a bane and realistic optimism is a spur for success.

PART VIII

Mountaineering and Tourism

- Fifty Years of Indian Tourism
- Mountaineering in India

34

Fifty Years of Indian Tourism

Dr. G. Sundaram

THE WORLD TOURISM Organization lays down the following objectives for tourism:

- Poverty alleviation
- Environmental regeneration
- Job creation
- Advancement of women and other disadvantaged groups
- Preservation of monuments and heritage sites

So, in this context, it would be worthwhile having a look at the development of tourism in the country since Independence.

Tourism in the World Context

Recently there was an advertisement in 'The Economist' of London by the World Travel and Tourism Council giving the pictures of fifteen world leaders(not one from India) starting from President Nelson Mandela to President Clinton to John Major, the then Prime Minister of the United Kingdom to King Hussain of Jordan and President Carlos Menem of Argentina stating that they have all identified 'travel and tourism' as a strategic economic and employment priority for the 21st century. 'Travel and tourism' is expected to create employment for 262 million people, or 10.5% of the global work force this year, growing to 383 million people by the year 2007. A gain of 121 million jobs or one new job every 2.4 seconds.

Tourism is considered the world's largest industry with 593 million people travelling and the industry accounting for an earning of $ 423 billion excluding air fares. A small country like Spain had overtaken the United States in the number of arrivals in 1995. France has an arrival of 60 million per year, more than her population. Even small countries like Singapore, Hong Kong and Malaysia are in the big league of tourism attracting more number of visitors than India.

Tourism is also world's largest export industry. It accounts for about 8% of the total exports - more than 30% of international trade in services.

The Indian Scenario

The international tourist traffic of the country during 1951 was just 16,829. Over a period of 44 years, the arrivals increased to 2.12 million in 1995, half of which is accounted by ethnic Indians from the United Kingdom and the neighbouring countries. Tourism is presently India's third largest export industry after ready-made garments and gems & jewellery(in the case of gems & jewellery, the import content is very high). The foreign exchange earnings from tourism during 1995-96 was of the order of Rs. 10,000 crores.

The direct employment in this sector during 1994-95 was about 7.8 million persons accounting for about 2.4% of the total labour force. The multiplier effect of tourism in employment generation is fairly high and as such the total employment including indirect employment is 18.4 million. It would be possible to generate additional direct employment for 4.73 million persons within the next five years if the international tourist arrivals could be increased to at least five million.

The labour-capital ratio per million rupees of investment at 1985-86 prices in the hotel and restaurant sector is 89 jobs as against 44.7 jobs in the case of agriculture and 12.6 jobs in the case of manufacturing industries. In the case of tourism industry, taking all individual segments together the ratio is 47.5 jobs and is still higher than other industries.

But whatever India has achieved so far is abysmally low as compared to even small countries like Maldives, Singapore and Malaysia.

Governmental Efforts

The importance of tourism as an instrument of economic and social change was recognised only in 1946 when a Committee was formed under Sir John Sargeant to advise the Government on the development of tourism. As a result of the recommendations of this Committee, a Tourist Traffic Branch was established in the Ministry of Transport in 1949. However, tourism did not figure as an entity in the Constitution and no separate plan allocation for tourism development was made in the First Five Plan(1950-55).

However, in 1952 the Government of India opened a Tourist Office in New York and the Air-India established a Tourist Cell at their headquarters in Bombay. Later a Government of India Tourist Office was also established in London. The first Hotel Management Institute was also set up in Bombay in 1954.

During the Second Five Year Plan(1956-66), a sum of Rs. 3.4 crore was allocated. But the expenditure was of the order of only Rs. 2.2 crore. The emphasis was mainly on providing accommodation and facilities at important tourist centres including transport. The Tourism Section in the Ministry of Transport became a full-fledged Directorate of Tourism in 1958.

The Third Five Year Plan(1962-66) also concentrated on creation of the same type of facilities with an expenditure of Rs. 5.1 crore against an allocation of Rs. 8 Crore. However, the major scheme was the establishment of a Winter Sports Complex at Gulmarg. A Committee was also appointed under the chairmanship of the late Shri L.K. Jha in 1962. The Committee was asked to assess the requirements of tourism in respect of hotel accommodation, transport, the rules and regulations regarding visas and customs formalities, a suitable publicity programme for promotion of tourism and the increase of foreign exchange earnings from tourism and its protection against leakages. The Committee submitted a fairly comprehensive report. Following this, the India Tourism Development Corporation (ITDC) was established in 1966. It was also agreed in 1965 to allow tourist charters by non-scheduled carriers to come to India though the number was restricted to 50 per year.

The basic approach remained the same during the Annual Plans during 1966-69. During this period the expenditure was of the order of Rs. 4.2 crore as against the allocation of Rs. 7 crore.

Also during this period a unique 'Operation Europe' scheme was launched and the national carrier Air India functioned closely with the Department of Tourism in these promotional efforts from Europe.

The Fourth Five Year Plan (1969-74) laid emphasis upon the importance of tourist facilities with a view to promoting 'destination traffic' as distinct from 'transit traffic'. The outlay was also stepped up to Rs. 46 crore. The Central Government also provided loans to the hotel industry in the private sector including funds for purchase of vehicles and integrated development of selected centres. The ITDC's role could not be minimised because during this period the Corporation constructed a number of hotels, motels and cottages with transport facilities at a number of strategic centres. This is valuable property even now and at that period of time the ITDC did play an important role particularly in the overall economic and social objectives of the Government.

The Fifth Five Year Plan(1974-78) laid emphasis upon integrated development of tourism centres like Gulmarg, Goa and Kovalam. The outlay was of the order of Rs. 60 crore. This was followed by the Annual Plans of 1978-80.

The Sixth Five Year Plan (1980-85) laid emphasis upon the optimization of the existing investment and increase in tourist accommodation both in the public and the private sectors. The third airline company, Vayudoot with small aircrafts was started in 1981 with the objective of providing air-links to the inaccessible areas particularly in the North-East. The fate of Vayudoot later was well known. But it should not mean that a feeder service with small aircrafts should be given up.

The Indian Institute of Tourism and Travel Management was set up in 1983 as an apex institution for tourism education.

The Government came out with a written policy on tourism in 1982. The policy recognizes that "the many attractions of the India hold virtually an unlimited potential for tourism development". The cultural aspects of tourism were also recognized. The employment opportunities, income generation, etc., were also spelt out for the first time. There was also emphasis upon domestic tourism. In this context, it should be remembered that tourism is of the order of about 100 million people and religious tourism is of the order of 150 million people in the country today. This is growing with increase in income and urge to travel although many places face the onslaught of the unregulated domestic tourists.

The Seventh Five Year Plan (1985-90) recognized tourism as priority sector and accorded the status of an industry to it. It was included as a plan objective for the first time in the planning process. The allocation was stepped up to Rs. 326 crore and the expenditure actually amounted to Rs. 437 crore.

The Annual Plans of 1990-92 accounted for an expenditure of Rs. 191 crore.

The National Action Plan for Tourism was evolved and presented to Parliament in 1992. The Action Plan recognized tourism as the fastest growing industry in the world and underlined its economic significance for the growth and progress of India. It laid emphasis upon the preservation of national heritage and the environment. It equally laid emphasis upon international tourism and the potential for foreign exchange earning. The proposal was also to diversify the tourism product. These objectives could be achieved by improving tourism infrastructure, integrated development of areas of tourist interest and restructuring and strengthening the institutions for development of human resources. (There are a number of catering institutes.) Private investment was also to be encouraged.

The Eighth Five Year Plan carries all these aspects of course with emphasis upon private sector participation because of constrainsts on public funds. However, plan allocation should be stepped up considerably.

Tourism Strategy

In spite of all these efforts over five decades, the performance of the tourism industry is dismal in the country today. To cite an example, the Andaman & Nicobar Islands are very beautiful. But the tourism infrastructure and access to these islands are poor. On the other side of the sea, Phuket in Thailand is a great attraction in the whole world. Thailand has also increased its total hotel capacity by 40% within two years. In the Atlantic, Las Palmas, an Island belonging to Spain is only a rock formation. There is no drinking water which has to be imported. For other purposes, the sea water is desalinated. But the

Island attracts 7.5 million tourists every year. Cuba's increase in hotel capacity is tremendous and tourism is the leading industry today replacing the traditional sugar. Whereas, with our vast heritage of temples and monuments and scenic splendour from the Himalayas to the numerous beaches, our international arrivals is hardly two million per year. This would mean that we need to have not tourism plans, but tourism strategy.

When I was Secretary in the Department of Tourism, I got a strategy paper prepared. Although the allocations indicated in the paper looked high, these were mainly meant for the infrastructural Ministries like Surface Transport, Railways and Civil Aviation which in any case had to make allocations. Some incentives were suggested in addition to the present incentives in the Income Tax Act, etc. The outgo per year would have been only Rs. 300 crore which would have earned another Rs. 10,000 crore per annum. But we at times follow a general policy and try to apply it even to nascent sectors like tourism. This may not be right. We have rightly stopped incentives for other sectors including exports. But, for a nascent sector like tourism, we have to provide small incentives to have big gains because almost all other countries including the neighboring countries do so. The private sector too should play an active role and increase the hotel rooms without looking at short-term gains in the form of very high hotel tariff as of today. They should go for foreign collaborations in a big way.

Besides, our Civil Aviation Policy has to undergo a drastic change. We have to improve our present airports within a short period of time. There are 121 airports with the Government of India and 139 airports or air-strips with the State Governments. It is necessary to revive them which is not difficult and encourage the private sector, if necessary by reducing the tax element for the aviation turbine fuel and giving small financial incentives so that these strips are properly used. For instance, there are 44 airports in a small country like Nepal. There are 21 airports in Mongolia of which only five have regular runways; others use the hard ground. This does not mean that we have to run risks and sacrifice the public interest. But the Director General of Civil Aviation should not come up with grandiose plans of expenditure for each and every airstrip and as a result no proposal is approved. In Alaska, lakes are used as runways for small planes(float planes) and tourism is doing tremendous business by operating these planes.

It would be advisable to augment the flights of the Air India and the Indian Airlines. While we are not in a position to do it on a large scale for want of finance, we should allow the private sector to do it including allowing them to operate international air services. Similarly, if we are not in a position for want of aircraft or are not interested in going to a particular destination, we should allow that country to come here freely so that the tourist arrivals could go up. For instance, we are not interested in going to Ulan Battor, but they come to Almatti and want to extend the service to New Delhi. This should be permitted without insisting upon reciprocal rights. So is the case with Singapore, Nepal and Sri Lanka.

We hurriedly closed down our service to Australia and South Africa. A service takes time to pick up. At the same time, it could be extended to South America so that there would be adequate traffic. For instance, Malaysian Airlines did this from Kuala Lumpur to Johannesburg to Buenos Aires. So we have to think on new lines instead of following the beaten path.

Similarly, we have to promote cruise tourism. For instance, there are places like Poompuhar, Tranqubar and Karaikal and it is difficult for a foreign tourist to reach these places by rail or road because the journey is cumbersome and takes a long time. A cruise service on the Coromandel Coast would change the scenario.

All this shows that our policies of tourism have not yielded the desired results in the last half-a-century and we have to think and move fast on new lines with the Government acting as a catalyst to the private sector so that the Indian people could benefit a great deal from this important sector.

35

Mountaineering in India

Capt. (Retd.) M. S. Kohli

I HAVE BEEN fortunate, rather privileged, in being associated with the Indian mountaineering for over four decades, and with adventure since early childhood. While India celebrates 50 years of Independence and takes stock of what we have achieved during all these years and what we should strive to accomplish in the future, a focus on 'mountaineering and adventure in India', amongst other national aspects, is very desirable.

Let us, for a moment, look at the pre-Independence scenario. For centuries the majestic Himalayas, spread over 2,500 kilometres of our northern borders, have always held a strange fascination for our people from all walks of life — artists, writers, poets and scientists etc. They are one of nature's great wonders. In the words of Jawaharlal Nehru, "the Himalayas are not only near to us but also very dear: for they have always been part of our history and tradition, our thinking and our poetry, our worship and our devotion. According to our mythology, they are the 'abode of Gods'."

Ancient cultural and spiritual links have thus brought Indians close to the Himalayas. It was but natural that our holymen should undertake journeys, involving long and arduous marches, to be able to sit in the shadow of the gods to meditate and achieve illumination and fulfilment; even more natural that shrines should spring up throughout the length and breadth of the Himalayas to celebrate the glory of God and become places of pilgrimage for the devout among Hindus, Muslims, Sikhs and Buddhists for centuries.

Initial awakening of interest in mountaineering in India came in the wake of climbing activity in the Himalayas by the foreign climbers, some of whom also settled down in India later. It will, therefore, be appropriate to survey briefly the mountaineering scene in India during the second half of the Nineteenth century and the first half of the Twentieth century, which also saw the birth of the Himalayan Club. The Himalayan Club, which was founded in 1927, was an early landmark in the history of Indian mountaineering. The formation of the Club was welcomed by many, both in India and abroad. Those who responded immediately were made founder-members. These included Sir Francis Young-husband, Sir Martin Conway, Normal Collie, Douglas Freshfield, Bruce, Longstaff, Howard-Bury, Norton, Ruttledge and all other members of Everest Expeditions. Sir Geoffrey Corbett and W.Allsup, became Honorary Secretaries. A year after its establishment, the Club decided to publish the *The Himalayan Journal* more or less on the pattern of *The Alpine Journal.* This journal has become a major source of the history of Himalayan climbs.

The 1950s ushered in the golden era of mountaineering in the Himalayas. In 1950 itself, the French climbers — Maurice Herzog, Louis Lachanel and Lionel Teray ascended the first 8,000 ft. peak, Annapurna I. The event was acclaimed throughout the world as a magnificent feat of human courage and endurance.

Much of the credit for early interest in mountaineering among Indians goes to the Doon School, largely because of the presence of some distinguished British mountaineers on the staff — J. A. K. Martyn, J. T. M. Gibson and R. H. Holdsworth, and to some extent owing to the fact that the School nestles in the foothills of the Himalayas. In 1951, Gurdial Singh of the Doon School climbed the 7120 metre high Trisul. This was the first Indian summit. The ascent of Trisul may not appear much of a triumph now, but over four decades ago it was considered quite an achievement for the Indians. The Doon School certainly blazed a trail that introduced Indians to mountaineering as a sport and it provided the tinder that was to catch fire two years later, after the first ascent of Everest.

The real start of Indian mountaineering, however, was triggered by the maiden ascent of Everest on May 29, 1953, by Sir Edmund Hillary and Tenzing Norgay. This historic achievement was hailed all over the world. In India, the two great visionaries, Jawaharlal Nehru and B. C. Roy, saw in this achievement a glorious opportunity to introduce the sport of mountaineering in India. They immediately decided to set up the Himalayan Mountaineering Institute (HMI) in Darjeeling with Tenzing as Director of Field Training. Major Nandu Jayal was made the first Principal of the HMI. The Prime Minister himself decided to become the Chairman of the Exe-cutive Governing Council with Dr.B.C.Roy as the Vice Chairman. The courses of the Institute started from November 1954, and this paved the way for systematic development and growth of mountaineering in India. Soon after the establishment of the HMI in 1954 Nandu Jayal decided to introduce an advance course annually, which was in the form of an expedition to a major Himalayan peak. So during the next three years he led expeditions to Kamet, Saser Kangri and Nanda Devi.

I was lucky to be selected for the advance course expedition to Saser Kangri in 1956. We were the first outsiders in several years to penetrate into the unexplored Nubra valley of Ladakh. Though we missed the main peak we succeeded in climbing the 24,000 ft. high Sakang peak. For me it was a wonderful experience. In 1958 Nandu Jayal joined the Indian expedition to Cho-Oyu, led by Keki Bunshah, a Bombay solicitor. This was the first major Indian achievement. Unfortunately, Nandu Jayal died on the mountain. This was a great loss to the Indian mountaineering.

In 1959 an all-Naval expedition, led by me, climbed Nanda Kot (22,500 ft.). This was one of the better known peaks of the Kumaon Himalayas adjacent to Nanda Devi. Dr. Somervell, who examined its northern aspect in 1926, wrote: "It seemed to us that the whole mountain was in danger of slipping down in snowy crushes". In that year, on May 25, after leaving the last camp at 5 a.m. and after struggling through one of the most difficult and steep ice-slopes, K.P.Sharma and I tore through the summit cornice and heaved ourselves onto the summit of Nanda Kot at 2.20 P.M., muttering *Nanda Devi Ki Jai.*

With these encouragements the Cho-Oyu Sponsoring Committee decided to take up the challenge of Mount Everest and convert itself into the sponsoring committee of the Everest Expedition. This sponsoring committee was later reconstituted on January 15, 1961, into a permanent organisation known as the Indian Mountaineering Foundation with its headquarters at New Delhi. This was a major landmark in the history of Indian mountaineering. The main objectives of the IMF are to organise, support and provide a base for expeditions for mountaineering, skiing, rock climbing, trekking at high altitudes as well as to promote, encourage, support and execute schemes for all Himalayan adventures.

Membership of IMF is conferred upon persons who have distinguished themselves in the field of mountaineering or have rendered valuable service in the promotion and spread of mountaineering and allied sports.

The 1960 Everest expedition led by Brig. Gyan Singh and with Keki F.Bunshah as the Deputy Leader, was a near success. For the first time a lot of indigenous mountaineering equipment produced in the ordnance factories was used. Brig. Gyan Singh was a great leader. The first summit party consisting of Sonam Gytaso, Nawang Gombu and Narinder Kumar missed the summit by 200 metres in adverse weather conditions. The second summit party consisting of M. S. Kohli, C. P. Vohra and Ang Temba spent two frightening nights at South Col where they were caught in a heavy monsson snows and had a narrow escape.

In 1961, there has been two noteworthy Indian expeditions, which deserve to be mentioned. These are the Indian expeditions to Annapurna-III and Nilkantha led by me and Capt. N. Kumar. Annapurna-III was selected after I had come across a remark by the well-known British mountaineer, Mr. H. W. Tilaman : "Only from broad back of the main ridge west of Annapurna-II or of Annapurna-IV could either of these peaks be reached, while Annapurna-III, bristling with gendarmes and cornices, could not be reached at all". That was enough for me to accept the challenge.

The ascent of Annapurna-III by the Indian team was the most dramatic story of mountaineering during the last four decades, till then an unexplored and virgin peak. While the team was halfway up the mountain, the local Bhotias, who were hostile to mountaineering expeditions, looted the base camp and took two of the team members as hostages. It was only after protracted negotiations and on the intervention of the then Prime Minister Jawaharlal Nehru and His Majesty the King of Nepal, the two expedition members were released. During this drama the formidable peak was climbed. Troops from Nepal reached the base camp for rescue. Lt.Vijai Shekhawat, later to become the Chief of Naval Staff, was one of the members.

The Nilkantha expedition was another milestone in India's history. Frank Smythe called it the most beautiful as well as the most difficult peak in the Garhwal Himalayas. Mr. O. P. Sharma, two

Sherpas, Phurba Lobsand and Lhakpa Gyalbu Lama, under the leadership of Colonel N. Kumar, claimed to have reached the peak on June 15. Kumar was badly frostbitten and had to have three toes of his left foot amputated. The ascent was, however, disputed. Despite IMF investigation, confirming the ascent the controversy continues.

The second Everest expedition (1962), with Major John Dias as Leader and Lt. M. S. Kohli as Deputy Leader had unsettled weather during their summit attempt. After spending an extra day at South Col and another extra day at the last camp at 28,000 feet, the trio made a gallant attempt. But when just 100 metres short of the summit, they were caught in a strong blizzard and had to retreat. The journey back became a life and death struggle. Finally, at 10 p.m. crawling on all fours, they reached their last camp. They spent three nights at 28,000 feet, two without oxygen, an effort which has not been matched again.

In 1964 the IMF sent three Pre-Everest expeditions. A team led by Flt. Lt. A. K. Chowdhury attempted peaks in the Panch Chuli range. Another team, led by Colonel N.Kumar, climbed Nanda Devi. The third team led by me attempted Trisuli and Nanda Devi East. On the latter peak we had a near tragedy when three members, Balwant Singh Sandhu, Harish Rawat and J. C. Joshi, and three Sherpas came tumbling down over 2500 ft from the Longstaff Col in an avalanche and survived. It was during this period Jawaharlal Nehru died. Nehru has been instrumental in starting mountaineering in India.

The third Indian attempt on Everest (1965) was a glorious success. The team which I had the honour to lead, was destined to set up a world record. In nine days nine climbers, in four teams, reached the summit. There was rejoicing throughout the country. The team was accorded unprecedented welcome at Delhi, on being received by the Prime Minister and a number of Cabinet Ministers at the airport. I was invited to address the members of both the Houses of Indian Parliament. In 1971, the late Shrimati Indira Gandhi, commenting on the Everest expedition, had remarked : "The successful Indian Everest Climb in 1965, the military victory in 1971, the peaceful nuclear experiment at Pokhran, the achievement of self-sufficiency in food, the launching of Aryabhatta, Bhaskara and Rohini and this last with our own rocket — each one of these has added to our prestige as a nation and to the self-confidence of our people."

The glorious ascent of Mount Everest by members of the 1965 Indian team resulted in a sudden spurt of mountaineering activity in the country. Tremendous interest and excitement was generated among the youth of the country. Some other mountaineering institutes sprang up. Early in 1961 the western Himalayan Mountaineering Institute had come up at Manali. In 1965 the Nehru Institute of Mountaineering was established in Uttarkashi. The number of Indian expeditions registered an abnormal increase. In 1965 there were only four Indian expeditions but in 1966 their number increased to 15. It went on multiplying with 25 in 1975, 65 in 1980 and 101 in 1984.

The 1960s saw a new development. Apart from the Indian Army the Indo-Tibetan Border Police Force (ITBP) started mountaineering activity in a big way. This young paramilitary force, created in 1962, is deployed in the Himalayan region. To enable the men to function in the hostile Himalayan terrain, mountaineering was introduced right from inception. I was fortunate to be invited to join this Force even before it was formally launched. I had eight years stint with the ITBP from 1963 to 1971 as Commandant and five years, from 1991-96, as Advisor (I.G.). During the past 35 years the ITBP has climbed over 100 Himalayan peaks including Everest from both sides, Kanchenzonga and 43 virgin peaks.

The Indian Army too organised several expeditions with large teams, with the objective of instilling the spirit of adventure and camaraderie among the young soldiers. Col. N. Kumar, who worked as the Principal of the Himalayan Mountaineering Institute, Darjeeling, and later headed the High Altitude Warfare School, Gulmarg, led several expeditions himself. The greatest achievement of the Army was the ascent of Kanchenzonga, the third highest mountain of the world, for the first time from the difficult North-East Ridge. The peak was climbed by Major Prem Chand and Naik Neem Dorjee Sherpa.

The IMF too organised a number of expeditions on national level to major peaks, sometimes in collaboration with foreign mountaineers of repute. Some of the notable achievements are the Indo-Japanese expedition which for the first time traversed Nanda Devi, Indian Ladies Expedition to Kamet and 'From the Ocean to the Sky' expedition led by Sir Edmund Hillary. This heralded white-water rafting in the Himalayan rivers. H.C.Sarin, Commander Joginder Singh and I were the Indian members.

The climb of Hardeol in 1978, led by S. P. Chamoli of ITBP, was another remarkable achievement. Hardeol, the Temple of Gods, had always been regarded as a tough proposition. The 1964 team, led by me, had near tragedy while attempting Trisuli and Hardeol. A timely withdrawal had saved us from an enormous ice avalanche. Ten years later, in 1974, a joint Indo-New Zealand women's expedition had met with tragedy. Four climbers, two Indians and two New Zealanders, perished in an avalanche. The mountain earned the title 'killer'.

Indian girls also did not lag behind. In 1961 the courses of the HMI were thrown open to the Indian women. Prior to this, the only instance of Indian women taking to heights was the association of three Indian women with the International Women's Expedition to Cho Oyu in 1959, led by Kogan Claude. They were Nima and Pem Prem, both daughters of Tenzing Norgay, and Doma, a niece of Tenzing and sister of Nawang Gombu. During that year, Nima set up a world record for teenagers by reaching 6,842 metres on Cho Oyu. She was then just seventeen.

In 1981, a mixed team of men and women, under the leadership of Colonel Balwant Sandhu, was sent to Nanda Devi by IMF. This was a special expedition initiated by the late Rajiv Gandhi under the aegis of Sanjay Gandhi Adventure Scheme which I had helped setting up. Three girls, Chandra Prabha, Rekha and Harsha, and three men Palzore, Rattan and Lhatoo reached the summit.

May 23, 1984, will be regarded as a red-letter day in the history of Indian Mountaineering. It was on that day that the very first Indian woman, Bachendri Pal, reached the summit of Everest at seven minutes past one. It was not only an achievement for Indian women mountaineers, but it brought new confidence to Indian women. In 1993, IMF sent an all-women team, led by Bachendri Pal to Everest. Seven girls and ten men reached the summit. Santosh Yadav became the first woman in the world to climb Everest twice. She had climbed Everest before with the ITBP team in 1991 led by Hukum Singh. Today India is proud of having more women mountaineers than any other country of the world. After climbing Everest, Indian girls are not going to sit on their laurels. Bachendri Pal is now working with the Tatas with a mission to spread the sport of adventure and mountaineering among the Indian girls. She is presently leading the first all-women team to traverse the entire Himalayas from east to west.

In 1976 an Indo-Japanese team attempted the traverse of the twin summits of Nanda Devi. The Indian team consisted of Colonel Jagjit Singh, Major Prem Chand, Capt. Alok Chandola, and Pranesh K. P. H. Singh. The Japanese side had K. Kiryu, K. Kano, Yusuo Kato (who became the first man to climb Everest thrice and died after the third ascent), and ten others. Kiryu and Jagjit Singh were the joint leaders.

The Eastern peak was climbed on June 9 by Prem Chand, Shingehiro, Kiryu and Rattan Singh. On June 13, Hasagawa and Takami descended from Camp IV below the East peak to the ridge connecting the two peaks. The climbers finally managed to reach the summit of the main peak in gruelling conditions.

One of the important joint expeditions was the international expedition led by Norman Dyhrenfurth in 1971. It was the first major experiment in understanding and cooperation among nations. The team was composed of representatives from thirteen nations. IMF nominated Major Bahuguna, who had narrowly missed the summit of Everest in 1965 with the Indian team. The expedition planned a two-pronged attempt; one team was to try the South West face direct and another to ascend the West ridge beyond the American Camp IV-West along its entire length. In this expedition Major Bahuguna died and his Austrian companion Wolfgang Axt came under worldwide criticism.

Another notable joint expedition was the Indo-American expedition to the unclimbed North ridge of the Nanda Devi. The expedition, which was jointly led by Adams Carter and Willi Unsoeld, left Lata on July 14 and moved along the Rishi gorge. That year India has the most severe monsoon in 100 years. The weather on Nanda Devi was unusually bad. Frequent avalanches swept the face. Nanda Devi Unsoeld, Willi's 22-year old daughter, who had been named after the peak was one of the most valuable and lovable members of the team, fell in an accident and died on the very slopes of the mountain she loved and had dreamt of climbing.

In 1996, seven ITBP climbers are reported to have reached the summit of Everest from the difficult North Col. Unfortunately, three brave climbers T. Samanala, Paljor and Dorjee, who claimed to reach the peak on May 10, perished during their descent. A Japanese team which climbed Everest the following day was unable to help the climbers in distress. This became a major controversy. Most of the old climbers feel that saving the life of a mountaineer in the 'death zone' is the duty of any climber in the vicinity. Besides several major expeditions already mentioned, there have been quite a few exciting ventures led by Harish Kapadia, who has been climbing the Indian Himalayas for almost 3 decades and who has nearly 25 exploratory trips, including 30 ascents, to his credit.

Rajiv Gandhi was very keen to see an Indian team reaching the South Pole, and another Indian team yachting around the world. In

1985, encouraged by him, an Army Engineers' team completed the first round-the-world journey in a special boat 'Trishna'. Rajiv and I continued our efforts for sending an Indian team to South Pole. I was able to arrange for Col. J. K. Bajaj to spend a season with the Indian Antartica team. After his initial survey he joined an international group and managed to reach the South Pole on 17th January, 1989 — the first Indian to do so. It was a marvelous effort.

India today has emerged as one of the leading mountaineering nations of the world. The HMI, NIM and the Manali Institute are training over 1000 youth annually. There are over 100 Indian expeditions to the Himalayas every year. The IMF has already completed the Sport Climbing Wall and regular competitions are taking place. The IMF Museum is getting ready for inauguration. Over 100,000 youth are venturing out to various parts of the Himalayas for trekking. Over a million visit the Himalayan shrines annually.

To preserve the Himalayan environment, the Himalayan Environment Trust was started some seven years ago by the leading climbers of the world. In 1997 India will be joining some elite nations where the Outward Bound movement is operating. I have agreed to become the chairman of the Outward Bound India. Admiral V. S. Shekhawat and some eminent persons are on the Governing Council.

Mountaineering in India today has spread widely among all sections of our youth. It is no longer a privilege of a coterie. These years have also witnessed major changes in equipment, in climbing techniques, in attitudes towards climbing, and above all, the ever-growing number of the youth embarking on Himalayan treks.

Looking back, our thoughts go to several climbers who have blazed the trail, but are not with us today. The foremost among them is Major Nandu Jayal, Sir Harold Williams, Major John Dias, Sonam Gyatso, Avatar Singh Cheema, Phu Dorjee, Harsh Bahuguna and many others. In the past few months India lost two great stalwarts, Harish Sarin and Brig. Gyan Singh, both died at the age of 82, having fulfilled a lot. Mr.Sarin looked after the mountaineering institutes in India for 27 years and the IMF for 23 years. Appropriately a hall and the mountaineering store in the IMF Building complex have been named after Harish Sarin and Brig. Gyan Singh.

The story of Indian mountaineering during the last 50 years has verily come to be a record of three generations of Indian pioneer-climbers, starting from Gurdial Singh's first Indian Summit - Trisul -

in 1951 to India's glorious ascent of Mount Everest in 1965 and finally to Bachendri Pal's ascent of Everest in 1984 and continuing with an increasing number of small but bold and exploratory ventures. The story is packed with high adventure and exciting drama, with successes and failures, fulfilments and disappointments and heart-warming triumph and agonising defeats. And sometimes deaths; for Nature is as benevolent as unforgiving.

The phenomenal growth of the sport of mountaineering in the post-Independence India has been one of the most welcome developments, for it has played, though indirectly, a significant role in the life of the nation. The record of the Indian climbers is replete with daring exploits that hit the headlines. Indira Gandhi chose to bracket the achievements of our mountaineers with India's universally acclaimed achievements in scientific and other fields.

On March 24, 1997, I visited Darjeeling along with Sir Edmund Hillary where he inaugurated Tenzing Norgay's statue. Tenzing had died in Darjeeling in 1986. During the formal unveiling of the statue on March 25, I recalled the words of the great visionary Pandit Jawaharlal Nehru, who said: "Tenzing, I want you to produce hundreds of Tenzings." Tenzing had kept the promise he had made to Panditji.

Our performance in the field of mountaineering has been very creditable. Although we have achieved a lot and can look back with satisfaction at our achievements, there is still much more than that remains to be done. There are hundreds of virgin summits, miles and miles of unexplored areas, more and more ridges and unclimbed faces of peaks already climbed. There is no better sport for the character building of our youth. Mountaineering, in fact, is a way of life which should spread, not only to cities and towns but to the villages and to remote areas of our country where young boys and girls are still living without being affected by the modern society. Once this takes place, as well as other sports and adventures, the strength of the nation is ensured.

PART IX

Their Vision of India

- Tryst with Destiny
- Building a Strong India
- Make India Strong and Great
- Guarding the Flame of Freedom
- Forty Years of Independence

36

Tryst with Destiny

Jawaharlal Nehru

LONG YEARS AGO we made a tryst with destiny, and now the time comes when we shall redeem our pledge, not wholly or in full measure, but very substantially. At the stroke of the midnight hour, when the world sleeps, India will awake to life and freedom. A moment comes, which comes but rarely in history, when we step out from the old to the new, when an age ends, and when the soul of a nation, long suppressed, finds utterance. It is fitting that at this solemn moment we take the pledge of dedication to the service of India and her people and to the still larger cause of humanity.

At the dawn of history India started on her unending quest, and trackless centuries are filled with her striving and the grandeur of her successes and her failures. Through good and ill fortune alike she has never lost sight of that quest or forgotten the ideals which gave her strength. We end today a period of ill fortune and India discovers herself again. The opportunity, to the greater triumphs and achievements that await us. Are we brave enough and wise enough to grasp this opportunity and accept the challenge of the future?

Freedom and power bring responsibility. The responsibility rests upon this Assembly, a sovereign body representing the sovereign

---

Speech delivered in the Constituent Assembly, New Delhi on August 14, 1947, on the eve of the attainment of Independence.

people of India. Before the birth of freedom we have endured all the pains of labour and our hearts are heavy with the memory of this sorrow. Some of those pains continue even now. Nevertheless, the past is over and it is the future that beckons to us now.

That future is not one of ease or resting but of incessant striving so that we may fulfil the pledges we have so often taken and the one we shall take today. The service of India means the service of the millions who suffer. It means the ending of poverty and ignorance and disease and inequality of opportunity. The ambition of the greatest man of our generation has been to wipe every tear from every eye. That may be beyond us, but as long as there are tears and suffering, so long our work will not be over.

And so we have to labour and to work, and work hard, to give reality to our dreams. Those dreams are for India, but they are also for the world, for all the nations and peoples are too closely knit together today for anyone of them to imagine that it can live apart. Peace has been said to be indivisible; so that is freedom, so is prosperity now, and so also is disaster. In this One World that can no longer be split into isolated fragments.

To the people of India, whose representatives we are, we make an appeal to join us with faith and confidence in this great adventure. This is no time for petty and destructive criticism, no time for ill will or blaming others. We have to build the noble mansion of free India where all her children may dwell.

I beg to move, Sir,

"That it be resolved that:

(1) After the last stroke of midnight, all members of the Constituent Assembly present on this occasion, do take the following pledge:

'At this solemn moment when the people of India, through suffering and sacrifice, have secured freedom, I, ..., a member of the Constituent Assembly of India, do dedicate myself in all humility to the service of India and her people to the end that this ancient land attain her rightful place in the world and make her full and willing contribution to the promotion of world peace and the welfare of mankind';

(2) Members who are not present on this occasion do take the pledge (with such verbal changes as the President may prescribe) at the time they next attend a session of the Assembly."

FIRST SERVANT OF THE INDIAN PEOPLE*

Fellow countrymen, it has been my privilege to serve India and the cause of India's freedom for many years. Today I address you for the first time officially as the First Servant of the Indian people, pledged to their service and their betterment. I am here because you willed it so and I remain here so long as you choose to honour me with your confidence.

We are a free and sovereign people today and we have rid ourselves of the burden of the past. We look at the world with clear and friendly eyes and at the future with faith and confidence.

The burden of foreign domination is done away with, but freedom brings its own responsibilities and burdens, and they can only be shouldered in the spirit of a free people, self-disciplined, and determined to preserve and enlarge that freedom.

We have achieved much; we have to achieve much more. Let us then address ourselves to our new tasks with the determination and adherence to high principles which our great leader has taught us. Gandhiji is fortunately with us to guide and inspire and ever to point out to us the path of high endeavour. He taught us long ago that ideals and objectives can never be divorced from the methods adopted to realize them; that worthy ends can only be achieved through worthy means. If we aim at the big things of life, if we dream of India as a great nation giving her age-old message of peace and freedom to others, then we have to be big ourselves and be worthy children of Mother India. The eyes of the world are upon us watching this birth of freedom in the East and wondering what it means.

Our first and immediate objective must be to put an end to all internal strife and violence, which disfigure and degrade us and injure the cause of freedom. They come in the way of consideration of the great economic problems of the masses of the people which so urgently demand attention.

Our long subjection and the World War and its aftermath have made us inherit an accumulation of vital problems, and today our people lack food and clothing and other necessaries, and we are caught in a spiral of inflation and rising prices. We cannot solve these problems suddenly, but we cannot also delay their solution. So we

* Broadcast from New Delhi on August 15, 1947.

must plan wisely so that the burdens on the masses may grow less and their standards of living go up. We wish ill to none, but it must be clearly understood that the interests of our long-suffering masses must come first and every entrenched interest that comes in their way must yield to them. We have to change rapidly our antiquated land tenure system, and we have also to promote industrialization on a large and balanced scale, so as to add to the wealth of the country, and thus to the national dividend which can be equitably distributed.

Production today is the first priority, and every attempt to hamper or lessen production is injuring the nation, and more especially harmful to our labouring masses. But production by itself is not enough, for this may lead to an even greater concentration of wealth in a few hands, which comes in the way of progress and which, in the context for today, produces instability and conflict. Therefore, fair and equitable distribution is essential for any solution of the problem.

The Government of India have in hand at present several vast schemes for developing river valleys by controlling the flow of rivers, building dams and reservoirs and irrigation works and developing hydro-electric power. These will lead to all-round development. These schemes are thus basic to all planning and we intend to complete them as rapidly as possible so that the masses may profit.

All this requires peaceful conditions and the cooperation of all concerned, and hard and continuous work. Let us then address ourselves to these great and worthy tasks and forget our mutual wrangling and conflicts. There is a time for quarrelling and there is a time for co-operative endeavour. There is a time for work and there is a time for play. Today, there is no time for quarrelling or overmuch play, unless we prove false to our country and our people. Today, we must co-operate with one another and work together, and work with right goodwill.

I should like to address a few words to our services, civil and military. The old distinctions and differences are gone and today we are all free sons and daughters of India, proud of our country's freedom and joining together in our service of her. Our common allegiance is to India. In the difficult days ahead our services and our experts have a vital role to play and we invite them to do so as comrades in the service of India. JAI HIND.

TWO YEARS OF INDEPENDENCE*

Since I first unfurled the National Flag on the Red Fort, two years have been added to India's long history which began thousands of years ago. During these two years, we have seen achievements and failures, we have experienced joy and sorrow. The good work we have done will remain even though we pass away. So will India, though generations come and go.

Great questions face us and our task will not be over till we have answered them. Our objective is to make it possible for the millions of Indians to lead contented and purposeful lives. We cannot do that till we have solved, to a large extent, the problems that face us.

On a day like this we should try to detach ourselves from the problems of the moment and see from a distance, as it were, what is happening in our country and in the world. It is right that we forget our little troubles for a while and think of the major currents that are flowing in our country.

Thirty years ago there appeared on the Indian scene a mighty man of destiny who lighted our path. That light illuminated our minds and hearts and large numbers of our people, forgetting their own troubles and domestic difficulties, their property and family, responded to his call. It was not for personal gain of any kind. Among these there existed a friendly competition as to who could serve the motherland better and more effectively. Our consuming obsession was the liberation of our country.

The star of a free India beckoned us forward. We dreamed of freedom from poverty and distress. We gained our political freedom at last but the other freedom still remains for us to achieve. Before we could do much to achieve it, new problems came in our way. Sixty lakhs of people migrated to India as refugees. We faced this problem as we had faced others. I suppose we made some mistakes but no one reviewing these two years will fail to appreciate our forward march in the face of all kinds of difficulties.

Unarmed and peaceful, we faced a proud empire, not looking for aid to any other country and relying only on ourselves. We had faith in our leader, our country and in ourselves. This gave us the strength

* Translated from a speech in Hindi delivered at the Red Fort, Delhi on 15th August, 1959

that sustained us during our struggle for Independence. If we had faith and self-confidence when seemingly we were powerless, then surely we are much better off today when we are a free people with the strength of a great country behind us. Why then should our faith and our confidence in ourselves weaken us? It is true that we have tremendous economic and other difficulties to face; it is also true that while we have rehabilitated lakhs of refugees, large numbers still remain to be helped and rehabilitated. But we have faced even bigger problems in the past. Why should we not face these in the same way also? We must not let our minds get entangled in petty questions and difficulties and forget the main issues.

We belong to a great country, a country that is not only great physically but in things far more important. If we are to be worthy of our country, we must have big minds and big hearts, for small men cannot face big issues or accomplish big tasks. Let each one of us do his duty to his country and to his people than to dwell too much on the duty of others. Some people get into the habit of criticizing others without doing anything themselves. Nothing good can come out of that type of criticism. So, wherever you may be, whether you are in the Army or the Air Force or the Navy or in the civil services, each one of you must do your duty efficiently and in a spirit of service to the nation. If the vast number of our countrymen apply themselves to their tasks in their innumerable capacities and cooperate with others, forgetting the petty things that divide them, we shall marvel at the speed with which India will progress.

I want you to think for a moment of the days when we fought the battle for India's freedom without arms and without much by way of resources. We had a great leader who inspired us. We had other leaders, too, but it was the masses of this country who bore the brunt of the struggle. They had faith in their country and their leaders and they relied upon themselves. Today, we have more strength than we ever had. It is, therefore, surprising that some people should feel dejected, have no confidence in themselves and complain all the time.

Let us get back the purposefulness, the enthusiasm, the self-confidence and the faith which moved us at the time of our struggle for freedom. Let us put aside our petty quarrels and factions and think only of the great objective before us.

In our foreign policy, we have proclaimed that we shall join no power bloc and endeavour to cooperate and be friendly with all countries. Our position in the world ultimately depends on the unity and strength of the country, on how far we proceed in the solution of our economic and other problems and on how much we can raise the depressed masses of India. We may not be able to complete that task, for it is colossal. Even so, if we make some headway, it will be easier for others to complete the task.

A nation's work never ends. Men may come and go, generations may pass but the life of a nation goes on. We must remember the basic fact that we can achieve little unless there is peace in the country, no matter what policy we pursue. There are some misguided people who indulge in violence and try to create disorder. I wonder how anybody with the least intelligence can think in terms of such anti-national activities. Bomb throwing, for instance, can do the country no good. On the contrary, it further aggravates our economic situation, which is a source of great anxiety to us. Therefore, it is the duty of everyone, no matter what his politics, to help in the maintenance of peace in the country.

The people have every right to change laws and even to change governments and they can exercise that right in a peaceful and democratic manner. But those who choose the path of violence have no faith in democracy. If their way were to prevail, there would be complete chaos in the country and the condition of the people would deteriorate even more. All progress would cease and the next few generations would have to carry a heavy burden.

I am still more distressed by those who, while condemning violence, join hands with those who indulge in violence. They think only in terms of winning an election and forget that the cause of the country and of the people is bigger than any party. If we forget India and her people while pursuing our smaller objectives, then we are indeed guilty of betraying our country. I wish to emphasize that all of us must understand that our most important objective is the safety and security of India and the prosperity and advancement of her people. That can only be achieved effectively if we stop quarrelling amongst ourselves and try to solve the great problems that confront us by democratic and peaceful methods.

We must look at our problems in a proper perspective. If we are preoccupied with petty problems, we shall fail to solve the larger and more important ones.

We must learn to depend on ourselves and not look to others for help every time we are in trouble. Certainly we want to make friends with the rest of the world. We also seek the goodwill and cooperation of all those who reside in this country, whatever their race or nationality. We welcome help and cooperation from every quarter but we must depend primarily on our own resources. We should not forget that those who lean too much on others tend to become weak and helpless themselves. A country's freedom can be preserved only by her own strength and self-reliance.

We are not hostile to any country and we do not want to meddle in other people's affairs. Every nation should be free to choose the path it considers best. We do not wish to interfere with the freedom of other nations and we expect them to feel the same about our freedom. That is why we have decided not to join any of the power blocs in the world. We will remain aloof and try to be friendly to all. We intend to progress according to our own ideas. We have decided to follow this policy, not only because it is essentially a sound one from our country's point of view but also because it seems to be the only way to serve the cause of world peace. Another world war will spell ruin and we shall not escape the general disaster. We are determined to make every possible effort in the cause of peace. That explains our present foreign policy.

Perhaps you know that I am shortly going to visit a country which is great and powerful. I propose to carry with me a message of friendship and assurances of cooperation from our people. Keeping our own freedom intact, we wish to befriend other nations. Our friendship with one country should not be interpreted as hostility to another.

Asia is passing through a great revolutionary phase and naturally India has also been affected. In other parts of Asia there is struggle and ferment. This morning's newspapers contained the news of trouble and upheaval in a small but important country of West Asia. We do not know all the facts and in any event I do not wish to express an opinion. All I want to say is that the prevalence of violence and violent methods weaken a country and undermine her progress.

In East Asia, a great and ancient country is experiencing revolutionary changes of tremendous significance. Whatever our individual reactions to these may be, our policy, namely, that we do not wish to interfere in anyway with the internal affairs of other countries, is clear. Each country should have the freedom to go the way it chooses. It is for its people to decide their future. Any attempt at outside interference or compulsion must necessarily lead to evil results. No country can impose freedom on any other. The world has a great deal of variety and it should be no one's business to suppress this variety or to impose ways of thinking and action on others. We should, therefore, survey world events in a spirit of understanding and friendship to all.

Our Constituent Assembly is busy framing a new constitution for India and soon we shall adopt a republican form of government. However, laws and constitutions do not by themselves make a country great. It is the enthusiasm, energy and constant effort of a people that make it a great nation. Men of Law lay down constitutions but history is really made by great minds, large hearts and stout arms; by the sweat, tears and toil of a people.

Let us, therefore, learn to study our country's problems in the larger perspective of the world and let us not permit the minor questions of the day to overwhelm us. I have faith in India and her great destiny. A country must have military strength but armed power does not by itself constitute a country's real strength. Her real strength lies in the capacity of her people for disciplined work. Only hard work can produce wealth for us and rid us of our poverty. Each one of us, man or woman, young or old, must therefore toil and work. Rest is not for us. We did not win our freedom so that we might rest afterwards but in order to work harder to hold and strengthen that freedom. There is a great difference between the voluntary labour of a free man for an objective of his choice and the drudgery of a slave. Our labour as free men and women will lay the foundations for a great future and our labour of love for the cause of India and her people will endure; so will the fact that we are building, brick by brick, the great mansion of free India. There is joy in such work and even when we have departed that work will be there for future generations to see.

One of our most important problems today is that of growing more food. We must avoid wasting food at all costs. We must conserve our present resources with great care. We have to tighten our belts. If the co-operation of the people is forthcoming, we shall solve not only this problem but many others. Our petty squabbles and party differences can wait. What is vital and important for us is to keep before us the picture of a great India. India is enduring and will continue to be there long after we are gone.

37

Building a Strong India

Sardar Vallabhbhai Patel

YOU WANT me to talk to you in English. I shall obey your command; but take it from me that it will not be long before you yourselves will have to speak in our national language. If you do not do that, you will drag the country backward. We have to exert our maximum effort to go forward. Unless you do that, I am afraid, you will suffer.

After a prolonged struggle the country has secured the freedom, but it is not the freedom of the kind that we wanted. It is not the freedom of the kind that the deliverer of the country expected, and to our shame we have to confess that by our folly we have lost him. Now after his going we must do penance and try our best to deserve the freedom that he obtained for us.

Free India is only a child of one and a half year. It has yet to learn to walk; it has to grow, to be strong, and its future depends upon how we build today. Therefore, we have to nurse it carefully; we have to feed, clothe and strengthen it properly. It is our great good fortune that we have here a rare opportunity to build our own country in our own fashion. History will record what we are doing today.

The first requisite for building a strong, free India is unity and peace. If there is no unity in the country, it is bound to go down.

Speech at Madras on February 23, 1949.

Therefore we must first of all adjust our differences and behave in such a manner that there is complete harmony and peace in the country. You cannot expect the Government continuously to maintain peace by force. It would be an evil day when in this country the Government has to use repressive measures permanently. Today we are passing through a period of crisis and our young men have, in their impatience, not realised that the freedom which has been obtained with great difficulty is likely to be lost or likely to give no benefit, no advantage, if we do not appreciate that our present duty is to unite and consolidate our freedom.

We lost our leader because we forgot the very first lesson. If we do not realise even after his going that in unity lies our strength, then greater misfortune will befall us.

For unity, we must forget differences of caste and creed and remember that we are all Indians, and all equal. There can be no distinction between man and man in a free country. All must have equal opportunities, equal rights and equal responsibilities. This is difficult to achieve in practice, but we must continuously strive towards that end.

There is one other thing that we have to do to maintain peace and order in this country. For a few years at least, till we are able to stand on our own legs, we must forget that we can every now and then threaten the Government. We cannot function if the Government is to be challenged day after day by groups of people who want to have their own way. What they want may be, according to their own honest thinking, very good; but Gandhiji has put before us the ideal of obtaining what we want by peaceful methods and through truth and non-violence. If people begin to threaten and challenge Government's authority and try to overthrow it to gain their objectives by force, the latter would not be able to do anything constructive. Forces are existing in this country which would create chaos and disorder, which would weaken the country instead of strengthening it.

We in the Government have been dealing with the R.S.S. movement. They want that the Hindu Rajya or Hindu culture should be imposed by force. No Government can tolerate this. There are almost as many Muslims in this country as in the part that has been partitioned away. We are not going to drive them away. It would be an evil day if we started that game, in spite of partition and whatever happens. We must understand that they are going to stay here and it is our obligation and our responsibility to make them feel that this is their country. It is, of course, their responsibility, on the other hand, to discharge their duties as citizens of this country.

We must all understand that the partition is behind us. It has to come to stay. I honestly believe that it is good for both the new nations. In two hundred years of a perpetual source of trouble and quarrels, in two hundred years of slavery, the administration created a situation in which we began to drift away from each other. It is good that we have agreed to the partition in spite of all its evils; I have never repented my agreeing to the partition. From the experience of one year of joint administration when we had not agreed to the partition, I know we would have erred grievously and repented if we had not agreed. It would have resulted in a partition not into two countries but into several bits. Therefore, whatever some people may say, I am convinced and I remain convinced that our having agreed to the partition has been for the good of the country.

After the partition, we had a huge problem; those who partitioned the country with our concurrence had mental reservations; they thought that the partition into two is not the last word and they started their game immediately after the partition. They went to Junagadh located in the midst of the Kathiawar states, where nearly half the number of princely states are located. They took Junagadh and secured its accession to Pakistan. It was the first danger sign, the signal for dividing India again. Fortunately for us, we woke up in time and those who tried that game saw that we are not sleeping. Simultaneously, there was trouble in Kashmir. Although there were many difficulties, the Government of India, despite all the impediments, got the situation under control rapidly. I should say we enhanced our reputation by sending there our army, which, in spite of its complete Indianisation, has proved its mettle and proved its worth. It is a great thing that immediately after the partition of the army and the partition of the country, our army, manned absolutely by our own people, showed by their strategy, their valour and their organising ability that it can stand comparison with any army in the world. It is a great gain.

Then our neighbour gave us long sleepless nights. Often, people were angry with us and thought we were neglecting the South. They hardly knew our difficulties and our plans. These plans cannot be revealed. What would happen if Hyderabad was invaded from the outside or if Hyderabad attacked us. We had to make preparations all over India. You know now by the results that we have kept our promise to perform the operation in such a manner that there is the least possible bloodshed. This is what we have to show for the first year of our freedom.

People are impatient; they want more wages for labour. Do they think we want to starve labour? Are we foreigners? Some people say we are capitalist agents. One thing I learnt from Mahatma Gandhi is that a public man should not have any property and I can challenge any Socialist or any Communist to play this game with me. But my quarrel is with those who, contrary to the second part of Mahatmaji's advice to us, want to use violence. There should be no terrorism amongst ourselves. So long as people were playing that game when we were under a foreign power, we made allowance for it; we are paying for it also, because an evil once tolerated grows. That is what we see in Hyderabad.

Why are these Communists creating trouble there? How did they grow? It was because the Hyderabad government was foolish enough to allow them to grow for its own ends and we had no control over them then to be able to suppress them. And what is it that we want there now? In three or four months' time, 200 or more young Congressmen, their own brothers, have been murdered. Is it a sign of the freedom that in the first year of the freedom you got 200 Congressmen killed in cold blood in a small area? Once these terrorists are driven out from that area, where will they go? Inside your border. They will harass you, they will play the same game with you. To the Communists, my appeal may be in vain, because they do not listen. I told them immediately after my release from the jail last time that I was prepared to take all the Communists into the Congress, to forget the past and keep the doors open provided they give up violence and cease to draw their inspiration from the foreign countries. Even now our offer is open, but if terrorism is the only method they want to employ, because they cannot defeat us at the polls and separate us from the masses of India, then it is our misfortune that we have to put our own dear young men and women into prison or to drive them underground.

That is one section of the people with whom we have to deal; the other is the R.S.S. I have made them an open offer: 'Change your plans, give up secrecy, eschew communal conflict, respect the Constitution of India, show your loyalty to the Flag and make us believe that we can trust your words. To say one thing and to do another is a game which will not do. In one year of the freedom we have experienced many things and learnt many lessons. Whether they are friends or foes, whether they are our own dear young children, we are not going to allow them to play with fire, so that the house is not set on fire. It would be criminal to allow young men to indulge in acts of violence and destruction, to let the lessons that our neighbouring countries have learnt be wasted on us.

Thus I have spoken to the R.S.S. and to the Communists. Then you have our Sikh friends. Some of them have also begun to threaten us and throw challenges. They are the only community in India which is allowed, with the unanimous voice of the Constituent Assembly, to keep arms. No other community is allowed to keep a sword or a *kirpan*. Why did we do this? Not in order that they might threaten the Government with the use of force. Government is prepared to hand over power to anybody who can take the people with him. But if anybody is going to play false and threaten the popular Government, the latter will not fail the people.

These are some of the many forces we are handling simultaneously in the first or second year of our freedom. We know that we have your affection, your love, your confidence, but that is not enough. You have seen our friends in the Railways threaten us. They say there is going to be a strike in the Railways if we do not meet their demands. We are willing to do so if we can. We would be most anxious to do so. But I must point out to those who are in charge of the Railway union that there are millions in this country who do not get as much as the Railwaymen get; let them not create the forces which they will not be able to control; let the Railwaymen understand that it is also their duty to share the misfortunes of the people in a period of trouble. Let us tide over the difficulty first. After all, the Railway is a nationalised concern; it is not a private company. Imagine the consequences, in this period of trouble, if Railwaymen do not play their part. If there is a strike on the Railways and we have to move the army from one place to another with the Railway communications cut off, one place to another swiftly, as we are faced with the threatened famine. If during such a period the South Indian Railway, which has threatened to strike, goes on strike, who will starve, and what would be the consequences? When the Railway Federation suspended its strike threat and kept it in abeyance, the other group called them capitalist agents. Now these other people have called for a strike; they know that they are in a minority and they will not succeed in making the Railwaymen go on strike. So their only weapon is terrorism, sabotage, dislocation and disorder.

The Provincial Government naturally have to tackle these people and immediately the Federation comes in with a statement that it is a wrong policy. I would like to know what is the right policy. When a house is on fire, is it the right policy to throw petrol or kerosene on it, or water?

We are living in very difficult times; yet the heart of the country is sound. The whole country knows that we are carrying an unbearable burden. Yet if anyone wants to see what the country thinks, let him come to the polls; I am prepared to accept the challenge. I am prepared to vacate as many seats as you like and have a trial of strength. And if you are able to take the country with you, we shall bless you, because the country is not going to follow any path which is foreign to the Indian culture and civilisation and the path that Mahatma Gandhi has shown. But I want to ask you why a few people roundabout the border of Hyderabad are terrorising the people in Krishna district? It is the fault of Congressmen. Are they united? Why are they quarrelling? Why do they not understand their responsibility? We made all kinds of sacrifices all our lives. Why did we make these sacrifices? Let not South India lose its good name and reputation. I appeal to you to realise what is happening. Did you ever imagine that Gandhiji would hear of a Congressman murdering a Congressman, or a Congressman instigating or helping a Communist to murder another Congressman? If the South Indian Railway is threatened, or if those Railwaymen who work in South India are asked to go on strike, have you no responsibility? Everyone in India has to realise that, as a free citizen of India, he must shoulder graver and greater responsibility if India is to take its proper place amongst the nations of the world.

Yesterday, I was presented an address by the Chambers of Commerce. It was in fact a catalogue of grievances. I had to tell them the unpleasant truth that unless everybody in this country, i.e business-men, labourers, industrialists, students and Government, all combine and cooperate, we are not going to make progress . We have not yet put democracy on a sound basis. In a democracy, of course, it is the will of the people that prevails, but the people must have experience to make their own free will felt and must have the responsibility to see that everyone is going to fulfil his obligations.

In this country, the greatest need of the hour is food. We import millions of tons of food into our country. We have not got the ships to bring the food that we want. So we pay crores of rupees as freight charges simply to bring the food here. We have not enough boats even to catch fish. We have no mercantile marine. We have nothing left in this country; for the last 200 years it has been bled white; during the war years in particular, every ounce of blood has been taken out. Our Railway system has been completely disorganised. The Transport Member makes tremendous efforts to set it right. But the Railways are like a decrepit old widow. The Railway sleepers and rails were taken out and sent to various theatres of war. We cannot replace wagons which have been overused for so many years. We cannot get locomotives. We cannot make them here; we have yet to establish factories for meeting the requirements of our country.

We must have a good mercantile marine; so we are building a fine port at Vizagapatnam. But it is only a beginning. A small country like Portugal has got pockets on our soil; we also have French colonies. Our friends in these areas who are fighting for the freedom along with us ask us to first settle this question; others talk of the wages for labour; and still others want us to deal with the businessmen first and to give them their due. The businessmen are frightened of the talk of nationalisation. They say: "Unless you give us condition in which industry can thrive, we cannot invest money or we cannot get money." So production has been at a standstill. We cannot produce more wealth in this country.' The Communists and the Socialists say: "let us first divide whatever is left and be all poor." But if you do not produce anything, then neither you nor any other section of the people will have anything. Therefore, so far as food is concerned, I have a grievance against the Congressmen and against those people who are in the Congress and today are preaching to peasants not to help this Government in procurement and to ask for more money. They are not better than the other people who say: "Do not work, stop work, go slow, ask for more wages." Because if there is no procurement, then the only course open to us is to import more and more, and importing more is nothing but economic ruin of this country.

If we in this country realise our responsibility, there will be no dearth of food. Of course, there is scarcity to a certain extent; the shortage of food according to our statistics is 7 per cent; in a vast country like this, if we act up to our responsibilities, this is negligible. Many people waste their food and cook more than they should. Those people should put a stop to this wastage. Then we should produce more food. Every inch of land that is available should be used for growing vegetables, fruit and other food. Wherever there is waste land which can be reclaimed, it would be the duty of the Government, local bodies, zamindars, and every citizen of India to use all his resources in the immediate task of growing more food on it. Thirdly, whatever surplus you have got, give it to the Government. When your neighbours are starving, do not be selfish. That is not the way which Gandhiji showed us. That is not our culture. Let not our neighbour starve; we must share his misery. Educate the peasants; tell them it is a religious duty to give all of their surplus for Government procurement, so that the Government can decrease the imports.

There are many Congressmen who are indifferent to this matter. They think that the elections are coming and they will be unpopular if they ask for procurement. A greater crime is committed by those who teach the peasants to ask for higher prices and not to give crops for procurement. That is a crime against humanity. A real Congressman would say: "My friends, our neighbours are dying; our country is being ruined; let us share the suffering of our brothers." I am saying harsh things to the Congressmen because they have a greater responsibility, greater influence and a greater hold on the people.

Let us all put our heads as well as our hands together, tighten up our belts and be prepared to share the sufferings for a while. It is only for a while, because I assure you that the economy of the country is sound; the heart of the country is sound; there is immense wealth in the country. The country is full of mineral resources and wealth. We have simply to use our brains and our resources to take them out and use them. But it will take time; it is not an easy thing. We shall require experts, machinery and capital goods. If we tide over this short period, India will be flowing with milk and honey.

38

Make India Strong and Great

Indira Gandhi

A BIRTH ANNIVERSARY, be it of an individual or of a country, is an auspicious occasion and a day of rejoicing. All of us celebrate it, be it here or in our homes. In earlier years, the radio carried the voice from here to the other parts of the country. Last year, however, television began carrying the images from here to a few big cities. But today television pictures of this ceremony will reach many small towns also, marking the beginning of the programme to reach television to 70 per cent area of the country. This is how all progress takes place — gradually.

It is a day when we recall our struggle for Independence. We remember Mahatma Gandhi, his other colleagues and disciples and many others about whom you must have read. But there were hundreds and thousands of other brave freedom fighters who also sacrificed everything. A few thousand of them fortunately are still with us. We remember them all and when we remember them, we also ponder as to what lesson we should learn from their sacrifices.

There are some who say that whichever Prime Minister spoke from the Red Fort, repeated the same thing every year. What a strange thing to say! The ideals that we set for ourselves, the things

---

Free rendering of an address in Hindi delivered at the Red Fort, Delhi, August 15, 1983.

that build up character and raise the morale of the people, concern for the security, progress and development of the country -- are not all these duties incumbent on us today? Can our basic thinking ever get outdated? Should we not remember these duties each year, indeed each day? And repeat them to ourselves, in our hearts and minds? This is true not only of our country; it is true of all countries. This is not the occasion to talk at great length about our achievements, of the big things that have been done for raising the standard of living of the common people. But the record is there for everyone to see. Our own countrymen, as also people of other countries, know about it and you must have read how the leaders of big countries have been talking about it. It does not mean, however, that our task has been completed. It also does not mean that we have turned all our aspirations into reality. But it does not mean that we have progressed along the path shown to us by our great leaders and that we continue to advance despite all difficulties and dangers and despite the fact that at times we have also faltered. Perhaps many of the difficulties we face today are due to this fact.

Once enslaved, poor, oppressed and timid, this country is today able to hold its head high. You look at the achievements. Some of them are really big. We have increased power generation. Earlier, power was available in a mere 3,000 cities and towns, and hardly any villages. Today, three lakh villages have been electrified and, of course, power is available in all towns. This is only a small example of what has indeed happened. I have already mentioned about television. You also know how we have sent our own satellites into space and how we can utilize them for the benefit of the farmers and others. At Kalpakkam, near Madras, our engineers, with wholly indigenous know-how, have set up an atomic power plant. In another two months we plan to send another satellite into space. All these are big steps which have relevance to our life, to the lives of the working class and students and also the everyday lives of housewives. Since we met here last, the Asian Games were organized in this city. It was a show of young people. That was followed by the Non-aligned Summit, which was an indication of India's capabilities, and the whole world had occasion to witness it.

I also take this opportunity to congratulate our young sportsmen who have kept the country's head high. I specially want to congratulate our cricket team for winning the World Cup recently. Those young men remind us of the brave youth whose courage shone through during our freedom struggle.

But do not imagine that other young men, our children, our farmers and our workers, don't deserve congratulations. All of them sweat hard in their given field of activity and step by step they are carrying India forward. I congratulate them all. We do not know their names, we have not seen them, nor can we identify them. Yet, they are the foundation of India -- the poor, those belonging to the Scheduled Castes, the tribals and the backward communities. I myself do not believe in caste and I would wish that it is rooted out from our country. We should all consider ourselves one. We are equal citizens of a great country.

Today, when we look at our achievements, we should also cast a glance at our shortcomings. What are the things that have held us back and what are the stumbling blocks which do not let us progress fast enough? If we were to learn a lesson from the freedom struggle, we would find that only unity and discipline lead to success. We find today that intentionally or unintentionally some people and some sections of the community hurt society in the name of that community, hurt religion in the name of their religion, and hurt the country in the name of their region. These are our weaknesses. These are the elements that have held India back, eroded morale and sapped self-confidence.

There are agitations in many parts of the country and people are making demands. This is but natural in a democracy. We are always prepared to talk to people and also meet their demands to the extent possible. But we also have to be careful all the time that while meeting the demands of one group, we do not hurt the interests of others or weaken them. Therefore, while considering these demands we have to discuss with all concerned and take into consideration their interests. We cannot satisfy all, but the least we can attempt is to see that there is minimum dissatisfaction. Whether the leaders of agitations want it or not, experience shows that violence creeps in. We cannot always find out who indulges in violence. When we find out, we do punish such people. Sometimes the agitators themselves do not know who is indulging in violence, but it harms the country all the same and the developmental process stops. Thus, those who launch agitations complaining of neglect contribute to the slowing down of development.

Let us look at some of the problems that dog us. There is the problem of Assam, about which there has been some strange propaganda. There are certain aspects of the problem which have an element of truth. It is true that foreigners have come and our efforts is to stop their infiltration, identify those who have entered illegally and make some other arrangements for them. This is not something new. When I discussed it the first time, I made some suggestions to the leaders of the Assam agitation. They said, "Either you accede to all our demands or we will not let you go forward with whatever you want to do". The result was that the process of identification, which could have gone ahead in the last few years, was held up. Now they want that process to be started and this work has begun just as we had earlier offered.

There is another strange accusation. Many people lost their lives in the attacks that took place there. Many of them were our Muslim brothers and sisters. Their villages were burnt. But also those of Hindus, tribals, Scheduled Castes, labourers from Bihar and Uttar Pradesh. I have expressed sympathy towards all the victims and condemned those who took the law into their own hands. Yet, the propaganda is as though we had a hand in the killings. If you go and talk to the affected people, they will say clearly who was really engaged in rescuing and protecting them and making their lives secure. It is true that at places the security was lax which resulted in killings. To that extent it is our responsibility but the propaganda suggests as though we instigated the killings. Who are the people indulging in this propaganda? They are the very persons who delivered inflammatory speeches, instigated people and created an atmosphere of threat and violence.

There is also the problem of Punjab. I do not want to go into the details; they have been repeatedly mentioned. Our effort in this country has always been to see that every community and every region receives justice and a fair share of the total wealth and resources of the country. Whatever demands I could meet from my side were accepted by me at the very beginning, but will it be just on my part to take decisions which may concern other regions and on which there may be no agreement? I may recall that it is being alleged that I am deliberately stalling a decision. Can the Central Government gain if any region or any community were to remain weak? Won't it rather weaken the Central Government itself because our strength depends on the strength of our regions? What is the Centre? Is it only the city of Delhi or the Secretariat or the Prime Minister's Office? The Centre is that which holds everyone together and is responsible for the security of the country. It is also responsible for ensuring justice to all. Therefore, no one who is at a comparative advantage -- whether an individual or a State — should claim more than due. All the same, the real power belongs to our States. Whenever there are constraints on resources, it puts strain on us as well. There are cuts imposed on the Central Ministries and also on the States. We are not happy about it, but we are helpless. If there are rains, it immediately changes our prospects; but in the event of drought or floods we all suffer. If the agitations, on which so much money is spent, were not there, we would make headway faster.

I was speaking about Punjab. The problem came up before me about two years back. My Government came into power in 1980. I should like to remind you that the people who are today agitating and making demands were in power in Punjab for three years earlier. During those three years they had two Ministers of their own in the Central Government and their allies were in power in the neighbouring States. Thus, during those three years they had all the opportunities to resolve their problems and meet their own demands. However, they did not raise their voice then. I should like to ask them and also pose this question to you, as to why they did not resolve these problems? Aren't they guilty of failure to act when they had the opportunities? Why did they not act? Probably because even at that time they could not have got whatever they wanted. So, when we came to power the entire responsibility was thrust on us. We are ready to resolve the problem provided the agitators are willing to sit down and reach an agreement with those others also who are concerned with this problem.

There are many other voices being raised which make us feel that the strength and unity of the country may be threatened. Fortunately, the sense of unity in the country is very strong. In connection with Assam, another false propaganda is being carried out throughout India. When I spoke about the minorities, I used to be accused of being more concerned about Muslims, Sikhs, Christians and other minorities. It was alleged that I was not bothered about the Hindu majority. May I remind you that in our country one community may be a minority in one part and in a majority in another? Similarly, people belonging to one religion may be in a minority at one place and in a majority at another. The new line taken by the detractors is that I am not at all worried about the minorities and that I go along with what the majority wants.

All political parties want votes at the time of elections. But today, standing here on the ramparts of the Red Fort and recalling our freedom struggle, let us also remember the era in which we were born, the life we spent, the sacrifices we made and the services we rendered. While it is natural to rejoice in victory and be saddened by defeat, our tradition teaches us that there is something above victory and defeat, and that is our duty. Our duty is to take care of our country. Even though we may not be able to complete the task, we should proceed along the path of progress to the extent we are capable.

Many people laid down their lives during the freedom struggle. Many did not live to see Independence. When we were young we did not imagine that we would be able to attain freedom within our lifetime. Yet that thought did not let us falter in our step nor did it weaken our resolve. We knew that we would take the country up to the point we were capable of and that later others would carry the flag. Today we are engaged in the task of development in the same spirit and the same spirit moves us in making the country stronger.

The country faces many dangers. There are external dangers and our internal weaknesses. I do not want to scare you and I know that you are not the ones to be scared. It is our responsibility, however, to recognise the situation. Only when we recognise the crisis can we keep ourselves fully prepared to face it. Today imperialism is not of the kind it used to be. Today it does not intrude into a country with troops. It exerts a variety of pressures in a surreptitious manner, pressures which are economic, political and of other kinds, which are not less pernicious than armed intrusion and in fact more dangerous because the common people are not able to recognise them. We have seen what has happened in many countries. They are independent and yet there is a shadow over their independence. India does not want that. Our path is clear. We want to be self-reliant through democracy, socialism and non-alignment. Some say that we are tilting this way or that, but we take all our decisions keeping the interest of India in view as also the interest of world peace. We might be more friendly with some than others but we have not allowed friendship or disagreement to come in the way of our decisions. We take the right decision and it is that which accounts for whatever success we have had in all spheres. Everyone knows that we are a country with ideals. It does not mean that we are able to achieve all our ideals or that we do not have failings and do not commit mistakes.

Unfortunately, the problem of corruption comes up and we regret to say that corruption is there. But it will be wrong if we were to raise the issue of corruption to the level of a bogey and insist that it will grow stronger. We have to see how to eradicate this evil from our life. There is corruption in other countries, too, but we are not concerned with them. We are concerned with ourselves and we must fully strive to root out this problem from all spheres -- from politics, from among the officials, from traders and others. We must raise our sights above our own gains and ask ourselves whether we are prepared to weaken entire society for our own petty gain. We should ask ourselves whether we are prepared to bring in a situation wherein our future generations will be harmed. Every citizen has to give thought to it. Atrocities have been committed against women. This is not something new. The time has come when this cannot be tolerated any more. The time has come when entire society must see that no atrocity is tolerated either against women or against men. Our women, our young men, our farmers who are the country's backbone, our workers who are our limbs and all our people -- whatever region,language or religion they may belong to -- must be strengthened. All of them have the right to receive justice and they will be strong only when they do receive justice. This stupendous task cannot be carried out by the Government or the officials alone. It can be accomplished only when every citizen realizes that as a citizen of India it is equally his responsibility because that alone will ensure his future. And if the future were dim, it will not only hurt him but will also hurt the coming generations. This is the spirit that must be imbibed.

I said just now that the country faced dangers. There may be no direct threat to our borders at this time. But there is an atmosphere of war throughout the world. India has always been peaceful and that is why we have had a big role in initiating the Non-aligned Movement. We want friendship with our neighbours. There have been some recent developments and I should like to reiterate that we do not want to interfere in the affairs of any other country. Countries must resolve their internal problems themselves. But if there is a large-scale violence, killings and loot, we have to condemn it. And we have always done so. In our neighbouring country, Sri Lanka, with whom India has had close relations, things have happened which have also affected the Indian citizens there. It is natural for us to be concerned. We have no intention to interfere. We want to maintain our friendship and our relations. We do not want that anyone should suffer but because our people have been attacked, our own citizens and those who emigrated from here, we are particularly concerned and we express our sympathy with those who have been the victims of violence. We must deal with all these problems in the most responsible manner. One wrong step taken in excitement could lead to far-reaching harm, making it difficult to restore balance. By God's grace we have so far shown great forbearance in all these international problems.

We have always tried first to understand the problem and then take steps with great care and caution. In this way we have succeeded in our efforts. We should not do anything which may harm those whom we want to help. People of Indian origin are living in several countries and some of them have become citizens of the countries of their adoption but some have remained Indian citizens. We should keep the interests of all those people in mind. We do not want to interfere in anybody's internal affairs. When humanitarian aspect is involved, we must speak out.

As I have said earlier, I am not concerned with any one caste or religion. I am concerned for all, whether they are Hindus, Muslims, Sikhs or of other religions. I am concerned because they all belong to India, not because they belong to any particular religion. They are all human beings. Today's world is convulsed by an economic crisis. There are challenges everywhere. There is unemployment. Here, I want to say something about the unemployment in our own country. It is a serious problem and we have been paying attention to it. We have just evolved two schemes, one for the landless people who are the worst hit in our countryside and who bear the brunt of the problem of unemployment. We want that at least one member of each family should get employment. This programme is going to be launched shortly and a big sum has been provided for it. Initially, this programme was started in Maharashtra where it was a success. We are, therefore, now extending it to the entire country. But I would like to remind you that we cannot cover everyone all at once. We hope that initially we will be able to cover about 30 lakh persons and as we achieve success, others also will be covered by the programme.

Similarly, in the urban areas, the educated young men are under severe strain. It is our effort, therefore, to provide resources every year for 2.5 lakh educated unemployed young men to stand on their own legs. Thus, each year new programmes are introduced.

Many people have ridiculed our 20-Point Programme, but the fact remains that it has made an impact. There have been some shortcomings but generally it has benefited people and is continuing to benefit them. You can see its impact if you go to the villages. Those who ridiculed the programme perhaps don't remember what the countryside was like and what kind of poverty prevailed there. It is a matter of satisfaction that the old scenario has now faded out. We are progressing and we shall continue to progress.

We do not want to fight with anyone, but you know that we have been attacked in the past and it has been an experience which we cannot forget. We, therefore, have to keep ourselves in readiness. Here I want to say a word about the brave officers and jawans of our armed forces. They have defended our borders with great courage and bravery. With the same devotion, they are also helping our people during floods and other natural calamities in peace time. They deserve our congratulations.

We must forget high or low, we must forget where we live, what is our status and what are our views. But we must remember our motto is to make India strong and great and all our thoughts must be how to progress along that path. I greet you all once again, particularly our young men and women. In their eyes there is new hope, on their shoulders new responsibilities, and in their hearts new courage. We are all full of this new spirit, whatever be our age. In this I include myself. You and I are but servants of one nation. We must not think about our status; we must always think in terms of serving the weaker sections and those who, due to some reason, have remained backward. We must always think how to lift the downtrodden so that we may march forward together and make the country strong and great. We must strengthen the country not only from the economic or political point of view but also morally and intellectually. Let us today take a pledge that we will not do or say anything which may denigrate our country in any way. We must keep the common man's morale high, make him self-confident and self-reliant. If we take this pledge and act accordingly in the next year, then we can work wonders. Not once but many times we the people of India have shown that whenever we take a decision with firm determination, we can achieve success. Let us show this once again, my brothers and sisters.

39

Guarding the Flame of Freedom

Indira Gandhi

WE ASSEMBLE HERE on August 15, every year. It is not a mere ritual function. We assemble here in the memory of those of our brave countrymen who suffered during the long struggle for Independence and also sacrificed their lives. This movement had a long time-span and people today do not know about it as much as they should. The younger generation is hardly familiar with it. I cannot describe it all here. However, just to illustrate, how people belonging to different religions were associated with the struggle, I should like to mention of some of our leaders who participated in the freedom movement. Tilak, Dadabhai Naoroji, Dr.Ansari of Delhi, Tayabji Saheb were people of one generation. Then, Mahatma Gandhi returned to India and the course of the freedom movement took a new turn in which not only the intelligentsia and other distinguished people participated but also farmers, workers, the younger generation and people drawn from various walks of life became co-partners.

Why do we hoist the national flag on the Red Fort? This place had not been a symbol of Independence. In fact, it is a symbol of the olden days. Netaji Subhas Bose had declared that when we became Independent, we would hoist the national flag on the Red Fort. For this reason, the first Prime Minister of India, Pandit Jawaharlal

---

Free rendering of an address in Hindi delivered at the Red Fort, Delhi, August 15, 1984.

Nehru, hoisted the national flag here in August 1947, and since then, every Prime Minister is performing this duty. Prior to that, three of our brave countrymen were imprisoned in this Red Fort. They had not adopted our path. Although their path was different, they too were prepared to sacrifice everything for the cause of freedom and their love for the country. People of Delhi know Shri Shah Nawaz Khan. He was a Muslim. Then, there were Prem Sehgal and Dhillon. This selection was neither ours, nor of the alien rulers. Still, by coincidence, they belonged to three different religions. I am saying all this because I feel we should know how the country became Independent.

We got Independence because people of all religions, all provinces and all communities were united. There was only one objective -- freedom of the country. Freedom is our birthright. Today we have different issues before us. During those days, we had only one objective and we fought for it. Today, we have to preserve the Independence thus gained and the efforts for this cannot be less arduous. The obstacles, the barriers, the dangers and the threats we faced during those days are all present even today, though in different shapes.

Some people say that I talk of these external dangers in order to divert the people's attention from the domestic issues. There cannot be a greater misunderstanding than this, because we cannot maintain the solidarity of the nation and solve our problems without knowing fully the travails the country is confronted with and the difficulties that people of all walks of life are facing. We are glad that we are free, but our hearts today are not full of joy. We have sorrows and anxieties. We are sad because we have not learnt the lessons of our history. We are sad because such forces are again raising their heads which may endanger the unity of the country by spreading poison.

I would like to remind you that communal disturbances which take place in the name of religion and cost lives of numerous innocent people and lead to destruction of property, are not communal alone, though they appear to be so. Behind these are political and economic considerations and narrowness of mind.

Communal disturbances have occurred in Andhra Pradesh, Karnataka, Maharashtra and Uttar Pradesh in the recent past. Some have also taken place in other States. The sorrow is not only that of individuals, families or communities but of entire India. It is a black spot on the entire country and it is our duty to root out all such elements from our soil.

In our democratic system, there may be differences in many spheres but we rise above them. To achieve the objective of keeping the country united, we have to transcend political and party-based differences which create dissensions between one another. If we cannot remain united and the country does not remain strong, with whom shall we have differences? Against whom shall we fight? With whom shall we make friendship, if nobody exists? Brothers and sisters, if the country fails, nobody survives. When we were fighting for the freedom of our country, it did not mean only political freedom. It also meant social justice, equality and economic justice. Only one phase is over and another one is under way. We have to cover a long and difficult path. Whereas the enemies were visible during those days, now they are in disguise. Some of them are open enemies, but many become unintentional pawns of others.

Everyone of us has now Punjab in mind. I do not want to go into the story of Punjab here. I have spoken about it a number of times. However, since some sinister propaganda is being carried on, I would like to say a few words. At the moment, I would like to say that whatever movements are conducted in one or another State with any ostensible purpose, in course of time these pass into the hands of elements who do not subscribe to the objectives of the movement or have something else in their mind, giving a new turn to the entire movement. They bring violence, murder, intimidation and so on into the movements, and the organizers of the movement lose control over the situation. This is exactly what has happened in Punjab.

Propaganda is being carried on, specially in foreign newspapers and television, giving the impression as if we did not even discuss the demands that had been put forward. You all know how long-drawn-out the discussions were. Differences were narrowed down to only a few points. As taught by Gandhiji, Jawaharlal Nehru and Maulana Azad, it has been our policy, whether within the country or in the international field, to reach the maximum possible extent of understanding, thus maintaining friendship, and not giving any offence from our side.

Whosoever has any demand, be he pro or against me, I have always listened to it and have tried to meet it as far as possible. But I have my limitations. The resources are limited. Funds are limited. We cannot go beyond these limitations. Sometimes there are demands which please some sections of the people but annoy others and can lead to serious discontent in other States. Therefore, we have to consider all the relevant factors. I should like to request those who have some demands either in the name of a State or a religion or a language or some other issue, to look around to ensure that the fulfilment of their demand does not aggrieve others. They should think whether their demand would not impose an economic burden on the country which may weaken the country or crush it altogether under its load. Economic hardship will not spare them either. We have taken care of everyone in our plans and it is our effort to help all sections of the people and States, so that they may all progress and develop.

Nowadays, the relations between the Centre and the States are being discussed. I, too, have said that we can discuss them and I am confident that if the issue is approached sincerely, a compromise can be arrived at easily.

In 1960-61, the States were getting a sum of Rs.500 crore from the Centre. Now, they are getting Rs.12,000 crore. A stupendous increase, indeed. Still neither the States are happy nor the Central Ministries are contented. They all say that they are not getting enough. I agree that amount does not suffice for their needs but we must also not forget that even in rich countries, the needs of all cannot be met fully.

Demands will not only remain, but will in fact increase. What we have to see is that while meeting the demands of those people who are comparatively well-off, we do not ignore or cause harm to those people who are weak and underprivileged. They must not get poorer as a result of the fulfilment of the demands of the affluent. The country will become strong only if the poor people of the country also become strong. In their strength lies the welfare of the affluent as well.

I hope that demands will be put forth not to further self-interests but to secure the welfare of the country and for helping the relatively weaker sections as well as for the all-round progress of the country. This is why our emphasis has been on helping the weaker sections as far as possible. This is the objective of the 20-Point Programme through which 15 million families have been helped to raise their standard of living. Many countries do not have even a total population of 15 million. But in a country with a population of 700 million, the figure is not that impressive. There is no magic that can benefit all these 700 million people immediately.

The 20-Point Programme was initiated only recently. Employment has been arranged through it and successes have been achieved in providing employment to a good number of young men, rural as well as urban. Progress has also been made in providing loans as well as in other fields. I know there are shortcomings. I know that some people have made mistakes. Some people have complained to me in this regard.

Those who do not reside in Delhi, or are listening to me for the first time, may be surprised to know that whenever I am in Delhi, barring the holidays, I meet people in my house every morning, ranging from a few to a few thousand. These people come from all walks of life, all religions and all parts of the country. Some people say they come just to see me, some others narrate their woes, a few others lodge complaints and some other praise the progress made. There are people who think that I waste my time by meeting them. Many leaders of other countries do not do so. But I feel that this helps me in getting an idea of the true picture of the country and the feelings of the people. It is certainly not a waste of time.

The area under irrigation has increased considerably. Some of our farmer friends have launched agitations. But whatever we could achieve for the farmers during the last four years remains unparalleled. Of course, the farmers were always given due consideration during the freedom movement as also afterwards. Actually, they were at the root of our movement. They are our food-givers. I know that the prices of some of the commodities that they consume have gone up. We are trying to help them, have actually done so. Chemical fertilizers are being supplied to them at rates lower than the actuals by providing subsidies to the extent of Rs.800 crore. This is not an easy task for a poor country. The prices of their products have also comparatively increased. It is, however, true that the commodities that they need have become dearer in our country as well as in other countries. It is also true that along with progress, demands keep on increasing.

People who could not even think of tractors and threshers and were not using chemical fertilizers or pesticides two or three years ago have now started using them and their demands for these commodities are on the increase. Demands, however, outpace production. This results in rise in prices. We have to take all these factors into consideration. If we are dependent on them, they too are dependent on the production of the factories. We have to pay attention to the industrial workers also and ensure justice to them. Sometimes we are at fault. The existence of many unions in a factory or a unit and their internal rivalries not only result in wastage of time, but also harm production. We have to pay attention to such things.

Every section should view its problems in the larger perspective of India to be able to appreciate the difficulties of others -- farmers, industrial workers, housewives, etc. Housewives are trying to run their households most economically in these days of rising prices. Not only the people of India but of the entire world are victims of rising prices. We are trying our best to make available essential commodities to the people throughout the country.

A sum of Rs.850 crores is being spent to help the rationing system to carry foodgrains to the remotest areas. We are trying to augment this amount. If somebody indulges in dishonest practices and corruption, stringent action should be taken against him. For this, however, it is necessary to know immediately who did what and where. If people say it is done by all and everywhere, it will be difficult to take action against the culprits. Local people have to be vigilant in this regard. If they remain alert, no atrocities can be perpetuated on the members of the Scheduled Castes, people of the minority communities and womenfolk. Alertness will help solutions to problems. We are trying to further tighten legislation in this regard. We also try to foresee the problems and solutions thereof, even before they come to the surface.

This is an age of self-reliance. Our slogan is that our nation should be self-reliant. What does a nation mean? It is not the land, but each one of you wherever you may be living. We want all of you to be self-reliant. We are trying to help you to become that. It casts a responsibility upon you -- the responsibility to do your duty. Please see that violence does not take place. Please see that holy or religious places are not converted into focal points of violence and crime and accumulation of arms. It is your duty to see that communalism does not raise its head. Wherever there are indications, please go there, as our workers used to do during the days of the freedom movement. They used to bring about peace in the area pacifying the people's anger.

This is feasible, because we have done it in the past. India has accomplished many tremendous tasks in the past and I am confident about the future as well.

Dangers always exist in a country. In a country of diversities of religions and languages, beliefs and traditions, internal rivalries are quite natural to an extent. But we have never considered diversities to be a symbol of weakness. On the contrary, diversities enrich us and add to the picturesqueness of our society. We do not want any religion or tradition to be curtailed. Everyone should be able to follow his own path.

But all the paths should merge in the ocean of Indianness, as the rivers merge into the sea. The synthesis of different beliefs and traditions constitutes Indianness. We must follow our faiths sincerely and should not impose ourselves on people not belonging to our own faith. If the people follow their faith sincerely, they will prove to be better citizens. No religion preaches violence. Every religion urges brotherhood, love and compassion. If the country follows this path, we shall be able to build a new society.

A new society is even now being shaped, and modernity is emerging out of the old traditions. This is one reason why some problems have cropped up in our country. Some pressures and problems have also come from outside. Life is a mixture of joys and sorrows. To rise above our sorrows or to be crushed under them lies in our hands. No Government or political party can offer help in this regard. It is our self-confidence and the internal power that help us to overcome them.

During the last four years, as you would have seen or heard or read, some events have taken place every year which enhanced the prestige of our country in the community of nations and also in our hearts. We, however, do not take advantage of that as other countries do. By 'we', I do not mean me or the Government, but the people of India. We did not make use of them to strengthen further our unity and the national pride, as all others do. This has been our shortcoming.

When the Asian Games were held here, I know how pleased the people of Delhi were. Young men belonging to Opposition parties also came to me and expressed their happiness and thanked me for holding the Games, although they said they did not agree with me in many other matters. A propaganda was, however, carried on that so much of money was being wasted without any useful return. You saw recently, in what spirit another country took up the same job. We have to see in what spirit the entire country should utilize such occasions so as to strengthen the unity, morale and self-respect of the country, instead of viewing events from a partisan angle. This is the greatest need.

Now, another responsibility has devolved upon us -- the responsibility for some other countries besides our own. People call it leadership. I am not fond of becoming a leader. I would only say that we have been provided with an opportunity to serve a hundred other countries in the best possible manner. I admit there are differences amongst us.

Fighting is going on in some countries and we are trying to stop it, although we have not succeeded so far. For example, the war between Iran and Iraq. We are in constant touch with the leaders of these countries. We are also corresponding with other leaders to explore possible solutions.

Recently, disturbances have broken out in one of our neighbouring countries. As you know, our policy has been of friendship and we have not ignored any avenue that leads to improved friendship, whether it is Pakistan, Bangladesh, Nepal or Sri Lanka. They are our close neighbours. Many years ago, when Jawaharlal Nehru was Prime Minister, he had suggested that India and Pakistan should enter into a No-War Pact. The same thing was repeated by the late respected Shastriji and myself in different forms and on different occasions. Pakistan, however, did not respond. After I became the Prime Minister again, and they acquired sophisticated weapons, they linked it with the idea of such a pact. We are not against it. We ourselves want it, but we said: So far you had been ignoring our suggestions and now, since you have raised this issue, will it not be proper to have a treaty of friendship, co-operation and peace naturally; there will be no war. Otherwise also, all these were part of the Simla Agreement. These have been recorded and duly signed by the two countries. If, however, you do not like that agreement, we can have a new agreement on these lines. But to say no to a treaty of friendship, co-operation and peace, and still ask for a No-War Pact, I ask you, my friends, how is it possible? How can we take it seriously? Still, we are trying to have something. I am sorry to find that their TV and newspapers carry reports about India which are far from reality and which may also be termed as interference in our internal matters. Still, we are taking up matters with them in all courtesy and in a friendly manner. But no government can overlook the interests of the country and its self-respect.

The situation in Sri Lanka is quite grave and my heart is full of grief for those innocent people who are being attacked without having done anything wrong. There are extremists and terrorists there as well and it is evident that a government is required to counter them. But the manner in which a particular community is being attacked for the last so many years has come in the way of restoration of peace, and the situation has gradually deteriorated. We do not want to interfere. We do not want to put any obstacle in the unity of another country. That would not be in our interest. We want our neighbouring countries to be stable and friendly towards us. We extend our hand of friendship and have offered help in having a dialogue and arriving at some conclusions acceptable to all.

The grief is of our entire country, although our Tamil brothers are affected most by the happenings there. Already 40,000 refugees have arrived. It is possible that people other than the sufferers may also have come with them and there may also be some spies amongst them. I cannot say what is the actual position. Our frontiers are such that in spite of our best efforts, such intrusions cannot always be checked. Still, we are making efforts. Patrolling has been intensified. I urged the President of Sri Lanka to have a dialogue somehow. He had himself suggested this and we had hoped that under his leadership progress would be made and an agreement would be arrived at. But so far I find only reports of unpleasant incidents. We are fully seized of the problem and we have all sympathy for the suffering people.

Our sea frontiers are vulnerable. But when I talk about these, it is not for diverting attention from our internal problems. I want our internal problems to be solved expeditiously so that we remain united and strong enough to face any danger. By accusing each other, or by lowering the morale of the police force and the army, we cannot make the country strong. Whenever aggressions have taken place, our jawans have faced them bravely and sacrificed their lives. Whenever a calamity has occurred, whether in the form of floods or something else -- our jawans have participated in the fight for peace and helped people. How can we not praise them? It is natural for a human being to err sometimes, whether a jawan or a politician or a public servant. Just because of the fault of one, we should not weaken the morale of the country. This will be neither in the interest of the country nor that of a citizen, or a political party. I am very sorry to see that some people do not hesitate in raising any point if it helps them get some publicity or benefit. I do not think that will really benefit them. On the other hand, this will harm the country and our morale.

We must remember, on this Independence Day, that just to attain Independence is not enough. We have to strive consistently to preserve it. We must guard this flame of freedom from every storm through our labour and, if necessary, by laying down our lives. Each one of us must take this vow today.

Earlier, when I referred to the 20-Point Programme, I stated that the uplift of the poor people and weaker sections of society and to help the small farmers were our objectives. More than Rs.1,000 crore have been allotted for these programmes. If a problem is faced in any part of the country, we take care of it. Soon the Seventh Plan will be launched. The objectives of this Plan are already known to you. These are: food, employment and productivity. All these are interrelated. If production does not increase, there cannot be employment, as also food. To achieve these objectives, we have placed adequate funds exclusively for the purpose. This will strengthen further the foundations of our country. Simultaneously, we have to help each other.

The struggle for the country's freedom had started even prior to our movement, but it did not succeed, because it was not a combined effort. You know what happened in 1857. You may hear more about it this evening. Why did not that revolution succeed? Because the people, in spite of sympathizing with it, did not step forward as soldiers for the cause.

We know that the last phase of the movement led by Gandhiji started on August 9, 1942. We celebrate the day every year. Why did we succeed? It was not because of violence, or enmity towards anyone. Our enmity was not towards Englishmen or England, but towards imperialism. We fought against imperialism and even today we are with people fighting against imperialism, as in South Africa. Besides the local population, Indians too are there. They do not have any freedom. They do not enjoy even the elementary rights of citizenship. Therefore, how can we not raise our voice in their favour?

You have to think over all this. One great leader had said, if one person is deprived of freedom, all of us lose our freedom. If any country is enslaved, the shadows of slavery fall on us all. Freedom and peace must prevail universally. Their blessing must be available to all.

India had been trying for peace everywhere. Recently, along with the Presidents and Prime Ministers of five other countries, I issued an appeal to the nations of the world against nuclear weapons. A one-hundredth part of the nuclear weapons now in store is enough to annihilate the entire humanity. Still, these weapons are being manufactured and accumulated. And India is blamed. India has some nuclear capacity. Our scientists have proved that they can do it. But we do not want to develop our nuclear capacity to produce a bomb. We do not have a single bomb. We want to use nuclear power to produce energy so as to help the farmers, we want to use it for medical science.

No programme of ours, whether it relates to space, sports, or science, can succeed if our young men do not come forward. Had they not enough capability, we could not have advanced. We are doing all this to minimize the sufferings of the poor people and the middle class people of the country in whom lies the nation's strength. In some fields we lag behind. This is but natural in view of the fact that the industrial revolution took place in some major countries 200 years ago. Now, how do we catch up with them, if our young people do not engage themselves in constructive work but indulge in destruction?

I am repeating this time and again because I know the creative capacity of our new generation. Our young people who are at school or college or in other institutions, have constructive talents. We have only to bring them out. We are forgetting our ancient ideals. We talk of religions and traditions, but do not pay attention to their basics. Their spirit calls for being good to others, helping others and creating a peaceful atmosphere. If we forget these ideals, we cannot advance. We have to bring about a social change and improve economic conditions. At the same time, we have to develop our spiritual strength without which we cannot be a great nation. We have to develop our moral values which are in abundance in India. We must not lose them.

This flag is a symbol, and not a mere piece of cloth. It is a symbol of the Independence of India, the sacrifice of India and the bright future of India.

40

Forty Years of Independence

Rajiv Gandhi

EACH ANNIVERSARY OF Independence is sacred to the country. On each anniversary we remember our freedom fighters. On this day we recall the builders of modern India. Today, standing on the sacred soil of the Red Fort, I recall 1857, when our first freedom fighters came to this Red Fort. I recall 1945, when soldiers of the Indian National Army were prosecuted here. Their only crime was that they fought for the freedom of the motherland. In 1947 at this very place, Panditji hoisted the flag of Independent India. Today, when we are assembled here, we remember the ideals, the principles, the values, and the dreams which inspired our freedom fighters to win Independence for the country. Today, all of us assembled here rededicate ourselves to that cause. Jawaharlal Nehru had said, "If we want to achieve great things, if we want to build a great India of our dreams, we shall have to become great ourselves and be worthy children of mother India."

On this fortieth anniversary, we naturally think not only of the events of the last one year but of the last 40 years. At the same time we look forward to the future as well.

Free rendering of the address in Hindi from the ramparts of the Red Fort, Delhi, August 15, 1987.

Our elders got us freedom and entrusted us with the responsibility of safeguarding and maintaining that freedom. It is our responsibility to protect it.

During these four decades we faced many situations, a number of threats and also pressures. We faced conspiracies, we faced aggressions. We did not bend, we protected the unity and integrity of India with our courage, our blood and our sacrifices. We showed to the world that India is strong, India is one and it cannot be divided. We demonstrated to the world that no one can enslave us again. We made it clear that nobody can weaken the unity of India. We made it evident that no sacrifice is too big for the security of our country, the Independence of our country and the unity of our country. No amount of labour, no amount of sacrifice is too high a price to pay for this purpose. Our soldiers, our officers give the best years of their lives to guard our frontiers and to defend us. In return we look after them, we provide them with the best of weaponry and ammunition. We see to it that they get the best tools they need. We are pledged to do so. The freedom of India means the freedom of the people of India. The freedom of India means that we should strengthen the roots of democracy, and hold impartial elections in which every citizen can participate. We conduct Parliament in such a way that the voice of the people of India is listened to. It looks after and builds the future of the country. The meaning of free India is that it has an independent judiciary and rule of law. Free india means that it has a free and unfettered press. But it is not so easy to protect democracy, especially when we find that there are people who endanger our freedom through irresponsibility and indiscipline, who show disrespect to the Constitution and its institutions through their behaviour. Still we have demonstrated that the roots of democracy in our country are deep. Our people must remain alert. It is only a Government based on democracy that can function in a country like India.

Our great economic achievements have been acclaimed all over the world. Gandhiji had taught us that the process of development and the task of building the country should begin with the poor people by eradicating poverty. He taught us that the moral duties should be kept in the forefront in our national life.

We have taken the country forward towards these very objectives. Eradication of poverty has been given the highest priority. We have used our entire energy in eradicating poverty. Indiraji gave a call for eradicating poverty. She brought about a new awakening in the country as a result of which there was reduction in poverty. Because of her 20-Point Programme and other programmes for rural development, be it NREP or IRDP or any other, there has been improvement in the lives of the poor people of the country. We see that the picture has changed during the last 40 years. Forty years ago two-thirds of India's population were below the poverty line. Today two-thirds of the population have come above the poverty line.

This achievement is due to our anti-poverty programmes. They have also smashed the hold of feudalism. Eradication of poverty has been carried forward through the Green Revolution. As a result, in just a few years time our production of foodgrains tripled. I remember the time when there was drought 21 years ago, and Indiraji had to seek foodgrains from foreign countries. How small she felt when she had to bow down to others for foodgrains. It was then that she decided that never again would India appeal to foreign countries for foodgrains. She overruled her technocrats and her other advisers and took steps which brought about the Green Revolution in the north-western part of the country. Indiraji's foresight and her determination coupled with the sweat and hard work of farmers of India, produced these desired results. Today we can say with pride that India will never go to others for food.

Similarly, at the time of Independence, our manufactures were restricted to a few simple things. Today, with the development that has taken place during the last 40 years, our industries have progressed to such an extent that India can manufacture products comparable with those of advanced countries. We have today reached a stage from where we can leap forward with greater energy and compete with others. Our scientists have shown to the world that they are capable of achieving the highest in the field of science. Our technocrats have proved that they can master all types of technology successfully. The path ahead is long but none can say that we have not traversed far enough during the last 40 years. We are building the India of our future on the foundations of development that have been soundly laid during these 40 years. We shall see to it that our industries grow and expand rapidly. We shall see to it that our youth get new and more opportunities of employment. We have to see that our productivity rises, prices go down and quality improves. It should be our effort to associate our workers in the public sector units with management. We should ensure that our science and technology are not borrowed from foreign countries but developed in a way that benefits the country and also the poor people of the country. They should be able to meet our demands and requirements. We also have to see that they go ahead and see the work done in other parts of the world, meet the challenges and show the way to the world. The most important thing, however, is that we should not allow our attention to be diverted. Our attention must be concentrated all the time on the poorest and the weakest person.

In the field of agriculture, production has increased a great deal, it has reached 15 crore tonnes. But we find that it is stagnating at 15 crore tonnes for the last three years. It is true that the monsoon has not been good during these years. Farmers in many regions and parts of the country have to face difficulties but we are resolved to ensure that the farmers' produce is not affected by the vagaries of weather in the future. We have to take steps to ensure increase in agricultural production in spite of adverse weather. Some 70 per cent of our population reside in rural areas, and almost the same percentage of people are poor and they earn their livelihood in the agricultural farms. The number of agricultural labourers is much more than that of farmers. We have to pay special attention towards them. If we want to eradicate poverty we have to begin with the farmers' fields. We have started spreading the Green Revolution and we are happy to see that during the last two years, an improvement has been noticed for the first time in Uttar Pradesh. Improvement has also been noticed in Bihar, Orissa and Bengal where the output of farmers is increasing. Poverty has been reduced in the rural areas. At the same time we have to pay special attention to the production of cotton, oilseeds and pulses. In this way we will see that with the spread of greenery poverty would be gradually reduced and would ultimately vanish.

This year we have provided more resources than ever before for programmes meant for the eradication of poverty. At the same time we have strengthened the administration as part of the poverty eradication programme. I have myself travelled far and wide, and after seeing the work with my own eyes and discussing the matter with the officers, strengthened these programmes and intensified them. Most important of all we have treated education as a part of the poverty eradication programme because as long as the children of the poor people do not get good education, poverty cannot be eradicated.

Today, however, we find another problem before us, a very serious problem, that is of unemployment of the youth. We find signs of pessimism in our youth. Millions of our young people do not succeed in getting employment and millions remain dissatisfied even after getting employment because they do not get what they want. We have to concentrate on the employment scene. There are some weaknesses and deficiencies in our set-up. There is employment, there are jobs, but the education, the skills that are required to fill up the vacancies are not there. Millions of boys and girls are matriculates, millions of them are degree holders but all cannot get white-collar jobs. We have taken care of these things in our new education policy. It has been our endeavour to make up the deficiency in our set-up. Through this policy we will ensure that the boys and girls coming out of schools and colleges, get such education which provides them employment. At the same time we will have to see that the rural employment programmes and other developmental programmes are implemented in such a way that the maximum number of people get jobs. But this will be possible only when we make a rapid progress in all fields -- agriculture, industry, infrastructure and services. Most important, perhaps, is the fact that we should succeed in the matter of self-employment. It is not so difficult to give jobs to all if we work with determination, if we examine things properly and if we see to it that our education matches the required skills. If we increase the pace of progress, bring maximum number of young people to the technical trades and inspire them to start small enterprises, place maximum number of people in services, then that objective can be achieved. We have to see that all people do not aspire for just government jobs; they should also go elsewhere. This can reduce unemployment and we are determined to eliminate unemployment. We shall place programmes before the country in the coming years to ensure that unemployment is eradicated.

This year we are facing a difficult situation because of drought. Such a widespread drought has not been experienced for many years. We had faced a drought in 1965-66, that was grave but was confined to only one or two regions. This year's drought has affected virtually all parts of the country. However, thanks to Indiraji's far-sightedness which increased the production of our farmers, our economy today is quite strong and we can face the drought. There will be no shortage. No doubt there is drought, but we can face it today because of the Green Revolution brought about by Indiraji. In many States this is the third or fourth year of drought. The poor are facing great hardships. Their basic needs are uppermost in our minds. Our minds also go out to the landless people and the marginal farmers who have been rendered unemployed and who are not getting any work today. In many

States there is a scarcity of drinking water as well. In many States there is a shortage of fodder for the cattle.

We will face the situation with all our might. As the head of the Government, I pledge that we will concentrate all our attention and accord the highest priority to deal with this drought situation. We will see to it that we are able to supply foodgrains to every nook and corner of rural India from our granaries. We will ensure that enough employment is provided to the poor people through relief works. We will also ensure that employment is provided to all those who really need it. We will see to it that there is no dearth of food. Nobody will have to go hungry. We will strengthen our public distribution system so that foodgrains reach all parts of the country, at the doorsteps of the people, especially in the rural areas so that people do not have to go far for food. We will ensure that there is no scarcity of drinking water. We shall also pay special attention to the problem of fodder scarcity so that our cattle wealth and animals are also able to face this difficult situation.

We have to make a large collective effort to deal with this drought situation. At the Centre, as also in the States, we will see to it that all required assistance is provided by us. At the same time it is also to be seen that the State Governments act firmly and with speed because it is they who reach the villages. We will give all assistance but the State Governments will have to move fast. I have written to the Chief Ministers of the States which are facing the drought situation. But since the country is strong, we will accomplish the job and successfully face this challenge.

It is, however, necessary that we devote our full attention and energy to this problem. Our granaries are full. We have the experience and capacity today. We can face this challenge without any foreign assistance, but we must be clear that it is not necessary to slow down the pace of development in order to deal with the drought situation. By stalling development, by suspending development, we will have to face a greater crisis in the days to come. We have to find resources so that without reducing or slowing down the pace of development we can face the present challenge. There is need for economy, austerity; it is necessary to reduce or eliminate non-essential expenditure.

This is the time when more fortunate people should come forward to the rescue of the less fortunate ones. We have to see that no anti-social element takes advantage of this situation to earn money and exploit the miseries of the poor people. We will have to deal firmly with such elements. Hoarding will have to be stopped, profiteering will have to be eliminated. If we face the anti-social elements resolutely we will be able to keep the situation under control. We will not spare any efforts. With all the might of the Government, we will see to it that the anti-social elements are kept under control. Any lacuna in the law that may come in the way of dealing with such people will be removed, and the Government will acquire the powers necessary for dealing with them, but I appeal to all to co-operate fully in raising resources and facing this national challenge boldly. We want constructive co-operation from every quarter -- from legislators, from Members of Parliament, from the Opposition, from experts, and from the press. In the context of this challenge, it is necessary to forge a national effort to meet the situation effectively.

India has made remarkable social progress during the last 40 years. We find that casteism has decreased during these years. Our women have become stronger. We have provided more opportunities to our girls to go to schools and colleges. We have specially encouraged them to go to schools. Last year, we consolidated further the anti-dowry law to strengthen the hands of women and we find that since then the number of girls killed because of dowry problem has gone down. We hope to further increase the strength of our women. We also have to pay attention towards our labourers and their problems. During the last two years, we have passed a legislation to prevent child labour. This law prohibits all employment of children in hazardous industries. The legislation provides for the education of children and also takes care of their food and health. The problem of agricultural labourers had been attended to during the past 40 years. We have set up a National Commission to study the problems of agricultural labourers and suggest programmes to deal with their problems.

The tribal people have their own problems. I have myself visited those districts, the villages and also their huts to have an idea of their problems and the way government programmes are being implemented, where these programmes need to be strengthened and where there is need for assistance. We have paid special attention to the problems of our Dalit brothers. We will see to it that the hands of the Commissioner of Scheduled Castes and Scheduled Tribes are so strengthened that he is able to deal firmly with the situation wherever the Dalit and the tribal people have not been given their due.

We will see to it that the legislation intended to uplift the Dalit and the tribal people is strengthened, the provisions are effectively implemented, and nobody is able to stall this work. We have implemented very effectively the 15-Point directive of Smt.Indira Gandhi relating to the minority communities.

The middle class population has increased in the country because of increase in the economic opportunities. A large number of people now go to different parts of the country to find employment. More and more people are now undertaking journeys in the country. People from one part of the country are going to other parts in search of jobs; they are getting employment outside their homes, their villages, their districts and sometimes even outside their respective States. This consolidates the unity of the country as such for the people are able to see the vastness of the country. The unity and integrity of the country is strengthened through these people. We have achieved a lot during the last 40 years but even then, in spite of the social progress, a lot still remains to be done.

Some of the problems are old and many new ones have cropped up. Communal feelings have come to the fore in some places. We see the misuse of religious places. The religious feelings of the people are being toyed with. We find one community fighting with another community, a brother fighting with his brother, a man fighting with another man; all these cause danger to our secularism.

Communalism and sectarian forces were causing harm to the unity and integrity of the country during the days of the freedom struggle. We had fought on the basis of the concepts denouncing communalism. People belonging to all religions and all thoughts have resided here since time immemorial. We have seen that people of all traditions and all faiths have lived like brothers in our society. There is no room at all for communalism in our society, our democracy. We have to face this challenge. It is the duty of every citizen to ensure this by all his actions and thinking. Each one of us should maintain cordiality in society. A majority of the people who are deeply religious believe in true religion, and are secular and they should come forward and face those few people who weaken the country, who believe in sectarianism, who believe in fundamentalism, who believe in violence and who believe in looting and terrorism. There is no place in India for those people who try to weaken the country in the name of religion. People of different communities have lived in this country for centuries, peacefully working together, playing together and participating constructively in each other's lives. Sometimes, however, hatred raises its head all of a sudden and things are on fire and there is terror.

Generally, outsiders are responsible for this, and sometimes because of religious leaders. These people weaken us by spreading rumours, creating misunderstanding and spreading falsehood.

Normally, innocent people fall victim to such conspiracies. Whenever such sectarian conflicts come to the fore, maximum harm is caused to the innocent people. They are the worst sufferers. Our war on sectarian forces cannot, however, be fought only through the machinery of law. This should be a people's war. It must be fought in every locality, in every area. We have to ensure that all of us are one in this war against dangerous criminals, and stop the misuse of religion, and eliminate the people spreading hatred. Those who are sowing the seeds of hatred among us must be crushed. We must face such people who are out to destroy our society. Communalism gives rise to separatism. Communalism produces terrorism and conspiracies are being hatched to destroy our democracy through communalism, separatism and terrorism.

We notice that all sorts of methods are being employed to weaken our country and to disturb peace in our country. Attempts are being made to create ill-feelings among the tolerant and peaceful people of this country. We do not have to submit to separatists; we have to face them. We will face all of them with all our might. We will face those who try to weaken our freedom, our security and our future through threats, pressures and causing infights. We will not allow them to succeed. We will not rest till terrorism is completely eliminated or till the terrorists do not return to the country's mainstream laying down their arms. We need not lose heart, we do not have to be fearful. Gandhiji has said: "Independence means fearlessness against death. A nation afraid of death cannot become free and even if it attains freedom it cannot protect it."

The words of Gandhiji should resound in our ears today and we must face this challenge boldly. We must remember that we will not counter them for taking revenge. If we try to take revenge, then it will only serve the designs of the terrorists. Revenge would only bring victory to terrorism. If we use restraint, terrorism will weaken and will ultimately be defeated. We must not fall into the trap of terrorism. Gandhiji has said that violence cannot be an answer to violence. Only non-violence can be the answer. India holds its head high in the world today. The voice of India is heard in the world with respect. Why? How is it that a country which was a slave, poor till 40 years ago, and about which people used to think that it would never stand on its own and could not safeguard its freedom, now speaks out in such a strong voice? It has been possible, because we moved forward taking with us the concepts of Gandhiji, principles of Panditji and the path shown by Indiraji.

We have learnt to seek fearlessly, we have learnt not to submit under pressures, we have learnt to move forward on the path of non-violence with courage and face the challenges boldly. We launched a movement against the atomic weapons in the world during the last 40 years. Today many powerful countries are attracted towards it. The feeling that Gandhiji and Panditji had brought to the fore before our Independence, is now spreading throughout the world after 40 or 50 years. It is just insanity that we continue to manufacture weapons while the available weapons alone can extinguish the entire world 50 times over. It is really madness that 15 to 20 million rupees are spent every minute in the world on the arms race. Even a small fraction of it can be of great help in eradicating poverty, disease and unemployment. India is paying attention to these things. We are paying attention to human rights and human dignity.

South Africa, where Gandhiji had started his first *satyagraha,* is still reeling under slavery. The flag of freedom has not still been unfurled there. It is shameful that 100 years have passed, hundreds and thousands of freedom fighters have made sacrifices including the sacrifice of their lives, but the place from where the flame of freedom rose is still under slavery. We have raised the question of poor people in the world. We have taken up the cause of suppressed sections of the world. We have demonstrated that our voice is that of sanity, tolerance, truth and non-violence.

Last month we signed an agreement in Sri Lanka -- an agreement that proved the correctness of our policy, which demonstrated that the impact of our foreign policy is good and that India was moving on the right path. This is an important achievement in these 40 years. The latest agreement that we have reached and signed has brought peace and cooperation in Sri Lanka. This has strengthened the cause of peace and cooperation in the entire region. We have checked the activities of those who were endangering the security of the entire region and have prevented rivalries of the power blocs reaching our neighbourhood. This has strengthened the cause of non-alignment. It has been proved that countries can solve their problems through dialogue without allowing the big powers or other sections or parties to come in. We have seen that whenever outsiders interfere, the problems become more serious and difficult. Today, on the 40th anniversary of our Independence, we have to re-dedicate ourselves to these ideals and concepts.

Our greatest asset is the system given to us by our forefathers. We have seen that the system is in tune with our ancient traditions and our culture, which have flourished uninterrupted for thousands of years. We used that spirit in our struggle for freedom and should use it in building a new India. Today, our greatest achievement is our democracy. We have to safeguard it, consolidate it. No weakness should be allowed to permeate it. Still, we find that certain elements are trying to weaken it in a bid to destroy it. This system has existed for the last 40 years, and we have found that under it India has gained in strength, it has remained one, it has progressed and has been able to face the world. If some people for their own petty political ends want to disrupt the faith of the people and harm our democracy just for their own development and benefit, we must stand up to them. We have to see to it that they do not gain in strength. We have to ensure that they are not able to divert the attention of the country. We must also see that they do not succeed in conspiring internally or from outside to weaken the country. It is true that a few things are not well in our society and our system. We will see to it that the people who are doing wrong things are dealt with promptly and firmly and are punished. Our concentration today should, however, be on national reconstruction and not on rumours. We must pay attention to national reconstruction and take the country on to the path of progress. We should correct the flaws in our system and promote such policies which will further strengthen our society and the system. We are doing so and we are trying to move on the path of progress. We would like to see that all sections of the people, especially the youth, start a national campaign against complacency, sectarianism and corruption. We have to abide by the principles which Gandhiji placed before us. We must safeguard our freedom. We must strengthen our society. It should be our endeavour to see that people belonging to all sections of our society work for the welfare of the poor and the weak, and maintain communal and religious harmony. We must ensure that Dalits, tribals and women progress in all respects in our society and consolidate their position. We have to be guided by Gandhiji's principles of truth, non-violence and human unity.

At the same time, we have to ensure that we remain self-reliant. We must remember that only right means can ensure the right end. Gandhiji's message was not meant for his generation alone. It was for all the future generations. This message is as important for the reconstruction and consolidation of the country as it was for the achievement of our freedom.

Our unity is sound, our integrity is eternal. We take inspiration from the past, to move confidently into the future. It is our firm resolve that we will unitedly move ahead on the path of progress to safeguard our freedom, our democracy, our secularism, our socialism, our security and our non-alignment, stage by stage, and make India really great.